DATE DUE

WITHDRAWN

DEMCO, INC. 38-2931

NOT MADE OF WOOD

NOT MADE OF WOOD

A Psychiatrist Discovers His Own Profession

JAN FOUDRAINE

Translated by Hubert H. Hoskins

MACMILLAN PUBLISHING CO., INC.
New York

For those who have shared with me the
depth of their mistrust and loneliness

Great care has been taken to insure that the
identity of the patients and employees remains concealed, and
therefore all of their names, occupations, residences and
family relationships have been changed.

Macmillan Publishing Co., Inc.
866 Third Avenue, New York, N.Y. 10022
Collier-Macmillan Canada Ltd.

Library of Congress Cataloging in Publication Data
Foudraine, Jan, 1929-
    Not made of wood.
    Translation of Wie is van hout.
    Includes bibliographical references.
    1. Psychiatry.   2. Schizophrenia.   3. Psychiatric
hospitals—Netherlands.   4. Psychiatric hospitals—
United States.   I. Title.
RC439.F6613   616.8'9   73-6057
ISBN 0-02-540200-5

First Printing 1974

Printed in the United States of America

CONTENTS

ACKNOWLEDGMENTS

I wish to thank my teacher, E. A. D. E. Carp, for his inspiration. To P. A. H. Baan I am indebted for some conversations that were just the help one sometimes needs.

Thanks also to my friends John Waage, Pier Engelsman, Louis Tas, jnr. and Andries and Berta van Dantzig. All in their own ways have been both sounding board and support to me.

I am grateful, too, for the advice which my friend Thijs Chanowski gave me. As a specialist in communication he said to me once: 'Stop talking about it, you should just write that book.'

I thank Loek van Vollenhoven, Pim Eijgenstein, Ron van Vleuten and many other friends for their help and support during the preparation of this book.

I want to thank many friends in America, among them the director of the institute where I took my training together with his staff. They and many other psychoanalyst colleagues in America gave me a great deal of warmth and friendship. In particular I want to thank Kenneth Artiss who in several encounters opened my eyes to the significance of linguistic science. His knowledge and his searching and questioning mind have been of major importance to me. I would also thank my mentors at the Washington Psychoanalytic Institute and in particular Edith Weigert – my training analyst – for her deep understanding and capacity to empathize.

Since my return to The Netherlands I have owed to Willy Arendsen a relationship with contrarieties and conflict in it, but one also of understanding, which has never detracted from my respect and admiration for this pioneer in the field of the organization of the modern psychotherapeutic center in The Netherlands.

I want to thank René de Monchy, who has been ready to support me as a psychoanalyst in dark times.

Babette Röschlau and Fleur Kemper have helped me with all the typing work. For their enthusiasm and support I am very grateful.

In the process of preparing the manuscript for publication in America and England I was offered the help of my good friends Dean and Doreen Eleuthery. They, a psychiatrist and his wife, both gifted in the art of psychodrama, understood that this book was also my psychodrama.

INTRODUCTION

You will certainly know as well as I the sense of helplessness that can descend on one in a book shop. You stand in front of the shelves marked 'Social Sciences' and an avalanche of titles comes hurtling at you: Man this, Man that. . . . It seems that everyone who has managed to do a bit of thinking nowadays immediately has to write a book about it. Psychiatrists, psychoanalysts and sociologists turn out one book after another. You take a few books from the shelves, flick through them, put them back, and usually exit with a tight pocket and a stiffish hangover.

I am always comforted by the thought that one doesn't really need to be so very well read and that those bookshelves don't actually hold that much original material. Many authors say precisely the same thing over and over or else just repeat what others have said before them.

There are, of course, writers with an authentic desire to bring about change. Indeed, in the treatment of individuals in some kind of psychic distress there is a lot that must be changed. We are faced with an enormous lag, not so much in knowledge as in our ability to organize the sort of help we should be providing – and that leads me back to the psychiatrists, psychoanalysts and social workers, in short to the help-givers.

Psychiatrists write a great deal, and some of their books are readable. Yet a lot of their work is simply indigestible. This is true not only of books, but also of the flood of articles in psychiatric and psychoanalytic journals. And – something the layman probably doesn't realize – psychiatrists don't always understand each other's publications. This is partly because many psychiatrists lack the ability to write (which is nothing to be ashamed of – after all, it is, or ought to be, their special job to listen very carefully to what is being said and what is being left unsaid, and then at the right moment be able to say something . . . as little as possible). But there is another reason why so many psychiatric and psychoanalytical books and articles are unreadable. Their authors have an irresistible tendency to drift into abstractions, to get away from the concrete experiences they have had with particular people in particular situations. As a result they create a fog of words about words, statements about statements about statements, and so become quite unreadable.

'Good,' you will be saying. 'So you're going to try to give this book a form and content that after a dozen pages or so won't put me to sleep. You intend to make it intelligible and, if possible, even gripping. And if it has something to do with psychiatry, may I be told first what it's all about? Who are you, anyway?'

Let me start by answering the second question first. After seven years spent studying medicine and five specializing in psychiatry I became a psychiatrist and then left The Netherlands because I was given an opportunity to join the staff of the psychoanalytical sanatorium known as Cedar Haven in the town of Westover, Virginia. It was one of the most progressive psychiatric centers in the United States. I worked there for four and a half years and during that time got my training as a psychoanalyst in Washington, D.C. When I came home in 1965 I worked for two and a half years as clinical director of the psychotherapeutic center known as the Veluweland Institute at Ederveen. I wrote a part of this book while I was there. I then put it aside, but after a couple of years started working on it again because I thought: Well, really, why not?

Now something about the content of this book.

I propose to write about my own career in psychiatry, the experiences I accumulated in America, my encounters with people described as 'schizophrenic' and what I have learned from them. 'Adventure in Psychiatry' might have been a good title for this book; but Dennis Martin has already used it for a study in which he describes how he tried to reform a traditional psychiatric institute.[1] 'Essays on Schizophrenia' would have been another possibility, but that, too, has been used,[2] and on further consideration I would have rejected it anyway as too literary. Yet both titles suggest what I want to talk about. Up to now it has been a long adventure; and over the past twelve years I have been deeply involved with the problems of people labeled 'schizophrenic.' By 'involved with' I mean I have encountered them, not 'observed' or 'investigated' them. Early in my training as a psychiatrist and psychotherapist I struck up a relationship with these people, and tried in the course of often long drawn out contacts to understand them. I came to realize that it was quite possible to do so. However apparently bizarre, however absurd their behavior, it became intelligible in that form of engagement between human beings that we call psychotherapy. I uncovered the sense in their 'nonsense,' the significance of delusions, hallucinations, aversion to every human contact; and the wherefore of it slowly became clear to me when I understood how much they had suffered during their early years when neither father nor mother had been capable of giving them positive help and guidance, entangled as they themselves were in the unresolved conflicts within and between them. My experiences in these psychotherapeutic relationships taught me that 'schizophrenics' are people like you and me, and not 'different' or 'uncontactable.' Just people in profound, existential need, dire need . . . and for that reason all the more human. 'Much more simply human than otherwise,' as the American psychiatrist Harry Stack Sullivan once expressed it. Official psychiatry, known also as clinical psychiatry, put the emphasis more on the 'otherwise,' as though the psychotic person were in fact qualitatively different and suffering from a 'disease.' I discovered that this latter idea was a delusion entertained by a lot of psychiatrists and very much harder to tackle than the 'fantasies' of people I met in the psychiatric institutions of The Netherlands and America. In short: I found myself rebelling and soon lost all confidence in the psychiatry I had learned from textbooks and even from some of my mentors.

In particular, I set my face against sticking labels on people in trouble and acquired a downright aversion to the habit of classifying 'mental syndromes' as though they were botanical specimens. Step by step, assisted by the literature, my own psychoanalytic training and trial and error, I developed a degree of technical competence in the field of psychotherapy and in the encounter with so-called schizophrenic persons in particular.

These psychotherapeutic experiences form the background to this book. Especially in America my interest became focused on the psychiatric institution as a whole and the social system of what the sociologist Caudill has called 'the psychiatric hospital as a small society.' [3]

The main stress in my story, therefore, is on the process of getting to know the very luxurious psychoanalytical sanatorium Cedar Haven, the staff of which (consisting of twenty-two psychoanalysts and the psychiatrically trained nursing personnel) was entirely devoted to the psychotherapy of 'schizophrenic disturbed' persons. For four and a half years I was in contact with all the problems that presented themselves on a ward of this sanatorium, a ward to which, as a psychiatrist ('administrator' was the term used there), I was expected to give leadership. It was a fascinating experience. What it amounted to was that on a small ward with nine 'chronically schizophrenic' women and the psychiatrically trained nursing staff I attempted to change the organization and to bring about a far-reaching reform of the whole milieu. Kurt Lewin said on one occasion: 'If you want to know how things really are, try to change them.' Thus I found out how things really were.

What I instigated for good (and ill) in my drive to reform this ward constitutes the major part of this book. 'Good,' you will say. 'But there is an extensive literature on the subject of the psychiatric institution and what goes on there, as well as attempts to reform it. There are a lot of books and academic theses on this topic. I usually find them unintelligible. They bristle with technical jargon, and I'm a layman.'

Fair enough: the specialized literature is enormous. But in telling what I have to tell I should like to get it across to the nonpsychiatrist as well. I have in mind a hypothetical reader who really wishes to be informed. I believe that information about the psychiatric institution, psychiatry and insanity (I have in mind what is referred to as 'schizophrenia') can be conveyed without a great deal of specialist jargon. I also think there is a real need for this. It is about time psychiatry was stripped of its mysterious and magical properties, that the psychiatrist (and physician) came off his pedestal and that the layman, too, learned to think about what psychiatrists are wrestling with. And that is quite a lot.

The story of how psychiatric institutions have developed (from the most progressive down to the 'snakepit' where thousands of people go almost totally without any kind of personal care and attention) has been told often enough. It can be found in many books and articles.[4] I shall content myself by making a few comments on that story.

Having at one time been tortured and burned, more recently 'lunatics' were chained up in cellars. A climactic and positive point in this otherwise sad story of the way 'demoniacs' were treated came with the actions of the French psychiatrist Pinel. He got rid of the chains and gave back a little freedom and dignity to the occupant of the 'asylum.' A hopeful and positive development in the psychiatric institution is known as the period of moral treatment, championed in America by, among others, Dorothea Dix (a sort of Florence Nightingale for the insane). This period (from c. 1817 to 1850) was followed by a most disconcerting relapse into miserable conditions in psychiatric institutions, which we have not managed to change drastically even now.[5] I say this advisedly, because despite all the ballyhoo about 'occupational therapy,' the advent of tranquilizers, the alterations being made to our psychiatric institutions, the situation is still far from satisfactory.

Attempts to reform the mental hospital fundamentally have generally failed. When it comes to the literature, we may distinguish two kinds: the writings of those authors who want to create new forms of organization, and the publications of those who say: 'No, don't. This form of organization cannot be changed because it is based on false assumptions.'

Foremost among the contributions of the 'reformers' is the work of the British psychiatrist Maxwell Jones.[6] He set up a sort of model farm and showed that change was indeed possible. He planned a quite different type of institution and community (he called it a therapeutic community). Joint decision-making engendered a spirit of openness at the daily community meeting (the very core of this organization), with patients and nursing staff in a circle together; the dividing line between 'healthy' doctors and nurses and 'sick' patients was blurred; the organization was horizontal and people were held responsible for themselves and for one another. They could discuss quite openly the relationships and conflicts that were developing between them and in that very process of reflecting together start to learn how to achieve relationships and genuine contact . . . or how relationships are rejected and contact lost as a result of anxiety. This was an ambitious attempt at reform, which came up against enormous resistance in traditional vertically and hierarchically organized psychiatric institutions where the doctor-psychiatrist and the nurse, male or female, occupied the seat of authority and had no intention of getting off it.

Regarding these attempts to reform the psychiatric institution by introducing the principles of organization propounded by Maxwell Jones there is, as I have said, an extensive literature available.[7] One feature of it is conspicuous. More often than not the reformers are lone operators (sometimes, if they get the chance, working with others) and what they achieve are minimal modifications in the social system denoted by the term 'psychiatric institution.' The reformers struggle against a mountain of opposition, and when, disillusioned or not, they eventually depart, the organization often rapidly sinks back into its bureaucratic, hierarchical, doctor-knows-best structure. This literature makes fascinating reading, but the striking thing about it is that it so frequently appears to be hammering away at the same old last: 'democratizing,' changing the vertical organizational structure into more horizontal forms, promoting co-responsibility and giving a bit of real encouragement to the category of people who form the lowest echelon in the institution's chain of command: the male or female nurse and . . . the 'patient.'

Because these attempts at reform encounter so much resistance, and progress is so infuriatingly slow, a counter-current has appeared in the literature, which has been operative for quite a time and is growing stronger. One of the major representatives of this type of literature is the American sociologist Erving Goffman, who in 1961 published a number of essays containing a scathing critique not only of the conditions prevailing in psychiatric establishments (whether progressive or not) but *in particular of the premises on which those institutions are built*.[8] It is significant that Goffman worked for some time as an occupational therapist in one of the biggest mental hospitals in the U.S.

My experience has convinced me that our present psychiatric institutions are extremely difficult to reform and that we shall have to look for alternatives to them, and that the training of psychiatrists and everything else that is involved in psychiatry needs a complete overhaul because they are riddled with faulty, not to say logically untenable, traditional basic assumptions.

You see, writing an introduction is a risky business! You start giving away what you intended to say later on. There are still a few points I need to explain. My experiences as a psychiatrist with people labeled 'schizophrenic' form one element of this book. But I had to impose certain limitations on myself in this respect. In particular, there is the ethical problem, which inhibits a lot of psychotherapists from describing in detail and very concretely their experiences and emotions in the often very protracted relationship known as psychotherapy, in which so many intimate things are disclosed and made intelligible. Psychotherapists who want to impart what can be disclosed of the unique life history and experiences of their clients tackle this problem by modifying and condensing their account in various ways. Thus they try to safeguard the anonymity of the client. I shall do that in some places. But I shall stick as closely as I can to the facts, without abstracting and generalizing too much. This is certainly not, therefore, a book about the problem of 'the schizophrenic person' (there is in fact no such being). At times it will touch on the course a client's life takes, the distress and confusion he expresses regarding himself, the group in which he grew up (the family) and finally the society in which he lives and has his being. I shall keep my speculations in theoretical psychology (the kind of thing known in the theory of psychoanalysis as metapsychology) to a minimum, but I cannot dodge this area altogether.

Now something more specific about the form of the book. I intend to take the reader with me on my journey through training as a psychiatrist, to share with him the experiences I accumulated in America and how my growing convictions about psychiatry and its institutions were conditioned by a number of 'chance' events. The subtitle 'A Psychiatrist Discovers His Profession' indicates that I want also to give my narrative the character of a personal history – the record of how I became a psychiatrist. So this book will be part narrative, part personal testimony and part scientific work. An impossible combination, but I want to have a shot at it all the same.

Most of the specialist literature I deal with is American, because it is with that that I feel most at home. The notes are at the end of each chapter. In most cases they are followed by a supplementary section containing a broad survey of the literature. To that end I have chosen not to provide a bibliography but instead some brief (occasionally not so brief) excerpts from articles and books, with commentaries. An account of the sources, the material on which I have drawn for my book, is given. I kept a sort of diary about my experiences and my encounter with the specialist field of psychiatry, and I have learned a great deal from my own recollections. During the period 1956–1965 I kept a written record of the psychotherapeutic experiences I shared with 'schizophrenic' clients, and a few of those notes are used in this book. For my account of the shaping of a therapeutic milieu on a ward of Cedar Lodge I have employed field notes made over a period of four and a half years (1961–1965) and tapes of conversations with clients and with the psychiatric nursing staff. In addition I collected everything that was relevant in the way of typed material and observations – for instance, all observational reports kept from day to day by the Cedar Lodge personnel. Rereading these filled in the gaps in my recollections. Lastly, I have made use of earlier lectures that have not so far been published.

And now, let's clear up that title *Not Made of Wood*. Enough, by way of introduction.

In most general terms,
we are all much more simply human than
    otherwise,
be we happy and successful,
contented and detached,
miserable and mentally disordered
or whatever.

HARRY STACK SULLIVAN

Part 1

The Netherlands

Two roads diverged in a wood, and I –
I took the one less traveled by,
And that has made all the difference.

ROBERT FROST

1. TRAINING

You take up medicine, as a student you come into contact with 'psychiatry.'

Usually that happens in the shape of lectures given by professors or readers in reputable lecture theatres. Sometimes these lectures are understandable, sometimes they swamp the student in a torrent of words, either making him feel that something very abstruse is being proffered here, which he is too much of a blockhead to understand, or that the lecturer is talking so much nonsense that it is hard to squeeze the sense out of it. Alas! the second conclusion is much rarer. Quite often during these lectures on psychiatry people are used for purposes of 'demonstration.' In the final years of medical study you do a spell of practical work as a clinical medical student in various clinics, including a psychiatric institution.

Of my time as a clinical medical student I can only recall that I struggled with mounting admiration through the thick tomes written by clinical psychiatrists on 'psychoses.' What the various authors had committed to paper by way of expert knowledge, observations, minute and subtle descriptive accounts, and how they larded these with a great mass of profound philosophical thinking and theorizing, often made my head reel. I nearly became convinced that I did not have the cultural background for this, and worse, that my intelligence was too limited to enable me to cope with such profundities.

As a clinical medical student I helped to collect 'schizophrenics' from the various wards, whom we – dressed in our white coats and preferably out on the lawn in the sunshine – then interrogated about their delusions, hallucinations, mental blocks, thought-disturbances and whatever else had to be investigated. In short, we would inquire how their 'craziness' was getting on; and they (who had gone through all this before) would show us how crazy they were. 'What sort of voices are you hearing, then, male or female? What about those obsessional ideas of yours? Just tell me now – there's a row of sparrows on the roof, I shoot one of them with a gun – how many are left . . . ?'

In this way we considered and examined the 'intelligence,' the 'emotional life,' the state of the 'erotic drives.' We jotted it all down and then convivially brought this 'study material' of ours back to the ward, where we would plunge into a discussion about the 'diagnosis.' Since we were not dealing with anyone who had a demonstrable physical disease (epilepsy, senility, etc.), we would discuss the problem of 'contact.' How was the emotional contact? We had not the faintest idea that in this sort of situation any genuine human contact, any interchange of feelings, had to be difficult to achieve.

We had all our technical terms down pat: the 'defect,' the absence of *Austauschaffektivität* ('exchange of feeling'). We peered into our books and registers, which listed a fair number of labels, made the diagnosis and went off to impart our findings to a drowsy resident (someone, that is, who was already a doctor and was doing the practical part of his training as a psychiatrist in the institution), who listened to it all for the umpteenth time. Occasionally, in a moment of enthusiasm, this long-suffering man would launch into an even more profound and extensive argument that was supposed to convince us that we had not yet made a proper diagnosis.

During the first stage of my training as a psychiatrist I came as a resident to the same establishment where I had been a clinical medical student. My various attempts to enlighten the students by my comments gave me the uneasy feeling that I knew little more about the problems than they did. In that sort of situation you develop a certain adroitness in dodging the really awkward questions. Here I gradually got to know the traditional mental hospital: the white jackets, the crowded wards (closed or open), the director of the place who made his weekly rounds, uttered kindly words of encouragement, slapped people on the shoulder and spent the rest of his time behind his new EEG apparatus. He was interested in electro-encephalography, the business of tracing and reproducing on graphs the electrical activity of the brain. I suppose he was in pursuit of the mysterious 'process' that would explain deviant behavior (so deviant from the cultural rules of the game called living that it earns the title 'schizophrenic'). The 'process' was apparently some form of physical disease and the feeling he created was that the discovery of this 'process' was just around the corner.

I was sufficiently indoctrinated at that time – through the study of medicine – to believe in that 'process' myself. Certain people had a disease known as 'schizophrenia,' and it was caused by a 'process.' What the 'process' was nobody could explain to me, but it served to account for the periodic occurrence of an extraordinarily baffling kind of behavior. Waves of 'schizophrenia' were therefore described as *Schübe*. After a whole series of these *Schübe*, it was suggested, a person would gradually withdraw more and more, become less and less accessible to human contact and finish up permanently housed in a mental hospital. These permanent residents were specifically denoted by the term 'defect schizophrenics,' and the impression I got was that the *Schübe* of the 'disease process' produced a sort of scar defect in the functioning of the human being.

It strikes me now, fifteen years later, that this is still the way a lot of psychiatrists think.

As a resident in psychiatry I did little other than treat physical illnesses, behave portentously during the daily rounds and avoid clashes with the head nurse. I occupied myself with filling in records and firing questions at the bewildered newly-admitted 'patient,' a procedure followed by the completion of the 'diagnosis,' a sort of christening on which a lot of psychiatrists expended much time and energy. Tranquilizers had made their appearance; I prescribed them. From time to time I pressed the button of an electroshock apparatus. (Electroshock treatment entails placing two metal plates on the patient's temples and sending a current for several milliseconds through the brain. An anesthetic is given in advance. The patient loses consciousness, sometimes there are jerking movements of the body, and after some time he wakes up. He has a total loss of recall of the electroshock. Miraculous results have been recorded in patients with certain forms of very severe depression. There are theories, of course, but no real explanation for this. The insulin treatment involves lowering the level of sugar in the blood by administering small quantities of insulin so that the patient goes into a subcomatose condition. He is roused from it when given sugar and is then sometimes much more approachable. But that depends rather on the psychiatrist. Both types of treatment are being used less and less. So it is said.)

The advice the director gave me was: 'Just keep your eyes and ears open.' Advice well meant but doomed to failure, as I did not know what I was supposed to see and what I was supposed to hear. I saw and heard little besides a considerable deprivation of human dignity. The totally arbitrary way in which people were provided with this or that diagnostic label, the use of the electroshock apparatus and the administration of large quantities of tranquilizers gave me no sense of satisfaction whatever. I did not understand the reasons for this marshalling of behavioral phenomena, nor did the medical activities I was engaged in give me the feeling that as a person with help to offer I was doing anything meaningful. I felt I was occupied in a totally haphazard way with constructing an identity for myself as a psychiatrist, but there was no meaningful content to that identity. I felt like an automaton obeying a number of conventional notions, and that by slavishly following a number of medical procedures I was surrounding myself with the aura of a psychiatrist.

I describe this reaction to you to make it clear that my search for the meaning and significance of types of behavior

6

dubbed 'psychotic' or 'schizophrenic' was closely bound up with striving for a certain measure of personal authenticity. I wanted to give my own professional identity as a psychiatrist an authentic significance.

I remember a man who came past my ward every day in blue overalls behind a coal cart. His face attracted me: finely formed. His diagnosis: 'schizophrenia with marked compulsive-neurotic traits.' I invited him to call on me one evening in the hospital apartment where I lived. He accepted my invitation, and when we had begun a tentative conversation I was struck by his sensitiveness. That impression was strengthened when he suddenly started quoting passages from the *Rubaiyat of Omar Khayyam*. I had just made acquaintance with this poem and we each of us read a stanza that evening. He left me astonished and deeply affected – a reaction which intensified as I pursued my conversations with him. Here was an extremely sensitive man who for years, in clothes provided by the institution, had been pushing a coal cart, apparently resigned to his lot and (as I came to understand later) to the shelter and security which life in such an establishment gave him. His mother came to see him every day, but I had no idea how great her influence on him was for I was still thinking in terms of 'disease' and of some physical cause or other as the explanation for his behavior.

Another important springboard for my development in those days was afforded by a series of conversations I had with a youngster classified as suffering from a 'puberty psychosis.' In fact this denoted little more than that he was psychotic, and it was suspected that he was unable to integrate the problems of puberty. As our conversations led to a deepening of the contact between us, I was struck by the inconceivable loneliness and confusion in which this boy, not yet twenty years of age, had spent the greater part of his boyhood and early adolescence. He gave me fleeting glimpses into the drama of his family, his relationship with his father and mother and that of his parents with each other. His feelings of inferiority and degradation were almost impossible to envisage. This time I learned something about the parents' marriage, divorce, his yearnings for his father, the hold his

7

mother obviously had over him and from which he could not wrest himself free. But I did not know how to evaluate properly what he had presented me with, nor how to preserve the contact which his withdrawn and defensive posture gradually made more difficult. I saw him ensnared before my very eyes in a whole host of delusions, and the image he presented was that of a young man irretrievably lost in an abyss of loneliness and bewilderment.

I was reading at this time a book by the American psychoanalyst John Rosen: *Direct Analysis*.[1] It made such a deep impression on me that I used it as a guide to the literature on the psychotherapy of 'psychoses' up to that time. I would like to go into what this book contains in some detail.

Rosen does *not* concern himself with those forms of behavior caused by one or another demonstrable physical disease: senile atrophy of the brain or, in younger people, dementia or shrinking of the cerebral cortex, alcoholic delirium, encephalitis and meningitis (inflammation of the brain and cerebral membranes), lead poisoning, cerebral hemorrhages and tumors, syphilitic cerebral disorders and many others. The term 'psychosis' Rosen reserved for those forms of behavior for which *no* physical cause could be adduced.

With characteristic and refreshing succinctness Rosen defined a 'psychotic' as someone unable to stand on his own two feet in life and to get ahead. If one can do that, even though with great difficulty, then the term 'neurotic' applies. Rosen was (and is) averse to sticking labels on everyone and uses the term 'schizophrenic' as being synonymous with 'psychotic.' Very odd behavior (deviating from the written and unwritten rules of a given culture – in other words 'clear-cut craziness') is for Rosen like a dream from which one cannot wake up, a nightmare, and also a flight from a 'reality' experienced as cold, threatening and bewildering, and from the tasks and responsibilities which this reality presents. It is primarily a regressive phenomenon, therefore, a retreat into childhood. Rosen declined to call this a 'disease.' Since his book was written in 1953 (he began publishing in 1946), he was something of a visionary, as I hope to show later in the course of my story.

8

Rosen also insisted that the behavior of the 'psychotic,' however bizarre, can be *understood* and that intensive psychotherapy (exerting influence via a purely psychological, personal and empathizing method) is the only right approach. The origin of the condition he traces back to some very adverse experiences suffered by the child in its early years and especially in its relation to the mother. In the later formulation of his thinking the concept of the 'bad mother,' who is felt as a poisonous experience and yet as someone to be recovered ('seeking the mother one knew'), broadens into the 'early maternal environment.' [2] Not only the mother but also all literal or symbolic substitutes (grandmother, aunt, little brother or sister, baby-sitter and even . . . father!) can be 'mother' in this sense.

Rosen was critical (correctly, in my view) of Freud's overemphasis on the importance of the father in the emotional development of the child. The child, Rosen argues, does not know that we are living in a Western patriarchal culture. To the child everything in the very *earliest* phase of his development, everything outside himself, is 'mother.' Thus he says:

In this sense even the father is a 'mother.' In the same sense the symbolic substitutes for 'mother' can include the electric night bulb which the infant sees, the air he breathes, the blanket which he chews, the urine which soaks his diaper and irritates his skin, and so on.

As a psychotherapist, Rosen takes vigorous intervening action, searches after the meaning of various delusions, hallucinations and bizarre contact-avoiding lines of behavior and presents himself as an omnipotent and good 'father-mother.' In that way he forces the psychotic person to realize just how much he has suffered. He forces the 'dreamer' to confront anew a reality that had been shunned; and helped by assistant psychotherapists, the client obtains an insight into his condition and how it arose, plus sustained care and attention in which reeducation and a process of relearning all sorts of social skills play a considerable role.

The book *Direct Analysis* startled and convinced me. From then on I read everything there was to read in this field – the

9

psychotherapy of the psychotic person. Séchehaye's dealings with Renée,[3] for instance, the impressive account of a psychotherapist who struggled for years on end with a completely withdrawn (autistic) girl and brought her back to the world of humanity and relatedness. This literature was fascinating, and I discovered to my surprise that for years psychotherapists had been making contact with people who had rejected every form of human contact; they took a hard line with their patients if necessary, cherished them like a loving mother, shared with them experientially the depth of their isolation and discouragement and – what struck me most about their efforts – *did not give up*.[4]

As I searched for more literature I could see a world unfolding before me. Thus I read the work of Schultz-Hencke, who flatly described the schizophrenic condition as a 'neurosis variant,' as well as the work of Christian Müller, Benedetti, Racamier, Winkler, Harry Stack Sullivan and Frieda Fromm-Reichmann.[5]

All these psychoanalytically trained psychotherapists had been convinced by their work that what is called 'psychotic' or 'schizophrenic' behavior is the outcome of a life the course of which was set initially in a family full of tensions and disturbing, psychically injurious interactions between the child and its parents. This sort of life, if the individual should end up dissociated from the family structure, is marked by persistent failure to relate to other persons or to accomplish ordinary tasks and by a profound inability to perform the roles (husband, wife, father, mother) expected of the individual within our culture. These psychotherapists have described the isolation, the predominance of fantasy over reality-oriented action, the profound doubt regarding one's own sexual identity, the problems connected with aggression and a great deal besides. They have stressed the all too human element, have pointed to the often insupportable situations within the family, and have reported the very positive results of the help they were able to give (though therapy was difficult and protracted), thus rejecting step by step the hypotheses of the 'progressive disease' and 'heredity.'

One day I asked to see the very amiable medical superintendent of the institution and put the pile of books I had been reading on his desk. My question was as sincere as it was naive: 'Why don't we do this here? These authors know what they're talking about. They don't believe in a "disease" and a mysterious "physical process." They are struggling to bring about at least a minimal interpersonal relationship and are beginning to comprehend what has seemed incomprehensible.'

The director declined to share my veneration of these writers. He was not all that interested. I can clearly remember his reply. 'Look,' he said, 'a radio set has so many wires. If one of them snaps you get those queer noises coming out of the set. Well, a human being has got millions of brain cells. If a few of those break down, people make queer noises, too. That's schizophrenia. I think it derives from brain damage, maybe from the hormones. One way or another we shall discover this process, perhaps the biochemical cause of the "disease," and until then we must offer the "sufferers" of this "disease" as humane a shelter as we can. Occupational therapy is a good thing, creates self-confidence. Sports and recreation, better furniture and decor for the institution, every so often a drama night and an occasional organized excursion to the zoo.'

He swept my books, amiably, from his desk and that evening I walked home with the feeling that something very important had happened to me. I had come to realize what the background, the philosophical assumption, was on which the whole of clinical psychiatry à la Kraepelin, of which I had once taken so exalted a view, was based. Who was Kraepelin?

Kraepelin was the founder of syndrome psychiatry (also known as nosological psychiatry), and for the present that may be summed up in the proposition of the German psychiatrist Griesinger: 'Diseases of the mind are diseases of the brain.' An endless succession of psychiatrists had thought, inspected, observed, classified in that way . . . and some still do. Thus a psychiatrist had to be a medical man and a neurologist, a neuroendocrinologist and a biochemist. As a neuroanatomist, after his schizophrenic patient had died, he sometimes cut the brain into small slices and put them under a microscope.

What people talked about, their experiences, their life history, were relevant, of course, but this was 'content.' The *way in which* they expressed and conducted themselves, the *form* of their behavior, the absurdity, the element of the bizarre, were 'in principle closed to empathy,' a warrant for the radio-set theory. The chief example was the behavior exhibited by those in the final stage of syphilis – dementia paralytica. Since the spirochete that causes this venereal disease eventually attacks the brain, in the final stage of the disease the sufferer not only evinces paralysis of the central nervous system but behaves in a strange way as well. Typical is the onset of delusions of grandeur. The sufferer thinks he is worth a million, identifies himself with great figures in history. Because of the physiologic basis for abnormal behavior in syphilis, it had been conveniently assumed that in the presence of other kinds of incomprehensible behavior one is bound to find some bacillus or other, a poison or metabolic disturbance.

The sentiments expressed by the medical superintendent of the psychiatric institution where I was training came to be of great significance to me. He was a very humane person who really cared about the patients and the life they led in his institution. Under his administration, even if the process was painfully slow, the institution's closed and open wards, conversation rooms and isolation cells did acquire a somewhat more cheerful look, and he did not neglect to visit the occupational therapy department, where he would utter words of encouragement. Indeed he was a great believer in putting as many patients as possible into buses and sending them off for trips and holiday excursions; and his sympathy was also apparent during his rounds through the wards, although these were somewhat perfunctory. And what he had said to me was partially true. I could accept his philosophy insofar as it referred to people suffering from dementia paralytica, cerebral atrophy, tumors and other forms of organic dementia, idiocy and profound mental defectiveness. But he simply threw onto the same pile all those who had been provided with extravagant labels such as puberty psychosis, degeneration psychosis, hysterical psychosis, manic-depressive psychosis, real and less real (!) schizophrenia. My conversation with him served to confirm my suspicion that despite all the respect shown in clinical psychiatry for psychoanalytical and psychological ways of looking at things, psychiatry was still governed by the fundamental starting point of physical disease.

If the 'schizophrenic' process was in fact seen as a mysterious illness, the concepts 'endogenous' and 'degenerative constitution' (these terms are still very much in use) were not just considered as hypotheses but had come to be used as though they referred to tangible realities, as though they had been demonstrated and experimentally proven. And the 'heredity' cause, especially for those conditions described as 'manic-depressive' and 'schizophrenic,' was obviously believed to have a very real significance.

Once I realized that the starting point was fundamentally organic, it gradually became evident to me why there were so few encounters with psychotic people that really engaged the parties at a human level. Why all the attempts to make the wards somewhat more attractive made such a superficial impression. Why there was so much complacent talk about the results of the massive doses of tranquilizers administered, which 'had given the institution quite a new face.' I could now see why there was a singularly expectant atmosphere: the moment when biochemists, neurophysiologists, pathologists and endocrinologists would finally prove their point about the 'disease process' was being awaited as a kind of happy event after which, with a sigh of relief, we would at last be able to go to work combatting all those psychotic conditions on a really causal basis.

I left the mental hospital in a state of considerable perplexity, with misgivings about my 'heroes' – and got lucky.

I continued my training at the psychiatric clinic of Leyden University. I call that 'lucky' because this clinic, under the direction of Professor Carp, was the only one in The Netherlands that was organized consistently for psychotherapeutic ends. Carp obliged his residents to read and write reports. He opened the doors to an enormous literature: Adler, Jung,

13

Freud, Buber, Gabriel Marcel, Carl Rogers, innumerable philosophers whose names (apart from Sartre) I have forgotten. In this clinic there was reading and there was discussion. People labeled 'neurotic' were 'accepted for therapy.' The approach to psychotherapy was Adlerian (tracing the source of the inferiority feelings, discovering the life-style that would obviate failing, and then just interpreting) – amateurish, perhaps, but with one substantial advantage. One *read* Adler (not *about* Adler), acquired a feeling for the holistic, purposive aspect of his view of things; and this made more accessible the work of Karen Horney and Sullivan.[6]

Submissively, I made myself conversant with the techniques, acquired a feel for them and gradually found my way through the literature. That psychotherapy was a discipline which also calls for an extensive technical training was something I had all but failed to realize. That through the seeming neutrality of the therapist many of the clients' desires and longings come to the fore, that old wounds are exposed, that the pain of unassimilated and forgotten memories of early experiences can be mobilized – this was the type of technical training that we residents had not come close to coping with. The emergence of powerful emotions, re-experienced by way of and within the relation to the psychotherapist ('transference'), and their clarification vis-à-vis past and future – all that still had to be experienced, and the proper way to 'handle' these emotions was an 'art' which we were still a long way from mastering.

The advantage of this avalanche of psychodynamic reflections and practical experience was that I first went through it, floundered – and then read and, intellectually at any rate, got an overall view of what the literature had to offer. I read the lot, quite indiscriminately, and Carp went on feeding me more. We engaged in psychodrama and sociodrama; and not least of all, my mentor introduced the residents to the work of Maxwell Jones and the sociotherapeutic principles that flow from it. The whole clinic was presented as a therapeutic community and I was confronted with all the ups and downs of that community and so with a little bit of 'administrative psychiatry.' Now in retrospect I realize the clinic was far from being a genuine therapeutic community; and yet one did get a whiff of organization principles, and they stuck.

'Responsibility,' 'responsibility for the other,' 'a person is what he does' – these were slogans used sometimes by enthusiastic residents in the most irresponsible way, but one was learning. However abstract all these philosophical reflections on the encounter with the 'mentally disturbed person' may sometimes have been, however limited, too, the knowledge which the group of residents had of themselves, and however many the ups and downs in psychotherapeutic relationships with which they operated, there was an unmistakable thread running through it all. The encounter of two human beings and what unfolded in the field between the two was presented to me as fundamentally the only form of meaningful action on the part of a psychiatrist.

During this period I was put in charge of a man who had manifestly been passed from hand to hand. Full of enthusiasm, a resident had gone to work on this student, who was fear-ridden and tied up in compulsive rituals, on 'orthopedagogical' lines. From behind his desk he kept pointing out to the client how the latter was trying to dodge his 'responsibilities.' What did my colleague know of his own sadism, which was lurking behind all that psychotherapeutic enthusiasm? What did I know about it myself?

However that may be, the anxiety-ridden student became gradually more anxious, for he saw himself cut off from every avenue of escape. Under the effects of this 'psychogenic barrage,' the automatic fire of pedagogical interpretations, the man became more and more anxious and one day he stopped making any reply at all. Indefatigable, the resident persevered for some time, pointed out to his client that he was 'ducking his responsibilities,' but eventually became alarmed over the situation that had arisen. The patient seemed petrified and numb and evinced no emotional reaction at all. He appeared to be without any feeling. After much discussion the diagnosis was declared to be 'schizophrenia.' It was decided (for inscrutable reasons) to administer some electroshocks. (The patient had previously stated that he felt his psychotherapist to be the devil.)

A number of splendid theories relating to death and rebirth have been written about sleep cures, insulin cures and electroshock cures, but what you really get is the shock of your life. The client did not react to his electroshocks in any way – at any rate he did not evince any sense of rebirth. On the contrary, he made an even more deathly impression. In this state he walked around the clinic for a year, replying to questions only with a 'yes' or a 'no.' The man remained without any expression of feeling and gave the impression of being made of wood. Absolutely no form of contact with him was possible.

So he was assigned to me as a sort of nuisance item, a part of the clinic's furniture. The diagnosis – originally 'obsessional neurosis' – had been altered to 'defect schizophrenia,' which meant that this man neither talked nor wept nor laughed. The experience I had with him turned out to be really crucial to my further development as psychiatrist-psychotherapist. Every day I would invite him to come and have a chat, force him to read the newspaper, to recite poetry, took him for walks in the park, tossed him a football (which he had a hard job throwing back) – all to no avail. However, my earlier experience had made me obstinate. I just would not be put off. There were occasions when we were walking through the park when with tears in my eyes I would seize him by the shoulders and give him a good shaking. He should and he would respond to my appeal for contact; I refused to accept his total rejection of me. I saw him every day for six months, except on weekends, brought Adler's whole theory to bear on him, filled in the silences, and slowly became overwhelmed with a sense of discouragement (referred to in the literature as 'therapeutic despair').

Leslie Farber has written very movingly about the deep despair through which the psychiatrist-psychotherapist passes in his attempts, lasting often for several years, to bring about a human contact with his schizophrenic client. I quote Farber:

What of the weeks, months, years, when these two sit together for an hour a day, immersed in a silence broken only by obscure mouthings or posturings conveying no secure meaning; or by earnest professional adjurations which draw no response? How much easier it would be during these desolate periods to abandon what must often seem a bitter mockery of relationship.[7]

I was getting nowhere with Karel. I felt that I was not seen, not acknowledged – indeed our relationship was a mockery of any form of togetherness between people, a situation from which I wanted more and more to run away. I began to dread these sessions. I then took to reminding myself that Karel was classified as a 'defect schizophrenic,' and I found a measure of relief in this 'diagnosis.' I believe now that *this very relief of the psychiatrist might well be one of the major functions of making diagnoses.* When we see that our stubborn attempts at restoring contact are not being crowned with success, falling back on attaching a name to people, linked with the associations 'sick,' 'defective,' etc., affords a feeling of relief, because we then think we are dealing with a mode of human existence so disrupted by the processes of a physical disease that a human encounter *can never* take place and therefore need not be pursued. I recalled, too, the convincing way in which my former instructor – the director of the mental hospital – had consigned all psychotherapy of 'schizophrenics' to the realm of illusion. My colleagues likewise advised me to reserve my energy for more accessible people, and my convictions began to waver.

That is how the deliberate and stubborn defensiveness of an individual with whom one is seeking contact can tempt one into accepting certain 'conclusions,' hypotheses about the 'organic origin' of deviant behavior, when that behavior exceeds certain proportions. Once again, it seems to me likely that the whole of (neo-)Kraepelinian clinical psychiatry has been a sort of desperate attempt on the part of psychiatrists to whom their clients consistently denied any form of contact, or who were nonplussed by utterances they could not or would not understand, to explain something by giving it a name.

During one of our sessions a bird was singing outside. We had been sitting in silence for some time. More or less without thinking I said: 'Do you hear that bird, Karel?' I looked outside, expecting no reply. But as I stood by the open window, at my back I heard my client say: 'I hear it all right. It makes me sad.' I stood in front of the window as if rooted to the floor. The words, the tone, the feeling they conveyed had taken me by surprise. As I turned to look at him our eyes met, and when I asked: 'What do you mean by that?' he replied: 'It's scalding under the sand.'

I did not need much sensitivity to symbolism to interpret that remark. It was a vital expression of the sandlike quality of his defensiveness.

The rest of the session was spent in silence, but from that moment there was no holding me back. In the evenings I would invite Karel to my room, would talk to him about Buber, Jung, about myself, my life, my ideals and disappointments. He held me at bay, relapsing into silence again for a couple of months, till the evening when, quite spontaneously, he started to talk. He talked for four hours, while I listened. He told me he was living in hell, surrounded by infernal watchmen. Everywhere there were omens reminding him, with exultant glee, of his lost claim on life. He was already dead – or not yet quite dead. To him I was the devil who during all those months had been refuting, though with a sadistic ambiguity, his right to life, had been holding out to him something which I knew very well was over and done with for good as far as he was concerned. The flower kiosk by the clinic, and a mattress that was floating in the ditch near the kiosk – that contrast was not there for nothing. It signified: 'The flowers are finished, you go *that* side, the side of the mattress, of decay.' And I myself, his therapist, had I not often said: 'I want to help you' (Dutch: *helpen*)? It was obvious to Karel what I meant. *Hel-pen* – to *pen* somebody inside *hell*.

Karel described to me a psychotic mode of existence in which everything was set into one single mode of meaning: guilt and expiation. He told me how, as an only child, he had been brought up a strict Catholic, about a weak father, his relationship with an anxious, oversolicitous mother who clung tightly to her son, felt any manifestation of independence on her child's part (sex included) as an imminent danger and so arrived at a state of close mutual attachment with him (identified in the specialist literature as a 'symbiotic relationship').

18

In the background were the priests, confession, the threat of hell, masturbation as a mortal sin – an atmosphere that made the conflict within the family even more dramatic and alarming. Karel described to me in those four hours his life history. His repeated failures as a student, fear in his contacts with girls – everything ridden with anxiety and guilt about his sexual feelings.

Gradually he became a total prey to anxiety, which permeated all his relationships. He ended up addicted to alcohol, to obsessive thoughts and compulsive actions. Strong, aggressive and sexual feelings made themselves felt all the same (people remain healthier than you might suppose), thoughts like: 'Even Jesus masturbated.' He talked about the battle against these thoughts, his urge to wash himself, to purify himself from guilt and so on.

He described to me in detail his experience of the 'ortho-pedagogic therapy,' the barrage of guilt-resuscitating interpretations produced by his former psychiatrist, who seemed to cut off every way of escape. I glimpsed a part of the psycho-dynamics, but the whole of his inner conflicts and their interaction escaped me.

I was able to share his feelings about the 'transformation' of the earlier therapist into 'devil.' Though the aggressive character of this type of psychotherapeutic intervention was unmistakable, Karel had also very likely projected his tremendous rage (repressed) onto his psychotherapist.

His account of the electroshock treatment convinced me that this procedure sumply *cannot* be the answer required by a person in dire need. Ringed around by grinning faces (the residents at the clinic), he faced electrocution, the ultimate penalty for his guilt. I have seldom heard such a lucid and totally clear account of what went on inside someone being 'treated' with electricity in this way. He talked the whole evening. I listened, now and again put in a question, understood a great deal, and we finished by shaking hands. Karel said: 'I thought you were the devil, or God. Might have been that, too. But I see now that your hand is moist. That's anxiety, I know. Were you feeling anxious?' I admitted my distress at everything I had been listening to, and Karel observed: 'Then there is a third possibility. Neither God nor the devil can know anxiety. But a human being can. I'm glad you are human, and yet . . .'

I replied (too hastily): 'You're afraid that because I'm human I won't be strong enough to be able to help you.'

We walked back to the clinic, and from then on we spoke together every day. Four months later his rigid psychotic world faded away. Other significances became possible. As I remember, it all seemed to me very much like a stream which, long frozen and still, was at last thawing out. Karel had a great sense of humor (he would send me into fits of laughter) and he became able to cry.

It will be obvious to the reader that this startling experience with Karel made me from that moment on a convinced supporter of the hypothesis that the psychotic person can (and must) be understood and approached on psychotherapeutic lines. Henceforward I was lost to classical clinical psychiatry for good. Confidence in my 'heroes' (Rosen, Müller, Séchehaye, Sullivan, Fromm-Reichmann, etc.) had been restored. I felt myself to be a kind of Rosen. Then, when Karel eventually managed to express fury and smashed a teacup, the director of the clinic promptly discharged him. At the moment all was going well!

I was about to continue my training in Amsterdam. I left for the city, and I saw Karel regularly for his psychotherapeutic session. His 'psychosis' had gone; anxious and soon addicted once more to alcohol, he struggled with reality. I made a lot of technical blunders in the psychotherapy (it is a skill that has to be learned), and Karel made me fall into every trap he could set for me. I yanked him out of the Amsterdam pubs, found work for him to do, and somehow or other we kept our relationship going.

The next step in training was supposed to be neurology. I chose Amsterdam for several reasons. 'Anthropological psychiatry' was being taught there as part of the psychiatric curriculum, and that sounded humane and wise. Also the clinic in Amsterdam was licensed to give neurological training. Here I must give a brief explanation.

Psychiatry and neurology did not in my view go together. Gradually – after 1956 – I had become convinced that this was a kind of freakish alliance, a product of history but a logical incompatibility. Logically, as I saw it, psychiatry had nothing to do with neurology (the theory of diseases of the nervous system). Training in this combination, I thought, led only to the creation of 'nerve specialists,' who failed to attain the degree of competence that would enable them to offer adequate help either as psychotherapists and psychodynamic psychiatrists or as neurologists. I found these ideas reflected in Sullivan (who was outspoken in his opposition to the misalliance of psychiatry and neurology),[8] and later in the work of other writers. As things stood, however, the future psychiatrist had to spend a year and a half in a neurological clinic. I opted quite deliberately for Amsterdam in order to *dodge* my term of neurology. I knew that though the university clinic was equipped to give training in neurology, very little came of it in practice.

That is just how it was. There was practically no neurology. My plan to get myself registered as a specialist in psychiatry without hanging around for a year and a half in a neurological department was a hundred percent successful. For the rest, the expectations I entertained of the psychiatry taught there were high. It would not be the same as it was with Carp, but it sounded all very 'anthropological' and 'enlightened' and I still cherished a naive faith in 'professors.'

The experience of discovering the real state of affairs was nothing less than appalling. The clinic turned out to be a sort of antiquated department of a large general hospital. The pavilion had a gloomy aspect – no garden, no lawn. On the wards the physically affected (with dementia, epilepsy, etc.) lay in beds side by side with people with grave problems in living (also in beds!). There was no group atmosphere at all, the psychiatry practiced was a sort of organic Kraepelin-nosology, with an almost ludicrous concern with 'diagnosis' and a staggering absence of any form of psychotherapeutic treatment, let alone training.

The weekly rounds consisted of going from bed to bed, the professor in the van, chief residents and junior residents filing along after him. The chief resident-instructors managed to perpetuate a low morale by their lethargic or authoritarian behavior. Everybody went around in a white coat or nurse's uniform except the patients: they wore blue hospital clothes and pants too long for them.

Of 'anthropological psychiatry' I heard little. Quite evidently it existed in the books and various documents, but I learned there in Amsterdam the truth of Einstein's remark: 'If you want to know what people really believe in, don't listen to what they say but look at what they do.' And what did they do, and what did the instructors ask us residents to do? To this very day it still is not clear to me.

In this clinic there was a quite explicit interest in the importance of the brain, its volume, the thickness of the cerebral cortex. The term 'air-insufflation' was much in use. By introducing a certain amount of air into the brain it is possible to photograph tumors or shriveling cerebral tissue. I certainly familiarized myself with a number of organic diseases there: pronounced shrinkages of the cerebral cortex, leading to extreme dementia, delirium tremens, dementia paralytica (the final stage of syphilis), the brain tumor that causes abnormal behavior. The purely psychiatric activities consisted of filling in forms containing an extensive psychiatric and physical record and making 'diagnoses.' Apropos of those, what struck me at this time was that in Amsterdam they had a much greater variety of labels. 'Booking out' morning was a sort of last judgment which consisted of hawking labels (degeneration psychosis, schizophrenia, puberty psychosis, debility psychosis, manic-depressive psychosis, reactive, neurotic, endogenous depression and so on), after which the patient's stay was administratively terminated. The patient was then either sent home or off to some psychiatric hospital or other.

The university's psychiatric clinic in fact turned out to be a reception center as well as a sort of road sign pointing to various mental hospitals in the country where 'treatment' could begin. It also functioned as an instructional center where the residents were able to see a large number of patients and where patients were put on show in the lecture room before the medical students, who listened to the commentary provided by their instructors.

The most striking thing in this bizarre world was the conduct of the teaching staff, who had very largely or even completely finished their psychoanalytical training. Their behavior puzzled me. In the mornings they would walk through the clinic in their white coats, and in the afternoons they would sit behind a couch, ostensibly functioning as psychoanalysts. Thus they stood with one foot in clinical organically-oriented psychiatry and exhibited patients in crowded lecture rooms and doled out labels as required, and one foot in psychotherapy, with all the respect and consideration for people in trouble inherent in the psychotherapeutic situation (in my fantasy, at least). It was not until later that I understood the reason for this peculiar division of functions and the background of what was an extraordinarily chaotic operation, both in organization and in the types of remedial action. So far as the latter are concerned – they were minimal.

In any event I came to one conclusion: there was no training. The best course, it seemed to me, was to go my own way and not be too conspicuous.

On the first count I succeeded, on the second I did not.

[1] J. N. Rosen: *Direct Analysis: Selected Papers* (New York, 1953).

[2] J. N. Rosen: *Direct Psychoanalysis, II* (New York, 1968).

[3] M. A. Séchehaye: *Symbolic Realization* (New York, 1951).

[4] The study by Gertrud Schwing, for example, has become classic. This psychotherapist (like Rosen and Séchehaye) stresses very much the recovery of a sense of maternal security.

A couple of quotations from *Ein Weg zur Seele des Geisteskrankheiten* (Zürich, 1940):

> My work has probably been successful because – as I later recognized – I instinctively gave the patients what they had at one time missed in the child-mother relation: motherly feeling. The mentally sick person who has escaped from reality into the unconscious condition of early infancy will apparently allow a motherly hand to lead him back into the real world.

Another passage:

> We have to give patients the maternal affection they lacked in childhood and which, usually without realizing it, they have spent their whole lives searching for. I do not refer here to the deprivation noted by Freud, which is tied up with the child's ineluctable, unquenchable yearning for love. For that involved the parent of the opposite sex. But the patients I am writing about here were exclusively frenzied, they would remain inaccessible to any therapy and every human effort to get close to them. Through the 'mother-experience' it was possible to reach them.

This writer shows great understanding, too, in pointing out the problems of the psychotherapist who feels himself called to this 'work.' In his wish to help, his 'motherly' dedication, the psychotherapist may also be expressing an attempt on his own part to compensate in others (his patients) for the mother love which he himself (or she herself) had to go without.

[5] References to this literature are to be found in the Notes to Chapter 3.

[6] There is not so much difference between the defensive forms of anxiety engendered in relations between people. Adler has called them *Sicherungsstreben*, Horney later described them as 'neurotic trends' and Sullivan as 'security operations.'

[7] L. Farber: 'The Therapeutic Despair,' *Psychiatry*, vol. 21, no. 1 (1958). Farber has had some noteworthy things to say about this important subject. For these the reader is referred to the Notes below.

⁸ H. Stack Sullivan: *Conceptions of Modern Psychiatry* (London, 1953). Lecture 1 in particular provides an illuminating survey of the whole range of problems.

NOTES

A simple but very clear survey of the psychiatric view of 'schizo-phrenically disturbed people,' the vague outlines of which have been presented in this chapter, is to be found in J. Rattner: *Was ist Schizophrenie* (Zürich/Stuttgart, 1964). Regarding the despair of the psychotherapist as an almost necessary ingredient of any psycho-therapeutic relation with people who reject every deep emotional contact, Farber says:

When faced with the inevitable despair, which I am suggesting must sooner or later overtake the conscientious therapist, it will not matter how indomitable or inventive may be his efforts to keep going: he cannot hope that his despair will be entirely unnoticed by his patient. Although perceptiveness may be severely impaired in the schizophrenic, he knows that it can never be extinguished – a knowledge which may, in fact, add the final straw to his desolation. What I would suggest here is a possi-bility which, since it has been overlooked, may offer some truth as well as solace. To the extent that the therapist becomes 'present' for his patient, that patient is capable of pity for his friend's distress. . . . In response to the therapist's despair . . . the patient will often try to confirm the therapist's image of himself as therapist. And insofar as the therapist is sincerely dedicated to his work – paradoxically, just because he is so dedicated – this will also have the effect of confirming him as a fellow human being. (Once again there is an awesome split between the 'human' and the 'scientific.') . . . In therapy the paradox is inescapable that the man who is incapable of arousing pity will find it hard to help another. I attempted to describe the peculiar and painful nature of the therapeutic life with a schizophrenic patient – its emptiness, meaninglessness, lack of confirmation – in short, the circumstances which lead to a particular despair on the part of the therapeutist, which may evoke in the patient a response of pity for his doctor's plight. I suggested further that such pity might very well lead the patient to assuage the thera-pist's anguish through therapeutic movements intended to confirm the therapist as therapist.

It seemed to me then, as it seems to me now, that despair is more or less intrinsic to the therapeutic life with schizophrenia, and moreover that such despair, if acknowledged rather than dis-owned, if contended with rather than evaded, *might* (the word is important) have a salutary effect on therapy.

I would like only to suggest in passing that the avoidance of despair by reducing it to a merely 'morbid' or 'unhealthy' state of mind, thus refusing to conceive it as belonging inescapably, in some measure, to our lives as human beings – that such avoidance may be more malignant than despair itself. (It was Kierkegaard's belief, you will recall, that the worst of all despairs is that in which one does not know he is in despair.)

It sometimes happens that despair itself provides the very conditions of seriousness and urgency which bring a man to ask those wholly authentic – we might call them tragic – questions about his own life and the meaning and measure of his particular human-ness.

When despair is repudiated these questions go unasked, and it may be exactly here – in the failure to confront these questions – that there occurs a turning in one's development which is inauthentic.

L. Farber: 'Schizophrenia and the Mad Psychotherapist,' *Review of Existential Psychology and Psychiatry*, vol. 2, no. 2 (1962).

2. WALTER

The day I begin working at the university clinic I am taken down the lines of beds by the chief staff psychiatrist.

Some patients are wandering about the closed ward, which in many respects presents a gloomy sight. The wooden floor, iron bedsteads, high windows looking out on a small inner yard covered with gravel. The patients wear faded hospital clothing, some sit around wooden tables in the marble-floored corridor, smoking.

We stop at Walter's bed and the case is explained to me. He was admitted three weeks before, after a bizarre attempt at suicide. It seems that he tried to slit his jugular vein with a sharp axe, and had also injured his hands. When admitted, he was very confused and bewildered. Tranquilizers did little to improve his condition . . . so the next step was to administer electroshocks. When he had had four of these Walter threw himself like a log on the marble floor of the corridor. Asked why, he is alleged to have said: 'I wanted to help a bit. I wanted to bash my head on the floor. Now I've given myself the fifth shock.' It was then decided to stop the electroshock treatments for the time being. The staff psychiatrist tells me to 'see what you can do.'

27

Walter is lying there in bed, his eyes filled with anguish. He seems to be listening to our conversation. Jet-black, curly hair, a round Indo-European face. He is nineteen, but looks closer to fourteen. When I get back from visiting the ward, my first job is to unwrap the bandages from Walter's neck and hands and remove the sutures. When I bend over him I hear him whisper: 'I'm so much in the jungle. Get me out.' I feel at once profoundly moved. That same day I ask the male aide on the ward to bring Walter to the small consulting room.

Before I describe what happened during this first session I think it would be a good idea to pause for a moment and reflect on this immediate sense of contact. I am describing the situation twelve years later, and as I cast back in my mind to this first contact, what strikes me is just how direct it was. The whole outset of this therapy had something very emotional about it and in many respects was unrealistic. As the most recently arrived resident in this clinic I had the job of filling in the records, producing brief life histories and summaries, investigating and 'making diagnoses.' My job was to classify and describe, and if the tranquilizers and electroshocks failed to work, I was supposed to insist on a rapid transfer to a mental hospital in the country.

Where Walter is concerned I seem to forget all these duties. I ask for permission to stop the electroshocks, and that same day – September 5, 1958 – I start with the 'psychotherapy.'

The consulting room is small, with a marble floor and high walls, painted white. A couch, two chairs, a table and a small wash basin in the corner comprise the furnishings. There I receive Walter, who comes in wearing an oversize white hospital shirt. One hand is holding up the long pants. I give him my hand, which he clutches tightly throughout the session; and he begins to whisper:

Little balls are hopping around everywhere, leaping and dancing in the body. I have a great world of ideas, hard as stone. The ball that is me has got separated from the world of atoms. It is hovering about now in the universe. The youngsters were in high spirits and the little ball hasn't been able to keep going. It has to come back into the middle; it has to recover its compactness. The ball has imagined itself a father.

My train of thought is quite mixed up. I am in the jungle. When the ball got cut off from the nucleus, life began. When one ball ground against another, it would burst apart. I try to lose energy, for in that way the nucleus may come all right again. I was dreaming away in that world of quick, nimble little balls. The ball had a charge just as big as the other balls. It got feelings, flesh, carnal feelings. It didn't want them. How will this nucleus be able to come into place again? Will it again have contact with the other little balls? We couldn't look one another straight in the eye anymore. I was ashamed of the badness in my body.

All at once there is light coming into the world. I must not remain isolated like this. I just let myself go. In military service they were all so keen and lively. I started to feel a bit cut off. I must do something to help. I really must manage to find the nucleus again myself. The world has become a labyrinth.

During this session I do little but listen and repeat Walter's sentences. I want to try and analyse it in rather more detail. Practically all the important strands in his complex of problems are there.

I assume that Walter is trying to give an account of his loss of the 'ego.' This would appear to be the major theme. He is describing this psychotic condition as a loss of the unity and compactness of his personality. He uses the language of atomic fission. Not only do the balls hop and dance inside the body, but the 'ego' ('the ball that is me') floats around in the universe.

The second theme includes a lot of what Walter evidently feels is the cause of his condition. He is quite clearly indicating that he feels himself engulfed by aggressive feelings: 'When one ball ground against another, it would burst apart.' He describes his world of thought as 'stone-hard,' there is 'badness' in his body. In the course of this session he also says: 'There were small birds, and later on a bear.' In the subsequent sessions it becomes evident that this just about sums up the essential nature of his problems. Walter has been a dreamy and lonely child for too long, a child preoccupied with little birds and the tender things of nature. He often speaks in diminutives as well. Then suddenly the 'bear' threatens to overwhelm him. Carnal feelings and aggressive feelings. During his military service he can no longer shut his eyes to the enormous difference between him and the 'quick and nimble little balls.'

His description 'I was dreaming away in that world of quick, nimble little balls' suggests how enormously backward he was in reaching maturity and in developing the ability to relate to other people. The loneliness is clearly indicated: 'a little isolated.'

But the world did not really become a labyrinth during his military service. As I am to discover later on, the labyrinth had been there presumably since he was two years old.

By way of a third theme, Walter indicates the lines on which the psychotherapy should proceed, and he puts these suggestions to his therapist. Walter proposes as the primary task that he must recover his 'ego,' his compactness. He says: 'I really must manage to find the nucleus again myself.'

Looking back, this seems to me one of his most crucial statements – and how blind I was to it! Walter, with his feeble sense of identity and independent selfhood, is telling me to take it easy. To recover the nucleus is the primary task; but an undue amount of psychotherapeutic activity, born of an impulse to give help and give it quickly, can at most only increase the threat to his autonomy. Walter is asking me to be a catalyst and to leave it to him to fit the various parts of his self together again. He is indicating what role he is prepared to assign to the therapist.

Twice during the session the 'father' theme occurs: 'The ball has imagined itself a father.' We shall see that he missed his father enormously – a bond that could have given him masculine self-confidence.

The advice Walter is giving me I would sum up as follows: 'Help me to become a man, keep your distance and leave most of the psychotherapy to me.'

During the next two weeks Walter utters bits and pieces of

his life history and his nexus of problems. The contact is now deep and open, now fearful and withdrawn. Walter recognizes me, seems apparently less confused, talks to the male nurses on the ward and says: 'I didn't know there were so many good people in the world.' I see him every day and continue to explain and encourage. Walter persists in talking about his 'savage nature.' At the age of six he had shot a bird and scooped fishes out of the pond and these were thoroughly mean things to do. As a session is beginning he picks an insect off the floor and studies it attentively, seeming upset because it is dead. He is anxious and tense and speaks slowly. 'I'm afraid of myself, of my rough nature.' The theme of the big, wild body that threatens to get out of control turns up again and again:

Walter: I've been frightened by my growth. I've got a treacherous body, not a good one. I would like to have no body, actually, to go on being just a shadow, and yet be in the world. A body with less weight, which merges with other people. My body is so big and I have to control that from inside.

That body of yours has been growing fast in the past few years, eh!

Walter: You bet! (And he laughs heartily.)

Walter also talks about the instructional films he saw during his military service, the sex instruction that threatened him (he didn't want to know about sexuality). The theme of his feeble selfhood keeps recurring: 'Everybody pushes me back, I can't keep my end up, I am afraid about what will become of me.'

The sessions are full of tension and anxiety. Sometimes Walter leaps around the room, screaming: 'I mean to do something, I'm nobody's fool!'

I give him a folder and paper for drawing and writing things down. In my notes for October 7 I find: 'A very striking change. Walter is speaking relatively fluently and starting to tell me more about his life history.' Before I present you with that I want to give you some more facts about those first sessions.

31

Almost without embarrassment Walter begins to talk about a radical doubt as to his sexual identity: 'All my life I've been uncertain whether I was a boy or a girl.' It started very early on, in his second or third year. Walter recollects his mother giving him a white shirt with a small bird embroidered on it. This recollection he uses as a symbol marking the onset of his confusion regarding the body: Was he boy or girl?

Walter describes a sense of being alienated from his own body, which 'just sort of hung there' and which 'grew so fast.'

You were afraid of that growing body with all that energy and all those desires.

Walter: Yes, I've got such a big body, anyway, and then to have to control it.

I want to help Walter take control again.

Walter: My father was a vigorous, robust sort of man. He had a pushing way with him, and that really made me somewhat afraid of him.

I enter in my notes: 'Walter has doubts about his own sex and has presumably never had the feeling of being a man. He feels small inside and his growing physical nature distresses him. The body is part of all that. He wanted to get into the big world and be a man, just like the rest of the lads in military service, with a job to do and something to aim at. But inside he feels like a 'little ball,' with a yearning, maybe, to remain a sexless child.'

October 20: Walter (comes in and says in a mimicking tone of voice): D'you smoke cigars? Myself, I used to smoke a cigarette or so. On my military service I saw a film, *In Privacy.* Walter comes from God. So a baby is brought by the stork, is it? I saw the film and I didn't like it. It shouldn't be allowed.

You didn't want to come from father and mother? No sex.

Walter: No, from God, and then out into the wide world. I didn't want to be tied to people. *They did nothing but get you glued to them.*

You would rather not come from people, because that creates a tieup, of sorts.

32

Walter: Yes, mother was real warm, and she kept making lovely little socks for me.

What kind of socks?

Walter: Oh, lovely ones, you know, really lovely.

Sometimes you got fed up with these socks, I suppose? (Walter suddenly bursts out laughing, really laughing, and his eyes fill with tears. Crying and laughing all at once.)

October 25: Walter wants to talk about nature again. By nature – I am now beginning to understand his language – he means the earth and the body. (Lewis Hill has called this process of grasping a highly idiosyncratic use of language 'to schizophrenese.')

It got so big and heavy. Can it really be light as well? You should do something with that body. I find it marvelous to have got a body like that. The earthly side of it was getting so terribly big. I wondered if I should be allowed to live so long from God. I had been claiming such a lot of life already. I felt such an egoist. I felt so mean and I couldn't come up to what people wanted.

I understand, I think, that Walter feels like a child in a great big body and feels guilty about his inability to give and to act. He also gives expression for the first time to a feeling of unlimited inferiority in regard to his brother Bill, three years his junior, who can do everything so much better. On the ward he becomes more active, talks to the nursing staff and says he is feeling better. He tried to help a fellow patient. What strikes me as I work over these notes is how Walter is presenting me with further bits of advice, which I persist in ignoring. He says: 'I didn't want to be tied to people. They did nothing but get you glued to them.' Here he is presumably expressing his tremendous fear of being committed to someone, the effect of which would be to dissolve the boundaries of the 'ego' and undermine his extremely weak sense of autonomy. My motherly dedication, my deciphering of his symbolic language, do of course provide contact and 'light in the world,' but they are also alarming. Walter fears that he

33

will 'get glued' to me and I to him. A more distant attitude would, I suppose, have helped him more at this stage than my dedication and affection, which reveal how much I am touched by the appeal he makes in the role of an anxious child.

Time now to tell you more about Walter's life history. I begin with what his mother had to say about it. During the three and a half years I was working with Walter I met with her regularly. One of the things she taught me was to reject the notion that there is any value to the concept 'schizophrenogenic mother.' Her story convinced me that a great deal of what at a later stage is called 'schizophrenia' is the outcome of a tragic combination of circumstances. No father and mother deliberately act to ensure that their child ends up in a psychiatric institution. They are people with enormous inner conflicts which they often try to resolve through their offspring. Admittedly, in the battle fought between the parents (and in-laws and grandparents) the children are often the battlefield. But the psychotherapist who concerns himself in real depth with all the members of the family loses any tendency to single out a 'guilty party,' though in the case of parents who harshly reject their child and keep hurting it mentally he finds it very hard not to.

As regards this particular drama, at any rate, it must be said straightaway that what Gertrude Schwing calls *Mutterlosigkeit* ('lack of mothering') did not come into it. Quite the contrary. In my talks with this mother she emerged as a plucky woman, battling with herself but also with circumstances that were often overwhelmingly difficult. The loss of her husband, the war situation in Indonesia, in which she saw her two children grow up, the life there in camps and later on in The Netherlands, the process of adjustment, the absence of any kind of help in bringing up her two children, the poverty, the obtuse decisions of this or that 'authority' and then afterwards . . . absolutely no form of psychiatrically effective intervention that might have given her as well as her children something to lean on. Walter's mother is a rather attractive Indonesian half-caste who never raises her voice. She cries softly, at times.

She has a passionate affection for her elder son and talks of what has come upon them both with a mixture of sadness and despair. She is evidently a woman who has felt overwhelmed by life and shows in many ways that she is oversensitive.

She comes from a family of three children and grew up in Indonesia. Her father was of Indonesian origin and her mother white. There were a good many conflicts and she felt strongly attached to her mother, whose behavior in the face of her stern and sometimes tyrannical husband was always rather helpless. Walter's mother grew up in an Indonesian village where she was very unhappy, and for as long as she could remember she had been obsessed with the idea of being 'all white.' She felt inferior because of her half-Indonesian half-European appearance. She is always bringing up the subject of being white, completely white, pure and clean, an aristocratic white woman, opposed tooth and nail to life in a black, primeval forest.

She got engaged and her fiancé often lost his temper badly and beat her on occasion. Although everybody tried to dissuade her, she went ahead with the marriage, for she had 'an unshakable faith in love.' This 'love conquers everything' theme recurs again and again: 'Without love I'm nothing, I can't manage without love, I feel paralyzed and sad.'

She lived with her husband in a town in Sumatra. The marriage was a bad one from the start. She longed for a child, and when it failed to arrive quickly enough, she went to the doctor about it. Then Walter was born. 'He was so handsome, doctor, so handsome. Rosy cheeks, a fine baby, the doctor said. He was everything to me, he was my glimpse of heaven. His hair was fair, like an angel's. As a mother I was worried and nervous, because I hadn't a clue. Other women know instinctively what they have to do, I didn't, I was anxious all the time.'

Breastfeeding became something of a nightmare. An inflammation of the breast kept making it necessary for her to switch to bottle-feeding: 'It was so painful every time.' She never dared leave her child, as other women in Indonesia often did. 'The responsibility was so great, I was upset every time he cried.'

35

Three years after Walter his brother William was born.

The mother tells me all the worries she had: For instance, Walter talked so little, and she recalls how the doctor set her mind at rest and said: 'He'll never be a great talker.' Her husband was out and about a great deal, and the mother seldom accompanied him when he went to a bridge party or visited friends. She did not dare leave her children with the *ayah* (native nurse). Often there were violent scenes which very likely derived in part from the fact that her husband found her overprotective about the children. Sometimes she would pack her bags and threaten to leave with the children.

When Walter was five the family moved to Surabaya in Java. Throughout this period, both in Sumatra and later on in Java, there was a lot of anxiety. These were the years prior to the Second World War. During the Japanese occupation her husband was interned, and the mother moved with the children into a house belonging to a member of the family.

This is what she has to say about Walter's clothes: 'He was fair, he was nice to dress. When he was small, he had on a nightie with a little bird embroidered on it, little red socks and shoes, a silk blouse with a collar and some nice pleating. Everything you put on him looked so good. His father found it all too effeminate, and we frequently quarreled about it. But after all he was just a child. Later on I gave him a white shirt and a pair of shorts with two little green birds on them. They stood out against the surroundings. Once I saw a Javanese woman peering over the fence at Walter and I heard her mutter: "Is it a child or a puppet?" She gave me such a fright and I thought she might do something bad, so I quickly pulled Walter out of the garden.'

The mother got more and more worried about not being able to give her children enough to eat, and so went short of food herself. As a result, she got into a poor condition, and her sister took the children for a month's holiday: 'I took it very hard, the children being away from me. Every day I looked at the photos and burst into tears.' Later on both the children suffered from an acute form of amebic dysentery and there were no medicines for it. The family lived in a pretty isolated spot, but the mother, although emaciated and ill herself, made a long journey on foot with her two children to a hospital, because she feared for their lives.

During those years – it was the time of the Japanese occupation – the little family lived with various relatives and usually in isolated places high in the mountains, where the mother earned a living by embroidery and needlework. Everywhere there were Japanese soldiers by whom, as a solitary half-European woman, she was frequently molested: 'I was living on edge all the time.' Yet from the stories she had to tell it is clear that the Japanese soldiers were particularly kind and nice to the children. I got the impression that the children, because they were well dressed, made a striking contrast to the totally impoverished people all around them, whose reaction was not at all friendly.

This latter point seems to me very important – the fact that the children were isolated among others of their own age group. The lack of playmates, of a single real pal – 'chum' is the word Sullivan uses – was not only the result of the mother's aversion to the 'natives' and the care she took over the children's clothes; it was also plainly rooted in the situation, and as an element in the story it crops up over and over again.

The mother was also afraid of being murdered by the locals. A very realistic fear, because the half-caste population of Indonesia was despised not only by the whites but equally by the natives. Such a lethal attack was a very concrete possibility, therefore, and this half-caste woman could not look to the Japanese for protection if the local population were to vent its hatred upon her.

The white population, too, lived in the same fear, but they found some protection as long as they were obliged to stay in the camps. Eventually the anxiety proved too much for the mother, and she asked to be interned. Her fear of the Indonesians and her abhorrence and shame regarding her 'peculiar blood' and appearance she expressed in many forms: 'It always seemed to me very bad for Walter to play with the Javanese children. I have always felt such a distaste for the native Indonesians. I detested their mentality, the shiftiness, the lack of straightforwardness. I'm sold on a fair complexion, and

Walter was fair as fair, though when he was six or seven he began to get darker.'

When the family was interned in 1945 Walter was eight, and that period must have been especially difficult for him. Most of the children, according to his mother, were 'riffraff.' 'They were European, so called, but then entirely by Javanese standards.' They used to set upon Walter. He had no life at all, and he gave up speaking. He was also very fearful, timid. His brother William knew how to stand up for himself and had a better relationship with the other children; Walter was always being teased and seemed to be a very different sort of child. During this period in the camp Walter got malaria, so his mother again brought him to a hospital, thus probably saving his life once more.

When the war ended the mother and children traveled a long way together in search of the husband. The boys were looking forward to meeting their father, whom they had not seen for three years. However, he appeared to have already gone to The Netherlands and had established a relationship with another woman.

Thus disillusioned, in 1946 the mother left with her children for The Netherlands. Walter was ten, Bill seven. The boys were very debilitated; meningitis broke out aboard ship, and seven children died from it: 'You lived in a state of anxiety all the time.' It was the depth of winter when the family arrived in The Netherlands. There the mother continued to look after the two children, and in 1948 the marriage was dissolved.

During the negotiations over custody of the children the mother became very depressed. She had no fight left in her. Without a lawyer and with very little knowledge of affairs she had signed a number of documents turning over the guardianship of the children to her husband and his second spouse. Although she tried later to get this rescinded, she had from that moment lost her rights to the children. Walter and his brother started living with their father and stepmother, and from then on they were positioned between the father and stepmother on one side and the mother on the other. Both parties made demands on the children's loyalty. The battle started in real earnest. The children felt the full force of it, and Walter grew increasingly shy and taciturn.

Some years later the mother succeeded in getting the children put under her care again, as their legal guardian: 'We were crazy with happiness at being together again. Walter was happy and was making plans for the future.'

A social worker connected with the court had a different idea, however, and proposed that instead of living with their mother the children should go to an orphanage, so that they would no longer be bandied to and fro in the tussle between the mother and her former husband.

In March, 1951, when Walter was fifteen and his brother twelve, the boys went to an institution. The struggle then shifted to between the mother and the administrators of the orphanage.

During the entire period so far described Walter was moving, evidently with no more than reasonable marks, through elementary school. Not long after he was placed in the orphanage he took the entrance exam for secondary school and passed it.

The mother visited the children frequently and they often came to see her at home. Walter felt very unhappy. 'It was like being shut up in a cage,' he said later. He moved up into the second form with good marks but then the trouble started. The mother continued to assist her son with his lessons, as she used to in Indonesia during his elementary schooling. Walter was finding it harder and harder to go to school, and in September, 1953, in the third form, it became obvious for the first time that he was having great emotional difficulties. The mother refers to this as 'his first breakdown.'

Walter lay in a darkened room, had severe headaches and wanted to be in the dark all the time. 'He lay in bed, stiff as a board.' In that period he became aggressive, and because of that he was admitted to a university psychiatric clinic. A year prior to that event the mother became acquainted with a man whom she married. All the time Walter was staying in the university clinic she visited him once a week. She had no contact with a doctor there, nor did she get any sort of help or guidance. Walter had a few talks with a psychiatrist and his

39

case was diagnosed as 'puberty psychosis.' If only something effective had been done at that time, a good deal of misery could have been prevented. Walter stayed in the clinic for five months, visiting his mother and stepfather on weekends.

The mother describes her son as being 'different' after his stay in the psychiatric clinic. He showed an enormous fear of returning to school. She persuaded him to start again in the second form of the secondary school and asked her new husband to allow Walter to live with them. Walter failed to move up from the third to the fourth form and with the help of a social worker took an exam to be admitted to a course of instruction for laboratory work. The mother found Walter more and more depressed, and when he failed this exam as well, he appeared quite distracted. For a few months he managed to hold down a job in a factory and in August, 1957, was called up for military service . . . and was certified as medically fit!

On weekends he continued to see his mother. Although Walter often said to her: 'I need a good father so much,' his stepfather was totally nonplussed by the passive and childlike behavior of this 'soldier.' To all appearances Bill's development throughout this period was very much less disturbed. Bill had a better understanding with his stepfather and was moving on through secondary school. The tension surrounding Walter grew daily. Then he struck himself with an axe.

After that he was admitted to the psychiatric clinic of the university in Amsterdam.

My contact with Walter in the clinic continues to be of an intensive – much too intensive – quality. Walter communicates with hands and feet, drenches me in a tidal wave of memories, bits and pieces of his life history. There is an element of despair in his whole style of communication, as like a drowning man he grabs and clutches at my outstretched hands.

I shall try to put before you, in as orderly a way as possible, whatever he is able to tell and I to hear: the chaos of memories, experiences, terrors that he expresses and articulates – sometimes in a confused, symbolic way, at other times with surprising clarity. I shall point out a few aspects here and there.

40

Walter: Right from the start I was scared of this great big world. I felt repulsed, pushed away by everything and everybody.

Pushed out of the world?

Walter: Yes, they were always pushing me away.

Here we have a fundamental motif: finding oneself weak and helpless in the world, being overpowered, unable to stand up for oneself with any degree of strength. This theme (called in psychoanalytical literature 'ego weakness') will assume a central place in this story.

Walter: I came to feel very early on that children didn't want to play with me, and before long I was in a strange world of my own. After all, a little kid has to have some outlet.

It was some sort of a shelter where you could creep in and hide because you felt rejected.

What Walter is expressing in one form or another is the feeling of *weakness*. At times he says of this feeling that 'you can't put it into words.' He never had the feeling of being a boy, was totally unskilled at playing with other boys. He describes a whole succession of discomforting experiences, to which his brother, three years his junior, provided a glaring contrast by fitting in much more successfully.

Walter tells me about his bashfulness, embarrassment, his sense of inferiority, of being the odd man out, laughed at by everybody. But the quality of what he is describing is not adequately covered by terms like 'embarrassment' or 'feeling inferior.' What he is trying to get across to me often has such a dimension that while listening to him and trying to interpret, I frequently experience an anxiety at being confronted with the depth of this isolation. Again and again he would repeat: 'I was giving out so very little.' Often he would attempt to describe to me his inability to assert himself as a human being (and a man) in symbolic language: 'Too little light was radiating from me.'

He describes his sense of weakness even in his body as a

'lack of cohesion,' as 'being transparent.' He describes himself as a 'dullard' or a 'little pekinese' as opposed to the 'great hound of the world.'

Sometimes I come across him in the ward, frantically busy with gymnastic exercises and handstands. On various occasions I have to be called because he is trying to eat gravel from the garden – 'stocking up with energy,' as he calls it.

Quite often what he is describing strikes me as a desperate struggle to continue in existence, simply *to be*. He is dead scared in the bath, he says, that he will 'dissolve.' It is spelled out by slow degrees how tremendously guilty Walter feels about his growing dependence on me. He describes himself as a 'parasite on my mother,' saying he had the feeling that through his need for food and care and love she had been gradually scraped hollow.

His growing anxiety is manifest when he starts to eat his feces. I am repeatedly being called to the ward to find Walter with his mouth full of feces. He writes about this:

I have acquired my shit from my feeding and must not pretend that I have not got it. My shit is digested food and I am not afraid of eating it. My shit is what is left of the food and I still hope to get energy from it. Once I've finished it I don't feel sick, but swallowing it gives me a lot of trouble. I regard my body as a pump that has to go all out to get that food and shit down inside.

A pig, after all, eats its own shit and my body wants it, too, just like a pig. I think one can get into the habit of it. It isn't palatable or healthy or sensible to reuse the shit from your ass and take it in again with your hands, but if somebody eats and uses up energy, then he is bound to value what's left over. And that's what I have done.

Later on he writes:

My shit is sawdust with quite a lot of energy particles still in it. The structure of the food has gone, and it is hard for the moisture in the body to seep through the digested food. The food must circulate more through the body. Food, eating, is the body's building bricks and can provide for building up body and mind. I shall be scoffing food for many a long year and I shall remain a man and not pine away in bed like a fly in a spider's web.

What strikes me most about his accounts is that his eating his feces (coprophagy) looks like a desperate attempt to obviate the loss of the 'ego.' With the help of bits of gravel, food, gymnastic exercises and the magic potency of urine (which he also tries to drink) and of feces, Walter is trying to *energize* himself. He is trying, it seems to me, to ensure his existence by drawing to him every source of energy. Eating excreta also has an element of self-punishment about it. He feels he is a pig, and so he wants to consume his own excrement.

I get the impression that Walter is becoming increasingly anxiety-ridden, yet I persist in my intensive contact with him, without realizing that it is probably his own growing and overwhelming dependency on me that is instilling in him all over again the fear of dissolving and losing his feeble identity. A light breaks upon me when he calls out on the ward: 'I'm not a homosexual.' He makes it even clearer to me through bouts of unloading aggression on the ward. He explains that a drawing on the wall is upsetting him a great deal. It turns out to be a drawing of a skier in a descending glide. It feels to Walter as though the man were gliding into the abyss.

He becomes more and more confused and anxious and seems to be disintegrating before my eyes. He gives me the following letter:

The number of crystallines, rock-hard steel iron nuclear spheres, minuscule molar christian marbles, adhesion and cohesion, forces of attraction and repulsion, equally large, a constant quantity which we can count and furthermore with our steel rock-hard iron eyes can see, count and observe, especially in a watery solution. Two equally heavy, steel, hard balls of molecules can be revolving around the rock-hard steel balls of nuclei.

He can hardly express himself any more and once more puts on paper: 'Hard balls, hard double balls, steel-hard eyes.'

Then at last it becomes clear to me that in the whole range and depth of our contact I have got much too close to him. I see with my own eyes what 'the terror of closeness,' this panic that is bound up with our deepening contact, really means. Walter can feel himself dissolving once more and melting symbiotically into me. In the course of a dramatic session I explain to him that at last I understand this terror he has of merging and melting away. Matching the deed to the word, I push my chair as far as possible away from him into the corner of the room, and it seems to me that he suddenly quiets down. He starts to nod approval: 'Yes, it's much better like that, we must keep our distance. Your eyes are blue and mine are brown. Walter wouldn't like to have blue eyes.' Pointing to his brown shoes he says: 'You wear black shoes and I wear brown shoes.'

I am I and he is he. That is what he wishes to tell me! He wants to be himself, to become himself, not a part of me. Then, too, he doesn't want to get entangled in a repetition of the passionate attachment he experienced with his mother – an attachment that had deeply undermined his own sense of being a unique individual (his 'brown eyes').

So throughout the past few months I have completely failed to appreciate that Walter needs distance, and 'must recover the nucleus for himself.' Once I have become more aware of his fear of being engulfed, Walter tries to give me a better idea of what that fear really means to him:

Walter: Yes, doctor, you really haven't managed to understand me all that well in this respect. Look, if I stare at this ashtray, then the energy flies out of me into the ashtray, and then the moment will come when Walter will *be* the ashtray.

You feel that you are transferring to the ashtray, then, that you are changing into an ashtray.

Walter: Just so. The energy flies out of me in that case, and it mustn't. The energy should come *to* me. Do you know what always upsets me?

Walter sometimes feels he is shrinking completely, and then it seems as if all the electrons start clattering in the body and then food has to be pumped in again. There must be a nucleus, a central core, in this body that keeps it all going, otherwise I can see it happening that everything will go to pieces.

When I see you, it is at the expense of the energy I get from eating. I don't want to talk about feelings anymore, I'll push them away now, look, like this. (He makes violent gestures, as though pushing everything away.) I only want to talk about math and physics. I used to like that: $(a-b)^3-a^3=3a^2b + 3ab^2-b^3$. (He laughs.) Yes, math is clear, it's intellect, pure intellect.

Intellect, unclouded by feeling.

Walter: Right. A world of spheres and bisectors, perpendiculars and triangles and parallels.

I believe I am beginning to understand things better. You are scared of coming under my influence and of becoming what I want you to become.

Walter (nods approvingly): Yes. Just so.

2. THE THEME OF DEPENDENCE AND INDEPENDENCE [1]

When I literally stand aloof, Walter feels he is recognized in his terror, but that does not settle the problem. I am now reaching his fantasy world as well, through which he has been trying to resolve the problem of dependency and his own condition of weakness in the world. I am discovering the function of these fantasies, 'delusions,' experiencing them with an increasing degree of empathy and understanding.

Walter continues repeatedly to express how anxious he is about his dependency on me and in this context gives me some insight into a number of worlds he claims to have constructed inside himself. He describes three such worlds:

The first world, that is just nature. I call it the world of nature proper. The sun, the plants. There are no people there at all, only Walter. Of course, in all its clarity it's a bit dead, but it's certain.

The second world includes people, it's 'the ideal world':

45

In this world if you knock two pieces of stone together there's no fire.

The people in this world, he tells me, are tall, strong and masculine and grow beneath the sun. They never lose energy and have what he calls a 'pure intelligence.' They have no feelings. The people are totally independent of one another and merely 'confer together on the basis of reason.' There are no love feelings, either, and no fire, that is to say, no feelings of hatred, and there are no 'Arabian' feelings (of sexuality and dependency).

The third world, he explains to me, is this one. In this world are loss of energy and hate and sexual emotions and grief and loneliness.

In this session Walter also articulates his dread of dying, which he fears as a being reduced to nothing. So often in his relations with other people he has been reduced to nothing.

In his second world Walter is drawing a picture of the totally self-reliant human being. In the first world, too, where Walter is alone but still amid trees and plants, this theme comes to the fore:

Look, doctor, a tree, in the autumn, its leaves fall off and with those leaves the tree nourishes itself again through its roots. We call it humus.

Yet another part of what is signified by the coprophagy is becoming clear to me. Walter is using his excrement as humus. He is trying through coprophagy to realize anew this 'ideal' of total independence:

I had the idea that I could make everything. I wanted all objects to come into being through me, from the bundle of energy that you are yourself, I also made myself. You are actually God.

What I detect here is the omnipotent one-man's-world as a defense against feelings of helpless littleness and powerlessness. I have since heard this more often, of course, but seldom so clearly – this 'megalomania') (delusion of grandeur) or 'fantasy' (those are the technical terms) by way of defense

46

the 'Baron Münchhausen maneuver' whereby a person pulls himself by his own hair out of his feelings of littleness, nothingness and dependency.

Walter presents me with a short letter containing this passage:

> Is another world, a life other than this life possible? The bedstead is strong as steel and hard, the cohesion is considerable. A person, too, it seems to me, may become great and then greater. Beginning small at first and then building up with love and in the process of seeking for love becoming greater and greater. Keep your eyes open all the time and it will get light then from outside, and through seeing well with the eyes is much seeing and thinking, more in fact than hearing thinking.

I get a lot of these sometimes muddled notes from him and try to concentrate on the essence of what he is attempting to convey. Having read it, I say: 'The bedstead isn't dependent on the other bedsteads, is it?'

Walter (laughs and says): No, there's a vacuum in between. I'd like to ask you something. This life is made for everyone, so is yet another life possible, then?

  You mean the fantasy world?

Walter: Yes, another life in this universe. A separation between this one and the other one. The universe is so big. This life here is so much of a jumble. Might there be another life, a different life, with *real* nature?

  You didn't want to live in this life with all its jumble?

Walter: Yes, I was busy catching shrimps one day and then people went by, laughing. I don't know why, they didn't say why, either. It was a regular mix-up.

This is one of the many examples of how Walter feels he is ridiculous, queer, immature. But I sympathize with him in the complaint, the accusation that emerges, the criticism of people's hypocrisy, of the farrago in which so many people end up rigidly confined.

Walter: I want to be off to that second world in the universe, which is the world of the sun. There are no school desks there. In real nature you only worry about good health and you get food straight from the plants, no preparation.

Yes, and in this life you're dependent on the doctor as well.

When I go off at the weekend?

Walter: Yes, that hurts, because then you're all alone.

And when I speak with other people here on the ward?

Walter: Yes, then you feel left out of it – kind of abandoned.

Now I understand, it hurts all around, eh? In that other world you're independent. There isn't so very much pain out there.

Walter: Exactly (He laughs.) That's for real.

The fear of losing energy, of disintegrating, is being brought out now all the time. The coprophagy and urine drinking gradually become less frequent, but Walter continues doing his handstands on the ward and sometimes he holds iron objects in his mouth. He keeps trying to explain to me the second world of nature:

> For my part I think it does exist. It's a world where everything is pure and clear. The objects there are purely abstract, are dead, self-subsistent. It's a shame that in the second world everything is abstract and there are no fine nuances.

Walter has told me several times already that by 'fine nuances' he actually means people and the love there is between people. Obviously, he wants to let me know that this natural world of totally abstract independence is not, after all, his ultimate choice. Sometimes he says to me, almost as though to offer me comfort: 'This life is a good one, too, you know. We do belong together. That little basin in the corner, for instance, is yours. I see it as though something quite jolly was coming from it, as though there were music in it.'

It is a moment (there are so many of them) when I feel deeply moved. I know what he means by the 'fine nuance.' That whole indissoluble core of tenderness between us: a feeling of affection which for me has a much more paternal

48

element to it by now; the craving for a father which he somehow exudes. A feeling, too, of being deeply moved by the comfort he gives me in my efforts to reconcile him to the world in which he and I are living, with all its contradictions and conflict.

Then the second world of nature is back again:

> That second world is really the converse of this one in which we live. By working hard the people there become that much taller and stronger and more masculine.
> Everybody there stands on his own feet.

I am beginning to understand it better now. The people in this fantasy world are independent of one another, they have no feelings of hatred, no feeling of distrust toward one another, no sexual feelings.

So we wrestle in our conversations for months with these different variations of the one-man's-world which Walter does and does not want to abandon, because of all the risks attaching to what he calls 'putrid reality.' It is impossible to repeat here all the details of his experiences in Indonesia, in the camps, in The Netherlands at the secondary school, which he relates at some length. The feeling of being 'crazy' and 'different' leads to a succession of expulsions from groups in which he sought in his shrunken way to establish a connection. As soon as the feeling of weakness and dependency floods over him, or he feels he is being coerced by someone, Walter returns to talking about the world of 'true nature' or, as he sometimes calls it, 'the great universe.' 'There the gods are indestructible and the people are of iron. Then I think that I am God sometimes.'

August 18:

> Being born I find a wretched business. I would have liked to have been born independent, free, to have gone into the wide world on a course straight to the center of the universe. But my route was one that landed you back just where you started.

Then he mentions his mother and the little shirt again. He

49

remarks that his mother invariably turned his 'straight line' into a 'curved line.' The straight line indicates a total self-reliance and independence. That way is indeed a lonely one. Sometimes, he says, it is like walking through a tunnel with iron walls, or like being imprisoned in plaster. But sometimes he finds it preferable to the curving line, by which he symbolizes the feeling of being bandied to and fro in his encounters with other people.

When on October 13 I go with him into town for the first time and we watch a football match, he tells me subsequently that he felt like a son with his father:

> Not free, though. I felt I was on a string. I would like to do it all over again and be alone. I'd like to preserve the way of thinking I've had since I was four. Everyone for himself. You want to have me living with other people again, but I don't want that. Why won't you go with me, doctor, into the world of true nature?

Sometimes he will express his desire for total independence by saying: 'Living in the little house of river clay.' From the river clay he makes his own house, denying and repudiating every form of dependence on any product made by human hand. If this world, and fantasy, of independence are threatened, he is anguished and enraged.

Walter: I'd like to give you a real shaking up. I wish the light between us would go away so that I couldn't see you anymore. In the old days, in my nice little world, at least I still had what seemed like happiness. I don't want to think any longing thoughts, only about geometry. I'd like to put a bullet in you. I shan't do it, mind you. The nurses, too, take them all for a ride. I'm not free. Nurses aren't human beings, they're women. Look, a straight line, that's what a person should be like, see. That's godlike, perfect, but in this putrid real world lines are bending and curving.

    Breasts?

Walter: That's it. A person shouldn't have any sex organ. They give you feelings. I'm a pig, I don't want to be a pig. Shall I draw a pig? (Walter draws a pig with big genitals.) A nurse is a pig. I'm a pig. When I see a pig, I'm always scared stiff.

On January 18, 1960, he voices very dramatically the terror he has of his relationship with me, a relationship of dependency:

Walter (screams): I want to be off, damn it! Just you beat it! I damn well won't put up with it. I'm not doing any more talking. We've had an idiotic conversation. I want to be a straight line, with no beginning and no end. Straight through the universe. I want no bending lines, I don't want to talk about the pig. I went away from mother in a straight line, and then I started zigzagging and turned back again. I once did the four-day walk, but that ran in a curving line too. In Druten, that's where we got the milk.
      Druten is the breast?
Walter: Yes, the mother's tit, that's what I'm terrified of.

And on January 20 he again expounds the meaning of the straight line:

Women are curved lines. I had the straight line in my head the whole time. I never wanted curving lines. Goodness is the curving line, too. I don't want either good or evil, the straight line doesn't belong to this human world. You don't look right and you don't look left: I always have to look right and left, that's everything crooked.

Yet some change is taking place. One day he says:

That nature-world is hard to imagine, really. I would like to try and find it and then it will be fine if our world can be fused with that second nature-world. I'd certainly like to live in that.

For the first time our worlds make contact. He is prepared to leave his one-man's-world, but is asking me to take a step in his direction as well.

On the ward he tries to romp around sometimes in the restricted space, to act tough, for instance, by 'rolling a cigarette,' and he walks around with a black bootlace around his neck, which is meant as a mark of his individuality, his black hair. There are weeks when he shows obvious improvement; and on one occasion I hear him telling a chuckling fellow patient a rather shaggy 'service anecdote': 'Yes, and I said: "Get stuffed with your big neck."'

On January 24 I note that the coprophagy and urine-drinking have stopped completely.

Walter has also acquired his long-awaited new black shoes. He puts them on with enormous pleasure, for he had not taken easily to wearing slippers the whole time. As we pass on the ward he says to me: 'Well, there's some sort of footing, anyway.'

I should add here for the reader's benefit that the whole environment in which our relationship is unfolding is far from propitious – and that is certainly an understatement! The hospital clothing, the frequent lying in bed (at visiting time), the constricted space – a nonsensical hospital setting that does nothing to further the psychotherapy.

Sometimes during our sessions street noises filter into the room. Quite often he listens to them and then says: 'Life out there went at such a pace. That's what I'm so afraid of.' A new drawing that he gives me shows a window with some flowers; he has drawn himself gazing out of the window. He tells me about his new sense of security inside the hospital walls, but also about his fear of ever having to make another start outside.

Many psychotic turns of phrase which he had used during the first month of therapy he now retracts. 'Oh, yes, those little balls, they were people, of course.'

Walter seems to be defending his fantasies of omnipotence with the courage of despair. On the ward he sometimes looks at me accusingly and says during the sessions:

'I don't want to belong to father and mother. I'm myself. This ashtray here I made, the food that I get I made. I am God.
　　　You felt you were a pinhead in the world and now you feel you're God. You make everything?
Walter: Yes, I'm better than I've ever been. I know now that I'm able to think. I'm reading, here. (He points to a book he has been reading for some days.)

No mix up of the feelings.

Walter: Ah, feelings, there are so many, so many.

When he sees me on the ward one day wearing a new pair of black shoes, after five minutes or so he puts on brown ones. He talks fluently enough now in the sessions, but during one of our talks he rubs himself across the chest.

What does that mean?

Walter: Well, that I'm not a woman. I've been scared all along of turning into a woman. I've been scared of losing my sex.

Go on.

Walter: Yes, with that little silk shirt. That whole period up to my tenth year. I was afraid of not being a man. I am afraid of women, because I'm afraid of becoming a woman to them. Could I become a woman? Can I become nothing? I had a feeling that I shouldn't play with the boys, and I really wanted to and perhaps they did, too. You know, I struck myself later on with that axe because I felt so God-forsaken. I've got more of a feeling of companionship now.

But you're also afraid of feeling close to me!

Walter: Yes, because you might change me. Then I'd get blue eyes. I'm not a bit like you. I'd rather stay apart.

Am I sitting the right distance away?

Walter: Yes, that's fine. How are you, in fact? Are you better again?

(On several occasions already Walter has expressed the fear that I might go mad, that he might infect me with his 'madness.')

At this point I conclude the theme of dependency and go on to another theme, closely connected with it but justifiably calling for separate discussion.

3. THE RELATION TO WOMEN

Now that the theme of an overwhelming need for dependency and the fear of being engulfed and dissolved in the other person is becoming more evident, Walter starts talking more about women:

> Women don't really exist you know. The woman who was born from the rib of man was really a man, too. I want to be quite independent!

He tells me in subsequent sessions how in the earliest years of his life he would often sit playing alone on a Dutch lawn, surrounded by a Dutch brick wall. Outside were the lofty trees of the jungle and the voices of the Indonesian children who were playing together, while he felt that he was not supposed to have any contact with them. With much difficulty and fear he goes on to say that he can remember an anxiety-ridden fantasy. It was that the trees suddenly swung towards him with a swishing movement and engulfed him in their upper foliage. A fantasy of being sucked away, sucked in, which he also frequently experienced as a fear in the toilet. As we make our way through the ward after a session, we hear on the radio a female voice singing.

Walter: That chap has a fine voice.
    But it's a woman.
Walter: No, I said that women don't exist. They're men dressed up. Women give one feelings.

This brings us face to face with Walter's attachment to his mother. The sacrificial love of this woman, the absence of a father, the war conditions which made the mother even more of a central figure in Walter's life, her need also for love and her abhorrence of vulgarity, force and aggression – all that colored the attachment and made it a matter of 'never being able to shake free of the mother figure.' This is referred to in the literature as 'symbiosis.' It leads to still greater anxiety and confusion regarding the subject's own identity as a boy. There is no father to identify with, there are no little friends during the Indonesian period, the extraordinary clothes used by the mother to enhance the non-Indonesian, white, angelically blond appearance of her child (and thereby also ensure his isolation) – all this has considerable consequences for Walter's sense of sexual identity. Alongside this persistent doubt as to his sexual identity an enormous ambivalence toward the female has developed.

Frequently during the sessions he will get up, look at his face in the mirror and touch his hair:

Walter: I've got a damned fine head of hair, you know, only it should be even blacker. I'm glad that I've still got my head, though. It was dangerous, that head-bashing, and then all that blood. (He is speaking here for the first time of the self-administered 'shock.')

Yes, your head's still in the right place.

Walter laughs and then gives me a gentle butt on the chin.

A striking description of how he felt minuscule, tiny as a molecule, and of his fear of being a dependent 'girl' I find in a letter he gives me at this time. In it he describes himself as a molecule wandering through a world of space and goes on to write:

For myself I am a colossal woman-hater, have been from my very earliest years, and would rather help further the contact between man and man, so that each may nourish the other, than that between a strange woman and me. When I was received into the Baptist Church, I found it a bloody abomination that a baptist woman should come to the congregation and dare to mount the rostrum. I wasn't prepared to stomach it, that they should say I was a girl! I am a man, of Dutch extraction, a boy scout, and believe in God, the very image of man after which we humans are created.

From now on, in his gestures, his bearing and his verbalizing, Walter begins to fight against the sense of dependency and the gentle femininity within himself. He has in fact been doing so from the very start, but I had not taken it sufficiently into account. He had now put on about thirty pounds and is beginning to look like a real sturdy fellow. Quite often he comes in with a soldierly air and gives me a vigorous, exaggeratedly male handshake. He talks about 'raving' and 'romping.' He is elated to be able to show me a few hairs on his chin; and his feeling of being drawn to women fires his anger. One day he says with a sigh: 'Why doesn't the nurse have legs like a football player?'

So far I have said little about his anger. Of course, there is angry resentment as a result of all the hurts and disappointments he has had. There is also enormous rage, functioning partly as a defense against his tender and dependent feelings toward me, feelings that fill him with so much anguish.

His tremendous repressed rage had made the nursing-staff quite fearful of him. That is probably why he was prescribed the electroshocks. More and more I have come to believe that electroshocks are administered to schizophrenic patients on the principle that the first blow counts for double.

Walter is beginning to formulate more aggressive feelings toward me. He is sometimes unwilling to come for our session and says: 'I damn well don't feel like it, that's all.' In a variety of ways he lets me know that he 'is fed up with toeing the line': 'Okay, then, I'd like to push your face in, kick you in the crotch. You give me so much attention and then I get the feeling that I'm ever so inferior. I don't want to tag along after you.'

The fear of dissolving into nothing prompts him to protest violently whenever he has to conform to the rules of the ward. Every rule (and there are some highly unreasonable rules in this traditional university clinic) he feels as a major threat to his sense of autonomy. At times he has violent outbursts of rage. In the occupational therapy department he lifts a man up, chair and all, and then lets him drop.

June 18: Walter enters and whistles loudly through his fingers. As he sits facing me he goes on blowing hard through his fingers and gives me a daring look as though to show me how free and independent he is. Then he says: 'When I die and my body is absorbed by the plants and my offspring eats those plants, he'll be eating me and I won't disappear.' He tells me he wants to weigh three hundred pounds in order 'to carry more weight on the scales.' He describes his body as a little ball and asks: 'Besides my body, have I also got a little ball that controls everything? My own linking apparatus?' Then he says: 'Have I an "I," am I an entity in my own right?' He expresses, too, the fear that he will eventually wither away in bed in this hospital, and in the middle of the session beats himself furiously on the head. 'I want to have my own switchboard in here.'

On June 19 we take our first walk together through the hospital grounds. Walter seems in a happy mood. 'It's as though you've been living for a long time in a dark winter. You think: Will I be blinded if I stand in the sunlight again?' Time and again he says: 'Mighty fine, mighty fine.' When the walk is over: 'I can stand another three months of it.' And before entering the ward he says: 'Doctor, I wish you more power with your work.'

June 20: He comes in whistling again and, acting the man, starts to roll a cigarette. Then he says, almost nonchalantly:

Well, what would you like to talk about? I'd like to go for a bike ride, no sense in all this chattering. What I crave is independence, that's the most important thing. If I was independent, on my own, all my problems would be over. I want to go my own way. When I talk to you, I'm not dependent on myself and yet I wouldn't like it if you just made me go away.

It is in this session that he refers explicitly for the first time to the similarity between his relationship with me and his relationship with his mother:

I kept running to her all the time, but when I was there, I hurried to get away again. Yes indeed, I got very angry with her, I wanted to smash her place up. I mean, damn it! Way back, with that little shirt. I had no pals I could play with. There I was, I saw nothing, doctor, nothing but the inside of the house. That huge country, and I saw nothing.

More and more Walter experiences his being shut up in the hospital and his relation with me as a kind of stranglehold.

June 27: 'Sometimes I don't believe you, because when you say something, I think: Shall I accept it? Won't it take away my independence?' During this session he refers to himself as an unpiloted plane that has to be operated by people in a control tower on the airfield. I feel that in these sessions I am beginning to understand the springs of what has been called in psychiatry the 'influence delusion,' the feeling of being completely controlled by others.

At the end of June Walter is transferred back to the closed ward because of his explosive rages. After a lot of trouble he manages to say: 'I hate you. Don't take me seriously.'

'Force it out, just toss it out,' I say.

'I'm so scared of my rattling crazy feelings.'

Walter has a kind of antenna attached to his ear and explains that it is to enable him to hear better. He is very anxious and fears he may lose contact. He explains that he is afraid of becoming a 'tame rabbit or a lazy swine' in the hospital: 'I'd like to be a football player, a professional football player. You should be on the go and working all the time.'

These are difficult moments, because I cannot altogether blame him. The small ward we are working in gives Walter few opportunities for activity. The occupational therapy is carried on in a cellar. There are no grassy spaces where he can run around, no place where he can give expression to his fury and the urge to be active.

August 7: Walter resists for all he is worth the need to declare his feelings. He is only prepared to chatter about playing football and about freedom, not about feelings. Then he starts to give vent to his aggression toward me: 'These psychiatrists, they get you nicely heated up like a coal fire and then flick you away like a heap of burnt ashes.' He expresses a tremendous suspicion of psychiatrists – the psychiatrist whom he had encountered previously and who had written everything down in 'neat, tiny letters,' and the psychiatrist in Amsterdam who had given him the electroshock. 'You're a shade better, perhaps,' he says to me. 'I want to get close to you and I don't want to get close to you.' He refers to his yearnings as a danger that distracts him and makes him weak: 'I'm afraid to talk for fear it will get me in its clutches, pull me down. That's why I want to play football and chess and checkers. So, doctor, just give it a rest, will you?'

August 13: Walter takes a checkers board along with him. He sets his piece in the corner of the board and says: 'Look, this is the most important piece in the game. It has to stay in the corner. If it should come out, among the other pieces, it would foul up the whole game. I was always getting into difficulties if I came out of my corner. No, I must stay in the corner. Talking to you about my feelings is coming out of the corner. I don't want that, it's a bad thing. I must keep my feelings in a gold casket.'

Walter is also conveying to me that he is more and more worried by the idea that he is having a bad effect on my life. Just as he feels affected by people and unfree himself, so, too, is he anxious lest he affect me and make me unfree.

On September 7 something occurs which helps me to see even more clearly the anguish he suffers in his relationship with his mother. She has given him a new shirt, and he comes in full of anxiety and indignation: 'Look here, doctor, I don't intend to let myself in for this. I must wear my own pants. Otherwise, nothing doing. I've got a fancy shirt and slacks from mother.' He goes on again about the nightie with the little bird on it that made him feel like a girl when he was three: 'I felt like a girl. I want to make my own shirt.'

Walter starts bashing the table and rages. During occupational therapy he breaks up a chair: 'I was due to be with you at four o'clock. I didn't want to go, and then felt I had to, and got all tensed up. Why do I feel I have to?'

At the end of September Walter is ready for his second excursion with me through the grounds:

Everything is beautiful and fresh now. I didn't know, I didn't see it before. I belted around all over the place on my bike. I didn't want to be a softie. I felt people were as hard as flint. I felt shut in by sheets of iron. I sensed I was a person with hardly any prospects. To me everything looked dead. Now there's life everywhere, and I feel quite different, too. I feel one percent good. So I can have feelings, doctor, can't I? It's all right for me to be soft?

Another interaction that I observe between Walter and his mother gives me a fresh insight into what is going on between them. At visiting time she brings him a couple of pears and starts to peel one of them. He consumes it meekly, and mother wants to peel the other one for him. He then smashes the pear against the wall. Later on he says to me: 'I wanted to have my

59

own pear, I wanted to plonk my pear down in front of me and keep it in my locker. But this way, doctor, it will *never be my own pear.*'

5. THE THEME OF LONELINESS

The degree of loneliness with which one is confronted as a psychotherapist is terrifying at times. The psychoanalyst Frieda Fromm-Reichmann devoted one of her last publications to this subject.[2]

On February 29, about a year and a half after I met Walter for the first time, he conveys to me in a few words something of the depth of his loneliness: 'There are variations. You get a figure 6 and you can still cry, but with a 4 or a 3 you can't cry anymore. Everything's frozen hard, then, everything's granite.' Now that I read my notes on this it strikes me that I didn't record what I was feeling during this session. That loneliness, uttered in more or less faltering words and phrases, terrified me as well. He told me about his loneliness over a lot of sessions. My account would be too long if I reproduced everything in his own words.

Walter has the feeling, he proceeds to tell me, that I am a bit impatient: 'That's your mistake. You want to go too fast, but that will keep me here even longer. I've still got so many problems. My youth was just four seconds ago.'

I am confronted with his loneliness during a phase when his behavior is very disturbed indeed. I discover later on he has been informed by a nurse that I am making preparations for my departure to America. Since I know nothing of this disclosure, his sudden regression is at first completely incomprehensible to me.

One day a worried nurse calls me to his bed, where he is lying under the bed frame. He explains that he is afraid of sexually assaulting the nurse. I visit him again that evening and sit by his bed for part of the night, because he says: 'Don't go away again. I was just left alone, I was just left behind.' Again I have the feeling that he is only now becoming aware of his loneliness. Fortunately, I learn what he has been told about me. This session spent at his bedside is in many respects the most moving experience for me, particularly when from time to time he utters the word 'two,' as though the world of his solitariness is ready to be abandoned.

A week later a regressive condition recurs, this time apparently much more acute. Having made a drawing of a horse and talked about his curiosity, he suddenly becomes petrified and starts eating excrement again. As he says: 'to provide his own keep.' It is 'obvious' to me, in retrospect, what it is that Walter is trying to tell me: that he cannot do without me, because he finds himself still trapped in a deep and terrifying set of problems.

He now becomes practically stupefied and appears extremely depressed.

May 1: He refuses food, lies quite stiff in bed, takes a long time to undress: 'I am aged nil.' He says something about 'drowning' and subsequently walks, a crestfallen figure, head between shoulders, through the corridor. Sometimes he will shut his eyes and groan. One day he drinks his urine and every so often lets himself fall to the ground. I have to be away for several days, and during this period he remains catatonic (in a state of rigidity), verbal contact with him is more or less impossible. He lies in bed, repeatedly putting the fingers of his right hand to his mouth. He bites his fingers and licks his own hand: 'That's tasty.'

It occurs to me that by refusing food and insisting on 'making his own breath' Walter is really saying that he has withdrawn into the omnipotent ball of a child feeding itself and rejecting any kind of dependency. All his gestures are slow and hesitant. His face is dreary and expressionless. He moves like a slow-motion film. Sometimes he tries eating his excrement again and speaks guiltily about the business of eating.

June 9: He explains himself a bit more:

I pinch my nose to improve my breathing. I want a new way of breathing, then I'll be better. Up to now my breathing hasn't been good, too much breathing in, not enough breathing out. I should be able to hold my breath. I want to go home.

Is he once more trying to express his rejection of dependency? The voice is thin and plaintive, he speaks with a minimum of words. He says he is ten years old. He offers me his dessert, for me to eat beside his bed. Then later he gives me his box with some candy he has saved. He insists that I take it all. When I thank him, he gestures casually, as if to say: 'It's all on me.'

What I realize more clearly now is that Walter probably wants to show that he feels responsible for my prospective departure. He has taken too much from me and is trying to give me something back.

On June 24 I begin to see the situation more clearly. He is lying under the bedstead, is very tense and motions me to go away.

Walter: I have sexy feelings, I have dirty feelings, I'm surrounded by a haze that I can't get through.

You feel guilty?

Walter: Yes.

What about?

Walter: I wrung a pussy cat's neck, a contented little pussy cat. I'm a murderer. I mustn't do that. Then off comes my head. You're a Jap. I was thinking that you hated me, too. That you'd bring me up before the military court. (Then Walter makes it much clearer.) No, no, no! I hate. *That* was it! Really terribly. My breathing's no good. Vapor.'

Come on, just breathe in my face.

Reluctantly Walter does so and I calm him down. 'Your breath doesn't kill me, you see?' Then he says, breathing in as he utters the words: 'I hate you because your jaw sticks out and I hate the nurse 'cause of her face. I've got such a load of hatred.'

'Just give it me, just hand it over.'

Walter puts his parcels of hatred in my lap, one and then another and another. He puts fifty parcels of hatred in my lap, all told. He then spits on the ground and on my hands. And now he begins to talk about his hatred, the words coming in torrents. Hatred for his stepmother, his father, his brother, his mother, the friends who made him feel ridiculous: 'I was on my own all the time, I couldn't talk about it.' He goes on spitting in all directions and says: 'Now I feel a bit relieved.'

There are moments in this dramatic session when he is somewhat fixed and bemused, but he is able to break out of that quickly enough. I am beginning to understand things better now. When he breathes out, this to him is like expelling a poisonous vapor. When the session is over, Walter and I together wipe up all the saliva from the floor.

On July 30, 1960, I find Walter much improved and quite collected in his manner of speech. He says: 'How can we discuss what is abnormal, if I don't even know about what's normal?' He then explains to me that in Indonesia he in fact knew only a couple of boys who spoke Javanese and would spend five or ten minutes with him from time to time: 'I didn't say anything. I wanted to, of course. I've been trudging the Sahara for so long.'

It occurs to me that I am not really aiming in this session at the central problem, that is, his fear of my leaving him. Clearly, I am not focusing on this problem because of some resistance in myself. Presumably I am unable to bear the thought of just how important I am to Walter (and he to me). I cannot fail to notice that during this period I do my best to keep in close touch with a friend and colleague, and to discuss Walter's therapy more and more with him in an attempt to find a therapist who can succeed me when I leave. (I left in fact in July of 1961.)

6. THE THEME OF SEXUAL FEELINGS

In the course of one session a somewhat ruffled Walter sits busy drawing (skaters) and after a considerable silence he asks suddenly: 'Why don't you let me go, then?' After which:

> I'm scared that you'll shove me into an institution. I want to go on being an ordinary boy. I don't want to live in this world, only study, in the ideal world, where I don't *have* to do anything, won't be dependent, won't need to eat, no women, completely free to walk and walk or linger around wherever I like.

63

He strides up and down the room:

I don't want to have to think. Mathematics.

Then out it comes:

On military service the boys were so out of the ordinary. They used to talk about being horny. They used to lie on the bed and then they would . . . they would say . . . something about a woman's appetite for it. I'm very frightened. I want to be myself.

It's difficult to acknowledge those feelings, isn't it, soldier-boy?

Still, he is gradually starting to talk more and more about the sexual feelings that have always threatened him. They run directly counter to his identity as the 'little angel' and the 'pure and innocent baby,' and he seems to be saying sometimes that for him being overwhelmed by sexual feelings constitutes a sort of threshold-of-hell experience:

I don't want to do any of those sexy things, it isn't normal. Sperm, there are millions, after all. Where's it found, in the earth or in the air? It's a combination of albumen. Can it mold away? This C-atom, which I was to start with, has it gone now or does it still exist? It *does* still exist? I sometimes think it's been broken down and different combinations have come about through the foodstuff that's been given me. Sometimes, too, when I lose urine I lose something of myself. I don't want to become somebody else. For instance, I don't suddenly want to find I'm Jack-quick-on-the-cunt or some sort of animal.

Now Walter is clearly becoming tense and excited:

Sure, I hate. Hack you to pieces, tear off your head and take a leg off, cut through your neck. Don't you soft-soap me. I have to keep on the go, so as not to be caught. You mustn't play with your pee-pee.

The growing contact between us permits a trust and intimacy which in turn help Walter to express his sexual thoughts. Just admitting to such a thing as sexual feelings, the mere fact of uttering words like 'sperm' and 'impregnate,' all this is a sign of his having been somehow deformed by me and seduced into using this kind of expression. Thus: 'Well, yes, I'd certainly like to cut your throat, but I think that you are going to slit mine now, that something dreadful is going to happen.' All of a sudden he feels me to be someone bent on cutting his throat as punishment for his turning out to have a sexual nature:

> It was when I was sixteen in Utrecht and in the hospital there. I handled my prick and then all sorts of horniness came out . . . that garbage. Then I thought: It's all over now, any hope of being myself. I had been ten months in a concentration camp, of course I had a feeling of inferiority, but that wasn't too bad. I was able to think, do some math, be by myself, and then it happened.

He tells me that in one of the camps he saw some boys showing their genitals to a girl.

> Because the ejaculation happened just after the psychiatrist had been talking to me in Utrecht, I thought the psychiatrist's talk had been the cause of it all. That was why I wouldn't talk to psychiatrists. Or to you, either. I did want to discuss it, but it was too soon. I am thinking now that you are thinking: That really is going too far, you wretched boy! That you are taking a poor view of me.

Whatever the reasons for his breaking down like that in his sixteenth year, his inability to ignore his sexual impulses is something he clearly feels to be catastrophic. He is unable to be 'himself,' his hopes of total independence, of clean, pure, mathematical lucidity can no longer be maintained as an ideal. From the turns of phrase he uses he is becoming aware that acceptance of his sexual urge means being driven irrevocably toward the other and entails being dependent.

February 14: He expatiates positively for a while on the progress of what is working itself out between us:

> I really would like to know more about women. A woman is not just a cunt. I never spoke, never dared to speak,

because I thought I couldn't. If I just so much as touch my prick, sperm comes out of it. Is that a good thing? It works all right, but . . . I don't want to stay in reality any longer, I'd prefer to be in a fantasy world. Then you can think about motors and math. A motor's got no prick.

Indeed in the progress of his psychotherapy Walter has become much more articulate. As far as I can judge, until his admission he had been a very quiet boy. Now what astonishes me in my encounters with him is his ability, despite his previous isolation, to put his troubles into words so lucidly:

I don't fancy talking, I can't let myself go. Talking's bad, change is bad. Imagine me beginning again. Then everything would start from scratch. I'd also lose my *certainty* that the world's lousy. If I speak French, then I'll be a Frenchman, I won't be Walter anymore. If I should change like that, I'd lose my I.'

Here Walter is quite clearly indicating how the contact between us and the very act of broaching this theme of sexuality is threatening to bring about an enormous change in him; and that change both threatens him and removes the assurance he feels regarding his fantasy world. I do not sufficiently recognize his growing terror in this phase.

During this session he remains on his feet: 'I don't want to sit down. If I do, I get ideas, an erection, and then I'm more sexy. I stand, and then just to talk. Go on thinking safe thoughts.' He now assumes a stiff military posture. 'This way I'm Walter, really me.'

In this session he is very anxious indeed and talks, though in a confused manner, from start to finish:

I want to be a boy, good, myself. At fifteen I was in despair, I thought I was all on my own, a real tramp. Will I ever be able to get away from my brains? Look, I was so desperate at school because I couldn't think anymore. Those feelings were shooting up into my brain. In the forces, during my service, it was thoroughly ghastly.
Sexuality is worse than murder. I don't want to be friends with you. These feelings must be pushed down, they come

66

squeezed out of my head. You want to sock me then? You want a fight?

Adopting a rather forceful tone, I explain to Walter that I approve of his having sexual feelings.

Really? But that's . . . that's . . . I thought you'd send me to an institution straight away. You don't think it's a bad thing, then? This is a very important point. I didn't realize the other boys had it, too. I don't want to be enemies with you, in that case. Yes, I must handle my prick. How should I pee? My prick used to be a friend when urine was coming but then it wasn't anymore. There was that other stuff.

Each time we meet subsequently he is out to show me that what he wants is to be an 'angel' and a 'boy scout' and that he is scared to death of losing my esteem and affection if he should reveal to me how 'bad' (i.e. sexual) he is. His sexual feelings are forcing him toward an adulthood from which he recoils: 'You're too onesided. I'm thinking of the future, of school and my work. This way I'm not getting any further. It's agonizing.'
Once more I explain to him the battle he is waging with himself, with his body, his male body, with sexual desire.
'Come on, you're just saying that. You don't feel bad about it then?'
I bring up the example of a rider and a runaway horse, and he responds enthusiastically:

All right, fair enough, if the horse bolts, I'm not there anymore. My brains are the rider, and then everything just fills up with sexuality. It was the same before the ejaculation. I was choked with thoughts. I lay there in bed, fighting them. I thought it could be heard in my voice, you know, in the way it was trembling.
              Was that why you used to rinse your mouth with water prior to the session?
Walter: Exactly. It makes me so frightened. Scared to death. I thought I was the only one. I thought I was crazy.

By the end of the second year Walter is able to relate in a

perfectly well-ordered fashion large chunks of his personal history from the age of two up to the most recent period spent doing his military service. For instance, he tells me about his anguished discovery in the orphanage of a girl's sex organs:

> She asked whether I'd like to make it with her. My heart was going, I was so scared she'd die, that *I* would die. My heart was thumping away so.

He describes the fight he had with this upsurge of sexual feelings at the orphanage in a number of variations:

> It was sort of a tremendous sense of inferiority, especially when I got all those thoughts running through my head. I thought I must be dim, some sort of weirdo, I thought I was the only one with sexual feelings, I was desperate at school, because I couldn't think anymore. I wanted to think properly, to learn, get things done, but those feelings went straight up into my brain. Then I got around to thinking. I took to lying in bed and I would say: Now I'm just going to think. And do you know what conclusion I came to? (Walter is clearly becoming very upset) I mustn't keep dwelling on this. I'm so scared of not being myself, ever again.

What Walter is saying here is that in his fifteenth year he was obliged to leave the paradise where he could 'be without sex.' Again I let him speak for himself:

> Then the sexual feelings came along and Jenny, the way I saw her, suddenly turned from being just another person into a girl. What's that then? How does that come about? All at once I was seeing sexual apparatuses instead of people. That was wrong and bad. There was nothing I could do about it. And then, at the climax, when I was sixteen, my world of illusion started up again. It was a retreat, of course, a retreat back into my second year. Reality was too terrifying for me, but that illusory world was getting stronger and stronger, and I was becoming so afraid of that. I was going crazy. So I was admitted, but in Utrecht nobody understood me, not the least bit. The sex urge was getting stronger all the time, too. I was soon out

68

of the hospital and nothing changed. My world of illusion grew and that went on till I cut myself with that axe. And now I'm returning to reality. Sometimes I used to swing back and forth between illusion and reality. As soon as I have horrible thoughts I escape into illusion, and then I'm a math professor and I have to write books about physics and chemistry.

This short summary passage is of exceptional relevance in that it reveals what has struck me over and over again during the psychotherapeutic treatment of schizophrenic patients: that what we call the psychotic world or the 'psychosis' entails in many respects a return to a world which had already existed at a much earlier stage and is reactivated when, later on, the demands of reality can no longer be met.

Despite his anxiety, he goes on talking and gives me the first names of various girls with whom he has had at any rate some contact:

Maria had a lovely figure. I was . . . completely bowled over. I kissed her too. I feel like a catapult going from side to side.
    What d'you mean by that?
Walter: The one extreme is the fantasy world and the other is reality, the real thing. How I longed for Maria, it made me tingle all over!

It certainly looks as though the process of coming to self-awareness and of sharing with me makes him, for the first time, more conscious of his loneliness and isolation.

I would so much like to be one of the boys. Make sure you get it, they used to say in the service. I wanted to all right, but I never could. I must move toward people, but so far I haven't got my own voice, my own character. What d'you think about my body?
    A decidedly Walter type of body.
Walter: (laughs happily) And you are most decidedly Dr Foudraine.

His anxiety increases. During our sessions he continues to stalk up and down, evidently not daring to sit. Pacing to and fro, he moves his arms about wildly; it seems to be an attempt to maintain freedom of movement and not to become completely petrified. It is as though he hesitates whether to go through with this or retreat into his fantasy world.

He tells me he wants to have more of a beard and would also like to have a shave. The ward nurses no longer have 'football legs' (that part of the denial he has given up). But his sexual feelings still continue to threaten him. On those occasions when he feels himself being attracted to a nurse, he thinks that the others can read his 'evil thoughts'. Yet, on March 3rd, I can record that gradually I feel he is addressing me as an entity. Walter has obviously changed.

My notes comment: 'He is becoming more normal, more human.' He usually begins a conversation on the topic of sexual feelings by uttering a magic formula: 'We must encourage common interests.' He uses this formula every time it reaches the point of expressing a sexual feeling or experience; and slowly I gradually realize that he is constantly anxious that our 'common interest' might be disrupted by the disclosure of his sexual feelings, and that I might punish him for being so open in displaying his carnal nature. In the army the soldiers used to tell dirty jokes, and one sex education film had the effect of a bomb going off. Everything became steeped in sex. If a man said, 'I'd like to empty my Sten-gun at the mountain,' it was sexual.

The 'dirty words' are brought out hesitantly: 'Joyknob, joystick.' He also explains why he had let saliva run out of his mouth during one of his regressions. To him the saliva represented semen, speaking ejaculation. In this connection he admits that he had wanted to mention masturbation but had felt this would inevitably trigger off in me a highly punitive and hostile attitude.

Gingerly and fearfully he tests my reaction. He comes in one day and, keeping his gaze fixed on me, slips his hand inside his trousers to finger his genitals. Still fearful, yet with a sort of happy feeling at having discovered his masculinity, he recites the first 'dirty joke':

Abdullah has the men line up naked. Then a handsome

lad comes. . . [At this point I frown, smile and raise my eyebrows.] Well, yes, doctor, er, no, not a handsome lad, a bird, and this bird has a big sword. Not a penis rises except that of the soldier's right in front. The bird cuts it off. Then the soldier starts laughing. The penis isn't his but Abdullah's, who's standing in the back row.

It turns out that Walter had his reason for choosing to tell this joke: it gives him a chance to express more openly his fears of castration.

When I was seventeen I heard a voice saying to me: 'It's all right, just go ahead, it's perfectly all right.'

      That was really your desires speaking, a wholesome bit of yourself.
Walter: Yes, yes, of course.

Immediately afterwards he seizes a piece of paper and draws a genital organ attached, with powerful bands (he calls them ligaments), to his skeleton. He is saying, in effect, that he has been afraid of losing his genital organ, or of having it cut off. Even though he is by now venturing to talk much more about girls, and even cuts out photos of them which he 'wants to enlarge five times', he remains frightened and says:

> I'm a woman, I have a womb. I don't take to the male side of it. If I was a girl, I would have had little girl friends and I could size them up better. Whenever I touched my prick I would have the feeling: that isn't mine.

Now he is clearly establishing an association between the girlish clothing he wore and the confusion he felt regarding his sexual nature.

August 2: This morning he is able to let me know that he has been masturbating. He first smeared his penis with toothpaste, 'to freshen it up.' He talks much more freely about masturbation, indicates that he considers his penis a very big one. 'Really good, isn't it? I felt the masturbation was a sort of safety-valve, I felt refreshed.'

But the next day, when I happen to go into the occupational therapy department, he is full of fear again, steps in my direction and hurts himself. After a good deal of hesitation he informs me that the day before he had been masturbating again, not with toothpaste but under the shower (he still has to wash away the sin). Then he heard someone outside say: 'Walter's at it again,' and a tremendous feeling of guilt came over him. When he saw me come into the occupational department, he was afraid of being punished, and the work tools suddenly took on the terrifying character of implements of torture.

Walter's mother visits him regularly, and I have a good many conversations with her. I even see them together sometimes. The father visits him only occasionally, but when Walter says he would like to spend a short holiday at his father's place and they have a really informative talk together in which Walter is able for the first time to convey to his father a great deal about his life, he makes his first trip outside the clinic.

A difficult situation now arises, because a week later his father rings me up and nothing will persuade him to bring his son back to the clinic again. But he *is* willing to cooperate fully in the continuation of the psychotherapeutic contact.

In my subsequent conversations with Walter I have a definite feeling that our contact has been ruptured in some way, and it occurs to me that Walter may have been feeling that I let him down when I consented to his father's taking him home on vacation. The first contacts he made with youths of his own age in the neighborhood of his father's house show quite clearly what major difficulties still lie ahead of him.

On top of it all, his grandmother, his father's mother, hardly made things easy for Walter by dragging him to a hypnotist. He dared not refuse, but all the same he is furious: 'It's no way to carry on, doctor.' Naturally enough, the hypnotist upset him a very great deal: 'I thought: He'll go and make a girl of me even now.'

By October 1 the setbacks seem more and more formidable, and Walter is starting to talk again about his solitary world: 'A straight path, that's my path in life, a currant bun to eat on the side and a gun to hunt with.'

72

His inability to make ready contact, the people who won't come to see him, the girls who seem unattainable, all give him a sense of powerlessness. Yet Walter sees quite clearly the danger of returning to his nice little world of fantasy: 'It cuts you off from reality, it's dangerous, oh yes, I know, I know.'

On October 7 I have my final session with him. For several sessions now he has been silent and downcast. Sometimes this atmosphere is broken by a single sentence, like: 'I'm perfectly healthy,' or: 'I would like more freedom, my world is too small.' Then it transpires that he is struggling against sexual desire and masturbation: 'As soon as you touch it, the sin starts.' 'I'm exhausted, I'm feeling down, I believe they don't want me in the football club because I'm like that. I'm scared that you'll kick me out, or else you'll think: "What a hopeless chap he is!"'

He leaves me in no doubt that what he really wants is to get back to the period prior to his sexuality, to his infancy. I try to explain to him how greatly he is still resisting his inexorable growth.

He says: 'Growth? I've never been against that. Growth. Okay, then, growth.' And later, during our session: 'But I used to be independent, doctor, and now I'm dependent. For if you accept those sexual feelings, you start longing and yearning, and so you're dependent.'

I have been trying to give an account of what went on in the course of three and a half years. There is a lot I have not been able to tell. My own feelings during this struggle were very intense. The last phase was painful for both of us.

For a time Walter managed to keep going outside the clinic, found a job, but was discovered one evening standing distracted in front of a ditch, and so he was readmitted.

At this time I was getting ready to leave for America. After I left he had a very difficult time, landed in the isolation room, but improved when he was eventually transferred to a mental hospital. There he came under the very good care of my friend and colleague, John Waage. They talked together a great deal, among other things about the separation and loss which my leaving for America entailed for Walter.

Recapitulating and theorizing about our relationship seem

73

to me unnecessary. The depth of Walter's loneliness, his confusion regarding his sexual identity, the extent of his 'ego weakness,' his terror of sexual and aggressive feelings, the problem of symbiosis and so much more – anyone interested will find aspects in my account that may be furnished with a lot of psychoanalytical annotations at the theoretical level and will find these corroborated in the literature.

Walter helped me to understand a great deal. Apart from the way in which psychiatrists started to give him 'treatment,' with the 'neat little letters' and electroshocks.

REFERENCES

[1] From the considerable body of important work that has been written on the anxiety about dependency needs I select one publication: H. F. Searles: 'Dependency Processes in the Psychotherapy of Schizophrenia,' in *Collected Papers of Schizophrenia and Related Subjects* (International University Press, 1965).

[2] F. Fromm-Reichmann: 'On Loneliness,' in *Psychoanalysis and Psychotherapy; Selected Papers* (Chicago, 1959).

3. TRAINING (Continued)

The reader will probably have realized by now that to go one's own way within the traditional setup of a university's psychiatric clinic was not always easy. The nursing staff, hard working in their way but without any psychodynamic training, understood very little of my relationship with Walter. When they saw me walking with him to the toilet, carrying his feces, and when they picked up snatches of our (to them) totally unintelligible dialogue, they must surely have thought: Who's crazy here, him or his patient? On top of that, my refusal to take part in the 'classifying procedure' and to fill out patient records – or at any rate my subtle sabotaging of this form of psychiatric practice – was beginning to be noticed by my instructors. I was hauled before the professor, who admonished me not to act like John Rosen but to stick to the clinic's rules of procedure. A situation not without its dangers, certainly; for it could mean dismissal from the clinic and an end to my specializing in psychiatry. As I write this (in 1970) I have by me a later work of John Rosen's in which he tells an amusing anecdote.

Rosen was working in 1943 as a resident in psychiatry at the Brooklyn State Hospital. At that time electroshock treatment was the big 'discovery' for 'treating' psychotic people. Rosen's efforts to apply psychoanalytical insights were considered ridiculous. He describes how the staff of this particular hospital used to brag that more electroshock treatments were being given there 'than in any other institute in the East.' Rosen, who at first had also prescribed hundreds of electroshock treatments, was trying to understand the psychotic person and was making a start with his psychoanalytically-oriented psychotherapy. He was running into difficulties with this. I quote:

> In the course of one memorable conversation with me the medical director slammed his fist on the table: 'I don't want to hear anything more of that Freudian talk in this hospital. From now on you just do physical examinations, urine, spinals and blood. And that's all.' [1]

'Just how risky' the purely psychological and psychotherapeutical approach to the psychotic individual is considered to be I also discovered in a passage written by Schultz-Hencke. In 1952, at the age of sixty, this psychiatrist who had started on the psychotherapy of psychotic people back in 1913 wrote as follows:

> So I would like just this once to say quite calmly what I think I am in a position to predict about the further development of psychiatry. I am perfectly well aware that in so doing I put my good name – in so far as I have one – to some extent in jeopardy. I know that I shall be vehemently contradicted. But it is my view that the whole future of psychiatry is really at issue here; and anyone who thinks that he can say something well founded about this should take part in the discussion which is happening now and will happen in the future. I will do my best to explain what I am getting at as precisely as I can and to describe accurately what I have in view. As a person already sixty years of age, I do not know of anything better I could do than to place the experiences that have been mine in the course of many, many years of analytical-psychotherapeutic practice at the service of psychiatric research and study. I know too that in this way I shall be able to lift many a burden from the rising generation of doctors.

Risking his 'reputation,' he wrote his book, which indeed contains much that can be of help toward a psychiatry of the future.[2] As to his being able to relieve a younger generation from the burden of prejudices regarding 'schizophrenia,' that alas! has proved so far to be unrealistically optimistic.

To get back to the situation I found myself in: There was only one strategy that I could discover for averting the 'dangers.' I decided to avail myself of the monthly lectures that were held in the evenings in the clinic. In that way I gave shape to my growing convictions and reported my psychotherapeutic experiences with Karel, Walter (and others with whom I had been working). In short, giving lectures seemed to me the best way of letting my views come out, as it were, 'between the lines.' My initial idea was to present to you two of these papers. However, on further consideration it seemed better to modify the form and content and to add a few footnotes by way of clarification. I now propose, therefore, to give you some basic information.

The term 'schizophrenia' comes from Eugen Bleuler, who in 1911 brought out a book called *Dementia Praecox and the the Group of Schizophrenias*.[3] The term 'dementia praecox'[4] had been used previously by Kraepelin. He made it his life's work to observe and listen, with the utmost precision (though at a distance), to people whose behavior seemed in some way crazy. Kraepelin's idea was to write a sort of textbook of psychiatric 'syndromes,' and he hoped that, like physical diseases, each of these syndromes would turn out to have its own peculiar mode of origin (cause) and development. He thought in terms of physical causes (a sort of disturbed metabolism). Thus he described people who rejected all human contact and who within the psychiatric institution gradually came to lead a totally isolated, almost vegetable existence as suffering from 'dementia' (an analogy with the dementia that occurs in aged people as a result of the process of cerebral degeneration). This, then, was the monumental work on which clinical psychiatry was based – a psychiatry put together by a rather obsessional German professor who provided his 'syndromes' with a large quantity of names.[5] A straightforward account of the derivation of these terms was written not very long ago.[6]

Using a new name – 'schizophrenia' – Bleuler did in principle the same thing, but introduced a lot of Freud's ideas into his observations from the very start. He attached much more *meaning* to behavior ('symptoms' such as delusions, hallucinations, bizarre and confused forms of verbal expression). For Bleuler the absence of emotional expression, the flood of associations and the predominance of 'fantasy' over relatedness to 'reality' (autism) were the fundamental or 'primary' symptoms. The more flamboyant forms of conduct which mark a person as being 'crazy' (delusions, hallucinations) he called the accessory (or 'secondary') symptoms.

Bleuler was more involved than Kraepelin with the people he was 'observing' and 'portraying.' He even went so far as to write:

Even normal persons show a number of schizophrenic symptoms when they are emotionally preoccupied, particularly inattentive, or when their attention is concentrated on a single subject. Among these symptoms are peculiar associations, incomplete concepts and ideas, displacements, logical blunders, and stereotypes.

It was Bleuler, too, who advanced the idea that the individual symptom (or mode of behavior) might not be so very important in itself, that more important was *its intensity and extensiveness*. In connection with that (and this was very modern) he stressed the relation of the symptom (or behavior) to the psychological 'setting,' thus to the situation in which the individual concerned found himself at that moment. Bleuler humanized the notion of 'schizophrenia' and so began to break down the traditional division of symptoms into distinct categories (nosology).

But there is much more to Bleuler's work. Helm Stierlin has devoted two important articles [7] to this subject. Stierlin made a hobby of investigating further into the background history of Bleuler and his actual ideas on 'schizophrenia.' The book *Dementia Praecox and the Group of Schizophrenias* had gone into six editions, but its author, who was the director of a major psychiatric institution, slowly became more confused. For although Bleuler was a contemporary of Freud's, he was entrenched in a tradition established by, among others, Kraepelin. Bleuler believed that one had to revere Kraepelin, and felt obliged to link up Kraepelin's settled views ('disease,' 'physical cause,' 'heredity' and the demarcation of various forms of curious behavior – a demarcation which had been so successful in the case of *physical diseases*) with the great insights of Freud, Jung and Adler, insights concerning the problems of human existence within a given culture. It is one of the myths in psychiatry that Bleuler's project actually succeeded.

To begin with, Bleuler leaned toward Freud and was therefore sharply criticized by the official clinical psychiatrists, who did not care to be informed about the emotional life and the unconscious of the human being. Bleuler could not stand up to their criticism, and though he was possibly on the way to seeing 'being schizophrenic' as a form of the conflict-ridden human condition, he dropped this insight and later made half-apologetic statements like: 'Critics should realize that far too much in my theory has been considered Freudian.' In the later editions of his celebrated book, as revised by him (I am still following Stierlin's account), he emphasized the idea of 'heredity' and argued: 'The essential cause, inherent in schizophrenia, lies in hereditary predisposition.' In yet later editions of his work he made statements that Stierlin describes as 'Bleuler's retreat.'

So gradually Bleuler sided with 'official' psychiatry and asserted with mounting assurance his conviction that everything referred to as 'queer' or 'strange' (hallucinations, delusions, dichotomous thinking and feeling, avoidance of reality, and so on) *had a physical cause.* Thus he argued in one particular passage 'that in acute stages there are noticeable defects in the brain-cells.' Bleuler fell back on a detailed consideration of the brain and reverted completely to talking like a neurologist.

So Bleuler's position became more and more pessimistic (or, if you will, subservient), and as far as treatment was concerned, he subsequently disowned the whole psychoanalytical-psychotherapeutic approach:

One must utter a warning against costly types of treatment that are of no conceivable use, anyway. Moreover, the economic and moral interests of the healthy members of the family ought not to be sacrificed to a hopeless type of treatment.

Bleuler went on to refer to 'work training' as the best remedy! The tone of this last quote is in fact: 'Work training, and beyond that, just living with the illness.'

When one notes in the passage quoted above the assertion about the 'moral interests' of the 'healthy relatives' (a highly questionable assumption of health according to research done recently on the family problems of the 'schizophrenic-to-be') Bleuler's work comes into better perspective. I believe that public opinion – of his professional colleagues, in particular – had a powerful influence on Bleuler. The time was not ripe, and linking his name with that of Freud, he evidently felt, was a risky business. Thus Bleuler arrived at the 'radio-receiver theory,' even though he contributed very substantially to our understanding of the persons known as 'schizophrenics,' in terms of conflicts in the unconscious.

We see the same thing happening with yet another contemporary of Freud's, who also worked with Bleuler. In 1907 Jung wrote a very important book entitled *The Psychology of Dementia Praecox*, a book full of insights into the unconscious complexes and motives of human beings, the purpose and meaning of all kinds of apparently bizarre modes of behavior. The psychoanalyst, van der Waals, gives Jung full credit:

Jung's is the honour of having been the first psychiatrist, guided by Freud's discoveries, to make a substantial contribution to a psychodynamic understanding of schizophrenic symptomatology.

In Jung's hands, Freud's concept of symbolizing turned out to be extremely productive. In accordance with this concept the symptoms are no longer accepted on a phenomenological level at face value, but as a substitute for something else which they symbolize.

The repressing forces of the ego influence the symptom

formation in a manner which render the symptoms unrecognizable to the patient as efforts to fulfil unacceptable desires. Jung's extension of the study of symbols to the area of schizophrenia yielded a rich harvest.[14]

But even Jung shrank from the logical outcome of his train of thought and continued to look for the 'cause' in some kind of metabolic disruption. Not until 1939 did he proceed to question this, and only in 1959 did he align himself with those who support the principle of psychogenesis. (Psychogenesis is an intricate term. It is used to indicate the causal effect of psychically injurious interactions in youth – and in later life – which lead to a marked defectiveness in an individual's capacity to live his own life and to enter upon a satisfactory relationship with his fellows.) Jung declared himself convinced of the value of psychotherapy as a principal method of treatment, joining a great line of psychotherapists, among whom Alfred Adler, Medard Boss, Christian Müller, Schultz-Hencke, Harry Stack Sullivan, Frieda Fromm-Reichmann, Federn, John Rosen and Séchehaye were the pioneers and with whom yet others have aligned themselves in growing numbers.

To return to Jung: He, too, recoiled originally out of fear of 'prevailing opinion.' On this the psychoanalyst Schultz-Hencke comments:

If, some forty-four years after the event, one reads C. G. Jung's work of 1907 entitled *Über die Psychologie der Dementia Praecox*, one is left asking in considerable bewilderment: How was it possible that Jung failed to implement his grand initiative at that time and build it up eventually into a correct theory of the psychology of schizophrenia?[2]

Thus both Bleuler and Jung remained bogged down in the traditional notions of the clinical psychiatry that surrounded them.

The name of Freud has been mentioned a few times already. Freud started with the concept of 'psychotic being' in his analysis of the 'Schreber case.' Since then, many people have wondered what might have happened if Freud had concerned himself more with the 'psychotic mode of existence.' Freud was very pessimistic regarding the possibility of communication. His belief that the psychotic's 'narcissistic libido organization' offered no 'possibility of transference' and that for this reason any psychotherapeutic contact was ruled out has certainly had an inhibiting effect on the development of the psychotherapy of the psychotic person.

The term 'narcissistic libido organization' is typical specialist jargon. What it amounts to is this: With his libido model (a sort of 'energy-activated' hand for making contact with others) Freud thought he could explain the total rejection of contact and the process of 'withdrawing into oneself.' The 'libido' withdrew into the person, who thus became 'unreachable.' The individual became wholly concentrated on himself ('narcissistic'). No emotional contact was possible in which the psychiatrist could be father-mother-brother (as the case may be) to his client (the 'transference' of emotions experienced earlier in relationship to father, mother, brother, etc.). Freud did, of course, alter his point of view, but his pessimism has certainly held things back.

At any rate, the work of Freud, Adler and Jung has provided a foundation for every other psychotherapist to stand upon.

I want to emphasize here that in regard to the psychotic mode of being Freud found himself in an unusually difficult position. Zilboorg, in particular, has referred to Freud's embarrassment concerning the relation between psychoanalysis and the traditional clinical psychiatry of his day.[8] Kraepelin and Freud were of the same generation. And Freud's mentor, Meynert, saw 'being psychotic' as a disease of the frontal lobes of the brain and could not countenance the idea that personality and psychic difficulties, after reaching a certain pitch, gave rise to apparently incomprehensible behavior. So Freud found himself amid a generation which in the Hippocratic tradition of medicine thought only in terms of 'diseases' and 'symptoms' and sought their origin in physical causes. The remarkable thing, according to Zilboorg, is that while Freud clung to the old clinical labels, he spoke the language badly: 'He couldn't care less about names.' It is clear to Zilboorg that despite all the contrary predispositions built into his preliminary training, Freud believed nonetheless that 'being neurotic' or 'being psychotic' (from the mildest degree to the most acute) were ultimately degrees of integration and disintegration of the total personality.

Quite early on there were psychiatrists who did not take Freud's pessimism about psychotherapeutically treating 'schizophrenics' all that seriously. The psychoanalyst Medard Boss asked Freud in 1935 whether he still stood by his old position, and when Freud advised him against psychoanalyzing a schizophrenic patient because a failure might harm the cause of psychoanalysis, Boss disregarded the advice and started therapy. He began with a feeding bottle and talking about the fear of castration. Typical of the climate in those days (and it has not changed very much) was the reaction of an eminent psychiatrist of the classical clinical school who said: 'You're quite a humorist, Mr Boss, and you've already permitted yourself a lot of jokes at the expense of classical psychiatry. But that you can actually affect the organic schizophrenic process with a feeding bottle and a chat about the fear of castration – that's going too far!'

That reaction sets us square in the middle of the problem raised by the psychotherapy of the schizophrenic person. One can hardly overlook the uncompromising nature of the standpoints, the markedly antithetical ways of stating the issue. To put it most sharply: There are psychiatrists for whom the 'scandal of psychiatry' resides in the fact that the 'physical process' has not so far been discovered; and there are psychiatrists who see the 'scandal of psychiatry' in the fact that some still believe in mental-disease-as-a-physical-process!

Manfred Bleuler (Eugen Bleuler's son) has in an extensive report pointed to the tragi-comical confusion of tongues that exists between psychiatrists. Opinions are enormously far apart. He writes: 'Without a necessary respect for even the most widely different views of others, we can no longer try to understand one another.' (I quote Manfred Bleuler at some length in the notes to this chapter. He has written a beautiful summation.)

So two types of psychiatrists (and 'psychiatries') have grown up; and if there is one thing I have no intention of doing, it is reconciling the one with the other. In fact, I believe that such a reconciliation is impossible.

Let us look further at these two types and schools of thought. The first one was very well expressed by my director of the psychiatric institution in Chapter 1. The man was dead serious in what he said: 'Psychiatry' is a natural science, the psychiatrist primarily a scientific investigator and then a physician, and one should not want to comprehend everything at all costs. There is a limit to empathetic understanding, the process of *verstehen*. Once past that limit (where that limit is drawn, of course, is the crux of the matter) one proceeds to 'explain' (*erklären*) in terms of the (still mysterious) cause in the body. Of course, one can understand this, that or the other factor, these psychiatrists argue. Naturally, the life-history is very important as are aspirations and needs. But the *form* in which an individual expresses himself (especially when that form comes under the notion of 'queer' or 'crazy'), that is beyond understanding. There are 'primary incomprehensible forms of behavior' and one can envisage these most usefully as the manifestation of a physical disease, the progress of which disrupts the coherence of the psychic structure.

It goes without saying that this type of psychiatrist applies this premise in his *approach*. This sort of latitude can never be concealed. Any person in great psychic distress who talks to such a psychiatrist notices it immediately.

What is this approach, this attitude? It is more or less patriarchal, the attitude of the scientific investigator and 'observer.' It is an attitude of 'interrogate and record.' Not only Kraepelin but also Bleuler and the philosopher-psychiatrist Jaspers (and an endless series of psychiatrists) have 'observed' in this way and have produced endless descriptions of the 'world of the psychotic individual.'

For this activity the term 'phenomenology' has been employed. It denotes a process of watching, listening and depicting very intently – a process resulting in minute accounts of the behavior and experiential world of the 'investigee.' The Germans especially have gone in for this. This 'static phenomenology' has been remarkably highly spoken of. One is at times lost in admiration, not at what someone says regarding inner afflictions, but rather at the literary accomplishment of the psychiatrists who, observing and 'empathizing,' are able to expound at length about their patients.

Ludwig Binswanger was an example of the philosopher-psychiatrist who scanned the papers his assistants had filled with observations their patients had made about their experiences and past lives. Binswanger proceeded to write a great work in which he most 'lucidly' illuminated the life and 'being' of these patients (Ilse, Ellen West, Lola Vosz and so on). Only he did it from behind his desk. Whether Binswanger ever 'saw' these patients himself, was involved with them as a psychotherapist, I really do not know.

This same Binswanger made an important admission during a conference of psychiatrists who believed that 'schizophrenics' could be understood, who accepted the hypothesis that these persons were suffering from their own 'human condition' and from what others had done to them. During this congress this eighty-year-old contemporary of Freud said:

> For me the breakthrough of the psychotherapy of schizophrenia into psychiatry is the second major event in my participation over more than half a century in the history of psychiatry. The first thing that I am so vividly reminded of by the current situation was the breakthrough achieved by Freud's psychoanalysis. Its triumphal progress may serve to that extent to console the present generation, because – just like the pioneers of the psychotherapy of schizophrenia – the then disciples of psychoanalytic theory not only encountered resistance but were rendered scientifically suspect, indeed, were even branded in various places as 'criminals.' [9]

An extraordinary statement by a man who changed his view very late in life.

But let us return to the 'phenomenologists.' Whether through their refined description of 'world-images' or minute accounts of a repertoire of conduct, these 'phenomenologists' always *observed from a distance. They entered upon no relationship, were not involved nor engaged as people offering help.* It is astonishing to realize that these investigators manifestly did not realize that a relation exists between 'knowing' and 'the known,' *certainly where human beings are concerned.*[10] The act of observing (however friendly the inflections of the questioner or investigator may be) affects *very considerably* the person who feels he is being made an object of observation (and ultimately of classification); and he reacts to this with conduct which the psychiatrist in turn interprets as 'typical' and describes in writing.

I would refer you to the work of R. D. Laing who has concerned himself at some length with the problems that arise when as a result of being observed people are made into objects.[11] I propose to vary an example that Laing gives. Imagine a lecture room where a professor, clad in a white coat, is 'demonstrating' a patient. The professor talks over the patient's head to the students and explains to them what 'syndrome' the patient is exhibiting. He gives a circumstantial account of the patient's behavior and world of experience. Then the patient suddenly shouts out: 'I'm made of wood, I'm made of wood!' The professor, kindling with enthusiasm, can now explain to the students that this expression is likewise typical of the syndrome (for instance, 'schizophrenia'). In a situation of this sort one may indeed ask (with Laing): 'Who is really wooden here, the professor or his patient?' The professor's attitude is aloof and objectivizing (reducing the person to a thing). In his investigatory and descriptive approach, therefore, and in the dehumanizing setting of the lecture room, it does not occur to the professor that the person sitting there, being gazed at by the students, is saying something perfectly sensible: namely, 'I feel I'm being treated like a piece of wood!' On the contrary, the professor is so little bent on deeper communication and human engagement that he is deaf to this irony and proceeds to explain once more to his attentive audience how the utterance of the 'demonstrated' patient fits in with his presuppositions as to what the thing 'is' that the patient 'has.'

If the amazed reader is now saying to himself: 'But surely

that can't happen,' I must assure him that it has happened and it does. In the clinic where I worked during my 'neurological' term the demonstrations in the lecture room were regularly conducted in the manner I have just described. And if the residents became so concerned about the fate of their patients that they actually started listening and talking to them (that is to say, if they took some form of psychotherapeutic action), they were rapped on the knuckles because their activities interfered with the 'purity' of the 'syndrome,' and that spoiled the professor's lecture and demonstration.

Let us turn our attention now to that other category of psychiatrists. These are the psychotherapists. They establish a relationship, they commit themselves, they 'forget' the labels. In the relationship the person sitting beside or across from his psychotherapist reveals himself – but in quite a different way this time. He exposes his misgivings and his loneliness, the sort of life he has been living, memories and feelings of earlier days (with father, mother and other 'emotionally significant adults') and relives them in the growing, deepening relationship with this individual who calls himself a psycho-therapist.

The psychotherapist actively intervenes, he presents himself with all the force of his personal commitment to his client, refuses to accept any failure of communication and thus shows another person a closeness, honesty, understanding and warmth he has never before experienced. In the human relationship now created, the client reveals much more of his subtle 'intrapsychic processes.' The revelation of the history of his private experiences can now take place on the basis of a growing confidence that the interest being shown here by the psychiatrist is primarily that of a psychotherapist.

Einen Schizophrenen verlassen, ist einen töten ('To abandon a schizophrenic is to kill him') is a saying that points to the maximal – or, if you like, libidinous – investment in the patient. In a relationship of that sort *more and more becomes intelligible*. The psychiatrists Siirala and Benedetti remind us that 'intelligibility' is not some attribute or other of a 'queer' phenomenon that we 'observe.' *Intelligibility, the quality of understanding, comes through the building up of a relationship with another person. It is something which passes through us.*[12] Indeed, Siirala goes further and preludes a theme to which R. D. Laing is later to give such a central place. Siirala wonders not only whether intelligibility is engendered but also whether the self-styled 'healthy' psychiatrist does not proceed to pose questions for himself – in other words, become less understandable to himself. Referring to what goes on between the psychiatrist-psychotherapist and his schizophrenic 'patient' he says: 'Or is it that we all share in this disease, this split condition, to which our society, our body politic, is subject?' [13] As 'schizophrenia' signifies a state of division, of brokenness, it is only in our struggle to restore contact and relationship with the schizophrenic that our *own* dividedness, *our* slice of unlived life, can become truly visible.

In this 'participatory understanding' (Sullivan puts it somewhat more drily: 'participant observation'), the psychotherapist stuctures an interpersonal situation in which the patient can at last become 'talkable,' because of the security he provides for him and his readiness and ability to give a helpful answer. Winkler speaks in this connection of 'dynamic phenomenology.' This is not some kind of free-wheeling activity. It has the character of dialogue. There is no investigator here, but a fellow human being who is sometimes restricted in his freedom, sometimes forced to struggle physically with his patient and sometimes even to model his own life upon him. Psychotherapy and dynamic phenomenology are a unity here and constitute a source of knowledge for the psychiatric discipline.

Regarded from these vantage points, a great many 'schizophrenic modes of behavior' can be interpreted in an entirely new light. Aversion to every form of contact, being totally immersed in oneself (autism), stunted feeling, a totally petrified attitude (catatonia), can now be seen as particular types of aversion dynamism. They are not 'properties' inherent in this or that 'matter' but are to be understood in terms of the dynamic process between the patient and 'the other.' They are relational forms, and for that reason the possibility exists of their being subject to influence. Regarded in this way, the stuntedness is something 'feigned,' a resistance to expressing the most intense emotion; the indifference is a pseudo-indifference designed to counter overwhelming dependency needs.

When one has seen autism of many years' standing melt like snow under the sun and the 'defective condition' unfold in the relationship with the psychotherapist in a rich diversity of emotions (as we saw in the case of Karel), one is no longer satisfied as a psychotherapist with the terminology employed in psychiatry. That terminology, used to express what we know about psychopathological phenomena, reveals *the way in which we have acquired that knowledge*. Is not the way the 'investigator' has set himself *over against* the schizophrenic patient the reason this terminology bears so markedly the character of 'the wasted and forlorn'?

Now something about the psychotherapy of psychotic people in general. As soon as one speaks about the prospects for development that exist in the psychotherapy of 'psychotic' people, one is invariably faced with the criticism that this psychotherapy is so difficult to put into practice. The critics point especially to the close and binding relationship between psychiatrist and client that arises in the context of a psycho-analytically-oriented psychotherapy and which is alleged to lead to situations extremely difficult to handle. The inter-pretative clarification of this binding relationship (the working through of the 'transference neurosis' or 'psychosis') is said to take a very long time indeed. A lot of people wonder, there-fore, whether the time and trouble demanded by a therapeutic process of this sort are economically justifiable!

The extension of psychotherapy must surely afford an adequate reply to this practical criticism. That reply is at hand. We are witnessing the development of family psycho-therapy, in which the emphasis falls not on one individual who is behaving in a 'mad' way (and is thus declared to be 'mad,' but on the *system as a whole*; we are seeing the develop-ment of strategies of change in larger subsystems of the com-munity; and we are seeing the growth of new types of institu-tion, where the extremely arduous work of individual psychotherapy is only one part of a 'total effort around the clock' in which a lot of assistant psychotherapists (and fellow 'patients') share. In that way a greater intensity is given to the therapeutic process.

During my period of training in Amsterdam I thought that this last aspect in particular, the fundamental reorganization of the psychiatric institution (especially the 'ward'), offered great possibilities. A large part of this book deals with this aspect. Before we get to that, however, I would like to give you one more very concrete account of my experiences in a brief but intensive psychotherapeutic intervention with a man I also met in Amsterdam.

[1] J. Rosen: *Direct Psychoanalysis*, vol. II, p. 8 (New York, 1968).

[2] H. Schultz-Hencke: *Das Problem der Schizophrenie, analytische Psychotherapie und Psychise* (Stuttgart, 1952).

[3] E. Bleuler: *Dementia Praecox and the Group of Schizophrenias*, 5th ed. (New York, 1961).

[4] The term *demence précoce* was first used by the Belgian psychiatrist, Morel, and what he observed in a fourteen-year-old boy he explained by means of a hereditary type of 'psychological degeneration.' B. A. Morel: *Etudes cliniques, traité théorique et practique des maladies mentales* (Paris, 1852–1865).

[5] E. Kraepelin: *Compendium der Psychiatrie* (Leipzig, 1883); *Psychiatrie, ein Lehrbuch für Studierende und Aertze*, 5th ed. (Leipzig, 1896) (6th ed., 1899; 8th ed., 1909–1915).

[6] R. Cancrio and P. W. Pruysen: 'A Historical Review of the Development of the Concept Schizophrenia,' *Bull. of Meninger Clin.*, pp. 61–70 (1970).

[7] H. Stierlin: 'Bleuler's Concept of Schizophrenia in the Light of Our Present Experience' in *Psychotherapy of Schizophrenia, Third International Symposium, Lausanne*, 1964, pp. 42–53 (Basle/New York, 1965); 'Bleuler's Concept of Schizophrenia: a Confusing Heritage,' *Am. Journ. of Psychiatry*, pp. 996–1002 (1967).

[8] G. Zilboorg: 'Freud's Fundamental Psychiatric Orientation,' *International Journal of Psychoanalysis*, 35, pp. 90–95 (1954).

[9] *Second International Symp. in Psychotherapy of Schizophrenia, Zürich*, 1959. Edited by G. Benedetti and C. Müller (Basle/New York, 1960.)

[10] Dewey and Bentley stated: 'The transactional is in fact that point of view which systematically proceeds upon the ground that knowing is co-operative and as such is integral with communication.' (J. Dewey and A. Bentley: *Knowing and the Known*, Boston, Mass., 1949.)

[11] R. D. Laing: *The Divided Self* (London, 1960).

[12] Benedetti puts it like this:

One ventures to wonder – and here I refer to the fundamental ideas of Siirala – whether the boundary of the intelligible can be drawn simply between certain self-contained series of symptoms of disease, or whether it does not rather run through ourselves. Intelligibility, understood in the latter sense, would not be a 'property' of this or that psychopathological phenomenon – an attribute objectively given-in-itself and theoretically available to knowledge – but it would only yield itself in virtue of the helpful 'forward leap' (Heidegger) as an event between one person and another. It could be experienced only if we personally stake a claim in the life of the patient, 'unintelligible' and defectively articulated in relation to others as it may be, and let ourselves be summoned to a helpful, for instance, interpretative response.

The passage comes from a major survey by Benedetti presented during the First International Symposium on the Psychotherapy of 'Schizophrenia.' G. Benedetti: 'Die soziologische, psychologische und psychotherapeutische Schizophrenieforschung, 1951–1956,' *Internat. Symposium über die Psychotherapie der Schizophrenie, Lausanne*, Oct., 1956, *Acta Psychotherapeutica*, vol. V, pp. 106–128 (1957).

[13] M. Siirala: 'Probleme der Begegnung in chronische Schizophrenie,' *Second International Symp. in Psychotherapy of Schizophrenia, Zürich*, vol. II, pp. 70–83 (Basle/New York, 1960).

[14] H. C. v. d. Waals: 'Schizofrene aandoeningen van volwassenen,' *Nederlands handboek der psychiatrie*, 4 (Deventer, 1970).

NOTES

M. Bleuler: 'Forschungen und Begriffswandlung in der Schizophrenielehre 1941–1959,' *Fortschritte der Neurologie und Psychiatrie* vol. 19, pp. 385–453 (1951).

In five years Manfred Bleuler read through about eleven hundred publications, visited a variety of psychiatric institutions at home and abroad, attended congresses and was struck by the enormous confusion concerning the word 'schizophrenia.' Everybody understood something different by it. For some it was a physical disease, for others *'eine psychologisch so verstehende Reaktion.'* Some called the psychoanalytical approach humbug and others said the principal was way ahead. There were psychiatrists who regarded the whole notion of a cerebral disease as a medieval old wives' tale, and others who considered it the only scientific basis. There was a corresponding confusion regarding 'the methods of treatment.' The prevailing view prior to 1941 Bleuler summarized quite simply (and correctly): Schizophrenia is a syndrome, a central group (the real thing!) and marginal groups with 'other' causes (what that 'other' might be is not indicated). But the core group is hereditary, a sort of metabolic disease, it does not have 'psychic causes,' but such factors are certainly an influence. Treatment is physical.

Then came the turnabout in the following decade which Bleuler characterized as growing doubt: Schizophrenia is *not* a 'disease entity,' *not* a hereditary disease, *not* the expression of a mysterious disease process that disrupts the body's functioning. It does *not* call for any one specific kind of medical treatment. Of the earlier and still persisting hereditary theory little remains beyond vague talk about *Anlage* ('bent'), 'sensitivity toward,' 'schizoid disposition' (a tendency to withdraw and encapsulate oneself). Bleuler attached a great deal of value to studies of the family system, which have provided a completely different outlook on things, supported the psychogenetic hypothesis and given a different aspect to heredity behaviour patterns, 'delusive ideas,' modes of thinking and so on, transferred not via the 'genes' but culturally from generation to generation (acquired by learning, in other words!). These studies allow more room for the concept of 'social heredity.'

Anyone who follows the way this has developed, when he looks through the older works will be deeply impressed to find it confirmed that generations of great investigators have without more ado taken the occurrence of psychoses in a family as proof of their hereditary character, without so much as stopping to think to what a great extent the psychoses in the family must affect its atmosphere and to what extent they may even act as a psychic trauma on the members of the family.

The whole body of pathophysiological research, the attempts, that is, to demonstrate 'the disease,' were summed up by Bleuler with the remark that they have not taken us one step further. He saw many more possibilities in the view that persistent emotional 'stress' leads to physiological changes.

After an exhaustive survey of all the physical treatments (the insulin cure, sleep cure, electroshock) Bleuler turned to psychotherapy, mentioning as prime examples the work of John Rosen and that of Séchehaye. All in all this is a most important article, in which Manfred Bleuler made no attempt to hide his personal preference.

A great deal of detailed information may be found in the survey by Gaetano Benedetti: 'Die soziologische, psychologische und psychotherapeutische Schizophrenieforschung 1951–1956,' *Acta Psychotherapeutica*, vol. 5, pp. 106–128 (1957).

The following selection of basic literature on the problems of 'being schizophrenic' ('psychotic'):

S. Arieti: *Interpretation of Schizophrenia* (New York, 1951).

H. Stack Sullivan: *The Interpersonal Theory of Psychiatry* (New York, 1953); *Conceptions of Modern Psychiatry* (London, 1955); *Clinical Studies in Psychiatry* (New York, 1956); *The Psychiatric Interview, The Fusion of Psychiatry and the Social Sciences* (New York, 1964); *Schizophrenia as a Human Process* (New York, 1962).

F. Fromm-Reichmann: *Psychoanalysis and Psychotherapy: Selected Papers* (Chicago, 1959).

H. Schultz-Hencke: *Das Problem der Schizophrenie* (Stuttgart, 1952).

G. Schwing: *Ein Weg zur Seele des Geisteskranken* (Zürich, 1970).

J. Rosen: *Direct Analysis*, vol. I (New York, 1953); vol. II (New York, 1968).

M. A. Séchehaye: *Symbolic Realization* (New York, 1950); *Autobiography of a Schizophrenic Girl* (New York, 1951).

L. B. Hill: *Psychotherapeutic Intervention in Schizophrenia* (Chicago, 1955).

Further basic literature:

S. Freud: 'Psycho-Analytic Notes on an Autobiographical Account of a Case of Paranoia (Dementia Paranoides),' *Collected Works*, vol. 12 (London, 1958).

C. G. Jung: *The Psychology of Dementia Praecox* and *The Content of the Psychoses*, both in the *Collected Works*, vol. 3 (London, 1960).

On the subject of static phenomenology:

K. Jaspers: *General Psychopathology* (Manchester, 1962).

G. Pankow: *Dynamische Strukturierung in der Psychose* (Bern, 1957).

P. Federn: *Ich-Psychologie und die Psychosen* (Bern, 1956).

4. JACK

In the clinic I encountered a man who had earned his living as a carpenter. He was thirty-two years of age, had been married for four years, after the birth of his first child he had become psychotic. Some months prior to his admission his wife had noticed that her husband 'had a wild look' and was gradually isolating himself. At work he spoke to no one, and alternated between working at a tremendous pace and wandering about the factory area. Most recently he had taken to singing songs, one after another. Now and then he was unaccountably aggressive.

The wife told me that as she neared delivery, her husband became very nervous. She said that he had always very much depended on her and that during their marriage she had had to help him with a great many practical problems. Because of his inadequate schooling she had also given him lessons in speech and arithmetic. This may have made him feel very inferior.

When Jack was admitted his main symptom, apart from a preponderantly manic disposition, was 'hearing voices' on a massive scale. The simplistic, highly concrete and in expression quaintly childish content of his 'voices' caused a psychiatrist whom Jack saw first to react as follows.

First, this colleague got the immediate and definite impression that the man he was dealing with was just 'dumb' and so Jack tended to provoke ridicule. This psychiatrist, adhering to the traditional system of 'observe' and 'diagnose,' gave Jack an intelligence test, and when he could not answer the familiar questions and do the arithmetic problems, and then revealed he had been left back in elementary school three times, he had his first label pinned on him: *debilitas mentis*, a portentous term meaning 'very stupid'! From this it was argued that because Jack could also be described as psychotic, the diagnosis 'debility psychosis' fitted him very well.

But . . . there is another way of looking at it. Jack functioned in relation to the other (in this case the psychiatrist) in such a way as to create the impression of being 'very stupid,' and because of the ridicule he provoked he simply increased the distance between himself and the other. One may wonder whether that was not just what he meant to do – create aloofness out of fear of a deeper contact, which might invite rejection (this type of behavior is in fact known as 'rejection courting').

So I asked myself whether Jack might not be using whatever was 'stupid' and 'ludicrous' about him as defensive maneuvers. By making stupid remarks and provoking general laughter the man was creating a distance in the sense of 'not being taken seriously' by others. At the same time a tendency to therapeutic nihilism was emerging in the psychiatrist: 'The man is too stupid to talk to.'

This pseudo-debility dynamic applies, I believe, to a lot of people who feel frightened and inferior. It is not without reason that the term 'poorly endowed' is constantly on the lips of so many psychiatrists and psychologists. When confronted with doltish behavior it is always a good thing to ask oneself whether somebody is not availing himself of the stratagem 'play it dumb,' with the aim of 'getting by unnoticed.' The psychoanalyst Mahler-Schönberger once spoke in this connection of 'pseudo-imbecility as the magic cap of invisibility.'

To get back to Jack: *As was discovered later, the description 'poorly endowed' did not fit him at all*; and his 'feeble intellectual functioning' turned out to be based, among other things, on the fact that at a very early stage his mother had assigned him the role of the 'dumb one' in the family and had fixed him in that role. While Jack was in extreme anguish under the influence of his hallucinations, he withdrew more and more from contact of any kind. He was sedated, and the clinic once again resorted to electroshock treatment, which seemed to make the situation worse.

As the months passed Jack became more and more inactive. In the occupational therapy department he sat all day smiling in his chair apparently immersed in an interior world. It was thought he would have to be transferred to an institution for more intensive care, when one day I had a conversation with him which suddenly gave an opening for contact to be restored.

The conversation started like this:

I've noticed that generally speaking you don't do much in the way of occupational therapy.
Jack: I don't want to carry on with being a carpenter I want to be a drummer in the army.
How do you mean?
Jack: I want to beat the drum. In the army, with a fine uniform on.
But you're a carpenter, aren't you?
Jack: I don't want to be a carpenter anymore. I want to go into the army to be a drummer and serve the Queen in a lovely uniform, with polished shoes.
But you can't go into the regular army just like that. You need to have some training for it.
Jack: I'll be a drummer with a lovely uniform on.

That is a typically 'stupid' conversation – but particularly on my side. I remained the objective 'questioner,' for I understood Jack's words in their superficial meaning, and apparently this only made the gap in communication bigger than ever. Jack was speaking a language that had to be decoded, and I was not trying to do that.

I shall not dwell on the problems of the very distinctive use the psychotic person makes of language. I shall restrict myself

to what took place between Jack and me, to our 'transaction.'
Bachrach, among others, pointed out a very interesting aspect
of the transaction with the psychotic person. The psychotic
who formulates a bizarre idea – a delusion, if you like – in
doing so confronts the psychiatrist with the job of *guessing
what really lies behind it*. That is to say, the psychiatrist is forced
to abandon his attempts to induce the client to conform to the
generally received and accepted use of language. *The psychiatrist is asked to come down to the level occupied by his client*, to
respond to the level of communication 'beneath' the level of
verbalized expression. This is what Lewis Hill called 'to
schizophrenese' and Sullivan 'to talk oblique.' In this process
of descending, of coming down, there is implied – and this is
the whole point – a very crucial act of turning toward the
other. In the last analysis it is a demand upon the psychiatrist
not to be an observer but a psychotherapist, that is to say, one who
wants to help and therefore achieve a deeper understanding.
In communication with psychotic people one sees how this
descending creates a sudden clarifying of veiled and obscure
forms of expression. A lad who talked quite unintelligibly
surprised me on one occasion by saying something I thought
I could understand. After I had put my notion directly into
words he said: 'A bird is known by its note, a man by his
talk,' and then resumed his unintelligible language in a somewhat less unintelligible manner.

The client, Sullivan once said, will momentarily drop his
'schizzy talk' and speak in normal language, an event which
the psychotherapist often regards as a sort of present. That is
how we understand Bachrach's observation that the habit of
using allegorical or symbolic expression *contains a test*. The
psychiatrist is tested on his 'willingness to understand.' Here
Bachrach arrives at the very interesting thesis that, for
instance, the 'delusion' can be regarded as 'an idea which a
patient gives out in a form which tempts the therapist to take
it literally.' He gives the example of a patient who every so
often asserted 'that she did not necessarily wish to go to
Rome.' The reply that she did not need to and that nobody
was forcing her to go was beside the point. The point was that
when she was young she had been compelled to be just like

the rest and to conform her behavior to that of 'the neighbors.' In this utterance she was protesting at the threat to her identity, using a modified version of the adage: 'When in Rome, do as the Romans do.' [1] So in Jack's case it made little sense to point out to him the difficulties joining the regular army would entail.

Our conversation now took a dramatic turn, as the result of a surprisingly simple 'decoding.'

You want to join the army to beat a drum?
Jack: Yes, and to serve the Queen in a splendid uniform, with polished shoes.
You want to work for the kind mother?
Jack: Yes.
A decent son, serving the good mother?

(Jack's eyes fill with tears. He seizes and clutches tightly the hand I extend to him at that moment.)

Jack: Yes, yes, that's right. My head's always been full of the Queen.
The good, ideal mother you've always been looking for?
Jack: That's right! That's it!

The bizarre 'you keep away' posture has gone. Our contact is warm and profound. A few minutes after this conversation, back on the ward, Jack has a tremendous fit of crying. When I ask him why, he replies: 'For the kind mother, I long for her so very much.' The effect of this conversation is amazing. At the next session he begins, *quite of his own accord*, to inform me that he has been hearing voices continuously for the past three months. The voices tell him he is the son of Charles Lindbergh and the Queen and that he must now prepare himself for his task as Crown Prince, for which he has been chosen. It appears that he has read an article on Lindbergh and seized on this notion as a way of giving expression to his desire for an ideal father-image. Jack describes his own father to me as a man who constantly took any kind of work away from him and would not allow his son to achieve anything on his own:

If I was mending my bike, I only had to go away for a

minute and my father would start to finish it off for me. When I got back it would all be done. A couple of weeks before he died I made a cupboard. I wanted to paper it inside. That cupboard was something I had done. I remember walking upstairs to the attic and opening the cupboard. It had already been papered. Ill as he was, father had finished off my work again, while I wasn't there. Now the voices say that Lindbergh will put me in charge of a technical workshop.

The conversations we have on this theme lead to a release of strong emotion, with impotent rage alternating with expressions of great distress.

In the course of the sessions that follow he tells me that he can also hear the Princesses' voices. They cheer him up and make him feel part of a happy family. This induces him to speak about the enormous loneliness in which he spent his early years. As the youngest of three children he had no contact with his two brothers or his parents. Just as Jack is talking about this loneliness, he reports that 'the voices are now telling him *I* am actually his brother.' These longings for a close brotherly relationship are persistently spoken of and this touches off an aggressive development: 'The voices cheer me up. Is all this just my desires? I don't want this to be just fantasy.' At the end of the session Jack hands me a cigar: 'For your brother, or father, maybe.'

That Jack is the Crown Prince-elect of his mother the Queen leads us quickly to concentrate the next conversation on his relationship with his mother. It comes out that his voices are in fact making a reality of a fantasy of long standing.

As a child he felt very much neglected and so isolated that fantasies in which he was a foundling (his own father and mother looked after him only in the most perfunctory way), were frequently used as a defense to ward off an overwhelming sense of loneliness and emotional neglect. His mother he describes as a very childish woman who always gave him the feeling of being very dull:

I would try and do my homework, but if I showed it to my mother she would laugh in such a queer way and start talking about the woman next door. She never helped me with it at all.

From his accounts it emerges that his mother imposed a sort of 'backward child' identity on her son and fixed him in this stereotyped role. Along with his father's influence this has engendered a crippling sense of stupidity, of thickheadedness, which he had partly come to believe in and use as something to cling to, and partly fights against with great obstinacy:

The Queen, that is, my real mother, is quite different. No, my boy, she says. Don't go away before you've shown me your homework. Just let me check it over. That's good, because she wants me to make something of myself and really get somewhere.

He goes on immediately to describe his mother as someone who persistently discouraged him from every form of achievement and at the same time consoled him by repeating the old saying: 'There's also a place for dull boys!'

It becomes clearer and clearer how the mother has tried to put a stop to any form of knowledge-seeking, and in particular has reacted with marked anxiety and fear to any attempt on her son's part to get to know more about sex. That this kind of blockage is a material factor in the emergence of pseudo-debility was noted a long time ago in the literature of psychoanalysis. The most striking feature is that the mother's influence is aimed at bringing about a sort of overall 'blessed ignorance' in her child.

Before I take my account of my dealings with Jack any further I would like to provide in some detail a description of his mother. I did not talk to her myself, but at my request my friend and colleague, Pier Engelsman, had a number of conversations with her. The following record of their acquaintanceship was written by him.

The mother is an odd woman. She has one, continually repeated, affirmation to make: 'At home everything is always cosy, quiet, cheerful and nice.' Everything she has to say over and above that serves to make the same point.

Questions about the darker sides of life, past or present, are resolutely warded off. Thus, for instance, she showed me a lot of family snapshots, all mixed together, with the sole purpose of demonstrating what fun they always had, her and the boys. When I asked whether her husband did not have a somewhat gloomy look in the photos, she did not reply the first time, and the second time said without hesitation: 'Yes, he was always so sociable, could come out with such wry remarks, you just had to laugh . . .'

The role she herself played in this scheme of things was that of the robust, efficient domestic 'mom,' the unexceptionable, always cheerful mother. This she demonstrates with innumerable would-be funny anecdotes, which she concludes with her extraordinary, sniggering laugh, to prove the point.

This cosy little world, in which there is no room for doubt or for problems, is, despite the air of apparent innocence, designed with a sure hand, in considerable detail; and there is no getting a foot in there. It is tiring just to listen to her.

After a time I quite lost the feeling that a motherly woman was volunteering to give me a lot of data and information. I felt on the contrary that she was all the time demanding approval, justification and agreement, or at the very least was bent on procuring an uninterrupted stream of attention.

In her anecdotes and tall stories one catches overtones of the hidden excitement, concern and fear of a very childish woman. Fear of the incomprehensible, complicated, fascinating big-wide-world of people. Thus the outward-directed function of this motherliness syndrome is: to save face. But one can also point to an inward-directed function: the warding off of one's own conflicts.

What she is also warding off, in a fairly broad fashion, is the experience of an unhappy childhood, about which one can only discover anything with great difficulty. In the end, though much disquieted at having to speak of it, she does admit that when she was at home as a child, she did *not* have it nice and cosy and peaceful and so forth. On the contrary. There was fighting and quarreling all the time. Father beat mother. Father died, oh no, father went off first, when she was ten, twenty, oh no, fifteen. She gets into a muddle.

When she was eleven, her childhood ended pretty abruptly. She started to menstruate, was very startled by it, remained silent and gloomy for a long time, her mother said nothing. At the same time she had to get her first job in service and therefore to leave school. She had not been a bright pupil, had once been left back. When she talked about school she giggled a great deal. She had been amazingly deft with her hands, would knit in a single afternoon what the other girls took a good three months over.

She was indeed fully aware that sex was still a great big a gruesome mystery to her. The lady for whom she worked about the house said to her one day: 'Isn't that nice carpenter who works over the way something for you? He keeps eyeing you, and seems to be quite a respectable young fellow.' – She married. – On the evening after the wedding she was alone with her husband in their nice new place, a record was being played of somebody singing in imitation of Handel's 'Largo,' but the words were: 'I want to go back to mother!' It was too much. She was very upset and burst into tears, so her husband, wishing to be kind, said: 'Put your things on and go to your mother, then.' But she was too plucky for that. Soon afterwards she got into bed and immediately fell asleep. For the next few days she went on crying a good deal, but was comforted by an older neighbor.

'You see, I've always been very much a child,' is how she concludes these confidences, which are brought in only at the very end of her list of subjects.

As a child she was considered dull, though good with her hands and fond of a joke. There is an obvious parallel, therefore, with our patient, her son. When she speaks about him as she has seen him in his psychotic state, it strikes one how impressionably and sensationally she describes this. Not without affection, but as though it had to do with a much loved pet that is making a peculiar or pitiable or comic exhibition of itself. She evinces nothing of the personal shock, the sense of respect, which someone would display who was capable of really identifying with her son as another person, as a personality. (I am very grateful to Pier Engelsman for agreeing to have his description of the mother included in this book.)

Because the business of 'hearing voices' was so material, I started every conversation with the question: 'What have the voices said today?' Whereupon Jack would proceed to relate the content of his 'hallucinations' in ever increasing detail. As the sessions went on, he disclosed, for instance, that the voices had told him his conception began at the moment Lindbergh and the Queen had gone walking together in the rain. This reminded me that the very day he was admitted Jack had spoken of 'sexual provocation in the bath' and also that among the voices offering him the prospect of sexual delights were those of many famous swimmers. Obviously, water and sexuality were in some way interconnected. When I broached this directly, Jack revealed (with considerable and mounting distress) that from the time he had first masturbated he had had a fantasy, a vision of girls lying in water with their clothes on. This fantasy kept forcing itself upon him during his attempts at coitus. So he achieved an orgasm only when he imagined his wife lying clothed in the water. He told me that he once wanted to duck his wife in water in order to stimulate himself sexually. This fantasy was accompanied by severe guilt feelings, and he had suffered from it a great deal.

You will notice that I put the term hallucination in quotes. I felt that Jack was now using his hallucinatory world to disclose to me, in a veiled way, all sorts of insistent problems and feelings.

When I examined the report of the first days I realized that even then – though in a far more obscure and 'droll' fashion – he had been using words to pose this same problem. He said, in fact, speaking about his 'world of delusion':

They have been with me, the three of them, they are swimming the relay, but when they are out of the race they come to me. I've made a little song about it. Can I sing it for you?

> Pong, pong, pong,
> here you have the harem,
> pong, pong, pong,
> wet hairs all,
> pong, pong, pong,
> all wet frocks,
> pong, pong, pong,
> here you have Greta Garbo,
> they float around
> pong, pong, pong,
> crazy girls all,
> swim all around,
> pong, pong, pong, etc.

How veiled and innocent this ditty seems. It's like 'all the little ducklings swim in the water'! And that is how my colleague, who was the first to see him, had taken it. 'Crazy' and 'droll' behavior, extremely excited (manic), 'stupid' and 'childish.' In fact, *what Jack was trying in his own fashion to express, even on that first day when he was admitted, was a frightful amount of misery and an enormous problem.*

At the same time as he was bringing out these fantasies Jack was revealing in the course of our conversations quite a bit about his sexual problems: his impotence during the marriage (about which his inexperienced spouse could do little to help him), acute guilt feelings about masturbation. During these conversations undisguised fears of castration would come to the fore:

I leaned against her. The first time, such a tremendous yearning, the first kiss lasted so long. I felt her teeth. I was terrified. I thought: She could very well bite my nose off.

My interpretations were moving at such a pace during this phase that for a short period Jack, in the context of his developing anxiety and terror, reacted with violent aggression and went for me. He explained later that he had not been able to follow all my interpretations and so was once more overwhelmed by a sense of being stupid. At the same time a fear possessed him that I might go off with his wife: 'I thought: They'll go away together one day.'

It was during the session in which he put all this into words that a deep and affectionate contact arose between us. He brought out his feelings of insignificance (especially intellectual insignificance) vis-à-vis myself and his wife and took occasion to refer to her, meaningfully, as 'Pascal.' It seemed that his wife sometimes tried to cheer him with the statement: 'I'm the head and you're the hands,' which he took to be a more or less definitive confirmation of his lack of intellect. Again we talked about the roots of his feelings of stupidity.

It was noticeable how intelligently and with what a wealth of diversity Jack was able to discuss his experiences. For instance, he explained how the birth of his son gave him the feeling that the latter would be 'just the same sort of imbecile' and that he even thought he could see it in the child's eyes. The situation at work was now becoming much clearer. He was trying desperately to prove that he was not a stupid carpenter; and this overwrought effort to get things done aroused in his co-workers, who were often amazed at his original way of tackling things, the inevitable envy, frustration and aggression. In this vicious circle his isolation grew and grew.

At one of our subsequent meetings Jack replied to my usual question: 'What have the voices said today?' that his hallucinations had gone. 'They disappeared after we had our talk yesterday about why I feel so stupid.'

What I noticed especially was that Jack used his 'hallucinations' as a *communicating bridge*, the only possible method he had of communicating. It struck me that under the influence of my interpretations he was gradually coming to refer to 'the voices' as 'my own voices' and to recognize them as projections of *his own complex of problems*. The 'voices' he had experienced as a frightening 'alien object' I had interpreted immediately as 'voices of your feeling' or 'pieces of yourself.'

His hearing the voices I also accepted as a method of communicating feelings, desires and problems which, in view of the terror associated with them, could not be admitted as his own. The following was a good example of this.

Jack was eager to see me as his brother, his friend, and expressed his need for dependence by saying: 'The voices now say that you actually are my bother.' At the risk of belaboring the point, I will again refer to the great difference in approach compared to the so-called objective method of inquiry into the available 'psychopathology.' Using the latter method, one would inquire about the nature of the voices, their character and content, note them as pathological findings, and thus put static phenomenology to work (Winkler). The patient would then feel that the investigator is not understanding his symptoms as an attempt to communicate, but is rather seeing them as expressions of a disease process, a sort of cerebral disturbance. To a person in difficulties this co-called objective approach, based on neutral inquiry, is to a high degree provocative and off-putting. It is also very noticeable that under this style of inquiry the stream of information slackens and the client begins to react very defensively.

The situation is conspicuously different in the psychotherapeutic conversation, where the psychiatrist at once accepts the voices ('symptoms') in their communicative significance, ascribes to them their value as enunciations of a nexus of problems and reacts to them as such with a meaningful, psychotherapeutically-oriented response. With this approach the stream of information increases. What Jack disclosed about his voices became more and more copious and detailed. Jack exposed his problems because he felt that I was not looking at his 'symptoms' as meaningless. This is what Winkler was getting at when he spoke of a dynamic phenomenology. Again and again, as we proceeded with this kind of conversation, I got the impression that in answer to the question: 'What have the voices told you today?' Jack understood he was being asked to describe large areas of his problems via the detour of reporting on his 'voices.' I could not escape the impression that the 'hallucinations' as such had already disappeared but were still being used as a method of communication that offered a great degree of security. It was as though client and psychiatrist stationed themselves attentively on either side of a third person (the voices), which represented the unintegrated part of the client's emotional life, expelled from the totality of his personality. For a time after he was admitted Jack hallucinated on a large scale the voices of film stars who assured him of their readiness to provide him with sexual experiences. During our final discussions, when the hallucinations had gone, Jack would talk about *his* strong sexual desires, which emerged particularly when he saw good-looking girls walking on the streets. These sexual fantasies filled him with a great sense of guilt in respect to himself and his wife.

Thus another function of the 'hallucinations' became clear to me. It was a guilt-shedding procedure, which can be described as a defense dynamism within the framework of the intrapsychic regulation. This intrapersonal function of the hallucination may be found in abundance in the literature (which is cited at the end of this chapter).

Besides the intrapersonal function, the hallucination also has an interpersonal significance, of the sort we described above as communicative-via-a-detour. It was much to the credit of Sullivan and his colleagues that they put so great an emphasis on this interpersonal function of the 'symptom.'

To sum up, therefore, one could say that the intrapsychic regulation function and the communication function were present right from the start; and in the course of the psychotherapeutic relationship the intrapsychic function diminished and the interpersonal communication function correspondingly increased.

When the hallucinations had disappeared, I pressed on with the psychotherapy, but to go into that at any length here would take us too far afield. One more point would seem relevant. Jack had been twenty years old and in military service (in Indonesia) when he disintegrated for the first time; and he was psychotic for five months. He had entered the service as a volunteer (without meeting the Queen!). Because of his tremendous urge to be 'on the ball' all the time and his exaggerated devotion to duty he soon made himself a laughing-stock. There, too, he found himself in a situation of being totally isolated within the group, which rejected him as 'queer.' After a whole spate of injections, sedations and electroshocks he was shifted, already in a hallucinating condition, back to The Netherlands. Those hallucinations had the same content as in the initial phase of his second psychotic crisis. We were able to discuss this whole phase, too, in detail; and Jack could even give a complete account of this experience in the presence of his wife.

It was the same problem that my voices talked about. To myself I called it at that time just a 'tropical fit.' Well, just to have something to hang on to, really. What else was I supposed to do? My voices stopped one day and I left the asylum without ever having uttered a single word about my problems and feelings. I was later informed that I was rejected for military service. I thought: You've been left back three times in school and now you've been turned down because of a tropical fit. From then on I started to work harder, just to prove that I was worth something after all.

During this period Jack was the only one of his set to get his carpenter's diploma, he met his wife and bought a houseboat with the money he had saved. When everything was set up and the child was born, he went to pieces for the second time. After his discharge from the clinic I acted on his insistent request that I come and inspect his houseboat. It was soon obvious why. Jack showed me the various technical improvements he had managed to introduce. They were original and full of invention. His son's room was decorated in a variety of shades – and Jack took the opportunity to give me a simple exposition of the functional significance of colors. We came to the conclusion that the houseboat, everything creative that he had put into it, was in fact a symbol par excellence of his protest at the label of stupidity that had dogged him for so long. And I recalled that the 'diagnosis' at the time of his first examination had been: 'manic-depressive, feeble psychopath,' and in the initial phase of the second one: 'typical debility psychosis.'

The label had pursued him right into the hospital. Who was 'wooden'? Who was 'stupid'? Not Jack, at any rate.

Just a few more marginal comments. The importance which this psychotherapeutic intervention had for Jack should not be overestimated. The ideal of psychotherapy, where psychotic conditions are concerned, consists of a modification of the personality structure. One aims at the psychotic side-stepping of vital life problems, but first and foremost the person in question must find release from the defensive structures that hinder self-realization and deep relationships with others. This constitutes the essence of intensive psychotherapy.

With this ideal in view, we may wonder what we can do for the psychotic individual. We encounter people who have become acutely psychotic and then after a brief period reintegrate. These shortlived psychotic conditions are marked by a disruption of the potentiality for communication, which is temporary and nonprogressive in character. I am convinced that in the present state of our knowledge of the psychodynamics of the psychotic person we have the wrong end of the stick if we discharge patients when they have returned to 'reality' as 'cured.' The psychosis, regarded as an *encounter of the individual with that part of his life which he has not ventured to live*, forces on the client and his psychiatrist the question of the *meaning* of this catastrophe. One can dodge this question. The psychiatrist may do so (by labeling the person and prescribing tranquilizers, which is less time-consuming and threatening than psychotherapy), and the patient will then try to forget very quickly the terrifying dream that descended upon him.

The psychosis remains a *Geschehnis*, a happening. That happening 'befell' the patient. Therefore, there is no obligation or commitment to understand it; one tries simply to become the same self, the 'old' self. The psychosis is thrust aside as a 'foreign body' and what was calling for integration remains unacknowledged. It is questionable, of course, whether the patient does become his 'old' self in this way. There is a scar, an enlargement of the constriction of the life process; a new defense structure appears in order to prevent the disintegration from being repeated. Alas! Sometimes the psychiatrist is too inclined to stress the alien element in the personality: 'It was a state of hypertension, a crisis, a product of your labile temperament, which could not stand up to this crisis situation in your life.' With the ideas of 'disposition,' 'constitution,' 'endogenesis,' 'cerebral disregulation,' the psychiatrist is searching for something on which to hang this attempt to expropriate whatever was experienced during the psychosis. Naturally the client goes along with this. Thus an individual struggling for integration can either be fundamentally helped or just left in his 'psychosis.'

Trying to integrate the psychotic experiences in a psychotherapeutic relationship was once called by Bodenheimer *Erlebnisgestaltung*, that is, a 'forming up of experience.' *Geschehnis*, what happens, can be transformed into *Erlebnis*, experience. A pointed inquiry can be made as to the purpose, the meaning, of the psychotic happening. The psychosis may be interpreted as the 'still voice' of one's existence, which has to be listened to. There are people who after termination of the psychosis undertake this attempt at integration on their own. They have the courage to transform what is 'foreign' and noncommittal into what is their own, is personal. Many, however, only have the nerve for this confrontation in the setting of a psychotherapeutic relationship.

In Jack's case the psychotherapy was brief; and he could very likely make only limited changes in his personality structure. At all events an autistic development was stopped and an emotional relationship created in the context of which he was able to discuss his emotional life. His fantasies persisted, but they were brought out into the open. In the presence of his extraordinarily tactful and sympathetic wife Jack was now able to talk about his conflicts, which were causing him so much inward turmoil. It remains a factor of the utmost importance that this psychotic phase of his did not entail a meaningless chaos of hallucinations, fears and isolation. Jack acquired some understanding of the fact that this (and the preceding) psychosis was not a scarifying 'alien object,' *but had to do with himself*; that it was to be understood against the background of his feelings toward his mother and father, his feelings of dependency on his wife, his feelings of stupidity and his sexual anxieties. This psychosis was *his* flight from reality, based on *his* fear of the other and himself. His delusion about being a child of the Queen expressed his desire for ideal and loving parents, a fantasy that existed even before the psychosis had taken on the character of reality. Jack could see that the forms in which he projected his world were not essentially different *before* and *during* the psychosis.

Here we touch upon what two such differently oriented experts as Ludwig Binswanger and Frieda Fromm-Reichmann have always stressed. A psychosis is a profound disruption in the continuity of a life. The question raised for us here is how to extend a helping hand. What help entails is restoring the continuity. Besides the insights and experiences which this brief psychotherapy afforded Jack and me, an attempt was made to achieve such a restoration. In this psychotherapeutic encounter a part of what was 'alien' was recognized as being the subject's 'own' and so was partially integrated.

The meetings at which I gave shape to much of the ideas described in this and the preceding chapter were held in the rectangular conference room of the university clinic, with the professor at the head of the table, instructors and assistants around him. Nobody was in a white coat and the atmosphere was rather sympathetic.

The meeting had, I am happy to say, a very positive effect. They went off well, and from that moment until my departure for America all was plain sailing. I was able to devote myself to starting on my own psychoanalytical training and pressed on with my psychotherapeutic work with a number of psychotic clients. To my astonishment no one put the least obstacle in my way.

It was now 1960. I had learned a great deal that was of value in the library and from periodicals, and in one of these periodicals I kept coming across articles that were identified by the words 'Cedar Haven, Westover, Virginia.' It was a sanatorium devoted entirely to the intensive psychotherapy of schizophrenically disturbed people. It had all the appearance of a sort of Mecca of psychoanalysis.

My work was smiled upon in Amsterdam as a blast of enthusiasm on the part of a young man (who would eventually grow wiser), but the climate was anything but stimulating. I had acquired (besides some goodwill) a sort of stereotyped image as the rash nonconformist with revolutionary traits. There was no question of supervision, of course – there was nobody with the experience to do it.

More or less on the off-chance I wrote to the director of Cedar Haven, Dr. Sebastian, promptly received a very friendly reply and as our correspondence continued there were two hurdles to be tackled. One, I would have to promise to spend at least three years working at Cedar Haven, as well as take an examination on medicine that would qualify me as a 'foreign medical graduate' to work in an American clinic. The second was money. I inquired about a grant, but neither the Dutch nor the American authorities were disposed to come across with enough money for such a long period.

My plan was doomed to failure. Dr. Sebastian came to Europe on vacation – and had it not been for my 'hero-worship' I would certainly have gotten no further. We arranged to meet in Paris, and for ten minutes I talked to him about my experiences. About Walter, Karel, Jack, the atmosphere in which I had been working and how it had all started. I was assuming it would be very much 'hello-goodbye' but suddenly Dr. Sebastian cut me short and said: 'You smell all right to me. You're a staff psychiatrist at Cedar Haven. I pay the salary. It's a deal?'

The whole conversation had taken no longer than half an hour. Now the future was wide open.

I wound up my work in Amsterdam, got myself registered as a specialist, transferred my clients to my friends and in June, 1961, left for the U.S.A.

The purpose I had proposed to myself was clear. Several years' training, supervision, experience, and then . . .

I was not emigrating. In the future, when everything would be different, there was so very much to be done for the psychotic person in my own country. At any rate . . . that was how I saw it.

REFERENCES

[1] A. J. Bachrach: 'Notes on the Psychopathology of Delusions,' *Psychiatry*, vol. 16, pp. 375–380 (1953).

NOTES

A couple more of the philosophical works referred to in the chapter are:

A. R. Bodenheomer: *Erlebnisgestaltung, Darstellung, eines Verfahrens zur Psychotherapie von Psychosen* (Basle-Stuttgart, 1957).
M. Siirala: *Die Schizophrenie des Einzelnen und der Allgemeinheit* (Göttingen, 1962).

Of the publications which refer to psychotherapeutic experiences and technical problems I give only a very small selection (the literature has become very extensive):

C. Müller: 'Die Psychotherapie Schizophrener an der Zürcher Klinik,' *Der Nerven Arzt*, vol. 32, pp. 354–368 (1961).

Müller thinks it is time for a survey of what has been achieved in the period between 1950 and 1960 in the field of the psychotherapy of 'schizophrenics.' He makes his philosophy quite clear: 'Our task, any help we are able to give, must start from the premise that we are to let ourselves get involved without prejudgments in a human relationship.' The publication deals with a follow-up investigation of ninety-four patients (fifty-six women and thirty-eight men) who were in psychotherapy for a year and were investigated five years afterwards. Müller (rightly) avoids the term *Heilung* ('cure') and leaves the impression that psychotherapy (carried on in this case by many of the clinic's assistants) is admittedly tiring and slow but certainly possible.

As regards the range of problems facing the psychiatrists who undertake this difficult work Müller reaches a considered judgment containing much that is essential. What is required especially of psychotherapists is a great capacity for empathy, an enormous degree of patience and . . . a lot of self-knowledge, if they are not to use the relationship with the patient for the purpose of trying to resolve their own unresolved inner conflicts. For the rest, one notes how Müller attributes to young psychiatrists (with their 'high degree of keenness and the cheerfulness with which they set about things') much more commitment, an enthusiasm that can open a deeper emotional relationship. The problem is that the 'more mature' psychiatrist (who has been through his own psycho-analysis), while he does have a more comprehensive view and does not so quickly become lost in these very intense relation-ships . . . has lost a touch of enthusiasm. Christian Müller is an accomplished psychiatrist, and I want to list here, with a few comments of my own, the subsequent publication by this pioneer in the field of the psychotherapy of 'schizophrenics.'

C. Müller: 'Is the Genesis of Schizophrenia Psychogenic, Multi-factorial or Unknown?', *The Internat. J. of Psychiatry*, vol. 31, pp. 411–413 (1967).

In this discussion Müller takes a firm stand against those who with respect to the origins of 'the schizophrenic form of being' hamper the development of our thinking by standing on their dignity and saying: 'We don't know what it is.' Since the term 'psychogenesis' is often equated with experiences of life and the events of living (especially in youth), it often acquires the implication 'traumatizing.' Müller rightly points to the fact that only now are we beginning to acquire some insight into the complexity of what Don Jackson called 'chronic enduring traumatizing influences.' What takes place within a family is very complex.

The following publications and books are devoted to the psycho-therapy of psychotic people. Again, a small selection:

C. Müller: 'Über Psychotherapie bei einem chronischen Schizo-phrenen,' *Psyche*, vol. 9, p. 350 (1955).

G. Benedetti: 'Psychotherapie einer Schizophrener,' *Psyche*, vol. 8, p. 1 (1954); 'Psychotherapie einer Schizophrener,' *Psyche*, vol. 9, p. 23 (1955); 'Analytische Psychotherapie der Psychosen,' in H. Hoff: *Lehrbuch der Psychiatrie*, vol. 2, p. 787.

P. C. Racamier: *Psychothérapie psychanalytique des psychoses* (1956). W. T. Winkler: 'Zum Begriff der Ich-Anachorese beim schizo-phrenen Erleben,' *Arch. Psychiatr. Z. chr. Neur.*, vol. 192, p. 234 (1954); 'Krisensituation und Schizophrenie,' *Nervenarzt*, vol. 25, p. 500 (1954); 'Dynamische Phaenomenologie der Schizophrenien als Weg zur gezielten Psychotherapie,' *Z. Psychother. med. Psychol.*, vol. 7, p. 192 (1957); 'Indikation und Prognose zur Psycho-therapie der Psychosen,' *Z. Psychother. med. Psychol.*, vol. 16, p. 41 (1966); with H. Häfner: 'Kontakt und Übertragung bei der Psycho-therapie Schizophrener,' *Z. Psychother. med. Psychol.*, vol. 4, p. 179 (1954); with S. Wieser: 'Die Ich-Mythisierung als Abwehr-masznahme des Ich,' *Nervenarzt*, vol. 30, p. 75 (1959).

S. Arieti: 'Psychotherapy of Schizophrenia,' *Archives of General Psychiatry*, vol. 6, pp. 112–123 (1962).

A lucid survey with a good list of literature.

Regarding the problems of the 'schizophrenic-to-be' as centered in the family I would refer the reader to my survey of the literature on this subject:

J. Foudraine: 'Schizophrenia and the Family: a Survey of the Literature 1956–1960 on the Etiology of Schizophrenia,' *Acta Psychotherapeutica*, vol. 9, pp. 82–110 (1961).

Part 2

America

5. CEDAR HAVEN

From New York I drove in my Volks-wagen to Virginia. A gas station attendant in Westover put me on the right road, and suddenly I saw the small sign: Cedar Haven. There was a large brick building, the center, among the trees. It contained the administrative offices and rooms for the therapists, a conference room on the ground floor; the second, third and fourth floors were for the patients; in the basement was a dining room for staff and patients. As a private clinic it was an example of private enterprise, owned by shareholders, and like every private sanatorium, profit-making. When Frieda Fromm-Reichmann published a series of classic papers on the psychoanalytic psychotherapy of psy-chotic persons the pioneering work really got started. Slowly the place became famous. The staff of Cedar Haven increased rapidly. When I arrived the number of patients was around ninety, the number of full-time psychoanalysts twenty-two, the rest of the personnel (administrative, psychiatric nurses, psychiatric social workers) totalled about 150.

Cedar Haven would have been inconceivable without the many fathers and mothers (some of whom were millionaires) who were prepared to invest practically unlimited amounts of money in this form of therapy. The patients came from many different parts of America; a considerable number had already spent many years in state hospitals, where under very unfavorable conditions and as a result of electroshock and insulin treatments they had grown steadily worse. In those days psychoanalytic therapy was generally considered only when, after many series of electroshock and insulin treatments, the family was faced with a final solution: lobotomy (surgical incision into the brain to sever nerve fibers). It was usually only then that some distant relative discovered there was such a thing as a sanatorium for psychoanalytic psychotherapy, and the patient was committed to Cedar Haven for this form of treatment.

The book *Psychoanalysis and Psychotherapy: Selected Papers of Frieda Fromm-Reichmann* (University of Chicago Press, 1959), contains the wealth of Fromm-Reichmann's psychotherapeutic experience. Her 'philosophy of mental disorder,' in part influenced and fertilized by Sullivan's insights, is illustrated in the Notes by a number of quotations. An impressive résumé of Fromm-Reichmann's philosophy regarding what she chose to call 'disorder' rather than 'illness' is to be found in an article: 'Remarks on the Philosophy of Mental Disorder.' [1]

Her main premises are:

1. Psychotherapy (a modified form of psychoanalysis) is possible and workable. It may take a long time, but 'disorder' can become maturation, disintegration can be productive, leading to unique individuality and a capacity for deeper and more enduring emotional relationship with the other.

2. 'Incomprehensibility' becomes comprehensible through the commitment of the psychiatrist as psychotherapist; bizarre behavior is a defense engineered by fear of contact with the other. This becomes crystal clear from the client's life-history and past experiences.

There is a great deal more in this skillfully compiled document. Fromm-Reichmann writes about one woman who remained in a catatonic schizophrenic condition for eight years, with fits of violence and self-mutilation. Besides tracts of concrete experience with Margherita, brief historical studies and discourses on the history of 'schizophrenic theory' (a story marked by pessimism and (psycho) therapeutic nihilism) there are a number of psychological insights in this article which are impressive in their originality and humanity. Particularly perceptive, I think, is the theme handled in the last section of this article. It is the problem of 'sane' persons who might not be so very 'sane' ('caricatures of what they might have been,' Sullivan would say) and of the 'insane,' struggling with themselves, but in their struggling also holding up a mirror to *us*. We could, says Fromm-Reichmann, learn a good deal from the *faulty capacity* of the so-called schizophrenic to dodge human problems in a magical way via rationalization. People who have withdrawn like this from every human contact are refreshingly impatient with compromises and hypocritical accommodations the so-called healthy allow to be thrust upon them by our culture. If we listened with respect to the person who does not conform (and so has to pay the price), we who think we are in our 'right mind' might well rediscover the ground of our existence, our deepest feelings, in direct confrontation with the 'mentally disturbed' person who has apparently taken leave of his senses. This theme (for the relevant passages I refer the reader to the notes at the end of this chapter) was later to be elaborated in some detail by Ronald Laing.

In her ideas and insights there is a clear evolution. What remains as the fundamental insight is that so-called schizophrenic behavior is very largely a warding off, a defense thrown up by overwhelming anxiety that develops in the relationships with other human beings, a terror that has developed from a very traumatizing situation in youth and comes out later, particularly in attempts to reach the state of 'adulthood.'

Originally even Fromm-Reichmann supposed that a persistent feeling of rejection by the mother was the source of the urge to ward off every deep emotional contact. Thus she adopted the ideas of Gertrud Schwing and Séchehaye and tried in psychotherapy to re-create a real motherly concern and care. Her attitude of profound empathy, warmth, tact and respect for the one who has fled from reality (regression)

123

remained, but her insights into the conflicts (psychodynamics) did change. After twenty years' experience she summarized her ideas quite briefly in a paper entitled 'Psychotherapy of Schizophrenia.' [2]

She states first the continuity principle. She has in mind here the business of integrating what has been experienced, lived through, during the psychotic phase, and of accepting instead of pushing 'the psychosis' out of one's recollection as some horrific and alien object.

The second theme is the mortal terror the 'schizophrenic' has of being rejected, abandoned and ignored. At one time Fromm-Reichmann's psychotherapeutic principle consisted of endless patience, motherly affection, tolerance and understanding. Rejection and disregard, or whatever form the obstruction of human development may take, produce intense hostility and rage and an overwhelming sense of one's own badness as a consequence of that hostility – Sullivan's 'bad-me.' Thus she says:

> Schizophrenics suffer, as all people in our culture do even though to a much lesser degree, from the tension between dependent needs and longing for freedom, between tendencies of clinging dependence and of hostility. For the above-mentioned reasons the degree of the schizophrenic's need for dependency, the extent to which he simultaneously recoils from it, and the color and degree of his hostile tendencies and fantasies toward himself and others are much more intense than in other people. As a result, the general tension engendered by the clash of each of these single powerful emotional elements becomes completely overwhelming.

Here she is clearly pointing to the quantitative difference between the anguish of so-called schizophrenics and those same conflicts in people who have suffered less, who have been better able to build up a measure of self-esteem. That quantitative difference in anguish does indeed give the impression of a qualitative difference, and produces innumerable symptoms which are both an expression of that anguish and a defense against it.

She returns repeatedly to the theme of dependency needs, fear of them and fear of one's own hostility (hate), which finds an outlet in fantasies or destructive acts directed against others or one's own self.

The 'fear of closeness' she sees mainly as a fear that the secret and intense hatred and anger, directed primarily toward people regarding whom overwhelming dependency needs and longing for security are manifested, will be *discovered*.

This applies also to the catatonic, stuporous condition which does not entail a total rejection and withdrawal but arises 'for fear of the patient's own hostility or violence in response to actual or assumed acts of rejection from other people.'

Another passage on the subject of stupor:

. . . withdrawal into stupor is more strongly motivated by the anxiety of patients who realize the danger of their own hostile responses to such neglect by people on whom they depend and to whom they are attached.

The stress throughout this article is on intense dependency needs, intense hatred (and a grandiose overestimation of its destructive effect on the other) and the warding off of fear engendered by this conflict through various forms of 'schizophrenic behavior.'

This has consequences for the psychotherapeutic approach. The idea that giving maternal love and attention (based on the idea that these were precisely what were lacking in earliest childhood) would cause the hostility and deep mistrust to disappear turned out to be unrealistic. We cannot really give an adult what was withheld from him as a child; it does not have the same value. A lot of Fromm-Reichmann's patients later admitted that her warmth and unending patience had only been important to them because it constituted proof that they were not so terrifyingly hostile in the eyes of the psychotherapist, and therefore not as bad as they themselves had supposed. One gets the impression that her approach became more robust, less interpretive and explanatory (when somebody ferrets out things for *himself* it is good for his self-respect), and that she came to view the so-called fragility of the psychotic person in a different light.

The therapy at Cedar Haven, the therapy ideology, really, was also influenced to a considerable extent by the ideas of Harry Stack Sullivan. His philosophy, too, was that 'mental disorder' is not something qualitatively different from the conflicts in any human being. Sullivan's starting point also was that what is alien, what is bizarre, sometimes over-whelming anxiety, are in fact experiences which anybody can go through in the early stages of his development. Only we undergo these processes fragmentarily, as unintelligible experiences in dreams or 'in our fleeting glimpses of what I call anxiety.'

Concerning the various views on heredity as a cause Sullivan is concise: not proven. And he adds, ironically: 'If anyone wants to discuss the heredity of eye color with me, I am delighted, except for the fact that it is not a very exciting topic.' Regarding the hereditary nature of so-called psychotic conditions Sullivan was very noncommittal. He declared: 'There is no shadow of doubt in my mind that mental illnesses arise out of life experience.' [3]

Back to Cedar Haven as I first saw it: Beside the main building, on the 120 acres of grounds, were a number of colonial-style bungalows that were wards for patients. Each had its own staff. Close to the main building was 'Rose Cottage,' a little further away was 'Cedar Cottage,' connected by paths leading to the occupational therapy building, the small kiosk (run by patients), and in the distance 'Hillside,' with two separate wards for patients on the first and second floors. All told, there were seven separate wards, three in the main building, the rest scattered about the grounds. Also sloping lawns, plenty of trees. Beside the extensive library in the main building there was a large conference area, lots of secretaries, tape-recording facilities and dictaphones. The atmosphere was of a Southern plantation, quiet in the damp heat typical of a Virginia summer. One mile away was the small village of Westover.

In addition to the medical director there was a director of psychotherapy. His job included consultation, apportioning the patients, assigning the psychotherapists with whom they might make the best combination and stepping in when a psychotherapist got into too much difficulty. On the staff were five candidate analysts, in training at a psychoanalytic institute; some of the staff were trained psychoanalysts. (The first thing I did was to become a candidate of this institute, and over the next four years I was engaged in an analysis and psychoanalytic training.)

The senior clinical administrator every day interviewed the psychiatrists in charge of the wards. Each ward had its own administrator. A clinical director was in charge of overall policy, public relations, contacts with other clinics, and also had the job of supervising the psychotherapists. Besides the dentist and house doctor (part-time) and five psychiatric social workers, there were the staff psychiatrists. Most had six clients assigned to them; and each client had his 'psychoanalytic hour' (lasting some fifty minutes) four or five times a week. Several psychiatrists had been made administrators and on top of that had three, sometimes four clients in psychotherapy. I was to join this latter group – but of that, more later on.

THE ACTIVITIES

Conferences were frequent. Besides the daily meeting of the group administrators, for every newly admitted client there was an 'intake conference.' During this conference a provisional psychotherapeutic plan of action would be arrived at, and as the conference was ending, it usually fell to the senior clinical administrator to exclaim: 'What about the diagnosis!' Then there would be a few vague comments: 'Schizophrenic reaction,' or 'Damn paranoid, I'd say,' or 'Stress the massive contact aversion' – and that would be that. A label was of secondary importance. Grist to the mills of my anti-nosological bent!

Once a week there was a major therapeutic conference. A report by a psychotherapist on a year's psychotherapeutic work with his client was followed by a discussion for an hour and a half, often with a sharp edge to it and right on target.

Twice a week the psychotherapists came together for an hour and a half in small groups. There would be discussion, guided by the more experienced analysts. A therapist would describe certain difficulties, and people would react, criticize, support each other. Besides being instructive experiences, these group gatherings provided a kind of mental hygiene for the therapists, for the group absorbed some of the stress and loneliness with which the therapist is confronted in his day-to-day psychotherapeutic work with schizophrenics.

The conferences, small groups and discussions during the lunch break ensured a fair amount of information sharing. What struck me most of all was the informal aspect of the discussions.

THE NURSING STAFF

A separate department of nursing was run by a director and her assistants, who had a very good preliminary course of training and instruction in psychodynamic, relational and sociopsychological principles.

Unqualified personnel, especially the male psychiatric aids recruited from the villages around Westover, had practically no training. They come into my story so very much that I shall say no more than that here. Very likely the scant attention given to the male aides had something to do with the philosophy of the Haven. This became clear to me with the passing of the years.

The psychoanalysts (during 'analytic hours'), working with their schizophrenic clients, looked for a fundamental improvement as a direct result of that psychotherapeutic relationship. 'Individual therapy' was central, residence on the wards serving evidently as a supportive, protective, and so far as possible, neutral *background*, to afford or restrict freedom of movement. Thus was engendered an atmosphere of 'waiting for the analytic hour,' with the implicit hope that the deeply regressed or paranoid or contact-rejecting schizophrenic client might eventually rise like a phoenix from his ashes and with some support and guidance from the psychiatric social worker go back into society, purified by the experience and with a profound insight into his own problems that would make him immune to a subsequent 'psychotic breakdown.'

After three months I realized that even in Cedar Haven, despite the esprit de corps, the talent of the psychotherapists, their experience, insight and respect for the psychotic mode of being, and not least their warm humanity, it was still possible to be on the wrong track.

REFERENCES

[1] F. Fromm-Reichmann: 'Remarks on the Philosophy of Mental Disorder,' *Psychiatry*, vol. 9, pp. 293–309 (1946).

[2] F. Fromm-Reichmann: 'Psychotherapy of Schizophrenia,' *American Journal of Psychiatry*, vol. 3, pp. 410–420 (1954).

[3] H. Stack Sullivan: *Clinical Studies in Psychiatry* (New York 1956); *Schizophrenia as a Human Process* (New York, 1962).

NOTES

The passage cited from Frieda Fromm-Reichmann about what so-called schizophrenics might teach us goes:

> If society could learn something from the schizophrenic's lack of any need or wish for plausibility or magic use of apologetic rationalization, it would make for much greater directness and frankness in human interrelationships.

> Mentally disturbed persons who have withdrawn their interest from their environment are refreshingly abhorrent of all kinds of cultural compromises, hence, they inevitably hold the mirror of the hypocritical aspects of the culture in front of society. For all these reasons it can be exceedingly valuable to deal with psychotic people for all those psychiatrists who are willing to learn from their psychotic fellow men. Considering relationships with mental patients from this viewpoint, it is no overstatement to say that the mentally sick, who allegedly have lost their minds in their interpersonal struggles, may be useful to the mentally healthy in really finding their minds which are all too frequently lost, as it were, in the distortions, dissociations, the hypocritical adaptations, and all the painful hide-and-seeks which modern culture forces upon the mind of man!

And she continues:

> However, this may become possible only if 'mentally disturbed' and 'mentally stable' people are no longer considered different in kind but only in degree, and if no moral disqualification is attached to mental disorder.

> Then and only then will so-called healthy but too well adjusted people become capable of hearing with respect, and with a consequent gain in growth, maturation and inner dependence, the message which comes to them from some of the culturally uncompromising and mentally disordered persons – a message none the less valuable because at times the price of their nonconformity is painful episodes of mental disturbance.

Regarding the continuity-principle she says:

> . . . *part of the work which a patient has to accomplish during treatment and at the time of his recovery is, in my judgment, to learn to accept and to integrate the fact that he has gone through a psychotic illness, and that there is a 'continuity,' as one patient called it, between the person as he manifested himself in the psychosis and the one he is after his recovery.* The discussion of the history of patients' illness and treatment after their recovery serves, of course, the same purpose. This is in contrast to the therapeutic attitude of some psychiatrists who hold that recovering patients should learn to detest and eject their psychotic symptomatology, like a foreign body, from their memory.

On the subject of the psychotherapeutic approach she says:

> *If our hypothesis about the interrelatedness between craving for and recoiling from dependency, dangerous hostility and violence against themselves and others, overwhelming anxiety and schizophrenic symptomatology* is correct, we must ask how the therapeutic approaches of consistent love and permissive care, as they used to be given to schizophrenic patients by some therapists, including myself, could be helpful. *We used to think that they were successful (1) because they gave a patient the love and interest he had missed since childhood and throughout life; (2) because his hostility could subside in the absence of the warp which had originated it; and (3) because the patient was helped to re-evaluate his distorted patterns of interpersonal attitudes toward the reality of other people.*

> We now realize that what we have long known to be true for neurotic patients also holds true for schizophrenics. *The suffering from lack of love in early life cannot be made up for by giving the adult what the infant has missed. It will not have the same validity now that it would have had earlier in life. Patients have to learn to integrate the early loss and to understand their own part in their interpersonal difficulties with the significant people of their childhood.*

> I also know now, and can corroborate this with spontaneous statements of recovered patients, that the love and consideration given to them is therapeutically *more significant because they interpret it as proof that they are not as bad, as hostile in the eyes of the therapist, as they feel themselves to be.*

On Harry Stack Sullivan's philosophy this quotation:

> In approaching the subject of mental disorder, I must emphasize that, in my view, persons showing mental disorder do not manifest anything specifically different in kind from what is manifest by practically all human beings. The only exceptions to this statement are those people who are very badly crippled by hereditary or birth injury factors.

There is probably no particular difficulty in grasping this notion except when the disorder picture includes the reappearance of processes that properly pertain to late infancy and early childhood.

From my viewpoint we shall have to accept as a necessary premise that what one encounters in various stages of schizophrenia – the odd, awe-inspiring, terror-provoking feelings of vastness and littleness and the strange strewing-about of relevance – are part of the ordinary experience of these very early stages of personality development in all of us. Most of us, however, experience these processes in later life only as strange fragments carried over from sleep or in our fleeting glimpses of what I call anxiety.

6. ROSE COTTAGE (1)

When I arrived at Cedar Haven, not only was I assigned a number of psychotic people as a psychotherapist, but I was also required to run a small ward with some thirteen chronically schizophrenic women. Thus my task became a dual one. Besides acting as a psychotherapist, my daily routine also included the running of this ward; and for some years past the title used at Cedar Haven for this function had been 'administrator.' [1]

All the clients at the Haven had dealings with two psychotherapists. Four or five times a week they would meet their psychoanalyst for an hour. It was his task to 'analyze' in a more or less orthodox fashion. The rest of their life on the ward was supervised by the administrator. He was responsible for making decisions about personal freedom, for giving or withholding his consent to visits to the nearby village; and at the same time it was his job to guide and direct the personnel who did the psychiatric nursing. It was also his responsibility, in collaboration with the social worker, to keep in regular touch with the patients' families.

This division of function between being a psychiatrist-psychotherapist and an administrator was a long-established strategy. One of its most boosted advantages was obvious. It enabled the psychotherapist to maintain his professional identity as a psychoanalyst because he was relieved of the obligation to intervene actively in the life of his client. Another advantage of the division of function was the possibility of a split 'transference.' The violently negative feelings that can manifest themselves in the course of psychotherapy could more easily be integrated if they could be partly diverted onto the administrator, who because of his daily mingling with the patients on the ward formed a welcome projection field for the intense feelings expressed by the patient towards his psychotherapist and parents. It enabled the psychotherapist to adopt a more neutral position from which to analyze and clarify, and the positive bond between therapist and patient was less threatened if some of the feelings of rage could be channeled to the administrator and the nursing personnel.

The tensions that had been experienced in the original family could be re-experienced in the relationships on the ward; and the split in function enabled the psychotherapist, who was much less involved in the day-to-day events, to bring his patient to a recognition of the connection between the original drama within the family and life on the ward.

This explanation of why a duality of function (between psychotherapist and administrator) was such a useful thing seems to me very much *post hoc*. A more convincing argument, in my view, would be that the division was established because it relieved the therapist of a lot of work and so gave him a chance to concentrate on the interpersonal and intrapsychic dynamics of his patient. The system in fact boiled down to this: the dirty work was left in the hands of a usually junior colleague – the administrator. He was charged with keeping the patient alive and kicking and protecting him from himself and the possibly harmful effects of others. After doing this job for a couple of years, the administrator usually joined the ranks of the psychotherapists and handed his normally rather thankless task over, with a sigh of relief, to a junior colleague recently admitted to the staff. In 1961, even in so progressive a center as Cedar Haven, the function of administrator was noticeably low in status. That there was little prestige attached to it indicates the rather small importance attached at the Haven to administrative psychiatry. Right from the beginning individual psychoanalytic psychotherapy had been held in such high esteem that sociotherapy had in practice been left far behind. When I arrived at Cedar Haven this lag in the development of sociotherapy came as a remarkable discovery. I had had quite different expectations about it. Stanton and Schwarz had by this time written their classic book, *The Mental Hospital*, which explored in detail the various powerful positive and negative factors that during 'the other twenty-three hours of the day' on the psychiatric ward either furthered or gravely hindered the patient's growth and development. Sullivan was renowned for his view that the environment in which his schizophrenic patients lived was of fundamental importance to the success of the psychotherapy. He was actually one of the first to attempt environmental therapy, a deliberate mobilizing of forces likely to further growth in the psychiatric ward. He called his endeavor 'institutional therapy.' [2] And though in her general reflections Fromm-Reichmann had not raised in detail the question of environmental therapy, its importance certainly did not escape her.[3] I had therefore expected that, in a sanatorium with exceptionally favorable conditions for developing a considered environmental therapy, one that was clearly guided by psychotherapeutic ideology, an active concern would be shown for this aspect of therapy. But on the ward there was a rather traditional atmosphere and the organization had an obviously hierarchical structure.

A head nurse and a registered nurse as her assistant, both in white uniforms, took their orders from the administrator, and after having given them their own interpretation, passed them on to the personnel lower down, the psychiatric aides and the male and female nursing assistants. Both were in the lowest position as regards prestige and salary. At the bottom of the ladder were – the patients !

The ward was housed, as I said before, in a small detached bungalow known as 'Rose Cottage.' Some stone steps ran up to a small terrace, which was railed in, and to the front door of the building, which was mostly of wood and painted white.

As one came in there was a small, rather narrow corridor with a door on the right saying: 'Nursing Office.' Facing it was a door that led to the living room, which struck me on entry as being too dark and too small. The walls were painted a dull, greenish color and, partly because of the trees around the house, the two windows let in insufficient light. Built into one of the walls was a television set, which a male nurse and a couple of patients sat watching in silence. There were a few cane chairs with plastic-covered cushions, a circular rattan table and a sofa, also of rattan. A patient was lingering in the doorway, apparently not venturing to go in, as though it were too oppressive and too small, or because she did not want to disturb the male nurse, who raptly sat in front of the TV set.

Going further down the corridor one saw on the right, next to the nursing office, a rather narrow staircase leading to the floor above. Behind it the corridor led to a fairly spacious room for one. Then the corridor divided to right and left. In that small, fairly dark area were two rooms for patients and a couple of bathrooms, one of them with a bathtub.

Walking back toward the main entrance one found at the end a door leading to the kitchen, which was painted white and had large windows looking out onto the terrace at the rear of the house. It contained a simple wooden table with chairs, electric oven, refrigerator, sink and cabinet.

On the second floor were the patients' rooms. Behind the house was a stone terrace, where several patients were sitting in the sun.

I shall give you in what follows a circumstantial account of how I made acquaintance with this ward and its history. Such an exposition will give you a better impression of the work that was awaiting me there.

The previous administrator, Dr. Fraser,[4] fills me in about Rose Cottage. In a fit of despondency about the very poor progress the patients were showing on this ward he had proposed that the clinical director relieve him of his job as administrator so that he could devote himself entirely to individual psychotherapy. Since a new staff member was just coming in, his request was immediately granted. A few days afterward he regretted his proposal because, as he told me later on, he had become very interested in this ward. He canceled his request but was given to understand that the decision had already been made. So Dr. Fraser's attitude toward me is rather ambivalent. On the one hand he seems relieved to be getting out of Rose Cottage, on the other he is obviously attached to the ward.

Rose Cottage has the reputation at Cedar Haven of being a difficult ward and in many respects a backward area. The main reason for that is the condition of the patients, seven of whom are among the most deeply disturbed schizophrenic women in the Haven. Dr. Fraser gives me a short description of each one.

Phyllis, a rather stout woman of fifty, has been in Cedar Haven now for twenty-five years. Five years previous to her admission – when she was twenty – she is said to have become psychotic. The therapy was in the charge of a senior analyst who has been working with her for many years. Phyllis can undoubtedly be described as 'chronically schizophrenic,' and has been in psychoanalytic psychotherapy at Cedar Haven ever since she first arrived!

Phyllis speaks in a mannered, childish way with a high voice, and what she says is mostly unintelligible. She is too fat and waddles past me. I meet her later on the lawn, where I make my first attempt to get into contact with her. When I ask her why she is at the Haven, she replies: 'Because I have an inferiority complex.' I do not know her yet and to some extent fail to spot the streak of burlesque in this reply, and so I follow up my attempt at making contact by saying: 'I guess I have feelings of inferiority as well,' whereupon Phyllis considers me for a moment and says: 'Is that so? Well, if you get over them, let me know,' and promptly wanders off, leaving me in a state of confusion. This exchange marks the birth of a new anecdote about Phyllis, for she seems to have hundreds of these wisecracks to her credit. Within the Cedar Haven community her buffoonery has won her a certain notoriety. All efforts to involve her in a deeper human contact have obviously gotten nowhere. And as she goes wandering about the grounds, she does indeed constitute a mockery of the psychoanalytic psychotherapy of psychoses. Her behavior is somehow indicative of a tremendous contempt. Dr. Fraser, when filling me in about her, makes no attempt to hide his discouragement. He compares her to a fort nobody can take, and I get the impression that her current visits to her analyst are more a pastime and recreation for him than a serious endeavor to help Phyllis at this late hour to emerge from her schizophrenic mode of living. Phyllis is obviously 'institutionalized,' and has her distinctive role in Cedar Haven, her circle of acquaintances, her room and her simple pleasures. Every evening she plays cards with the housekeeper. She is notorious for her habit of putting rubbish down the toilet of Rose Cottage. All attempts to stop her from doing it, all the interpretations of the symbolic meaning of this pastime, have manifestly led nowhere. Her conduct has more than once led to some pretty elaborate repairs of the sewage system, sometimes as far afield as the town of Westover. For the rest she does no one very much harm, although she was at one time well known for her enormous outbursts of rage during which she would turn blue. To these fits she owes her nickname the 'Blue Bull,' and even now people approach her with a degree of respect. It has struck me on various occasions that people give her a wide berth so as not to precipitate these outbursts.

The second resident whom Dr. Fraser introduces me to is *Julia*. Again I am shaken to hear that she, too, has been at the Haven for twenty-five years and thus also for twenty-five years in psychoanalytic psychotherapy!

When her psychosis first began Julia spent several years in another clinic, where she had electroshock and insulin treatments, and then she was admitted to the Haven. Once here, within a short time she totally regressed and lay in bed for years without speaking and had to be completely looked after by the nurses. Over the years five psychoanalysts have devoted their energies to Julia, but they were able to establish only a little verbal contact with her. Her 'record' comprises several volumes filled with the reports of therapists who from time to time detected a glimmer of hope, discussions of her case at therapeutic conferences and the observations of her behavior by innumerable nurses, male and female. She is now in therapy with her sixth analyst, who has apparently managed to get somewhere with her. An enthusiastic, go-ahead man, he has been working at Cedar Haven for several years now and runs a ward of his own in the main building. As I see Julia during these first days, she is a woman who looks younger than her years and speaks in a high-pitched, affectedly childish voice. She walks up and down the corridor, holding her hands aimlessly clasped together in front of her. Her face wears an anxious frown, and she avoids any contact with me. For her, too, Cedar Haven has plainly come to be 'home.' Her parents have obviously resigned themselves to the situation, because for reasons so far obscure she has not seen her father for ten years, though she is still visited occasionally by her mother and an elder sister.

The third inhabitant of Rose Cottage is *Sylvia*, who strikes me as being in many respects the most disturbed of them all. She has now been in Cedar Haven for fourteen years and is forty-six years of age. She hovers around in a half-crouching posture, more or less ignored, the remains of food adorning her sleazy dress, which is not properly fastened. She moves her hands in jerky, spiraling gestures and at intervals emits a sort of harsh noise, half-cough, half-groan. Her eyes are screwed up as though she can no longer see properly, and she evidently has only a few teeth left.

When I approach her she seizes my hand, and then with a tremendous effort – punctuated by stuttering, moaning noises – comes out with the words: 'Blood count, if at all possible.' Later I hear her say: 'Medical treatment, if at all possible,' and later still: 'Methyolate, if at all possible.' Her face is contorted by violent grimaces. Dr. Fraser tell me more about her. She asks for 'methyolate,' he explains, because she has repeated attacks of primitive rage during which she thrusts her hand, whenever possible, through a window. This produces cuts, which luckily do not usually have to be stitched but can be treated by the use of a bandage and Merthiolate (a kind of red iodine). Obviously, she is playing the role of a medically sick or invalid person and hence is always asking for some form of medical treatment. Dr. Fraser explains that during these fits of rage she will often throw herself to the ground; and on one occasion I see this spectacle. She rolls over in a frenzy, beats the ground savagely with her two hands and drools at the mouth. A nurse eventually manages to calm her down.

The people to whom I have introduced you so far are all described by Dr. Fraser as 'chronic schizophrenics.' Clearly he regards Sylvia as an exception. He informs me with some pride that the diagnosis applicable to her is 'adult autism.' It would seem that what he is alluding to here is the fact that as a child Sylvia was diagnosed as 'infantile autistic' and so now, being adult, must be called an 'adult autistic.' Thus Sylvia is presented to me as carrying a different label from the other inhabitants of Rose Cottage. I learn that before coming to Cedar Haven she had been in a psychiatric institution, was treated there with electroshocks and was also given insulin cures. After her arrival at the Haven she went rapidly down-hill. She, too, has had quite a number of psychoanalysts and has been constantly surrounded by nurses and male attendants. The sum of words uttered about Sylvia in countless con-ferences and the theories regarding her condition advanced by so many colleagues fill many volumes.

The nurses still bath her, and for the most part feed and dress her as well. She takes an occasional short walk on the arm of a nurse, clutching it fiercely. She cannot wear glasses because she smashes everything; and the idea of a new set of teeth simply has not occurred to anyone. She is repeatedly constipated, and then her request is: 'Enema treatment, if at all possible.' (It was not until later that I came to realize how enormously demoralizing Sylvia's presence was for that ward, for she set the tone. It is also clearer to me now why the rest of the community at Cedar Haven regarded Rose Cottage as the backward territory of the psychotherapy of schizophrenia, from which it was well to keep a respectful distance.)

Sylvia has now been working for four years or so with a psychoanalyst who on another ward is 'seeing' another more or less adult autistic for an hour four times a week. Sylvia goes for walks with her psychotherapist, takes short rides with him in the car now and then, seems to be attached to him and is able to utter the words 'analytic hour' when he comes into the ward. Precisely what that 'analytic hour' means to her is not clear to me, but as the months pass I discover that her analyst has been trying to maintain a verbal, albeit extremely fragmentary, contact with her and on the basis of a certain psychoanalytic psychology to arrive at some interpretation of her behavior.

The next person I meet is *Leslie*. She, too, has been at the Haven for a respectable length of time, fifteen years. She is a tall woman of a clearly masculine build. She has very pronounced features, with a rather large nose and a lot of hair on her chin. It does not need much imagination to conclude that Leslie must have a big problem with her sexual identity. She has thick, coarse hair, and Dr. Fraser calls my attention to her tendency to first twist it around her finger and then tug it out. A kind of tonsure has appeared on the crown of her head as a result, a circular bald spot which no care and devotion can get rid of. When I first see her she is walking about with strangely angular, twisting motions. She is like a colt on its first run in the meadow. The movements are skittish, but also have something defiantly jolly about them. Leslie has long legs, certainly not unfeminine but very hairy. Although generally speaking she looks as if she is in an aggressive and defiant mood, at our first meeting her approach is a fairly friendly one. When she starts talking to me I don't understand a word. She evidently talks in a completely symbolic language. Dr. Fraser explains to me that they are still engaged in decoding this language and that her psychotherapist in particular spends the main part of his sessions with Leslie decoding her verbal cyphers.

When I ask him to tell me more about Leslie, it turns out that when she was twenty-one she became acutely psychotic and stayed for one and a half years in a psychiatric institution. There she was given the familiar electroshocks and insulin cures and was, it is said, in a very poor way indeed. When she came to Cedar Haven, many regarded her as a sort of demonic manifestation. She was savagely aggressive and obviously repelled everyone. She now has in hand her second psychoanalyst, who has been working with her for ten years. He comes four times a week and holds his sessions with Leslie in her room. When I see her in her room later on, she comes appealingly toward me, making half-masculine, half-feminine seductive movements with the lower part of her body, and says in a voice that reminds me of Marlene Dietrich: 'Where is the key?'

Like Phyllis (the first patient I described to you), she turns out to have the unpleasant habit of tearing everything to pieces, especially her clothes. So Leslie is beset by a constant shortage of clothing. She also tears up paper, and her room is often in chaotic condition from the torn-up periodicals.

I am struck by the tremendously childish way Leslie behaves. She has to be looked after almost all the time, and she has a special nurse for this. This nurse takes her for walks, gives her baths, combs her hair and tries to do something with it. So far as I can make out, Leslie herself does nothing.

We resume our tour of Rose Cottage, and our next encounter confirms again that I have landed in a very special ward of Cedar Haven.

We meet *Cathy*. Cathy is now thirty and has been at Cedar Haven eight years. She is excessively fat, of small stature, and has a round, childish face. In essence Cathy's history is not so very different from the rest. She, too, is regarded as a chronic schizophrenic, and for some years prior to being admitted to Cedar Haven had been in another institution. Her history since she had been at the Haven is a dismal one. Up until about three years ago Cathy was one of the people most feared, and this myth has not died, for even now people are afraid of her. Cathy used to have fits of fierce frenzy, which seized her at the most unexpected moments, causing her to attack people in a most dangerous fashion. She is said to have injured a lot of people, and with only a few of the nurses and male attendants did she preserve a somewhat better relationship. Her method of attack marked her as a 'dirty fighter,' and student nurses who do a period of training at Cedar Haven every four months are therefore informed right away about her fits of rage and how dangerous she is. In recent years, Dr. Fraser tells me, Cathy had gotten very much better. She, too, has had a lot of therapists, but over the past five years she has been working with a forceful psychoanalyst who physically is every bit a match for her. A relationship of growing confidence is now developing between them.

The Cathy I observe during my first few weeks walks up and down a lot, and when not walking, constantly sits watching television. She makes a very passive impression and uses her pocket money to buy large quantities of sweets, which she can obtain at the kiosk. She is usually in a surly mood and seems to have identified herself with the role of somebody who is 'unreliable.'

The next person I meet on my tour is *Isabel*. Isabel is a small, not unattractive woman of forty-two. Already she has spent twelve years at Cedar Haven. She, too, has been through several psychotherapists, but for eight years now has been working with the analyst who is also working with Leslie.

As are most of the others, Isabel is the daughter of wealthy parents. When I meet her and remember the others, I am forced to note the extent to which Isabel has entrenched herself in Cedar Haven and how the role of 'let's go on being crazy' gives her the assurance to remain.

She is continually occupied with her body. She keeps bathing her eyes with water and blowing her nose – in the course of which she uses up a large number of tissues – and appears obsessed with her motions.

She has frequent fits of rage, during which she emits a stream of curses, and a harsh, biting tone comes into her voice. What she says at such times is extraordinarily confused, but what stands out is that she invariably harps on events in the past; especially during these attacks it is evident how unable she is to get away from the past and to let it go. She disregards every form of decent deportment, breaks wind in the crudest way and sometimes, in one of her rages, is capable of screeching: 'The shit is sticking, somewhere it's got to come out,' at the same time squeezing her bottom with her clenched fist. Sometimes she will make a crude show of her sexual desires by pinching her private parts, calling attention to this problem in a confused welter of screams and other noises.

In the weeks that follow I see her often wandering aimlessly about the lawn, usually with a tissue, a cup with some fruit juice in it and her handbag on her arm. Quite frequently she will hold long monologues with herself, and at times I see her shouting something into empty space. She will often sit crouched under a tree, as if wanting to keep out of everybody's sight. At the same time her conduct is evidently calculated to support a role that has obviously grown with the years: 'Crazy Isabel.' It astonishes me that Isabel is allowed to behave in this way, to 'play crazy' publicly on the lawn, and that nothing drastic and effective is done to put an end to this situation.

Her analyst sees her four times a week, but, like Leslie, she is not received in his own room. Her conduct there has been altogether too unmannerly, so he now visits her in her own room in Rose Cottage.

These six women constitute the nucleus of the ward and set their mark on it. I begin to understand better now why, during this tour of inspection, Dr. Fraser claps me encouragingly on the shoulder from time to time – almost with malicious pleasure – and counsels me to 'just take it easy.' He repeats his pronouncement that 'brilliant and well-trained psycho-analysts have been trying for many years to analyze these people and their behavior and to get them to return to reality.' The fact that they have not succeeded is evidence enough for my colleague that I should not have any high-flown notions about any contributions I might be able to make toward their recovery.

In the coming months I became gradually better informed about the story of Rose Cottage, not only through Dr. Fraser but also from hearsay I managed to pick up.

The story began on the fourth floor of Cedar Haven's main building, an upper floor where, I am told, the six ladies I just described formed the nucleus of the ward. This floor had had its succession of administrators, and eventually a European psychoanalyst arrived. This administrator was one of the few who had been trained in sociotherapy as well as psycho-analysis. He knew Maxwell Jones's work and in his initial period as administrator started gradually to introduce some kind of order into the situation. On his initiative the patients were moved to Rose Cottage; and for one year he tried to give his nurses and male attendants a new type of training and to construct something that could be said to resemble a 'therapeutic environment.' This effort took a great deal out of him, because he came up against great resistance from both the management of the clinic and his analyst colleagues who, one must suppose, found Dr. McBride's interventions too pushing. From what I was told I got the impression that Dr. McBride had obviously made himself rather unpopular. He decided to chuck his job as an administrator and devote himself to individual psychotherapy, a choice which relieved him of further difficulties.

He was followed by Dr. Fraser, who had set to work with a great deal of energy. Yet I got the impression that this energy had to make up for his lack of knowledge regarding the principles of the therapeutic environment.

I gradually discovered that the Cedar Haven management expected, if not a miracle, at any rate an original way of tackling the job, from a new European (me), and that this was partly the reason why after a moment of despondency Dr. Fraser ceased being an administrator!

After a few weeks Dr. Fraser handed the ward over to me – something it clearly hurt him to do. I never saw him on the ward again.

The first thing I did in my job as administrator was to watch in some wonderment how the nursing staff ran the place. During the first few months I did little besides observe the situation and sound out the views and opinions of the nursing personnel. I organized several meetings attended by the whole staff and discovered to my alarm that some of the male attendants were so ignorant that they thought 'schizophrenia' was actually a kind of brain disease! This was indeed a strange thing to find in a sanatorium that prided itself on rejecting the organic hypothesis as totally false. The two male attendants were young and not very dependable employees. They were pretty aggressive in their attitude, even toward me, and had had very little training. The head nurse was a fairly young woman who four years previously had done her spell of training as a 'student nurse' at Cedar Haven, and after getting her diploma had come back and been quickly promoted. She was warmhearted and well-intentioned, but very excitable and would complain about her high blood pressure. I got the feeling that she was really not up to this impossible task. I got to know the nursing personnel in this way. The day shift came on at eight in the morning and finished at four-thirty; the evening shift came on duty then and worked till midnight; the night shift worked through the night until eight the next morning. The personnel numbered about fifteen all told, including the reserves – which was a very considerable complement for the thirteen or so patients resident on the ward. The first conclusion I came to was that the staff was very demoralized right down the line. Working for so long in such a 'backward area' without any clearly visible improvement in the patients' demeanor, and the often disparaging way they were treated by the personnel on the other wards, had contributed a great deal to this. The rest of the personnel at the Haven obviously felt that being assigned to work in Rose Cottage was definitely not a privilege. Also the abrupt departure of Dr. Fraser had not been good for morale.

So the nursing personnel viewed their newly arrived administrator with mixed feelings. In addition to a certain amount of sympathy because of the task facing me at Rose Cottage, there was also a forlorn atmosphere; and no one had much confidence in a new administrator.

It is pertinent to describe how the demoralization had been handled by the personnel and by Dr. Fraser. I have mentioned the relapse into a 'physical disease ideology' that I had observed, particularly in the case of the two male aides. It also appeared that the personnel turned as much as possible to one another for support, for instance by holding lengthy discussions together behind the closed doors of the head nurse's room. Even the TV set in the living room was obviously being used by the personnel as a means of distraction. The male aides could get excited watching the baseball games, and thus find relief from the patients. Another method of keeping oneself going amid all the discouragement I observed at a picnic that was organized by Dr. Fraser and in which I took part. I give a rather extensive account of it here because it was so typical of the situation I encountered.

146

With Dr. Fraser in control, the nurses, male and female, took part enthusiastically in organizing this picnic. The kitchen supplied all the food, and along with the charcoal and the grill for the barbecue this was stowed in a car provided by the Haven. Not a single patient took part in any of these preparations. Dr. Fraser was a very energetic man. I heard later that he had been a scout.

When everything was ready, the patients were shepherded to the waiting vehicle. After an hour's ride they arrived at a lake, where Dr. Fraser and his staff removed first the patients and then the food and drink from the car. Before very long several patients had spread themselves on the grass, others were taken off by a nurse to go canoeing. With his two psychiatric male attendants Dr. Fraser was in his element; and he was assisted by the head nurse and the social worker, who laid out the hot-dogs and hamburgers on the picnic table. A male nurse got a fire going, and the meat was promptly cooked by Dr. Fraser in person, helped by the social worker. The patients lifted not a finger.

Before long Phyllis came to spy out the land, grabbed – under the very eyes of the nurses – three uncooked hamburgers and promptly ate them. No one made any attempt to deny the corpulent Phyllis this pleasure, apparently because no one was prepared to face one of her fits of rage, which might have thoroughly spoiled the atmosphere.

This account may perhaps indicate what I am getting at. One way in which discouragement and demoralization were combatted was the tremendous *activity* displayed by the nursing personnel, under the administrator's leadership. Now and then, of course, somebody would try to stir the residents of Rose Cottage into activity, but these were feeble attempts, mostly unstructured and doomed to failure.

It was about three months before I was through with my observations and reconnaissance work and had gotten over the shock of the initial adjustment. During that time I was no more than the head nurse's pupil, and in my ignorance I would turn to her, when necessary, for help and for further elucidation.

My first real move was to write a report of my conclusions.

In it I concentrated on the interior structure of Rose Cottage. By quoting various things said by patients and the nursing personnel I tried to make out a plausible case for rebuilding. One proposal was to remove altogether the wall dividing the small sitting room from the corridor so that there would be a bigger space where one came in. I also proposed the construction of an isolation room. At the same time I put in a request for the purchase of new furniture and for the papering and painting of the whole ward in lighter, fresher colors. Another part of my proposal was to rebuild the attic as a large conference room and to move the TV set from the living room to the attic.

Before submitting my report I discussed it with the nursing staff, who greeted it with hoots of laughter. The demolition of the wall, in particular, turned out to be no new idea at all. Dr. Fraser, when he had been in control, had asked for this, too, but without success. Still, I put my report in; and to everyone's amazement, including my own, it was not only taken seriously, but very soon an architect appeared, flanked by the directors of the sanatorium. All the proposed changes were agreed to, and two weeks later the work was in full swing. Evidently, the timing of my request had been just right; and I suppose they wanted to give me, the latest innovator, as big a chance to succeed as possible.

While the rebuilding was going on, I continued with my observations on the progress of events in Rose Cottage. In the next chapter I shall go into this in rather more detail. Even now it is possible to draw one conclusion. In this psycho-analytic sanatorium, imbued with an ideology I wholly agreed with, conditions had arisen (it was, of course, not only in Rose Cottage that they existed) which tended to encourage deviant behavior and to perpetuate it rather than go against it.

Those who were termed 'patients' evinced an improbable degree of passivity and were surrounded by a large number of workers whose urge to be active was realized by doing for, caring for, organizing for and thinking for these passive 'children.'

[1] For the original publications I refer the reader to D. M. Bullard: 'Problems of Clinical Administration,' *Bulletin of the Menninger Clinic*, vol. 16, pp. 163–201 (1952).

M. L. Adland: 'Problems of Administrative Psychotherapy in Mental Hospitals,' *Psychiatric Quarterly*, vol. 27, pp. 246–271 (1953).

The 'administrative service' is described by Adland as a structuring of the whole ward to ensure that it functions:

> first as a positive agent in itself and second as a stimulus to the patient's work with his individual therapist. These goals can be further defined as: first, nurturing the dependent needs and fostering the personality growth of the patient; second, through recognition of the total problem, setting reality limits; and third, structuring the environment so as to relieve the anxiety generated in the psychotherapy rather than forcing the psychotherapy to relieve the anxiety generated on the ward. By nurturing dependent needs the writer means: first, offering the patient relief from the burden of managing all aspects of his daily living; second, having recognition of his wants, responding to them, and if possible anticipating them; and third, giving the patient an opportunity to express wishes which are truly his own.

What is being described here is the philosophy of 'permissiveness,' even the *anticipation* of needs and wants. When one realizes that this article was published in 1953 and one sees the ultimate results of this philosophy as I encountered them – the Rose Cottage patient, regressed into totally passive dependency – one begins to understand where things have gone wrong.

For the rest, Bullard seems to have anticipated the problems. Not only does he point to the tensions that arose in his sanatorium as a result of the policies pursued by the various 'administrators' (some obliged the patients to conform to 'hospital policy,' other ward psychiatrists behaved too independently and created a sort of 'hospital within the hospital'), but he also shows his concern about the problem of the 'chronic patient' who goes on vegetating in total dependency. He argues thus:

> It would seem that there might be developed over a period of years an administrative psychiatry that has as its core the view that many of the patient's symptoms, especially the chronic ones, are in some way expressive of a pattern of interaction with the hospital staff and personnel, for which the hospital is as much responsible as is the patient.

One wonders why it took 'a period of years' before this insight was put into practice.

² H. Stack Sullivan: 'Sociopsychiatric Research,' *American J. of Psychiatry*, vol. 87, pp. 977–991 (1930–1931).

³ Although she wrote: 'A psychoanalytic hospital should be a therapeutic community' and stressed the cooperation between the psychotherapist-analyst and the administrator, yet she wrote primarily as a psychotherapist and her views about relationships on the ward remained rather superficial.

F. Fromm-Reichmann: 'Problems of Therapeutic Management in a Psychoanalytic Hospital,' *Psychoanalytic Quarterly*, vol. 16, pp. 325–357 (1949).

NOTE

Please note that in this and the subsequent chapters not only the patients' names but also those of members of the staff, nurses and so on, are fictitious.

7. ROSE COTTAGE (2)

The previous chapter contained an outline of the situation in Rose Cottage. In it I referred to the nursing personnel's 'urge to be active.' I would now like to describe this in greater detail.

MEALS

As is customary in any mental hospital, the food was prepared in the kitchen of the main building. The cafeteria was located in a basement area of the main building and the patients made their way to it on foot, usually under the supervision of a male or female nurse. In the cafeteria they would be handed a tray which they placed on a rail along the counter. I noticed that most of the Rose Cottage patients were content to point silently to the dishes they wanted to eat. Over the years the waitress behind the counter had acquired enough experience to be able to interpret every murmur or gesture correctly.

When the food had been served, the patient would pick up her tray and go to a table with it. When there was some hanging about, the attendant nurse would take firm hold of the tray and walk with it and the patient to a table. The patients' table manners were poor. At the end of the meal they were supposed to carry their trays over to a trolley provided for the purpose. Some would do so; but Leslie and Sylvia in particular would have none of this. Their trays were usually picked up by the supervisory attendant. This obviously saved time. After that everybody went back to Rose Cottage. The ward had a regular supply of fruit juices and milk in its own refrigerator. Tea and coffee were brewed in the kitchen of the main building and brought by the kitchen staff to Rose Cottage. In the evening a snack chosen by the head nurse would be prepared and brought over by the duty nurse from the kitchen of the main building.

CLOTHING

If one really intends to discover what is being done on a ward with regard to the most elementary requirements of the patients, what the nursing staff are actually up to – and how they are doing it – one really has to go and live on that ward. (The anthropologist William Caudill and the sociologist Erving Goffman have in fact both done this. The former even had himself admitted for a period as a patient.) Even though I spent a great deal of my time on the ward, it was still very difficult to get to know in any detail the various activities of the nursing personnel.

One of my most surprising discoveries concerned the activities of the night-duty staff. These people followed the routine obtaining in so many psychiatric hospitals: that is, they made their rounds during the night. This meant that they entered the rooms and used flashlights to satisfy themselves that everyone was asleep. But that was not all they did. When they went into the rooms they collected the dirty underwear scattered around, and made it a part of their night's duty to sort, stitch and repair it. When this underwear came back clean from the laundry, the day-shift personnel made sure that it got back safely into the closets and drawers of the various patients.

The personnel on the evening shift not only assisted with undressing the patients but also put out the clothes to be used the following day. That enabled the night shift, after waking and helping to wash the patients, to find immediately the clothes needed for the coming day. A clothing budget, created especially for the purpose, was managed by the head nurse in cooperation with the psychiatric social worker, and the purchase of new clothing was reported to the relatives concerned. As for outer clothing, to my surprise it was generally purchased by the day-shift nurses, although they were accompanied on these shopping trips by the patient in question, who usually behaved in a completely passive manner inside the store.

MONEY

The accounts department would send the bills to the parents; and the latter would pay also the cost of the extra budget for clothes and pocket money. A statement of the account was not sent to the patient.

I had some trouble finding out through which organization pocket money was expended. Someone on the staff of the domestic department controlled part of it and, working with the Rose Cottage head nurse, would buy a number of coupon books to be deposited in the kiosk. During their daily walk to the kiosk the patients could 'buy' their sweets or whatever by asking the person in charge of them for the desired article, either verbally or with the same silent gestures with which they chose their food. The article asked for would then be handed over; presumably the patients did not even notice that this 'financial transaction' was concluded by having a coupon torn out of their book. No patient actually carried the book of coupons on her person, and of the six residents I have described only Cathy carried some money in her bag and handed it out herself. The rest did not have any money at their disposal. Calculating the amount of money issued and returned was superfluous, therefore, in this system; and this disposed of the need for anyone to carry a purse or bag with them.

When I asked why this system was used I was told that some years before an irate father had alerted the Cedar Haven management to the fact that his daughter had torn up a number of dollar bills. This system had been devised to prevent that sort of thing, and it functioned rapidly and efficiently from the standpoint of the sanatorium.

It will be clear from all that I have been saying with what energy and expedition the staff of Rose Cottage, assisted by the personnel of various departments, kept the patients trapped in their total passivity. It seems to me a good example of how psychotic people's already weak sense of competence is further undermined, so that a condition of almost complete paralysis of the ego functions arises, with an accompanying total dependency on the various providers and supervisors and on the hospital as a whole. This phenomenon has frequently been described in such terms as 'institutionalization,' 'institutional dependency,' 'institutional neurosis,' etc. It would be wrong, however, to get a too onesided view of this. The schizophrenic people on my ward rejected self-reliance in every possible way and because of their passive demeanor invited the various attendants to fulfill their own need to offer help.

It struck me that the whole rebuilding and refurbishing was going forward without the patients who lived at Rose Cottage having any say and without any consideration at all of the specific needs and wishes of the nursing staff.

The head of the housekeeping department evidently regarded the ward as part and parcel of her particular territory. Now and then, in passing, my opinion might be asked for, but the nursing staff was hardly included in that sort of consultation. One could say that the ward as a whole was regarded as an irresponsible child, which should be resigned and uncomplaining about the novelties being thrust upon it.

The thing that struck me at this point was the lack of independence of the ward, and the paradox that while the nurses were given a great measure of responsibility, they were not given the authority to wield that responsibility to any real effect. In fact, the nurses and the entire ward were at the mercy of the different departments. The accounts department controlled all the money, the kitchen looked after the supply and preparation of foodstuffs and the housekeeping department (all these departments were ensconced in the main building) called the tune where cleaning operations on the ward were concerned. The housekeeping department employed a number of girls as servants, some of whom had been working at Cedar Haven for years. One could hardly call Carol a girl. She was an older black woman who had worked at the Haven for twenty-five years. Actually, Carol was one of the most stabilizing elements among the staff. She knew the patients through and through, and they appeared to respect Carol, who was a somewhat shy yet friendly woman. So Carol was assigned as a domestic servant to Rose Cottage but did not come under the nursing department, which saw to the staffing of the ward from the main building. It soon became apparent to me that Carol's activities were both extensive and important. It was she who kept the living room, kitchen, corridors and lavatories clean. She washed the windows, tended the woodwork, mopped the floors and, by working with the nurses, kept the patients' rooms clean, too.

If by now you are beginning to get a bit irritated and wondering what all this has got to do with 'schizophrenia' or psychiatry, I must ask you to bear with me a little longer. As an amateur sociologist or anthropologist I am trying to sketch a particular 'culture' – which is necessary as a starting point for the rest of my story, in which I intend to describe the building up of a 'therapeutic environment' or 'therapeutic community.'

My observations did not emerge in so neat and well ordered a fashion as they appear now in writing them down. On the contrary, much of what I discovered was revealed during a stage in which I was encouraging the staff to take a quite different path. Then resistance of various sorts loomed, and it was through having to track down the sources of this resistance that my observations increased and I was able to enlarge my insight into the formal and informal structure of the ward.

The transactions between the nurses and male attendants on one side and the patients on the other may serve to complete the picture.

There was one nursing assistant in particular, a middle-aged woman, who for years had taken Leslie under her wing. I shall call her, for convenience, simply Leslie's 'mother.' She bathed Leslie, washed her, brushed the obstinate hair, put curlers in it and went walking with her. Her activities were best summed up by Cathy, who once expressed it to me concisely and clearly by saying: 'Mrs. Care thinks for us.' Mrs. Care was indeed a textbook example of caring, acting and thinking for the patients; and in her relationship with Leslie she lived out this role fully. She was very much prompted to do this by Leslie herself, who seemed to have an indescribably adroit way of suppressing in herself every manifestation of self-reliance and responsibility and could produce such a strategically skillful posture of dependency that every nurse, assistant or attendant reacted to it almost automatically by taking over the responsibility themselves. I cite an incident I observed in the cafeteria as an example.

Leslie has finished her meal and her empty plate, cups, utensils and so on are lying on the tray. The male aide in charge of her sits beside her. She gets up in her characteristic way. As she does so, she moves the tray with her left hand almost imperceptibly towards the aide sitting next her. He automatically grasps the tray thus pushed in his direction, stands up and takes it to the appropriate trolley. Meanwhile, Leslie, with an air of bored superiority, exits from the room, with the aide trailing after her. A very cleverly executed maneuver.

Just as Leslie had been entirely taken over as 'her charge' by Mrs. Care, so was Sylvia tended in a special way by Mrs. Fee, who worked mainly on the night shift and so was able to give liberal assistance when it came to waking her up, dressing her, sorting out her clothes and washing her. In the daytime she would often be taken by Mrs. Fee on some excursion, and Sylvia was clearly very attached to her. Both her psycho-analyst and Mrs. Fee were frequently greeted by Sylvia with the words: 'Ride in a car, if at all possible,' or 'Peppermint candy, if at all possible,' two phrases in which she managed to give pithy expression to her need to be driven around passively and given some sweets.

The ministering, not to say mothering, activities of Mrs. Care and Mrs. Fee turned out to be only dramatic examples of what was happening on all fronts between the nursing personnel and the patients. Very telling evidence of this was the organized excursions to the open-air theater or the cinema.

In the head nurse's little room two telephones had been installed, one for maintaining communication with the various departments, the other an outside line. In general the head nurse had charge of these telephones, and there was a 'hospital rule' that patients must never be allowed to handle a telephone. Tickets for the movies or the theater were ordered on the telephone by the head nurse through one of the occupational therapists.

The architectural alterations were very soon completed and I organized a series of meetings with the nursing staff to brief them on the modes of schizophrenic development. Using plenty of examples I told them how I saw them as engaged in transactions which I tried to define in such terms as 'mother-child,' 'strong-weak,' 'healthy-sick.' I discussed with them my knowledge from the literature about the syndrome of 'institutional dependency,' that caused most of the patients to reject every kind of responsibility and self-dependence. I explained how the process of doing-and-thinking-on-behalf-of-the-other entrenched the patients even more in their role of helpless invalids. I tried to expound to the staff in greater detail the significance of the 'role concept' and pointed out the possibility that the conduct of 'a mad person who is totally incapable and cannot be held responsible for his actions' may become a *role* in which an individual seeks refuge as a source of security, a role in which at the same time he is confirmed over and over again in the controlling organization. I also talked about the inconceivably small measure of self-confidence that makes every schizophrenic person retreat before the duties and tasks of his life. I portrayed by way of example the fate of a person recovering from a physical disease who is forced to remain lying flat on his back by nurses all too keen and willing to help. In such a case the muscles atrophy, the process of convalescence and rehabilitation never takes place, and the patient remains in a totally passive and invalid condition.

The staff listened to my arguments and explanations attentively enough; but the two young male aides refused to cooperate at all in this new approach, and more or less said so. My reaction was a pretty emotional one and I fired them both. To my surprise this was taken in a very positive spirit to the head of the nursing department. (In fact I had no authority to take on staff or fire them.) When two new members had been appointed to my staff, I proposed putting into practice the theoretical notions I had been presenting. From that moment on the chaos was complete.

I. THE REACTION OF THE NURSING PERSONNEL

This could best be described as a growing bewilderment or confusion as to roles. Now that the staff were obliged, when faced with any transaction, to ask to what extent the patient was transferring responsibility to them and to what extent they were preempting it, they ended up in a state of considerable uncertainty. I made a practice of walking through Rose Cottage and instructing them on the spot; but in spite of the support and encouragement I gave them their anxiety was increasing all the time. For them the nurse's role was synonymous with caring-and-thinking-for-somebody. Again and again they would come to me and ask: 'What should I do? I don't know what I should do anymore.' They developed strong negative feelings toward me; and instead of gradually standing back and encouraging the patients to assume a degree of responsibility, however slight, a lot of them withdrew, apparently with the intention of scuttling the experiment completely.

They were also afraid that they, too, might be fired. At the frequent meetings I held with the nursing personnel (gatherings which later developed into a form of group therapy) they would express this fear. They felt threatened in their professional identity. The loss of their former role was such an enervating experience that for a time they felt themselves and their function to be without meaning or purpose. Then, too, they came to believe that if such an approach were to lead to real self-reliance and responsibility on the patients' part, that is, if my ideas were to prove correct, the number of nurses might quickly be reduced by half. I took the view that this fear of getting fired had to do above all with their intense confusion regarding their role during a phase in which a new role enactment had to be constructed that would enable them to assign a new rationale to their calling.

2. THE PATIENTS' REACTION

In this initial phase the residents of Rose Cottage did not, on the whole, make things easier for the nursing staff. Now that they kept hearing: 'I think you can do this for yourself,' they, too, felt increasingly anxious because their role, comprising modes of conduct that could be described as 'crazy,' 'helpless,' 'irresponsible,' 'invalid' and 'incompetent,' was being threatened. That role was their security; and in their anxiety they threw themselves fanatically into even more regressive and passive behavior. A number of them, Leslie in particular, became incontinent. Leslie started to excrete in bed – a habit she had stopped some years before.

An example of Leslie's behavior: It is decided that Mrs. Care will no longer put Leslie into the bath but will still help her to undress. Someone must give her her soap and washcloth and then leave the bathroom and shut the door behind them. After a few moments people walking past Rose Cottage hear Leslie screaming out the window at the top of her lungs: 'Is there nobody to wash me anymore?'

Another example of the situation created is the following description based on staff observations:

It was decided that the patients would be brought to the kitchen and encouraged to help with the cookout, but would not be told what to do. Sylvia immediately took the chairs out on the porch. Isabel saw the grill and talked and screamed about knowing a policeman named Mr. Grill. Sandy said, she did not have enough strength to help and got up and took a large can of beans and threw them on the floor. Julia fixed the hamburgers in large balls, which Isabel started playing with, throwing them in the air and catching them. Cathy stirred the beans. Leslie and Betty started yelling about killing and Isabel joined in and Betty finally had to be escorted out of the kitchen.

Isabel passed out raw onions, Cathy asked Leslie to keep out of the salad, and Phyllis said: 'Leslie, by the time you finish eating, everybody will be dead from starvation.' Leslie said she would pour the tea in the salad and Cathy stopped her. Leslie then ate an onion (skin and all). Julia just stood there and rubbed her face.

A nurse left, saying she couldn't stand it. Phyllis came in and said: 'Leslie is doing some funny business out there.' The beans started burning and Cathy removed them. Isabel told Betty she had lost her prestige at Rose Cottage. Dr. Foudraine arrived and commented on the confusion. Patients roamed in and out, picking on hamburgers and salads.

THE 'WORK PROGRAM'

After several meetings it was resolved to ask the patients to clean out the whole bungalow themselves. Not only were they obliged to keep their own rooms in order and make their own beds, but patients were allotted responsibility for various parts of the house and took turns at attending to these 'beats.' The 'domestic,' Carol, was asked to 'assist,' but not to do the work herself anymore.

At the same time we decided on a daily community meeting. This was attended by all the patients, the nursing personnel (members of the other shifts took turns so they could come) and the 'domestic help.' Any problems that cropped up were discussed at this meeting. By ten o'clock it was presumed everyone was getting down to her cleaning job.

It goes without saying that this initial part of the work

program ran into enormous difficulties. At first the patients refused to give a hand and showed in a most bizarre way just how incapable (and unwilling) they had become. The nursing staff felt paralyzed, enraged and frustrated. They simply did not believe that these activities could be taken over by patients; and it became more obvious as time went on that *they themselves were unwilling to give up* a great part of them.

Just to make things even more difficult, I asked those who had worn a white uniform to get out of it and do their job from then on wearing ordinary clothes.

The staff, still confused, angry and very anxious, felt all this (the cleaning-up operations, the community meetings, relinquishing their uniforms) was making them more and more unsure of themselves. I was not very democratic about introducing these reforms. In fact I dictated them. At times the problems were so great that (without my knowing it) the whole staff, ganging up together, convened a couple of meetings at which they quite seriously considered resigning en bloc and requesting transfer to another ward. I was not told about these meetings. An observation dating from that initial phase gives a fair reflection of the battle going on:

Leslie's job is to clean up the living room. She stands in the middle of the room, holding the dust mop and flapping it around childishly. Mrs. Care is beside her, coaxing her on without much conviction. Leslie keeps thrusting the mop into Mrs. Care's hand and Mrs. Care tried to give it back to her again. Mrs. Care clearly feels quite miserable; and I am told she has recently become very depressed.

After a time I arranged a private meeting with each member of the staff; and during one such conversation Mrs. Care told me more about it:

Yes, indeed, I had hoped you'd get discouraged and give up. There I was, standing with Leslie in the living room, and she had the dust mop in her hand. She started her job. She looked at me and I struggled to control my impulse to take the mop away from her and do the cleaning job myself. I hated you so much!

Leslie and I had been very close for many years. I used to dress her and put her to bed. I made her bed and brushed her hair. I did everything for her. Sometimes she would look at me and say, 'Mummy never did these things for me,' and that made me feel good.

I was living for someone, someone to be looked after. When Leslie started to do the job well, I can remember thinking: Now she's going to grow up. Now I'm going to lose her. It was as if you were pulling us apart.

This says more, I feel, than many pages of theory. Mrs. Care told me a great deal more on that occasion which seems to be of importance.

Before she became a nursing assistant at Cedar Haven she had looked after her husband and children. Especially after her elder children had married and left home, she became unwilling to part with her young daughter. She gave a lot of examples making it very clear how she had clung to this daughter and pampered her. She had never allowed her daughter to prepare a meal for herself, and she told me that even when grown up the daughter let her mother fasten her dress and tie her shoelaces. In spite of this coddling the younger daughter managed to get away from home and marry, after which Mrs. Care again became very depressed and felt she no longer had any purpose in life. It was then that she started longing to become a nursing assistant; and she told me how she had set about her job the very first day, on the fourth floor of the main building:

I remember Leslie was the first patient I saw, she was standing in a corner and crying. Then that feeling came over me again that I could be a mother to her. I can even remember thinking: Now you've got a daughter again! I've always looked after Leslie, from that very moment.

I learned more from what Mrs. Care told me then about the importance of a good integration between individual psychotherapy and creating a therapeutic environment (and that means especially the creation and training of a group of colleagues whom we shall continue for the present to call psychiatric nurses and aides), than from all the theoretical speculations in books that I have read on this subject.

Just imagine the situation. A brilliant psychoanalyst whose publications have made him famous sees his patient four times a week over a period of ten years and interprets what is going on in her and between them both. He hopes that she will become herself, will differentiate herself from the breeding ground of their mutual understanding, and find the strength to build up her self-reliance, her autonomy.

And at the same time, practically under his very nose, Mrs. Care is working during the rest of the day in the opposite direction. The bond between them is a kind of symbiosis – but of a quality we could describe as static and pathological. It must be very much like the drama of fearful clinging together on the part of mother and child, a relationship which stunts any sort of growth. The struggle that Mrs. Care described to me seemed only quantitatively greater than what I saw happening around me among the nurses.

It was precisely in this phase, when newer forms of relationship favorable to growth were being sought, that there began to arise what Lipsitt once called 'the conspiracy of symbiotic interdependent relationships, which destroy both the staff's and the patient's opportunity for growth and development of autonomy.' [1]

To my amazement Carol, that sage, mature woman, turned out to be quite able to interpret my suggestions properly. With certain ups and downs, of course, she switched from her role as the servant who does everything for everybody to that of an educator and instructor. Yet even Carol went through a phase of obvious confusion as to her role.

She was one of the oldest of the twelve maids. These people ate with one another and earned a settled wage. Now that Carol was not supposed to work in the same way and was gradually turning into a 'psychiatric aide,' she began to become part of the group nursing personnel. She told me how tremendously concerned the patients were, to begin with, for the welfare of the staff and about the anxiety shown by various nurses. Thus Cathy, when she was busy cleaning out the conference area in the attic, said to Carol: 'If I do this job well, you will be fired.'

So on this ward I was continually struck by the presence of static and pathological symbiotic ties between the 'nurses' and the 'chronic schizophrenic.' The 'children' were deeply afraid that 'mother' would be shoved aside as useless.

In many respects Cathy's observation was true enough; and such comments were made by other patients, too. As I have already said, there was indeed an obvious fear on the part of the nursing personnel of becoming unnecessary and useless, of being fired. It appeared to be a repetition of what had happened in the original family situation between the schizophrenic-to-be and one of her parent-figures, as so often described in the literature.

During this whole intensely confused period the community meeting in the morning was a particularly tense affair. There was a feeling of enormous anger on both sides, and often there were long silences.

The nursing personnel felt especially strange now that they had lost the security provided by their white uniforms. The registered nurse told me later on:

> The white uniform was for me the crowning glory of my career. I had done all my training, I had got my diploma, for this. When you asked us to take off that white uniform and turn up in ordinary clothes, I thought: Have I been working all those years just for this? [2]

Meanwhile the work program was slowly being extended. So as to get a bit of order into my presentation I shall split the various activities into the categories I wrote about earlier.

MEALS

With some assistance from the head nurse and under her direction one of the patients would make out a list of the food required; and this would all be brought by the patients themselves from the kitchens of the main building. After a lot of trouble it proved possible to get hold of a sum of money.

Then, instead of the ready-made evening snacks from the kitchen, the patients decided for themselves what they wanted to eat late in the evening and would buy the various items of food during the day (or evening) in Ashville and prepare them on the ward.

During the second year one of the male attendants managed to get a communal Saturday morning breakfast started up on the ward. Supplies of food were purchased, the breakfast was prepared and the table laid by the patients themselves. Other meals, too, were regularly organized on the ward. Everyone came to these communal meals, which gave an opportunity for some instruction in table manners.

CLOTHING

The patients themselves attended to their dirty underwear and to any repairs that were necessary. They sorted the clean linen and stowed it away in the closets. A lot of patients began to launder their own underwear; and at one stage during the second year, when morale had risen to unprecedented heights, an automatic washing and drying machine was procured and installed on the ward. The patients were taught how to make use of it, and from then on, under the direction of one of the nurses, all the underwear was washed and dried on the ward itself. By keeping a close watch it was possible to ensure that certain patients did not foul up the machine – a transparently obvious move meant to convince us that our efforts were all a waste of time.

It was interesting to observe that on the other wards the experiment with the washing machine *was not taken seriously*, because they were firmly convinced there that none of the Rose Cottage patients would be able to use such a machine. But they learned.

The patients took some money and went off to Westover or Washington to choose their own clothes and pay for them. Naturally, there were dramatic scenes in some of the Westover shops. I shall refrain from giving you the details.

Patients' pocket money, at one time managed with great devotion to duty by Mrs. Smith of the housekeeping department, was removed from her charge. This Mrs. Smith, who had toiled so zealously over the years, was deeply grieved by this measure; in spite of all my assertions that it was good for people to be responsible for their own money, she never forgave me. One of the patients became ward secretary and after a good deal of guidance and supervision from the head nurse took over the whole business of administering the pocket money. The scenes enacted when the inhabitants of Rose Cottage were actually handed their pocket money in dollar bills no pen could describe. Phyllis immediately threw hers down the lavatory, Leslie tore hers into shreds and Julia, with a dreamy expression, put all her money on the counter at the kiosk in order to get a bar of chocolate for it. No one except Cathy still knew how to handle money or was prepared to count or keep watch on the amount of change. The patients were obliged to buy handbags and purses and these vanished like snow in sunshine. The staff had to struggle for months to teach Julia what she could do with a dollar bill, and Leslie had to go without her sweets for months on end because she had sensuously torn up all her pocket money.

RESISTANCE

The cleaning activities gave rise to various difficulties. Two main sources of opposition have already been indicated, the nurses and the patients. But there were more – and I shall take them one by one.

In this connection a point emerges that seems of major importance in any undertaking of a so-called therapeutic community in an otherwise traditionally organized psychiatric institution. An attempt to create a new form of organization has innumerable repercussions for the rest of the establishment: it is like tossing a stone into the water and creating a lot of ripples.

1. When our program first began the leaders of the *housekeeping department* showed a friendly interest and a certain sympathetic response to my enthusiasm and the growing enthusiasm of the nursing personnel. They had a tolerant 'let's bide our time' attitude, with the underlying motif that 'the whole thing will collapse in the end.' But pretty soon there was trouble, especially since as time went on the ward really got filthy. The patients were desperately trying to dodge their tasks and the nursing staff, including Carol, could only prevent themselves from taking them over with great difficulty. The result was a ward in a state of total squalor. As luck would have it, it was during such a phase of thoroughgoing pollution that the woman in charge of the housekeeping department, accompanied by a female inspector, held a tour of inspection. (The said inspector was the overseer of conditions of hygiene in hospitals and therefore in psychiatric institutions as well.) The inspector was alarmed, showed not the least knowledge or understanding of the work of Maxwell Jones, and wrote a most unfavorable report to the director of Cedar Haven, in which she referred specifically to the 'conditions obtaining in a ward with the name of "Rose Cottage".'

This touched off a serious incident because the future existence of this private psychiatric institution depended on the granting of a license, and that in turn depended on the report of the inspector of hospitals! In general hospitals there are a lot of prescribed rules of hygiene; and since psychiatric institutions are still called 'hospitals,' they must in principle satisfy the same regulations. I was surprised to learn that the plates from which Leslie, Cathy and the rest ate had to be sterilized at the end of each meal. As if 'schizophrenia' were a contagious disease!

It goes without saying that the argument I put to the director of Cedar Haven had little success. I could indeed contend that in the last analysis his clinic was not a hospital but a school where people whose lives were afflicted with grave difficulties were involved in the learning process of psychoanalysis in order to get to know themselves better and live in a more efficient way. My argument did not convince him. He saw the danger that the license for his whole clinic might be revoked. We were trapped in a culture that had 'institutions' with laws and regulations applicable to hospitals. So a hospital inspector was on the point of bringing my 'therapeutic community' to an untimely end.

Before long came the news that the housekeeping department was planning to dispatch a number of 'domestic servants' to Rose Cottage to launch a bold attack on the pollution. The nursing personnel, now in a state of surprisingly high morale, rallied with great solidarity around the 'leader,' and we discussed the crisis at a number of emergency meetings.

In the community meeting our schizophrenic residents contemplated the crisis that had arisen with scarcely concealed pleasure and made it quite clear that they thought they had won the argument. The atmosphere among the 'educators,' who had closed ranks around me, evinced at that moment the mentality of a paranoid group trying to hold off an outside world threatening to destroy it. In the end a fairly simple solution emerged. The nursing staff cleaned up the whole house themselves and we asked the housekeeping department to inspect it regularly. With this proof of our cooperation everybody was placated and the 'licensing' of the hospital was no longer at stake.

2. I am in the middle of cataloguing what for the time being I have called simply the sources of opposition. As the second of these I must include the gardener and his staff. Of the various departments of the Haven, I have not yet mentioned the *groundskeeping department*. Cedar Haven consisted of a main building and three cottages, some considerable distance apart; around them were beautifully kept lawns and trees, a swimming pool, a building for occupational therapy, and kitchen gardens. The upkeep of all this, and especially of the gardens, was the responsibility of Willy, who had been doing the job with great devotion for the previous twenty-five years. He was assisted for the most part by casual employees whom he hired in Westover. Willy became a source of resistance. I laid it down as a component part of our program that the area around Rose Cottage be designated 'our' garden. This meant

that the patients were to be responsible not only for their house but for the garden surrounding it.

It was some time in the autumn when the first schizophrenic patients at Rose Cottage, supervised and encouraged by the nursing staff, started to rake up the leaves from the lawn. Before long this group of at first reluctant workers came to be known as the 'Dutch leaf-raking group,' and as far as I could make out, Sylvia was the only one who enjoyed it. Instead of: 'Medical treatment, if at all possible,' she was now often heard to say: 'Raking leaves, if at all possible.' I do not intend to describe in any detail the sort of pranks the schizophrenic patients treated us to on the Cedar Haven lawns.

When my twenty-two psychoanalytic colleagues beheld the Dutch leaf-raking group at work, led by the initially none too enthusiastic nursing personnel, naturally there was no end of comment. Things got rather difficult come wintertime, when one of the jobs on the agenda was to remove the snow and clear the paths. 'Our garden' (or 'our land,' as it was often called) was very soon invaded by a number of Willy's assistants who got to work, armed with shovels.

An observation by one of the nurses indicates what happened then:

I saw the head nurse from Rose Cottage come running along. She shouted to him, 'This is our land.' The gardener seemed not to understand and said, 'But ma'am, I've got a job to do.' The head nurse then asked him to give her the shovel, but he refused.

There they stand, on a winter's morning, facing each other. A perplexed black man come to do his work, and a head nurse trying to take his shovel and his work away from him. When we looked into this incident more closely, it appeared that when it came to other activities in the garden Willy had showed little regard for our program. 'Our land' had for twenty-five years been 'his land' and I was never able to convince him otherwise.

But the incident taught us a great deal more. This remover of snow was in the most literal sense fighting for his bread, his living. I began to realize there is every reason to suppose

169

that in a well-organized 'therapeutic community' a lot of the usual staff of a psychiatric institution *are indeed superfluous and so will be out of a job*. I shall not expound further on this point here, but put it to you as my conviction and as a proposition. (If the psychiatric institution still has a future – which I doubt – there is every reason drastically to *reduce* the size of the staff and not – as we are so often told – to increase it.) As I said, Willy never yielded to the need of the ward to become more autonomous. For four years he made a practice of going over again with his lawnmower the grass we had already mown; and no protest of mine ever made the least difference. Yet when I met him, he always wanted to assure me of his sympathy with what I 'was up to with these poor people.'

I have given two examples of resistance to the organization of a therapeutic environment: the account of the 'pollution crisis' and Willy's inability to leave any bit of his work to others. The housekeeping department and the grounds-keeping department were institutions of a hospital organization. Any large organization must have a division of functions; this would seem *to be a necessary mark of a bureaucratic form of organization*. It is obvious, though, that it does not exactly further the struggle for greater independence and responsibility on the part of the patients. The more Rose Cottage grew in self-reliance, the greater the resistance that was shown in various ways by the hospital departments.

It is tempting to speak again of static-pathological-symbiotic ties – this time between the 'mother' hospital organization and its 'child,' the ward, which had come to be completely dependent on departmental provision and therefore was essentially a minor, below the age of responsibility. A typical example of this was our total lack of tools needed for the garden as well as for keeping the place clean.[3]

3. *The nursing department* had a director of nursing, a woman who together with her assistants organized and ran the business of staffing the various wards at the Haven. She looked after all the salary arrangements, as well as acted as adviser to the nurses and aides on the various wards.

I realize that I am on the verge of representing this department as another 'resistance factor.' But I am bound in all honesty to say that in the building up of our therapeutic community in Rose Cottage we had no trouble at all with this exceptionally progressive director, who was very quickly persuaded that the experiment we had undertaken ought to be supported to the full. In fact it turned into an unusually happy collaboration between us.

From the very start what we were doing in Rose Cottage was called an 'experiment,' and under this banner the ward soon became more or less autonomous as far as its staffing policy was concerned. The head nurse at Rose Cottage was free to organize the personnel working under her. Any clashes that occurred among them were talked over in my presence at our weekly meetings.

The fact that we investigated the conflicts among the nursing staff *on the ward itself* meant that the Rose Cottage staff gradually obtained a large measure of autonomy. When it came to the question of leave, this was arranged by mutual agreement between the nurses, male and female, on the ward.

The psychiatric aides working on the ward, men and women, were no longer 'hired out' to other wards; as a result a much greater solidarity and sense of connection grew on the ward itself. When new staff members had to be appointed, the head nurse and I were in a position to select them ourselves and present them to the Rose Cottage permanent staff for their approval.

The director of nursing showed considerable understanding of what we were trying to do. Every time she was consulted by a member of the staff as their 'adviser,' she would listen and then would *refer the problem back* to the ward with such comments as: 'Why don't you talk the thing over a bit more with your administrator?' or 'I'd bring up this suggestion at your next meeting.' The director of nursing also allowed me to train my own staff; thus she relinquished her job as instructor as far as the Rose Cottage personnel were concerned.

Having given these examples of cooperation, I want to mention a source of trouble that was directly connected with the nursing department. In the evenings at Cedar Haven a supervising nurse was stationed in a small room in the main building. Part of her job was to make regular rounds of the various wards and give advice, if needed. Thus she was a nurse not belonging to this side or that side and not attached to any particular ward. I forgot to tell this nurse, whom I shall call Mrs. S., about our experiments. When Mrs. S. came into Rose Cottage in the evenings she usually found the members of the evening shift in the head nurse's room. Generally speaking, people would stand up when she entered. She expected and got a 'report,' presented verbally by the head of the shift on duty. The various patients were reviewed and sometimes Mrs. S. would give instructions. If a patient seemed aggressive and overexcited, Mrs. S. was supposed to be consulted, then she would either seek the advice of the duty doctor or herself stipulate what should be done.

Little by little Mrs. S. began to notice changes during her visits to Rose Cottage. No longer did she find the nurses and the psychiatric aides in the nursing office, but more often than not in the living room or outside, busy with one thing or another. She also noticed that no one stood up anymore when she came in. The person in charge of the evening shift kept calling her 'Lou' now instead of addressing her as 'Mrs. S.' It also struck her that she was no longer spontaneously given a 'report.' When she inquired how things were going on the ward, the usual reply was that things were well in hand and she had to listen to an account of the various activities lined up for the evening. There were times when she got no answer to her questions at all, because the Rose Cottage nursing staff were too busy and did not want to interrupt their work. Then she would normally be invited with a wave of the arm to take her pick of the snacks laid on for that evening. An account by a nurse working on the evening shift represents very well the sort of situation that had emerged:

At one time we relied very heavily on the night supervisor, Mrs. S., about what we should do, asking her for advice and that sort of thing. Now we seldom bother her with any-thing, unless it is strictly medical. We have felt wedged between the program and the supervisor. It's a hands-off policy in Rose Cottage now. I think it would have been much better if you had explained all this to Mrs. S. instead of her having to get the information from us. But at the same time, there is a much more relaxed atmosphere between the night shift and the supervisor. At one time the supervisor was up on a pedestal, now she is just Lou.

We sort of run our own show. I think that Mrs. S. gets phone call after phone call from other units asking, 'Can we do this, can we do that?' They have to get her permission before they can do anything. We feel we know our patients better than anyone else and consequently we do what's beneficial.

Mrs. S. did indeed feel that she had been dethroned and had the greatest difficulty in accepting this new independent attitude on the part of the Rose Cottage staff. The nurse was quite right to observe that I should have foreseen these conflicts and put things right perhaps by keeping Mrs. S. informed about everything in detail. This would certainly have had a favorable effect on the conflict of roles that had arisen, whereas now the changed relationship caused a lot of rancor in the supervisor, which she showed again and again.

[1] The term 'conspiracy' comes from Klapman, who in a discussion of the whole problem of the 'chronic hospital patient' declared: '. . . If we seek to make hospitalization truly therapeutic we shall not overlook to what extent hospitalization itself, as it is now so often constituted, *conspires with the patient* to produce a state which robs him of all incentive.' Dennis Martin ('Institutionalization,' *Lancet*, vol. 2, p. 1188, 1955) also suggests this when he argues that 'the institution has a strong power to mould patients into the type best suited for its purpose; and those who are predisposed stand in the most acute danger.'

Lipsitt approaches the problem of the extreme dependency which some patients develop toward the institution that admits them and looks after them ('institutional dependency') on the basis that there is a certain type of person who by nature already has extreme dependency needs. The way the institution functions corresponds very well with this person's needs. A relatively new idea is this author's attempt to view the situation as a form of collaboration. Dependent-conformative behavior is rewarded by the institution, manifestations of independence and nonconformism are blocked off. (D. R. Lipsitt: 'Dependency, Depression and Hospitalization: Toward an Understanding of a Conspiracy,' *Psychiatric Quarterly*, vol. 36, pp. 537–554, 1962).

See also J. Waage: 'On Symbiosis and Symbiotic Relations in the Mental Hospital,' *Psychiatr. Neurol. Neurochir.*, 71/2, p. 14 (1968).

[2] A. Goldberg and D. Offer: 'The Role of the Uniform in a Psychiatric Hospital,' *Comprehensive Psychiatry*, vol. 11, p. 35 (1961). The authors observe how little research has actually been done into the significance of the uniform (white coat, nurse's outfit) in the psychiatric institution: 'Uniform dress worn by certain professional and specialist classes of people helps to reduce role confusion and makes for an economy of relations.' In this way a relation is standardized. On these grounds alone one may assume that ordinary clothes permit a greater variability in the relation-forming process. Through interviews with nursing personnel these authors learned of the *need* nurses had to wear the white uniform in order to bolster their professional identity. That they believed the patients needed to see them in this uniform 'appeared to be a projection of their own needs.' Some nurses seemed scarcely able to function within the specified role of nurse without their uniforms. They were fiercely opposed to any change: 'To members of this group the lack of uniform means being naked.' The patients, after they got used to it, said they felt about the situation in a much more positive way. Without uniforms nurses and aides became more like

people: 'I could tell Miss B.'s moods the first thing in the morning by looking at the type of dress she wore,' says a schizophrenic man.

[3] Merton Kahne in particular has pointed out this facet of the bureaucratic form of organization. The organization as a whole is the owner of 'necessary tools, property and instruments,' which are loaned out when necessary to the specialized departments. (M. Kahne: 'Bureaucratic Structure and Impersonal Experience in Mental Hospitals,' *Psychiatry*, vol. 22, pp. 363–377 (1959).

8. ROSE COTTAGE (3)

It is May, 1963. The Rose Cottage program is a year and seven months old.

For six months now there has been a new head nurse, enthusiastic about the job; and six months ago Mrs. Care requested transfer to another ward. In the end she could not cope with the changes, and as morale rose and the patients' behavior and functioning improved, she became more depressed. The nursing staff now come together once a week, having initially met for an hour twice a week with myself in the chair.

There are no longer communication blocks between the three shifts, and as a result the conflicts between various members of the staff, which in the past were fairly frequent but never really settled or even openly declared, have been reduced to a minimum.

In what has become a classic report Stanton and Schwarz call attention to the field of conflict-laden tensions between staff members (often 'hidden disagreements') in which the patient gets caught and to which he reacts with symptoms such as acute excitation, aggressive outbursts and so on. Obviously, in their tendency to separate the 'good' people from the 'bad,' patients set at variance members of the staff who cannot get on well together anyway. When conflicts between staff are resolved – or at any rate opened up to discussion – there is, Stanton maintains, a notable improvement in the patients' behavior.[1]

Friendships are beginning to develop between staff members. The group solidarity is very noticeable. The staff persist in talking about 'our program' and refer to one another as 'we at Rose Cottage,' in contrast to the rest of the Cedar Haven personnel. Their colleagues in other wards do not make fun of them so frequently. Among the former there is a growing atmosphere of approval and sometimes of envy. The aides and nurses from these other wards often visit Rose Cottage. The staff like very much to welcome these 'spies' and take some pride in explaining the various new features being introduced. If at the outset my relations with the staff had been rather bad because my authoritarian way of dictating various reforms had shocked them, now a better relationship is gradually emerging.

The staff venture to criticize me more and there are moments, many moments, when I feel I am included in the group as their peer. The 'doctor knows best' atmosphere begins to disappear and there is less and less trace of a hierarchical setup based on status and prestige. The staff now work much of the time in their ordinary clothes, and there is an increasing awareness that between a nurse and a psychiatric aide there are no differences (except in pay!).

During this phase I try to evaluate the situation so far created. I am especially interested in how the nurses, male and female, are responding and feeling about the situation, comparing it with what has gone before. Various comments that have come from the staff make me think that there is a gold mine of ideas and insights among them which might deepen my understanding of the problems faced by psychiatric nursing personnel.

I am curious, too, about the effect on other departments and the reaction of those not directly associated with Rose Cottage. It has even crossed my mind that there just might be a book in it. But – with that idea in the back of my mind – I need more material. The social psychologist attached to the research department of Cedar Haven is not available. No other 'objective' outside person is anywhere about. I decide to set 'science' aside and with the help of a tape recorder let the Rose Cottage personnel and the staff belonging to other departments of Cedar Haven have their own say. Thus in what follows they speak for themselves. Their comments come across to me as genuine, and that is enough. They talk about the reforms and the new forms of organization. First a bit of theory.

I. THE OPEN WARD

Over many years there have appeared in the literature countless publications in which the terms 'open-door policy' and 'open ward' occur. What these referred to, among other things, was a literal opening of doors and getting rid of locks and keys. I believe that whether a ward is closed or not is not fundamentally relevant to the atmosphere prevailing on that ward. The open-door policy as an idea is right as far as it goes, but it does not get to the heart of the matter. An open ward is not a ward with doors that are open and have no lock on them, for open doors have little to do with openness. An environment is open when people (staff and patients) bit by bit arrive at open interpersonal relations, open expression of feeling and interchange of essential information. What is opened up in a therapeutic environment is the dimension of human trust and creativity. What has to be unlocked is not the doors but the spontaneity that leads to personal relations between human beings, in contrast to closed role-conditioned professional interactions. An open ward is a ward where a spade is called a spade in everyone's hearing. A ward where the nurses make their 'report' behind the closed door of the nursing office and where the distrustful patients try to catch the least sound is a closed ward, even if every other door is wide open. A ward in which a wall separates those who, dressed in white uniforms, do the nursing (the 'healthy') from a group of those who get nursed (the 'sick') is a closed ward, because it precludes personal encounter and so stunts for both groups the process of personal growth.

178

Greenblatt and Levinson have summed up very well the theme of the 'open door.' They reach the following conclusion:

Although a considerable improvement in staff-patient relations appears necessary before the door can be opened, ideal staff-patient relationships cannot be achieved except after the door is open, for the open door can undo staff embarrassment and conflict about being both jailer and healer at the same time.

With that conclusion I can only partly agree. The importance of a literal unlocking of doors is in my view made too much of here. What agrees more with my experience is their final conclusion:

Lastly we should emphasize that the open door is but one of many possible symbols of an institution advancing on the road toward more meaningful staff-patient relationships, and a better therapeutic climate. An open door without an open mind is bound to be a failure. An open door which is purely a fetish is meaningless.[2]

Rubin and others also give an extensive survey of the 'open-door policy' (which Dorothea Dix campaigned for in 1855 but which vanished along with so many other good aspects of 'moral treatment of the insane.') The relationship to the idea of a therapeutic environment is worked out and 'openness' is associated in this publication with 'freedom,' 'dignity' and 'responsibility,' while the 'closed unit' is above all linked with rigid behavior patterns on the part of staff and clients and the depreciation of the patients that results.[3]

An example of the connection between keys and openness comes out in the words of a psychiatric aide. Before I quote him verbatim, I should say that on the ward we had introduced a rule that at every opportunity the keys should be handed to the patients. Thus although the nursing staff carried keys on them, they never opened a door themselves. Keys were always handed over or in a friendly way tossed to the patients, who could then unlock a door or closet themselves. This broke a rigid hospital rule to the effect that 'one should never give the patients one's keys.'

When we broke this rather pointless regulation the effect was surprising. At first the patients were not very disposed to handle any key whatever, and it took many of them half an hour before they could manage to unlock a door! With Sylvia, for instance, it took months of practice and she had a great many temper tantrums before she was prepared to put the key in a lock and turn it.

Here is what a male nurse had to say on the subject:

Although Rose Cottage is my home base, I am what is called a 'floater.' I also work sometimes on other units. There is a freedom in Rose Cottage which gives you the feeling that you can take responsibility on your own, deal with certain situations. I feel the freedom on other units to be repressed to a great degree. I think this whole unit expands through this kind of freedom.

This ability to give the keys to the patients and to see what each patient will do with them. You don't get anywhere when you don't take any risks. When I go to another unit, I know right off that I can't give my keys out, so I am on guard. Just being restrained about the keys makes me restrain all my actions. I think the key is very important. The key is in a way – what do you call it? – the key to some kind of method of therapy. I really never give my keys out on any other unit because it's an overwhelming kind of feeling. It may be a small matter, but I consider giving the patient keys really something important and really the key to freedom.

It is an arresting statement. The simple fact that on other wards he was compelled by a certain regulation to hang onto his keys and never let them out of his hands stifles his spontaneity. He was 'on guard' and believed that his spontaneous human feelings were 'locked up,' too.

A registered nurse reported as follows:

When I started to work in Cedar Haven I knew you were supposed to never let your keys out of your hands. You should never give them to a patient. You shouldn't even lend them to another person on the staff. When we started here giving the patients the keys, we were all very scared. We were simply afraid we would be out of a job if we lost our keys. To start with – when we had handed the keys over – we would stand right behind the patient. As soon as the door was open we made sure we got our keys back again. The patients were extremely pleased to get their hands on some keys. They took to asking for them and some even asked for a key to their own room. At first, when they took hold of the key, they were so used to somebody else opening the door for them that they would just stand there right in front of the door. And every time I found myself wanting to relapse into the old habit and open the door for them myself, after all.

A nurse coming from another ward described the giving of keys to patients as *giving up her own authority* and in doing so provided a good example of her confusion as to her role:

I felt surprised about the way the patients are making coffee here, when they want it. They seem to get a kick out of making the coffee themselves and also offering coffee to other people. In the beginning, when I was here, I found it a little bit silly that people were urged to sweep the front porch. I found it silly, *because when you do it yourself, you can do it in no time at all.* I started ordering the drugs myself at Rose Cottage. At Hillside nobody touched the medicine cabinet but me. But then the head nurse came and said, 'No, Cathy will do that.' Cathy then came in and ordered the drugs. It made me feel kind of useless. I thought: Here I go through 3 years of nurse's training and I can't even order drugs. I used to work on Obstetrics all the time and I used to work with my hands and here I am at Rose Cottage and I didn't know what to do. Cathy could type out the doctor's orders just as well as I could. In fact, I was quite amazed.
When Leslie puts on her lipstick, I am in a real tizzy. *I get such a strong feeling to do it for her, because I could do it much quicker and more effectively.* Sometimes she smears it all over her face and then I have difficulty taking it off her face.
But what was especially odd for me was that people just

came in and out of the nursing office. They were all over the place. There is much less of a barrier *and when I give up my keys, there will be even less of a difference.*

What she described just about sums up the problems of a nurse whose training has drilled into her certain forms of behavior that in a therapeutic community she had got to unlearn; efficient and trained 'to do it quicker and more effectively,' entrenched in her role of white-uniformed official, dodging personal contact (and conflict) by retreating into the head nurse's room where she can busy herself with her technical and administrative activities, and now frightened by the thought that she will have to get down to working on a personal and educative level (and for that very reason exposed herself more as a person).

THE OPEN NURSING OFFICE AND THE OPEN REPORT

Not only was there a community meeting every morning from nine to ten, a meeting in which patients and staff took part together, but it was also decided that the door to the head nurse's room should remain permanently open. The result was that patients were free to walk in and out of this room and began to take over certain duties in the head nurse's sanctum. One patient got the job of manning the telephone, another that of accounting for and distributing the pocket money, and yet another was installed as secretary, helping the head nurse with her various administrative chores.

The fact that patients were invading the sphere of the nursing personnel not unnaturally touched off a good deal of anxiety in the staff. The nurse whose comments were just cited gave a good idea of the conflict that was going on. It did not mean that the nursing office was totally lost as a refuge for the nursing personnel; but the nurses now had to learn to make up their own minds if and when they wished to have a moment of privacy. Privacy within this organization was no longer automatically ensured by an 'institution' (the head nurse's closed room), but was gained by taking a personal stand, by insisting on having it. In this way the nurse became a person who in articulating her need for privacy provided the schizophrenic clients with a better model for identification. This was a particularly valuable model, for schizophrenics are people who have enormous difficulties in demarcating the frontiers of their own personality, in indicating their need for privacy and demanding it. These difficulties are connected with the persistent invasion to which they were exposed in youth by their parental figures.

Now a few remarks about the open nursing office. Carol put it very nicely:

> I thought it was splendid when that door was opened. For years people had stood listening at the door and so often they would say, 'Why do you close the door, then? It must be false what you are saying.'

A senior nurse (not attached to the ward) who sometimes acted as supervisor said:

> I like openness. On other wards the door is shut when I am being given my report on my round. As a matter of fact, it makes me feel somewhat uncomfortable.

I also had a couple of conversations with on-duty psychiatrists who once or twice a week joined the evening shift in Cedar Haven but were not on the sanatorium's staff. They gave two quite different impressions:

Dr. S.:

I've noticed that I stay sitting around in Rose Cottage longer than on other wards. It has something to do, I think, with a different type of relationship that has sprung up here between personnel and patients. Whatever's going on here is talked about much more openly, whereas on other wards the staff are often whispering to one another. There's more aloofness there, the patients are more like 'outsiders.' On my rounds at Rose Cottage they often invite me to have something to eat and one way or another I say yes to the invitation, I'm more at my ease, sitting here.

I make my rounds two to three times a month. On other wards I get a feeling that the patients are not supposed to come into the head nurse's room, and if they do, you get the idea they are committing an offense. Then I feel I am, too. In Rose Cottage any feeling that the head nurse's room is holy ground simply doesn't exist. Patients are obviously welcome. I find the way people here walk in and out very friendly. When I go to another ward, I get involved in a pseudo-intellectual sort of conversation with the nursing personnel about problems. I notice more emotional inter-action, people either like each other or hate each other's guts.

Dr. V.:

Patients started coming into the nursing office in Rose Cottage as the years progressed and it made me feel uncom-fortable. During the five minutes that I'm over there I have noticed that the staff seem to be more interested in dealing and relating to the patients than in giving me and the super-visor a report. The staff seemed to be enjoying the job too much[!].
On the other wards the staff start giving their report in much more official style. The brief time I spend in Rose Cottage I find a pretty casual affair. There's always a lot going on here. Patients doing this, the staff doing that. Cedar Cottage is dead quiet. The patients are certainly more gloomy. In Rose Cottage I feel like an intruder. On the other wards there are definite rules right down the line. When the Rose Cottage staff talk to me, they use a louder voice, almost as if to make certain that the patients can hear them. It's almost too much. I personally like the closed nursing office better.

When one examines carefully what this psychiatrist is say-ing, it is noticeable how threatened he feels by the informal atmosphere. He feels threatened in his function as a 'medical man' and shows irritation at not being treated politely and with due ceremony. The nurses on the ward, with their new style of behavior, were also breaking many of the rules of what

184

Stein called the 'doctor-nurse game.' In this game the doctor is maintained in his authoritarian-omnipotent role through a transaction which requires the nurse to take the initiative, to provide information and advice – without, however, detaching herself explicitly from her passive-submissive role.[4]

The game goes like this:

Doctor (on his round): So you're sleeping badly. Hm. Quite so. (Off the cuff, the doctor can think of no medicine, let alone the correct dosage!)
Nurse: What do you think about amytal in this case, doctor?
Doctor (pensively, as if he knew of something else): Yes, that would seem to be the best thing. Let's see – what shall we give?
Nurse: For Dr. X. I was giving 250 mg., doctor. (Clear hint, knowing that the doctor is for the moment at a loss for the dosage.)
Doctor (having reflected): Splendid! Let's do just that!
Nurse (grateful for the advice): Of course, doctor, as you wish.

In the preceding account a somewhat authoritarian colleague, in his role of 'physician,' is saying that he finds it all a bit too 'casual.' It is not formal enough for him, and surprisingly, he comes out with the remark that 'the staff enjoy their work too much.' The whole passage serves to corroborate something that Maxwell Jones pointed out over and over again: namely, that the process of organizing the therapeutic community means breaking out of the traditional hierarchy of command and that this is the hardest thing of all for nurses and doctors to accept.[5]

THE OPEN REPORT

It is a custom in traditionally organized psychiatric wards for nurses to 'report' to one another. That is how it was in Rose Cottage, too. At four in the afternoon the departing day shift would assemble in the head nurse's closed room and give the evening shift the day's particulars and instructions for the evening. It was a secret affair; and the patients would mostly stand listening at the door and peering in through the glazed window. This, too, was changed. We decided that the day shift should deliver its report publicly in the living room to the evening workers, that patients be free to listen to this discussion and, if they found it necessary, to add to the reporting corrections or comments of their own.

At first the nursing personnel felt threatened by this measure. The fact that patients were present and listening to their account of particular events made them realize more and more how subjective the reporting sometimes was; and again and again it happened that patients would interrupt and bring out aspects of a specific incident that had escaped a psychiatric aide or a nurse.

Along with the open community meetings in the mornings these measures helped to create an almost excessive climate of open communication and the spread of information. One result of this was the rapid disappearance of pronounced paranoid reactions on the part of the patients. The whole business of talking behind their backs became a thing of the past. The psychiatric social worker described the sort of atmosphere that began to prevail:

I remember quite clearly that the reporting was always done behind closed doors. What we had to say about the patients was always kept secret. I think getting this in the open was a great help to pateints. Actually there wasn't anything said that they didn't know in most instances. This kind of attitude has with me carried over into my family work, because I realize much more that there are not too many secrets that the patients cannot hear. I really think that what I learned in Rose Cottage is carried over in my work with families in which there is already much more freedom to talk in front of the patients. For instance, the other day I sat down with the family of Leslie at lunch. She was there, too, and we had a couple of martinis and they told me an awful lot of information about the family in front of Leslie. I found out about many more particulars in regard to the difficult situation the mother was in during the time that

186

Leslie came and I also understood much more about the function of the grandmother in this family.

Leslie, I think, listened more intently than I have ever seen her. The next day she said, 'Wasn't that a good time we had yesterday?' The family told me that their recent interview and the talks we had were the best experience they ever had. I think this is directly related to the openness in Rose Cottage and the open reports.

The social worker made a direct connection between the disclosure of 'family secrets' and the disappearance of the atmosphere of secrecy on the ward. The fact is that the interactions within the family which give rise to paranoid reactions are repeated on a ward organized on traditional lines, where doctors and nurses discuss the patients in hushed voices and in the seclusion of their own room.

The head nurse commented on the institution of the open report in these terms:

One thing it has done. It has given the patients a feeling that we are not in the nursing office talking about them. I've heard the more verbal ones like Isabel and Cathy on many occasions comment during these reports about incidents and the way they saw them. So the oncoming staff gets the picture not only from the staff but also from the patient.

In the beginning it was remarkable how all the patients really gathered at four o'clock in the living room, because they didn't want to miss this for anything. Now they gotten used to it. In the beginning it gave me a funny feeling. To sit out there and say what was to be said in private for so long. It was hard to hash over a certain assault or incident, when everybody was listening. I now feel perfectly able to say whatever has happened. I have no qualms about it.

Finally, the maid, Carol:

After the change that occurred I heard several aides say they had to be sure that what they had written down on the observation sheets was right, because the people were able to check it. So evidently, in the old days, certain things that were written on the observation sheets were not right. A

187

lot of patients have told them plenty of times, in the open, that what they were saying was not true. I was glad when the report was open.

OPEN EXPRESSION AND EMOTIONAL EXCHANGE

Right through this period, during the 'in service' training of the nurses as well as at our various conferences, I gave a lot of lectures, backed by practical examples, on personality development, schizophrenogenic interpersonal situations, symbiotic relationships and the principles of the therapeutic community.

My main purpose was to build up confidence in the staff to express their feelings as the normal human beings they really were – people with their own anxieties and particular sensitivity. In the context of this reform the disappearance of the white uniform was just a symbol; and in the process of training the personnel I got to know my staff members as human beings and brought them to greater self-acceptance. At the same time it was the staff gatherings that offered the best opening for instruction in personality development and interpersonal dynamics.

It is possible to explain to nurses the whole structure of psychoanalysis, but I think that there is not much to be said for this as a method of instruction. They had to discover for themselves what acute anxiety or terror is in the here-and-now situation of group therapy. Just as every psychoanalyst in the end experiences for himself in his own personal analysis what has been described in theory, so did the nursing personnel discover in this setting the reality of notions like defense mechanisms, anxiety, self-reliance, guilt feelings and so forth. What I kept in view was that the nursing staff in relation to the patients should behave as the people *they were and not as they had to be or ought to be*. The nurse who in a specific situation adopts certain procedures because she thinks they accord with 'doctor's orders' or with 'hospital rules' or 'because the head nurse says so,' and at the same time also hides behind the defensive façade of her white uniform, is acting in an extremely confusing way. She is acting like a robot with an implausible amount of hypocrisy. Schizophrenic people have been through all this before inside the family in which they grew up where they were exposed to bewildering emotional interactions between their parents. The entire literature on the 'schizophrenogenic family' describes the intense emotional confusion which the poorly integrated parents engender in their children.

Carl Rogers has helped to explain the importance of 'being as one is' in the psychotherapeutic relationship. He uses the concept of 'congruence,' which he defines as follows: 'When an actual experience which the psychotherapist has of himself and the relationship accords with his awareness of himself and the relationship, the therapist is congruent.' A condition of that sort is the opposite of presenting a defensive façade in relation to the patient. If the therapist experiences the relationship in a certain way but is trying to be something else, the condition which Rogers is attempting to define is not met. For Rogers this condition of nonambiguity, of 'congruence,' is basic to all psychotherapy.[6] Schizophrenic patients in particular are especially sensitive to what is *actually* happening in the relationship. In the symposium on the psychotherapy of schizophrenia in 1950, Brody pointed out the sensitivity of the schizophrenic patient to the nonverbalized and only partly conscious feelings of his therapist,[7] and Harold Searles also devotes an interesting article to this.[8]

What Rogers is getting at is that by freely being himself the therapist is prepared for and opens himself to the possibility of an existential encounter between two real human beings. In this context Rogers holds it to be more therapeutic for the therapist to communicate his fear or anger to his schizophrenic patient than for him to keep such feelings hidden away:

But it is one of the heartening aspects of psychotherapy that within the limits set by therapeutic relationships the therapist learns that he may justifiably risk being himself within those limits. A psychiatrist, a friend of mine, said that he never feels so complete, so manifestly himself, as in the therapeutic relationship; and I am sure many of us share that experience.

I was trying to create this condition of congruence in the nursing personnel, in relation to the schizophrenic people on my ward. The following interviews afford examples of what the staff had to say about it themselves.

Here is what two psychiatric aides, Sue and Mary, put on tape:

Sue: Two years ago the people here used to bawl and shout a great deal, smash things up rather a lot, and there were frequent fights, too. The 'cold wet sheet pack' was an automatic procedure. After that, we took to using the isolation room. When somebody had calmed down, we would go in and have a long chat. But that doesn't happen so often now.

Then again, we can express warmer feelings now and it seems much more genuine to me.

Mary: For me that's a complete change. Being able to show people that you like them.

Sue: It used to be that patients would ask us: 'What's wrong with you today?' A staff member would answer: 'Nothing,' or 'I'm fine,' but the patient knows and sees right through you. Now I feel much more free to say what is really bothering me, when something doesn't go right with my husband or when I have a headache or when things do not go my way. The patients seem to be much more satisfied by this. If you just say: 'Nothing,' they immediately seem to take the blame upon themselves.

Sue gave an example of this:

Isabel approached her and asked whether she felt unwell. Sue replied that she was indeed in a bad mood, because she had a fight with her husband. She was literally saying to the patient: 'You'd better keep out of my way a bit today, because thanks to the fight at home I'm in a bad mood,' to which Isabel replied: 'I'm glad you said that, otherwise I'd have had the feeling all day that I was somehow to blame for it.'

Here is a clear description of earlier attitudes compared to the developing 'congruent' ones of the nursing staff and their beneficial effect on the schizophrenic patients. In the subsequent part of the interview Mary continued:

> The staff members in Rose Cottage, as I have observed them, say much more what they feel and think about the patients directly to the patient. At Hillside [Mary came to us a few months before from another ward] I felt it very hard to express feelings of fondness, because I didn't see it done around me. Here I found it much easier to express feelings. Carol shows so much of her feelings just the way she talks to the patients. I experience myself talking much more about my work and the patients at Rose Cottage to my husband, who seems to become more interested in the work that I do. At Hillside I just didn't feel like doing that. My husband asks me what I did today and what the patients were doing today.

She then said:

> *I was trained to never lose my temper, never raise my voice and never show my emotions in relation and during work with patients* [!!!] Nothing about my family, my background, my likes and dislikes was to be communicated to the patients.

This latter comment exemplifies a process of indoctrination that gives to a nurse's behavior its undiscerning and robotlike character.

2. THE NURSING PERSONNEL: THEIR SENSE OF AUTONOMY AND RESPONSIBILITY

To further increase the nursing staff's ability to stand on their own feet, I assumed as administrator the stance of someone who basically does *not* know. I did not write orders in the doctor's order book (except for some medical prescriptions), and when instructing I did my best consistently to express my disapproval of all routine procedure and thus of any slavish following of rules (generally defined as 'hospital policy'). What all this amounts to is delegating responsibility *downward*.

(The literature on the therapeutic community is full of this principle.)

The one who is furthest 'below' on a psychiatric ward is the psychiatric aide. She comes into direct contact with the patients most often, and if she is to act 'congruently' she must take responsibility for her job in the knowledge that she has the necessary competence and authority. The status hierarchy, which in the traditionally organized psychiatric institution is vertical in character (responsibility is generally delegated upward instead of downward), leads to a state of tutelage and a sense of inferiority in precisely those workers who come into direct contact with the patients. Once the personnel got through the dangerous zone of role confusion and loss of the old professional identity, the development of self-reliance and responsibility slowly got under way. Here are a number of examples, taken from interviews I held with various members of the staff.

Stephanie:

> The moment you carry out orders, you just do not feel that you're making any contribution yourself. I am convinced the patients can sense very well when you are carrying out somebody else's instructions.

A concise enough summary of a whole flood of literature that has been published concerning the role of the psychiatric nurse.

Don, a male psychiatric aide, who after working for a year requested transfer to another ward, compared his experiences on his new ward with those at Rose Cottage:

> The differences between the two wards are fairly extreme. Where I am now the psychiatrist leaves his instructions and we carry them out to the letter. We go by the book and don't need to think very much. It all goes very smoothly – but it's dull.
> I feel I'm a sort of robot. But in Rose Cottage it became too tiring for me. Now the psychiatrist is the law and the head nurse the top sergeant.
> It doesn't give you any responsibility.

And now further comments from Sue:

I take a different view of this vicious behavior. Previously, if somebody lashed out, we were on to it at once with a 'pack.' But why – if the patient is already quiet again? Netty can go on striking and kicking – that's all right by me. If she can't control herself, she needs to do it. But if patients ask for it [a 'pack'], you have to get down to talking to them and finding out why they think they need it.

Sue's comments indicate her increased sense of professional prestige. She is beginning to develop her own ideas and her enhanced feeling of self-reliance releases her creativity. Her observations are original and interesting. She implies that violence has its own phenomenology. Just as a mother must be able to listen to her baby and learn by trial and error what the various implied meanings are in order to give a correct feedback, so, too, must the psychiatric aide attend to the various forms of aggression. According to Sue, the sudden manifestation of violence is far more often than not the expression of a desire to be heard, seen and acknowledged. That implies that in these cases it is not a question of a loss of 'ego control.' So if after a sudden eruption of violence the patient calms down and at the same time two psychiatric aides are bent on preparing the 'cold wet sheet pack,' there is then a situation of incorrect feedback. When such a patient lies for an hour or so wrapped up in wet sheets, he is in effect being told: 'You've asked for this control because you yourself lost it. You were asking for a sort of 'auxiliary ego' capable of supporting your weak "ego."' *Instead of reinforcing it* a measure of this kind *actually weakens the ego*. The loss of control occurs naturally; but without proper observation and listening there is always the danger that the schizophrenic patient will get a wrong and therefore confusing feedback that undermines the strength of the ego instead of reinforcing it. What Sue described is one of the chief factors that tend to reduce a schizophrenic patient on a ward to a 'chronically ill' state: *The patient is treated as a thing* and continually relives this de-humanizing and confusing feedback, which is so often the cause of the condition he is in to begin with.

193

What I learned from Sue's comment was that one is indeed wasting one's time and energy if one tries to teach nurses to think with greater psychological understanding and at the same time sets them to work in a bureaucratic setting. The number of creative ideas that the personnel gradually but spontaneously produced exemplifies what this is all about: a growing sense of professional autonomy. Having a communal breakfast on Saturday mornings was the idea of the male psychiatric aides. The night-shift staff came up with the idea of putting out all the lights at night time, except in the nursing office. It turned out, to my surprise, that this was not done throughout Cedar Lodge. After a time the patients went to sleep at night and no longer felt any need to work up to a high pitch of excitement or chitter-chatter with the nursing staff during the night.

A good example of the increased sense of autonomy is provided by the various accounts of a growing reciprocal respect between the ward and the other departments. Joyce (the registered nurse) said about this:

> If we have anybody off sick, Mrs. G. rings up and asks if we need someone, and whom we want. That used not to be. A nurse just arrived, and there was no discussion about it.

Here is what one more member of the nursing department, Mrs. G., had to say:

> I've been working here since September, 1961, and comparing things all the time. What the patients were like, and what they are like now. Cathy, who just used to walk up and down, Julia, who would sit for hours with her head down in a chair.
> Cathy now brings me the reports and we usually have a chat. Julia brings reports, and we talk. Her expression has changed from a dull, vacant look to one of awareness. Isabel helps me work out the weekly timetables of duty for the staff. At the beginning: 'I can't do that, I'm no secretary.' Now at the most she will ring to say she will be a bit late.
> A few days ago Phyllis came and asked, 'Let's just have a

cigarette together.' I can hardly understand it. Phyllis was never known to do such a thing.

The director, in her summing up, reflected a good deal of her own philosophy and her observation of how the members of staff had grown:

As you know, I've listened a lot to the staff and always referred them back to your consultations. God knows I had my troubles in the beginning. But what strikes me now is that no one has lost his professional identity and that they take much more responsibility. That's the trouble. In a bureaucratic and hierarchical organization people never get to be more mature and self-reliant. You must be able to grow; and I can see that it is happenings.

Then she took me to task a bit in the following passage:

You were very authoritarian at first, after all, and I sensed that you found the whole nursing staff totally incompetent. Plain stupid. But you are more relaxed now, too, and you listen better to what the staff have to say. You've been lucky with the selection of your staff.

Having given first thought to the aspects of 'openness' and 'autonomy,' it would seem useful to say a few things about the ward within the totality of the psychiatric institution.

The new things accomplished on the ward and the favorable effect this had on morale and on the patients' behavior gradually led to a change in the status of the ward. A few sentiments recorded by the nursing staff reflect this process.

The registered nurse, Joyce, said:

They used to call us 'that crazy bunch at Rose Cottage.' They would often say, 'What's Foudraine up to now !' Or with downright sarcasm, 'Can you get anywhere with God?'
Sometimes they would say, 'He's crazy. Has he cured anybody yet?'
There was a great deal of envy, too. Everyone thought we were off our nut – in all we were doing. Now the tune has changed. People are getting more friendly and showing more interest in what we are doing in Rose Cottage.

These remarks give a pretty good idea of how the personnel in the rest of the sanatorium reacted. I have not said much so far about my colleagues, my fellow-administrators. During the time Rose Cottage was in the process of growth a mounting degree of rivalry developed that often gave the administrators' meetings a very fierce character indeed. Besides justified criticism there was also jealousy. The overall success of the ward, the experimental changes and innovations, the deviationist ideology and the staff's growing enthusiasm aroused negative reactions in many people.

It was my good fortune that the personnel of the ward, after their initial strongly negative reaction, took such a positive and loyal stand. Without that kind of support the situation would certainly have been hard to assimilate psychologically at times. The fact that we kept going against traditional nursing principles sanctioned by 'hospital rules' naturally gave rise to conflicts with the management of the sanatorium. Here again, luck was on my side, in every respect. The freedom and the opportunities to experiment were in large measure given to me.

If you feel that this is turning into a sort of triumphal progress report, it is time to call your attention to the denouement. In the midst of these successes I became more aware of how *wrong* we are about the psychiatric institution and that it is going to be a very difficult job indeed to reform it.

But that comes later on.

[1] A. H. Stanton and M. S. Schwartz: 'The Management of a Type of Institutional Participation in Mental Illness,' *Psychiatry*, vol. 12, p. 13 (1949).

[2] M. Greenblatt and D. Levinson: 'The Open Door: A Study of Institutional Change,' in *Therapeutic Community*, H. C. B. Denber, ed. (Springfield, Ill., 1960).

[3] B. Rubin and A. Goldberg: 'An Investigation of Openness in the Psychiatric Hospital,' *Archives of General Psychiatry*, vol. 8, p. 269 (1963).

[4] L. S. Stein: 'The Doctor-Nurse Game,' *Archives of General Psychiatry*, vol. 16, pp. 699–703 (1967).

[5] Maxwell Jones argued:

Often the doctors themselves are the people who have had less training than either social workers or psychologists, and in any case their training in a general hospital has tended to give them a feeling of considerable authority and even omnipotence. To have their performance in these daily meetings questioned by their juniors and other professional colleagues can be extremely painful but is undoubtedly a valuable learning experience if the personality of the individual allows this to happen.

M. Jones: *Social Psychiatry* (Springfield, Ill., 1962).

[6] The importance to the psychotherapist of schizophrenics of an attitude of 'congruence' is further defined by Rogers in his paper 'A Theory of Psychotherapy with Schizophrenics and a Proposal for its Investigation,' in *Psychotherapy with Schizophrenics*, J. G. Dawson, ed. (Baton Rouge, La., 1961).

[7] Brody and Redlich, eds.: *Psychotherapy with Schizophrenics* (New York, 1952).

[8] H. C. Searles: 'The Schizophrenic's Vulnerability to the Therapist's Unconscious Processes,' in *Collected Papers on Schizophrenia and Related Subjects* (1965). In this essay Searles makes use of Johnson and Szurek's observations concerning the sensitivity of delinquent children to unconcious antisocial impulses in the parents.

The views expressed by Lewis Hill, in particular where he says: '[The patient's] life has been severely restricted, limited and invaded by the requirements of his parent's conscious and unconscious conflicts and drives. Anything in the unconscious of the parents which would produce anxiety must become a preoccupation of the patient in order to keep down parental anxiety and thereby reduce his own distress,' gave occasion for this interesting essay by Searles.

See also A. M. Johnson and S. A. Szurek: 'The Genesis of Anti-Social Acting Out in Children and Adults,' *Psychoanalytical Quart.*, vol. 21, pp. 323–343 (1952), and L. B. Hill: *Psychotherapeutic Intervention in Schizophrenia* (Chicago, 1955).

9. THE PATIENTS

It is time to speak more concretely about the patients. I will let various members of the Cedar Lodge staff speak for themselves.

One of the old hands in the kitchen, who helped with the distribution of the meals, had this to say:

They certainly were the sickest patients and they were waited on entirely. They didn't want to do anything for themselves. I'm talking now only about the dining-room situation. Julia at this moment is able to do practically everything in the dining room, getting her food, asking for certain articles, putting her plate back, and that sort of thing. Phyllis in the past year is able to sit down, carry on a conversation and she is for the most part sensible. Phyllis had no contact with any dining-room personnel in the old days. Seeing the way they were when they had to be helped, and seeing them now helping themselves is one of the biggest improvements. I've called it a miracle.

One of the old employees of the Rose Cottage, Mrs. Johnson of the night-shift, reported:

To me the patients were just vegetables. They stayed that

way for about a year after our program started. First you had to get the staff on your side. So long as we were still against you, nothing could alter. But now there's a feeling of a breakthrough. I can talk much better with everybody. How shall I put it? On a different level. There's a different feeling about. In the old days we all had our jobs mapped out. It was really rather easy. Now there's something happening every minute and yet the nights are much more peaceful. To begin with – when you were forcing the pace so much – we all felt: 'I wish he'd take the boat back to Holland.' Now instead of patients I can see people. I was afraid of Cathy. If anybody had told me earlier on that I would develop a kind of understanding with Cathy, I'd have said he was crazy.

She ended her account with the remark: 'For the first time there is just a glimmer of hope!'

She is right: 'For the first time there is just a glimmer of hope.' It is impossible to describe all the work done by the staff, which in many respects seemed to edge forward inch by inch into a practically impassable terrain of apathy, passive resistance, inconceivably profound discouragement and confusion. A few examples:

SYLVIA

As you will recall, Sylvia was reputed to be an 'adult autistic.' The head nurse described how she got Sylvia to make her own bed:

When the meeting is over, I go along with her to her room. She begins by throwing herself on the floor and produces her first tantrum. I have to stop her from smashing a window. The task, making her own bed, we perform initially together. In this opening period it takes about three hours. Thus I stand for three hours at a time giving directions, and she often comes up with one burst of rage after another.

Indeed we often heard frightful noises penetrating to us

below. Sylvia frequently screamed out: 'This is becoming a regular hell-hole around here! Give me back the old Cedar Lodge! I want to get back to the old Cedar Lodge!' The battle with Sylvia was joined on all fronts: her clothes, personal hygiene, going to bed, getting herself dressed and undressed, handling money, running errands, making coffee, etc.

I myself observed the following incident:

Sylvia wants to go to the movies and sits in the nursing office. After a lot of bother she finds the telephone number in the directory and writes it down. Now she is unwilling to lift the receiver off the hook and throws her first tantrum. Eventually, she lifts the receiver but hands it at once to the nurse, who has the greatest difficulty not taking hold of the telephone. Sylvia now flings the telephone down and produces a second tantrum. In the end she starts to dial the number. It comprises five figures. She dials four and asks the nurse to dial the fifth. This is again refused. Eventually she gets the connection and to our great astonishment she speaks out bold and clear and books two seats.

The battle was fought by all shifts – and this time consistently. Even so, every advance was won only with a lot of trouble. It was as though Sylvia shunned every activity that might help to bring her out of her regressive condition, as though she felt every action of her own as a threatening loss of security, which evidently was invested in the strong shelter provided by her role as a 'sick-invalid-crazy person.' During the morning meetings she would often retreat into herself and fall asleep. As soon as she was awakened, there was a new tantrum. She would then scream out: 'I'm damned crazy! I hate these meetings!' And we noticed, not without satisfaction, that Sylvia had slowly but distinctly begun to expand her vocabulary.

Dr. McBride stopped his work with Sylvia and asked me to become her psychotherapist. She then had just one person to deal with. I put her on a fairly low dosage of tranquilizers. It would take me too long to describe the psychotherapy with Sylvia here. She started to speak more and more, eventually went off alone to the hairdresser's in Washington, bought her own clothes, wore dentures and glasses and in the evenings attended plays and concerts in Washington. She took to reading the newspaper and surprised me with her flair for music and her considerable interest in politics.

She obstinately refused to face up to her real age (45); and we fought many a (verbal) battle over this question. Despair at the many 'lost' years of almost total regression and the confrontation with adulthood (and old age) – all these experiences with her would constitute a separate chapter. Sometime after my departure (at the end of 1965) Sylvia left Cedar Haven, and she now lives in an apartment with a private companion.

The change in her from a snarling, moaning, filthy woman who scarcely spoke, who shook convulsively with her whole body and was forever flinging herself to the floor, into one who was well dressed, had the affectionate nature of a child and spoke quite clearly with an extensive vocabulary, was one of the 'miracles' of Cedar Haven. So it was for me, too.

PHYLLIS

Phyllis was put on a slimming diet and we stuck to it. People stopped giving her a wide berth, and several times the former 'Blue Bull' showed what she was capable of: she did indeed go blue with rage and made quite an impression. But as morale improved, fear of her disappeared and along with it the myth of danger that grows around so many schizophrenic patients.

JULIA

Julia changed from a dreamy, completely passive and fear-ridden woman into someone who went every week to the beauty parlor in town and in many respects gave evidence of growing activity. She had to relearn everything: counting, telephoning, knowing how to handle money, all those little things that she had long since forgotten. Her therapist worked with her so enthusiastically that she was able to leave Rose Cottage and went to live at the home of a senior psychiatric aide after having been in Cedar Haven for twenty-five years.

CATHY

Her weight reduction made very slow progress. In many ways Cathy was of assistance to me, because during the morning meetings she was always pouring ridicule on our program, while her derisive behavior at the same time implied an obvious cry for help.

The myth that she was 'dangerous' died rapidly. She began to take piano lessons and before long was volunteering to work in an office in Westover. With each step forward she developed tremendous anxiety and so gave me an insight into the often inconceivably low degree of self-esteem which was a typical feature of many of these women, along with a great fear of any further success, because that would inevitably open into the future which many of them still saw as a huge black hole that exerted no attraction whatever. Why change the security of the Haven for the loneliness of a spinster in an apartment?

LESLIE

Her major improvement was the care she gradually gave to her appearance. The radical confusion she felt regarding her sexual identity (which went along with a markedly symbiotic relationship with her father, who did accept her as a son but never as a daughter) she would often express by saying things like: 'I'm a man. I don't want to be a woman.' After about two years' work she stopped pulling out her hair, ripping up her clothes, and once a week she would visit the beautician. She stocked up her wardrobe, and we eventually succeeded in persuading her to stop using her lipstick to tattoo herself red all over. In the initial phase Leslie would use her cosmetics in such a way that her face looked like a clown's. She colored her lips far too vividly and was obviously exaggerating their size. Her movements gradually became more rounded and less angular; her demeanor changed from provocatively aggressive masculine rebelliousness to silent depressions and despair at the loss of her femininity. As time went on she began to cry more. We noticed that she was gradually speaking in clearer language. We had rigorously refused to respond to her symbolic language, which she used to force those around her to continually 'translate.' For me the following was a moving incident:

There is to be a dance party in the occupational therapy building, and Leslie is standing in the Rose Cottage living room in her new cocktail dress, just back from the hairdresser's. When I come in, I am struck by how attractive she looks. I compliment her enthusiastically. She then starts walking toward me in a Marlene Dietrich fashion, with lots of seductive gestures, until she stands in front of me. She opens her eyes wide, slowly raises her long arms and in an amused tone, with a half-smile on her lips, says: 'Well, is something coming up?' I have no doubt as to what she means. She is asking whether her appearance has produced an erection on my part. It is, it seems to me, a moment for candor and I reply: 'Woman, you sure can do it!'

As we stand there facing each other, both with a laugh of recognition, the deep gulf seems to be bridged for a moment, and there is the shock of real human contact.

10. PATIENTS HELP
EACH OTHER

Some years ago, in the journal *Psychiatry*, Summer described the situation I found in Rose Cottage as a 'schizophrenic no-society.' [1]

A good name for a group which at the same time is not a group but rather a number of people without any mutual contact, without a shared ideology or commitment to a common task or goal. Summer and others are critical of the notion that there is such a thing as a patient 'society,' 'community' or 'culture.' Insisting that there is, Summer argues, may be due to the fact that we have trouble accepting the idea that people can live together as a sort of aggregate of individuals without any reciprocal solidarity, without any form of social organization.

If one postulates as the minimal requirements for a society: (1) a certain number of shared expectations; (2) working and cooperating toward a particular goal; (3) a certain number of rules of conduct, agreed to by the members of the group; and (4) having some knowledge of one another, then, Summer argues, the patients on a ward of a traditional psychiatric institution may be regarded as a kind of hotchpotch of separate individuals who sometimes do not even know one another by name and exhibit no form of cooperation at all. They are not 'a group of persons, whether or not in physical contact, who are aware of themselves as sharing a common ideology, interest, property, etc., or the fact of sharing something in common.' Summer therefore calls them a 'no-society.' The task is to transform this 'no-society' into a group.

And indeed that is how it was, at first, on the ward. What was particularly striking was that the various patients never mentioned one another by name. One of the surprising developments during our experiment was that the patients began to make more and more contact with each other and to call each other by name. That was also true of their relationship with the nurses. This development was fostered by a principle which I introduced from the very beginning. Why should patients, besides helping themselves, not be able to help their fellow patients, too?

The idea of encouraging patients not only to help themselves but also to offer aid to their fellow patients is not new. It is surprising, though, how little it has been put into practice. Many contributors to the literature have wondered why it should not be possible to persuade psychiatric patients to support and understand one another – and to stimulate these interactions.

Thus Esther Brown[2] has called attention to the potential psychological value helping a patient has for another patient. But a systematic exploration of this possibility is again and again frustrated by our prior assumption that patients are 'helpless.' Brown wonders whether it would not be possible to develop in the psychiatric institution an organization within which patients might indeed give their fellow patients psychological help. She points out that many people who have managed to recover from a psychotic phase have a very clear recollection and understanding of what other patients, then in the throes of a disintegration, are going through. Use can be made of this understanding and the principle of helping fellow patients should not only be permitted but actually structurally built into the life on the ward.

Brown states:

Are we encouraging the patient in his thoughtfulness of

others, are we giving him an opportunity to help others as he has been helped, or do we insist on doing things for the patient, on being always the givers of medical help when the patient is constantly the recipient and never the giver?

And she continues:

An impartial observer of typical ward-practice and patient-responses to it may have cause to marvel at how docile and submissive brave, bold, liberty-loving American citizens become when they find themselves admitted to our hospitals and even into some of our clinics. In a sense it would appear that we Americans are once adults and then become children – when we grow old and when we enter a hospital.

Robert W. White has raised a similar question.[3] It is also a well-known fact that in his psychotherapeutic work with psychotic people John Rosen put this principle into practice and would often seek the advice of the patients he had been treating as to the psychological approach he should adopt with others. Milton Greenblatt likewise calls attention to this subject.[4] He talks about the possibility of 'release of therapeutic potential from the patients themselves' and points out the advantages of a social structure in which strongly negative feelings towards authority can partly be given expression and partly be diluted through the development of peerlike relationships.

Lastly, there is Harry Stack Sullivan, who in his article 'Sociopsychiatric Research' (*American Journal of Psychiatry*, 1930–1931, vol. 87, pp. 977–91), and later on in his book *Schizophrenia as a Human Process*, gave us a brilliant analysis of the work that he had been doing in 1930 at the Sheppard Enoch Pratt Hospital in Baltimore. The article occupies an important but somewhat neglected place in the literature. It is the first classic account of the creation of a therapeutic environment for schizophrenic patients, referred to by Sullivan as 'institutional therapy.' In Baltimore Sullivan got an opportunity to organize a ward according to his own ideas, and he promptly got rid of all the women. When he speaks about nurses, it was in a characteristically biting tone:

Those never enough to be admired miracles, whose life is so glaringly illuminated by the professional ideal, often shining the more brilliantly and casting the more perfect shadows, because it is without any competing ideal.

About his work on the ward he wrote:

Instead of spending most of my time in denaturing minor atrocities and stupidities of the patient's life in the hospital, I could now devote myself to cooperative effort that tended to endure, instead of to end on the threshold of my office.

He called his ward 'a school for personality growth' instead of a 'custodian of personality failures.' Actually, the man speaking here is one who realized very well that social rehabilitation may sometimes be a necessary *preparation* for more fundamental treatment, by which he clearly meant psychoanalytic psychotherapy. The atmosphere on his ward he described as one of education, 'broadly conceived, not by verbal teaching, but by communal experience – good tutoring.' The 'milieu' should not create strong feelings of dependency on 'powerful' personalities, but broaden and deepen interest in interpersonal relations.

Helen S. Terry described Sullivan's ward as a 'pre-adolescent society' and reminds us once again of the fact that when he was growing up Sullivan himself felt very isolated from boys of his own age.

At this point there emerges the theme that Sivadon and Maxwell Jones have repeatedly stressed: the development of a social structure which will enable patients on a psychiatric ward to establish contacts with each other, that is to say, at the 'peer level' (the relationship between partners of similar age, brothers and sisters). This stress on 'peerlike relationships' derives in particular from Sullivan, who in his reflections on personality development stressed the importance of what he called the 'preadolescent phase,' the phase prior to physical puberty. Contact with people of one's own age is an essential aspect of the culturalizing and socializing process. For Sullivan, whether or not one has a positive experience during this phase more or less determines one's eventual 'socializing capacity.'

In the affection for the 'chum' with whom bosom secrets can be exchanged there lies for both Sullivan and Piaget one of the principal sources of the later adult love relationship; and this may also be the principal phase in which it is possible to compensate for and straighten out what has been distorted by traumatic experiences in the relationship to parental figures in early childhood. So, too, Boszormenyi-Nagi declares:

> The milieu of our unit helped to cultivate the peer-level, 'chum-like' relationships, even between very disorganized people. For many of the patients it was the first time in their lives that they had a friend. These friendships typically occurred as a rebellious alliance between patients against the authority of nurses, replicating a phenomenon which normally occurs during latency with peers.[5]

Now for my own observations in Rose Cottage. As we got more successful at stimulating patients to help one another, the staff began with mounting enthusiasm to report little incidents that exemplified interactions of a mutually helpful kind. What they noticed especially was the measure of tact and efficiency with which one patient would offer to help another. A few examples:

Sylvia (at one time the moaning and grumbling 'adult autistic') was asked to feed a very depressive fellow patient in the dining room. Sylvia, who two years before had often enough been fed herself, responded to this request in a way we had not thought possible. To everyone's astonishment she took her schizophrenic fellow patient by the hand and began feeding her with a spoon without any motory disturbance. Her movements were harmonious and flexible, and to the amazement of the bystanders she stopped groaning and grumbling and began to sing softly:

> My mamma done tol' me, when I was in knee pants,
> My mamma done tol' me, son:
> A woman'll sweet talk and give you the glad eye,
> But when that sweet talkin's done,
> A woman's a two-faced, a worrisome thing,
> Who'll leave you to sing
> The blues in the night.

As she sang, she completed the feeding of her fellow patient in a motherly, tender way.

Another incident took place in the main building. An acutely catatonic woman went shambling along to the dining room, which was in the basement. She was walking slowly, with her eyes shut. A nurse on the ward caught sight of a male patient and at once asked him to help the woman get down the stairs and to see that she got some food. I was struck by the gentle way in which this man, whom we shall call Donald, set about bringing this task to a proper conclusion. Alas! once they were downstairs Donald's task was hastily taken over by a student nurse.

Some months later I asked Donald about his experience and in particular inquired whether he remembered the incident. To my surprise he was able to come out with quite a number of thoughts and feelings on the subject. Donald was a very withdrawn man, who dodged all interpersonal contact by mumbling to himself. During our conversation he spoke with unusual clarity. He said:

> I wanted to help her, just like a boy scout. It was a desire to achieve something. I had a feeling that my interest would help to make her better. I was tensed up because I thought I must be in the way, that what I did would all be for nothing.

When I invited him to say more about his feelings at the time he was helping his fellow patient to get down the stairs he said:

> You should really get something done every day. But sometimes you feel a sympathy that goes further than that. That beats everything or nothing. I felt I'd got a sort of royal decoration, like being knighted with a sword. That's how I felt. Such a big success . . . nothing to touch it . . . I mean . . . what I felt and what I knew.

Our contact during this interview became considerably deeper when he went on:

> I knew where I was going. I felt that God wanted her to live and I felt like a king helping her. It felt like living.

At these words Donald smiled and when I inquired more closely about his smile, he said:

The feeling that you really were able to help somebody so much all by yourself and do just what she needed.

I also asked him about his reaction when the student nurse had intervened. Donald said:

It was everything I had to offer. I would have done absolutely anything for her that evening. I felt crushed when the nurse took over. I felt the institution coming back and that I had been put in my place. The institution works in a routine way – the way the staff wants it. I wondered later if I really had helped her. I thought later: Perhaps you didn't help her at all. Perhaps it was all just a laugh. When the nurse took over, I felt like I was a failure. I felt that I was not in a position to be a king.

What struck me especially was that after a successful interaction of this kind, in which help was given and received, a number of patients would suddenly function much better, would be less confused, and would usually display a more adequate type of behavior. One can explain this in a very simple way, of course. They suddenly felt they were no longer worthless, they dropped for a moment the role reserved especially for the inmate of a psychiatric institution: 'being a patient.'

I would like to put before you a few ideas prompted by these observations, a sort of hypothesis which cannot be verified and so is perhaps not worth very much. But psychoanalysts are given from time to time to explain simple phenomena in as complicated a way as possible. It is a form of excited fantasizing.

There are many ways in which one could account for the phenomena I have been describing. My notion was that *certain* schizophrenic patients, if they have been engaged in a successful 'helping' interaction, may experience a sudden recovery of their sense of identity.

We know that a lot of schizophrenic patients were brought up in families *where the needs of the parental figures dominated in an extreme fashion the needs of the child.* In these 'schizophrenogenic' families the future patient evolves an identity formed particularly around experiences of sacrificial giving – understanding, helping and supporting extremely anxious and very, very demanding parents. Once admitted to the psychiatric institution, the roles are reversed. Now the nurses and doctors fulfill the role of the helping, responsible, understanding and need-satisfying figure, and the patients have to assume the role of helpless 'patient.'

In the psychoanalytic sanatorium psychoanalysts who have tried to 'schizophrenese' have given a great deal of time to the business of interpreting mysterious symbolic communications offered with equal persistence by their patients. Donald Burnham, reminding us of the adage that doctors need patients in order to be doctors, cites this statement of Loeb's:

> The patient gets along best in the hospital if he accepts his submissive and dependent role and does not complicate still further the already existing conflicts and difficulties which the staff have with one another.

In the psychoanalytic literature we find an extensive discussion of the problem of the 'helping' child in Searles' publication on the positive feelings between the schizophrenic child and his mother.[6] The great emphasis psychoanalysts have put on the need to receive love is not repudiated by Searles, but he underlines the equally great need the child has to give love to others, especially to his mother. This emphasis on the need to give love provides Searles with a new dimension in his efforts to get an insight into what develops between the future schizophrenic child and his mother. Searles has an important predecessor. The psychoanalyst Sandor Ferenczi also showed great insight into the effect of overwhelming psychological traumata on the development of the child. He rediscovered seduction and psychological exploitation and was one of the first to describe the splitting process as a defence against acute and chronic traumata (a splitting off of the emotional life bound up with early experiences). In his 'Child Analysis in the Analysis of Adults' he shows how children who have had to put up with a great deal, psychically and physically, where attitude and expression are concerned, make an older, almost sage impression. They mother other people, as if they want to help others with the knowledge they themselves have so painfully acquired.

In his 'Confusion of Tongues Between the Adult and the Child' he returns to this theme and suggests that in the child subjected to sexual exploitation or serious traumata, emotions like those of an adult can be aroused, potential relational qualities that normally unfold in marriage, motherhood or fatherhood. Thus beside regression Ferenczi postulates the idea of a traumatic *progression*, a premature maturity. In this connection he cites the dream of the 'wise baby' in which a child scarcely out of the womb starts to talk and exhort the parents to wisdom. The fear of the unconstrained adult, balancing on the edge of psychotic disintegration, *turns the child into a psychiatrist*. In order to protect itself against dangers presented by people who threaten to lose control over themselves, the child must identify at a deep level with the potential aggressor.

In describing the bewilderment that parents engender in their children during the process of projecting upon them their own frustrated unconscious needs Ferenczi stated: 'Children have a compulsive need to create order in chaotic family relationships and to burden themselves with the afflictions of other people. A mother who is forever complaining turns her child into a nurse-for-life, a real mother-substitute. It is a process in which the child's real needs are ignored.' The theme of the prematurely adult and 'sage' child, the child-psychiatrist, is completely in line with what Searles notes in his account of the intense loyalty in the relationship between mother and child. I quote:

If the normal child feels concern and solicitude for the mother when the latter is anxious or burdened, the pre-schizophrenic detects in his mother, no matter how unable he is to formulate it thus, a tragically unintegrated and incomplete person. To his mother, tragically enmeshed in her own personality-problems, he responds with an intensity of compassion, loyalty, solicitude and dedication, which goes beyond that which a child would have reason to feel toward a relatively well mother.

I shall ignore here the extensive literature on the dynamics of the family, which often comes back to this point. I prefer to elucidate my idea with the concept of identity, as described by Lichtenstein, in his paper 'Identity and Sexuality.' [8] Lichtenstein maintains that the primary condition for the formation of identity is contained in the symbiotic unity of mother and baby and not in the gradual breaking down of this unity. This latter phase, in which the distant, increasingly self-reliant individual is gradually separated off, is called in the literature the 'separation-individuation phase.' Lichtenstein sees the child as an organ within the surrounding total organism of the mother. Just as an organ is *both* separate *and* symbiotic, so is the child one with the mother, while at the same time a part in relation to the whole.

Being an organ with the organism (the maternal *Umwelt* which also includes the mother's unconscious) gives the child the *function* of an organ, too. Lichtenstein sees in this function the nucleus of the unfolding human identity. Thus identity is here defined as the experience of potential instrumentality for another. In the symbiotic relationship the mother employs a combination of stimuli specific to her, and frustration of needs as well as the specific combination of stimuli are recognized by the child long before there is any question of an actual perception of the mother as 'other.' The way in which the mother holds the child, warms it and touches it, the way in which certain senses are stimulated and others are not, forms a kind of 'stimulus cast' of the maternal unconscious. The mother satisfies the child's needs, *but also creates needs which she then satisfies.*

Thus Lichtenstein sees the child during this stage being fashioned into an organ, *an instrument for the satisfaction of the mother's unconscious needs.* This way of conceptualizing the notion of identity is extremely 'other-directed.' But it is a fascinating viewpoint. So as not to define this 'instrumental identity' too narrowly Lichtenstein prefers to speak of an 'identity theme.' He then postulates that this 'identity theme' is irreversible, though capable of many variations. He even goes to the extent of regarding the conservation of this 'identity theme' as a compulsive need for achieving self-expression in a number of specific ways of being-for-the-other. Without going into this article in any further detail, one could sum it up by saying that in the symbiotic relationship the child is molded in a particular way into being-for-the-other.

This strongly instrumental quality of the concept of identity, so interpreted, can only reinforce the suggestion that *some* schizophrenic patients have a compulsive need to afford help and support to others as a manifestation of their identity theme as 'helpers.'

Let us now look at the examples again and try to elucidate them. Placed in the position of helper, Donald feels like 'a king, a knight who has received the accolade.' He suddenly feels – as he disclosed in a later conversation – as if he were of royal blood, guided by 'royal inspiration.' For a few moments he knows 'where he is going,' because under his own steam he is helping the other person 'just where she needed it.' I interpret this moving description as a sudden manifestation and recognition of a sense of identity. Erik Erikson uses the same words as our patient when he describes the sense of identity as 'to know where one is going.' [9] One can, of course, see the experience as one of accomplishment or of 'being worth-while'; but it may also be seen as a breakthrough and manifestation of the identity theme of 'helper.' This theme is then actualized in the helpful action. Donald not only has the *capacity* to help, but he actually does help and during the few moments in which the structure of the institution allows him to do so realizes himself. During our conversation Donald said: 'I felt born again. I felt gifted.'

But when the 'institution' enters in the shape of the student nurse, the act of helping is interrupted and a sense of failure and bewilderment replaces the growing sense of competence, tinged with a clear expression of omnipotence: 'From a king I became just an ordinary person.'

In conjunction with this idea, just a few more general

thoughts on the possible psychotherapeutic implications of what I have been describing. If 'being a helper' expresses an essential quality of the sense of identity of certain schizophrenic people, we could see their major problem in their early years as being put in a position in which they were asked to give help and support and at the same time were neither permitted nor considered competent to do so. The schizophrenic patient could be regarded therefore as an intensely frustrated savior. In the course of the psychotherapy of schizophrenic patients I have often been struck by the overwhelming sense of frustration which resulted from the experience of not being able to give expression to this need to give and to help. On the parents' side there is a standing invitation and demand to be helped; but at the same time they consistently refuse such help. After all, to accept it would force them to recognize and admit their own helplessness and dependency.

I mentioned therapeutic implications. How are we to assess this aspect of our schizophrenic patient's personality? We can quite justifiably see the caring, saving, omnipotent aspect of their behavior as a form of defense that evolved in the struggle for survival. If we stress this aspect, it makes sense to regard the prematurely mature and 'understanding-sympathetic' aspect as a masochistic subjection brought about by psychological exploitation.

In that case the helper and savior type of behavior will be a kind of pseudo-self, covering up the original core of the personality, the 'original self,' as the psychoanalyst, Winnicott called it, or in a rather different sense, 'regressed ego,' according to Guntrip.[10] Our therapeutic approach, then, will be on the lines of offering to clarify this form of defensiveness so that the patient can recognize his own intense dependency needs and the equally intense need for individuation and recognition of his own needs. From this standpoint it is the child's individuality that is severely neglected in the psychological vacuum created by the exploitive use the parental figures made of their projections.

Thus it would seem meaningful to force the schizophrenic patient to accept the idea that he is indeed a patient; the acceptance of his 'illness' can then be the starting point of the

216

therapeutic process. Correct though this theoretical viewpoint may be, I hold it to be a wrong approach for some schizophrenic patients. If I have understood Ferenczi rightly, the wise child is indeed a child, but wise with it. Thus, too, the pseudo-self is a part of really being oneself, just as a 'defense,' born of intense conflict, can be a real talent.

One of my patients described how he developed the delusion that he was Jesus Christ and that he had been assigned the task of establishing harmony and peace. He recalled how as a child he had had a fantasy about sitting on a throne. His parents would approach the throne and lay their difficulties and their despair, their conflicts and animosity before him. He then made peace and explained to the parents the cause of their troubles. His former analyst interpreted this fantasy as an 'omnipotent defense.' He pointed out to his patient that he 'was still sitting on his royal throne.' Although the patient accepted the gradiose aspect of this image of himself, his reaction to the 'power-powerlessness' quality of the interpretation was a very negative one. For him the fantasy was a very valuable aspect of his identity that had more to do with love, sympathizing and the profound need to help than with power and powerlessness. (I shall ignore here the intense hostility that likewise lurks behind this loving ideal.)

As part of a psychotherapeutic strategy I encouraged a number of the Rose Cottage patients to manifest this aspect of 'being themselves,' both in certain phases of the therapeutic relationship at the individual level and in their role as a member of a new community. It seemed sensible to me not to force them into the role of patient but to encourage them to assume the role of co-therapist. Such a strategy helps the patient to reintegrate himself around a mode of being peculiarly his own, and is perhaps essential to his efforts to rediscover his own sense of identity. In this I find myself in agreement with the therapeutic strategy described by Federn, at any rate during the opening phase of therapy as well as of the hospital career of the schizophrenic patient. The goal during this phase is recovery of the 'ego,' recovery of essential defensive structures. Allowing the patient to go through a number of experiences in which he succeeds in giving help to others might then serve as a kind of building block on which to structure the process of crystallizing his own identity.

Returning now to Donald, I was struck by two more comments of his. He said: 'The institution came to the fore in the shape of the nurse.' And: 'The institution operates in a particular, hard-and-fast way.' The prejudice on which Donald got shipwrecked was the deep-rooted conviction on the part of medical and paramedical personnel that they are the only ones in a psychiatric hospital who should (and indeed can) help and understand. That this obstinate prejudice is very hard to break down, anyone who tries to change this role definition of psychiatric personnel in a traditional institution will be aware of. We see here the other side of the coin. In their syndrome of 'chronic helpfulness' the staff very likely manifest a similar identity theme. Psychiatrists, social workers, nurses and priests are not only manifesting in the way they function their own need for help, but are also giving expression to a theme vitally bound up with their own sense of identity. Up to a point the psychoanalysis undergone by the psychiatrist can moderate his compulsive need to help – but helping remains a fundamental orientation. Though the psychiatrist may become conscious of a great deal, he still is a dedicated and stubbornly determined savior figure.

We conclude then that some schizophrenic patients are both our opponents and our collaborators. Opponents in the sense that they want to help just as much (and just as fervently) as we do, collaborators in the sense that their identity theme provides their life with a goal not unrelated to ours. The rivalry between these identity themes could be one explanation for the syndrome of chronic identity diffusion, which is the tragic lot of a great number of our schizophrenic patients in institutions.

I am thinking here in particular of Leslie, whose confused verbalizing often included the remark 'I want to go home.' In the way she behaved Leslie was almost a caricature of helplessness. Anyone who really set out to help her and understand her she drove to the edge of desperation. With clockwork regularity she would answer the question 'What's your trouble?' with an obstinately insolent look and the reply 'What's yours?'

Throughout the foregoing reflections I have centered the problem around the dialectic of giving and receiving. Some schizophrenic patients experience the role expectation qua 'patient' as completely at odds with their own identity theme qua 'helper.'

Goffman, in his brilliant sociological essay, brings out what it means to lose one's personal possessions on entering the psychiatric hospital. People lose their valuable papers, glasses, wallet, sometimes even their own clothes. There has been a big change, fortunately, in this respect and people are now allowed to retain many of their own things. Goffman calls these the 'identity kit.' I am suggesting that we let the patient hang onto yet another part of his 'identity kit': his capacity to help and understand other people.

I shall end this chapter with an anecdote. During the first week of my psychiatric training in the hospital I met a man who had been discharged from military service because he had been found to be psychotic. I asked him what his trouble was and if I could help him. He smiled and said that he had no troubles and had come to help me. He explained how the conviction had suddenly come over him that he was in fact a psychiatrist. He was actually glad to be sent to the hospital and asked if I could arrange for him to have a room so that he could get down to work. I was deeply puzzled. At the very outset of my career as a 'savior' here was my first patient telling me that he was a psychiatrist.

The director of the hospital gave me the support I needed at that moment. He told me that this was a typical schizophrenic delusion of grandeur. I felt relieved, avoided the patient and never forgot him. Now, ten years later, maybe I would give this man a chance to work along with me, as part of my therapeutic strategy. But my room I would not give up.

REFERENCES

[1] R. Summer, Osmond and Humphry: 'The Schizophrenic No-Society,' *Psychiatry*, vol. 25, pp. 244–256 (1962).

[2] L. B. Brown: *New Dimensions of Patient-Care* (New York, 1961).

[3] R. W. White and H. C. Solomon: 'Clinical Management of Psychiatric Hospitals,' *Connecticut State Medical Journal*, vol. 15 (1951).

[4] M. Greenblatt, D. J. Levinson and R. H. Williams: *The Patient and the Mental Hospital* (Glencoe, Ill., 1957).

[5] E. Boszormenyi-Nagi and J. L. Framo: 'Family-History of Hospital Treatment of Schizophrenia,' in *Current Psychiatric Therapies*, vol. 2. J. H. Masserman, ed. (New York, 1962).

[6] M. F. Searles: 'Positive Feelings between the Schizophrenic and his Mother,' *International Journal of Psychoanalysis*, vol. 39, p. 569 (1958).

[7] S. Ferenczi: 'Confusion of Tongues between the Adult and the Child' and 'Child Analysis in the Analysis of Adults,' in *Final Contributions to the Problem of Psychoanalysis* (New York, 1955).

[8] H. Lichtenstein: 'Identity and Sexuality,' *Amer. J. of Psychoanalytical Association*, vol. 9, pp. 179–261 (1961).

[9] E. H. Erikson: 'Identity and the Lifecycle,' *Psychological Issues*, vol. 1, no. 1 (1959).

[10] H. Guntrip: *Personality Structure and Human Interaction* (New York, 1961). *Schizoid Phenomena, Object Relations and the Self* (London, 1968).

[11] D. W. Winnicott: *The Maturational Process and the Facilitating Environment* (London, 1965).

11. BUREAUCRACY AND DEHUMANIZATION

Any psychiatrist who is interested and concerned about what is happening in a psychiatric ward will find himself gradually developing into an amateur 'social engineer.' In trying to investigate his ward as a social system he will make many of the kinds of discoveries I have been describing. The extensive literature on this subject will then become clear to him and will corroborate his own experiences. When the psychiatrist starts to play the role of cultural reformer and tries to produce *change* he will encounter forces he had not previously detected. The culture which he as a reformer is bent on assailing will present itself more and more as a recalcitrant and at times extremely rigid network of roles, embedded in a formal structure sanctioned by 'tradition' and the many fixed ideas of those who sustain it. He will become aware that just as every culture offers man possibilities of being human, it at the same time presents serious limitations to the full realization of true humanity.

Otto A. Will has said in an important article that man's greatest frailty may well be his overcautious respect for what he himself has created:

It may be that man's fatal weakness lies in his too tender

regard for that which he has created, and that his clinging to the spurious comforts found in the maintainance of a familiar and relatively unchanging culture, may interfere with his making the appropriate and timely response to the challenge of his existence. The delusions of the culture are costly – and maybe fatal – for men in general and for psychiatric patients in particular.[1]

If the psychiatrist does not show this 'tender regard,' but on the contrary assails and undermines established positions and traditions, his efforts may irrevocably isolate him and his conduct may be (and surprisingly often is) classified as 'crazy.'

Having registered my complaints, I want in this chapter to buttress them with some theoretical arguments. The moment has come for us to move away from the concreteness of unique human individuals and examples of human behavior to a form of generalization.

My guide where theory is concerned is an article by Merton J. Kahne.[2] I take it on the author's authority that the source, both theoretical and pragmatic, for his study of the bureaucratic form of organization is to be found in the work of Max Weber.

First, the essential structural characteristic of this organizational form consists of a hierarchical chain that has the form of a pyramid. Within the chain are certain aspects such as decision-making, task-assignment and forms of communication. Secondly, the bureaucratic form of organization is typified by the use of rules, regulations or 'official policies' which are defined by the blueprint of the organization and which delimit the actions and conduct of people within the organization in their official functions. Thirdly, there is a high degree of specialization in function and competency with a clearly defined division of labor, especially at the top of the hierarchy.

A fair number of authors have suggested that the bureaucratic organizational form develops in situations where very complex decisions lying beyond the competence of a single person are repeatedly necessary, and also in situations where a relatively small number of people must coordinate the behavior of a large number of people. It has also been suggested that as the importance of money as a status symbol is decreasing, another symbol is taking its place: namely, the authority to manage, to influence other people and to exert control over them. Kahne goes on to argue that the bureaucratic form is the most general administrative form of modern social organizations, and that it is the form most characteristic of present-day mental hospitals. That it is the *only* possible form of organization may be one of our 'costly delusions.'

Let us return to the sanatorium where I worked. It had the typical marks of a bureaucracy. The general task of the organization might be expressed as follows: to lead 'schizophrenics' via psychoanalytic psychotherapy to a radical reconstruction of their personalities and a state of immunity from subsequent psychotic disintegrations. There was a clear hierarchical organization and also a division of tasks and labor among a number of specialist departments. These were: 'Occupational Therapy,' 'Nursing Service,' 'Bookkeeping and Financial Department,' 'Housekeeping Department,' 'Groundskeeping Department,' 'Department of Clinical Administration' (the group of administrators managed by the senior clinical administrator), and last but not least, 'Medical Department' (the group of psychoanalysts and the house doctor who was attached to the clinic for purely medical tasks).

Kahne argues that the subtle, tacit, rational and administratively efficient aspects of bureaucratic organizations form a grave obstacle to any individual care and concern for people. By 'individual concern' one should understand all those measures that lead to social rehabilitation, reeducation and radical correction of interpersonal and intrapsychic defects. Thus individual care can be seen as working to release the full 'latent potentialities for living,' or the reactivating of a thoroughly disrupted process of becoming human. According to Kahne, the bureaucratic form of organization inherently harms and blocks this individual care. In effect his thesis is that a psychiatric institution with this organizational form simply cannot carry out this task.

How does the bureaucratic form of organization get in the way of this kind of care and concern for people?

Kahne gives a straight answer to this question: It results in *impersonal relations between people*. In this form of organization people labeled 'patient' are brought into relation with people labeled 'doctor,' 'nurse' and 'aide.'

At this juncture I have to decide whether to survey in detail the most important literature that describes this dehumanizing process, or whether to present some general conclusions that can be drawn from this literature and leave it at that. I think I would make my whole argument top-heavy if I were to survey in detail the literature on the subject of dehumanization alone. You and I, good reader, would soon feel lost, making our way through this great mass of literature. I think it would be wise just to mention a number of conclusions and describe them briefly.

1. In the hierarchically-structured bureaucratic form of organization those on the upper echelons have the duty and the tendency to issue general directives, orders, guidelines and rules of procedure. These 'top brass' are furthest away from the patients and have the least amount of information about the specific situations patients and staff find themselves in. Relevant information about the various aspects of the ward and the developing interpersonal situations either does not reach them or does so very inadequately. Vital information usually gets stuck at certain junctions in the communication channels of the hierarchy or becomes distorted. This distortion of information is a result of the mutilation to which it is subjected. The human perceptions of those who are part of the hierarchy contribute most to this distortion process. The actions of patient A are reported by psychiatric aide B to nurse C, via her head nurse D, who informs psychiatrist E. The psychiatrist who makes his rounds and gets a 'report' from his head nurse thus knows little or nothing about what is actually going on. Psychiatrist E does or does not report his available information to his superior, and so on. The medical or clinical director at the top of this communication channel may (and usually does) miss the bus entirely.

2. Since it is *taken for granted* within the bureaucratic organization that most subordinates are limited in their capabilities, the important decisions are made by those who are furthest from the patients and spend the least amount of time with them. The patient is entirely excluded from participating in these decisions.

The important decisions are made, generally speaking, by doctors, nurses and supervisors, or the 'nursing service.' In my earlier account this tradition of 'doctor knows best,' written orders and 'nursing care,' combined with the illusory helplessness of the patients, is a prominent feature. Many of the practical examples – for instance, the organization centered around the distribution of pocket money on the ward – exemplify what Kahne describes as activities of an administrative personnel who in a businesslike, efficient way (usually behind the scenes) make decisions whose import goes unnoticed. These decisions, made on the basis of scanty or incorrect information, then have to be communicated downward through the official channel, which leads to the process of 'misunderstanding.' A typical example:

The director of the nursing service at Cedar Haven, in her orientation course for psychiatric aides, would advise them to be very careful in handling keys and to make sure that keys never got lost. The various psychiatric aides whom I interviewed, however, believed they had been given a strict order that 'on no condition and at no time whatever are keys to be handed over to patients.' Thus a progressive director sees her liberal instruction turn into a caricature of a 'never-under-any-circumstances-allow-it' prohibition.

3. The lower-echelon personnel – the 'nurse' and the 'psychiatric aide':

The whole literature on the social organization of the mental hospitals, the principles of the 'therapeutic community' introduced by Maxwell Jones and Sivadon and also modern works dealing with forms of industrial organization show a striking uniformity with respect to the current role of psychiatric nursing personnel and what is desired for updating that role. It really all boils down to one thing: The 'psychiatric nurse' and 'psychiatric aides' are classified as lowest in status and salary; at the same time they are the main contributors to the (institutional) care of the psychically disturbed person. It is by their conduct that this individual care stands or falls. Their actions and behavior determine whether a period on a psychiatric ward is an experience calculated to further growth and self-realization or whether it degenerates into a gradually mounting loss of self-confidence and undermining of ego strength. In my account of the schizophrenic women of Rose Cottage you saw an example of people who have drifted off into a state of apathy and demoralization and have been 'institutionalized' into an unbelievable degree of dependency and passivity.

The lower-echelon workers have been placed in a very difficult position within the bureaucratic organization. Their problems are excellently described in general terms in two books: *Personality and Organization* by Chris Argyris and *The Human Side of Enterprise* by Douglas MacGregor.[3] Both these studies describe the failure of the bureaucratic form of organization in industry. Both confirm that this organizational form creates a climate of relations between people which inhibits instead of promoting growth and maturation of the human personality. Both refer to a growing volume of research on the problems of workers in lower positions in the hierarchical chain. It would seem that the bureaucratic organization, based as it is on the principles of job specialization and 'authorities' or officials in command, does not reckon sufficiently with people's psychological needs, as expressed during recent years in modern theories regarding the development of the human personality.

Argyris concludes that lower-echelon workers are inclined to passivity, dependence and to the development and perfecting of 'a few skin surface abilities.' Attempts to raise the workers' productivity level by means of financial rewards simply do not succeed. Even the well-known 'human relations' approach, which tries to introduce an element of democracy and a human touch into the boss-worker relationship, has not led to the desired results.

Argyris and MacGregor base their explanation for this failure on the fact that the assumptions underlying these corrective measures were wrong from the very start. Mac-Gregor sums up these presuppositions:

1. The average human being has an inherent dislike for work and will avoid it if he can.
2. He must therefore be coerced, controlled and directed, threatened with punishment, in order to achieve the organizational objective.
3. The average human being prefers to be directed, wishes to avoid responsibility, has very little ambition and wants security above all.

He criticizes these assumptions, and his main argument is that most human beings *do* want responsibility and to perform well in their work. What is more, he believes that the average person possesses more creativity and is more intelligent than we suppose. But the (potential) creative capacities of the individual are not utilized in modern industrial organizations. They are lying fallow.

MacGregor argues that people have a need for growth, responsibility, expansion of their own potentialities, creativity and self-reliance. When this personality growth cannot develop in a particular work situation, there is persistent low morale, passivity that lapses into daydreaming and eager anticipation of a well-paid vacation. The 'human relations' approach implies that *participation* and *some measure of democracy* should be introduced, it is true; but 'just to tell a worker he is important when, through actual experience, he sees that he is minor part (task specialization) with little responsibility (lack of control, directive leadership, management control) can only increase the employee's dissatisfaction.'

Both writers maintain that power, prestige, social approval, competition, creativity and independence are the strongest motives underlying human behavior. It is precisely in a bureaucracy that these motivational forces are blocked. When workers cannot get these incentives to personality growth, the outcome – as research has shown – is various attempts at adaptation, expressed in daydreaming, lack of interest and initiative, noninvolvement, etc.

What these studies describe in the context of industry is

familiar to us when we recall the behavior of the Rose Cottage psychiatric aides at the outset of 'the experiment' – daydreaming psychiatric aides, not engaged with patients, wasting their time in front of a television set in the living room on the ward. What MacGregor and Argyris found in industry is even more true of the lower-echelon personnel in mental hospitals. For they are without the chance of competitive 'upward mobility' as a potential stimulus to greater activity. They are given great responsibility but without any real authority – they have to depend on the directives of the head nurse and the doctor. Their activity degenerates into an anxious fending off of any form of responsibility, initiative and creativeness. This abdication of responsibility – 'passing the buck' – also happens in the hierarchical chain when superiors delegate decisions to those below them, marked 'unimportant' or 'for further consideration.' Thus the nursing staff on psychiatric wards are confused on the issue of authority. They end up with a poorly developed sense of professional identity and self-reliance, and consequently offer the psychiatric patient on the ward very few opportunities for normal and clear interpersonal interaction. The psychiatric aide, confronted with people who in the here-and-now situation are experiencing fear, despair, distress and longing, is tongue-tied. His conduct becomes stereotyped. He waits for directives from above, and by the time he gets them, the situation that had confronted him is already over and done with. Usually he is also in a position of 'multiple subordination!' Besides the head nurse, he sometimes has to fetch and carry for the doctor and the person in charge of the occupational therapy department. His attitude toward patients is robotlike. He attempts to translate human activities in all their color and variety into simple terms such as 'sick,' 'excited,' 'aggressive,' 'hallucinating' and so forth. These are his efforts to simplify his perceptual and action world, in order to cope with his own inner confusion.

Kahne describes the characteristic atmosphere of the bureaucratic structure in the mental hospital in Max Weber's words:

The dominance of a spirit of formalistic impersonality, 'sine ira et studio,' without hatred or passion, and hence without affection or enthusiasm. The dominant norms are straight-forward: duty without regard to personal considerations. Everyone is subject to formal equality of treatment; that is, everyone in the same empirical situation.[4]

Thus Kahne sees the mental hospital as a bureaucratic struc-ture with hard traditions that tend to promote primarily impersonal relations between people. Rules prescribe the conduct of personnel and encourage stereotyped attitudes and procedures toward the patients. A real interpersonal 'ex-perience,' therefore, only occurs in specific circumstances.

Eldred and his colleagues [5] refer to the highly stereotyped interactions between schizophrenic patients and personnel, and their research indicates, among other things, that quite often *subsequently to* these impersonal interactions episodic 'psychotic' behavior will suddenly occur. They note that the patient is treated as though he or she were a thing and not a person.

The element of respect is lacking in these interactions. They give, for instance, this telling example:

Mrs. Z seemed to react rather strongly to the contact with Dr. S on his round. The initial contact was brief. Later Mrs. Z called Dr. S back to tell him that her nose was broken. Dr. S refused to discuss this as realistic, and told her that her nose looked all right . . . to him, and again left her. Later, as Dr. S was leaving the ward, Mrs. Z called to him, but he evidently did not hear her and she received no response. Following this she talked to herself and became more and more verbally agitated. By the time Dr. S left, Mrs. Z was overtly hallucinating.

They point out that such a stereotyped form of 'treatment,' continued for months and years on end, is bound to erode the feeling of self-respect, however small, which the patient pre-sumably still had on entry to the mental hospital.

It is also an important item in this research that the number of contacts between staff and patients averages one moment of contact per 25 minutes for each patient. Strikingly enough,

229

personal interactions among the staff members were twice as frequent; and the authors' conclusions, briefly summarized, are as follows:

1. Both the qualitative and the quantitative data lend themselves to the preliminary interpretation, that all members (not just the patients) of the ward-population to some extent share in the attributes of chronicity, which we ordinarily think of as being associated only with the chronic schizophrenics.

2. It is our opinion, that these findings represent social and individual processes on the ward, which are relatively invariant and which can be altered, at our present state of knowledge, only with difficulty by any of the members of the ward-population. The personnel as well as the patients are in this sense victims of their culture.

3. The findings suggest that our contributions to chronicity lie somewhere in the area of relating to the schizophrenic, in ways similar and complementary to his way of relating to us.

Thus one clear observation of Eldred and his colleagues is that the psychiatric nurses and aides *begin gradually to react with just as much chronic schizophrenic behavior as the patients with whom they have to deal.* A fact which once prompted Artiss to write: 'It may indeed be, that the schizophrenic person on the hospital-ward has more control over our behavior than we have over his.'[6]

If we now turn back to the initial situation I found in Rose Cottage, we can apply the data from the literature I have just been citing. Embedded in the bureaucratic structure of the psychoanalytic sanatorium, the ward was conspicuously lacking in autonomy. The formal organizational structure was stunting all self-realization and growth of personal self-reliance, both for the nursing personnel and for the patients. Some six specialist departments (medical, nursing, grounds-keeping, bookkeeping, housekeeping and occupational therapy) had the real say and responsibility, and thus the nurse in charge of the ward was put in a position of multiple subordination. It became her job to satisfy the often very conflicting demands of these departments. Authority was centralized in the higher echelons of the departments, and the result was to constrict the competence of the personnel and their freedom to make decisions. It strengthened their sense of immaturity and promoted impersonal, stereotyped relationships with the psychotic residents. The hierarchical authority structure, inside as well as outside the ward, led to a blockage of communication downward as well as upward. There was an obvious wall between the personnel as a group ('the healthy ones') and the patients as a group ('the sick ones'). Any spontaneous interpersonal interaction at an emotional level, any forming of a group with democratic decision-making and participation on the part of all, was made impossible.

The personnel group had a low morale, which came out in the form of apathy, a lack of initiative and interest, and daydreaming. They tried to cope with this state of affairs through an intensified urge to work (cleaning up, administration) and would retire into the head nurse's room in order to find some human contact with each other. General regulations were obediently followed. In this situation the patient group had withdrawn into emotional isolation and apathy. Their behavior gave substance and form to their intensified self-definition as 'chronically crazy'; they expressed this in bizarre actions, extreme passivity and dependency. Between the two groups – personnel and patients – there was a tacit contract, which (quoting Lipsitt) I defined as a static-pathological-symbiotic interdependency. The 'healthy ones' fed, clothed, looked after and directed the 'sick ones.' The situation had assured the status quo; and the patients' goings-on had been duly categorized by a cultural term – 'chronic schizophrenic.'

REFERENCES

[1] O. A. Will: 'Human Relatedness and the Schizophrenic Reaction,' *Psychiatry*, vol. 22, p. 205 (1959).

[2] M. J. Kahne: 'Bureaucratic Structure and Impersonal Experience in Mental Hospitals,' *Psychiatry*, vol. 22, pp. 363-377 (1959).

[3] C. Argyris: *Personality and Organization* (New York, 1957). D. MacGregor: *The Human Side of Enterprise* (New York, 1960).

[4] M. Weber: *The Theory of Social and Economic Organisation*, E. A. N. Henderson and T. Parsons, trans. (New York, 1947).

[5] S. H. Eldred, N. W. Bell, L. J. Sherman and R. H. Longabaugh: 'Hospital Factors Associated with Maintainance of Chronicity in Schizophrenia,' American Psychiatric Association, Annual Meeting, St. Louis, Missouri (May, 1963).

[6] K. K. Artiss: 'Environmental Therapy,' *Current Psychiatric Therapies*, vol. 4, J. H. Masserman, ed. (1964).

NOTES

J. K. Wing: 'Institutionalism in Mental Hospitals,' *Brit. J. Social and Clinical Psychology*, vol. 1, pp. 28-51 (1962).

The title itself indicates the contents. An essay surveying the literature on 'institutionalism' and the shrivelling up of 'everyday social roles, which is the consequence of a social experience reduced to uniform dullness.'

S. H. Eldred, N. W. Bell, J. L. Sherman and R. H. Longabaugh: 'Hospital Factors Associated with Maintainance of Chronicity in Schizophrenia,' American Psychiatric Association, Annual Meeting, St. Louis, Missouri (May, 1963).

This paper comes straight to the point: 'That mental hospitals can contribute to the perpetuation of mental illness is by now a commonplace observation.' Chronicity is defined as 'stable, atypical interaction patterns, constriction of ideation and interests, flattened or inappropriate effect, and the maintainance of interpersonal distance.'

The syndrome known as 'chronic schizophrenia' is, alongside the existing nidus of problems, an adaptation to the social system of the psychiatric institution, the 'total institution' so brilliantly described by Goffman. The main emphasis in the work of Eldred (among others) lies in the description of stereotyped interactions with patients who 'have in common a quality of the patient being treated as if she were an object or a thing rather than a person.'

None of this has anything to do with friendliness, hostility or 'permissiveness.' It is concerned with the fact that 'the essential human quality of regard or respect is lacking.'

W. H. Dunham and K. S. Weinburg: *The Culture of the State Mental Hospital* (Detroit, 1960).

Besides the condemnatory verdict on the cultural climate of the 'state mental hospital' generally, this study gives a fascinating description of the culture of psychiatric attendants. The findings, that these employees are a sort of tyrannical group who force the patients into total submission, are hardly encouraging.

R. C. Carson, P. M. Marjolis, R. S. Daniels and R. W. Haeine: 'Milieu Homogeneity in Treatment of Psychiatric Patients,' *Psychiatry*, vol. 25, pp. 285–290 (1962).

The emphasis is on the change in the role of psychiatric nursing personnel:

> No longer merely a caretaker agent of the doctor, the trained psychiatric nurse is seen increasingly as a therapist in her own right with associated freedom and associated responsibility.

M. C. Moss and P. Hunter: 'Community Methods of Treatment,' *Brit. J. of Medicine and Psychology*, vol. 36, p. 85 (1963).

Here, too, is a description of a ward of chronic schizophrenic women. The authors' commentary on the role change of the personnel tallies with my own experience:

> This change of role for the nurse and loss of function as a near domestic was a very hard one to accept, symbolizing as it did the laying aside of a collective defense.

At first there was the usual frustrated, angry reaction from the staff, and then later the morale went up. Also a disappearance of what the authors call 'the traditional defence in institutions – the growth of the "we" (staff) and "they" (patients) attitudes.'

R. N. Rapaport: *Community as Doctor: New Perspectives on a Therapeutic Community* (London, 1960).

An important book with much detailed elaboration of the ideas of Maxwell Jones:

> The idea of the therapeutic community is not that one group of individuals (staff) is giving treatment to another group of individuals (patients) but the hospital is viewed as a community in which everyone is expected to make some contribution toward the shared goals of creating a social organization that will have healing properties.

This social organization (the therapeutic milieu) is seen, *not* as a 'routinized background for treatment,' but as a 'vital force'! Very extended consideration is given to 'democratizing' ('Each member of the community should share equally in the exercise of power and decision-making about community affairs, both therapeutic and administrative'), the creating of a horizontal organizational structure (which considerably lessens the negative devolution of responsibility onto 'those in authority'), an appeal to responsibility, ongoing confrontation with reality, the creation of openness and the availability of all information.

T. J. Cheff: 'Perceptual Orientation and Role Performance of Staff-Members in a Mental Hospital Ward,' *Internat. J. of Social Psychiatry*, vol. 8, pp. 113–122.

A publication which does *not* examine the structural problems, but rather describes types of conduct on the part of nursing staff toward patients:

A. H. Stanton and M. S. Schwartz: 'Medical Opinion and the Social Context in the Mental Hospital,' *Psychiatry*, vol. 12, p. 243 (1949).

The critique centers on the fact that the administrator actually gets no training in social psychology and yet must deal with a group and the structuring of this group (something also pointed out again and again by Maxwell Jones).

Ignorance regarding what is *actually* happening on a ward, the inability to *see* it (because the training and the conceptual framework are lacking) leads psychiatrists in institutions to make stereotyped generalizations, which are then doggedly adhered to. The psychiatrists are therefore prone to describe these institutions as oriented to the 'needs of the patient,' without seeing how the 'needs of the institution' really predominate.

J. Henry: 'The Formal Social Structure of a Psychiatric Hospital,' *Psychiatry*, vol. 17, pp. 139–153 (1954).

Next to the work of Kahne, this is one of the most important publications on the formal structure of the psychiatric hospital. Thus the emphasis falls not on people who are at fault (and should do differently and better), but on the structural quality of the *organization* which makes these failures practically inevitable:

> In other words, before one identifies certain people as operating inappropriately within the organization, some attention should be focussed on the difficulties inherent in the organization itself.

I want to emphasize Henry's stress on the principle of 'multiple subordination,' a situation in which the male attendant or psychiatric aide or nurse has to take orders from a number of 'people in authority.' This, partly because the orders are often conflicting, leads to confusion, and Henry quite justifiably wonders whether such an 'external system simply reproduces the internal system of the schizophrenic and, in no small part, the internal systems of many others suffering from mental illness.'

S. P. Kraus: 'Considerations and Problems of Ward Care for Schizophrenic Patients,' *Psychiatry*, vol. 17, pp. 283–293 (1954).

Kraus describes the same sort of situation as existed in Rose Cottage. 'Schizophrenic' patients of long standing become almost invisible, totally isolated, dependent, and as far as normal human activity is concerned, in a state of paralysis.

A. R. Frank and A. G. Centuria: 'The Therapeutic Community in a Private General Hospital,' *Comprehensive Psychiatry*, vol. III (June, 1962).

These authors warn us (as many others have) not to wrap the term 'therapeutic community' in a veil of glory so vague that it gets lost to sight. Activities defined as 'progressive,' 'reactivating,' 'democratizing,' the introduction of group meetings and heaven knows what other reforms – it is better *not* to include these under the term 'therapeutic community.' The authors stress the very clear responsibility that must accrue to patients in the *decision process* regarding how people live and are 'treated' within the institution.

A. H. Stanton: 'Milieu Therapy and the Development of Insight,' *Psychiatry*, vol. 24, pp. 19–29 (1961).

At the beginning of this article Stanton examines the work of a pioneer in the field of 'milieu therapy,' Ernst Simnel (the original publication: 'Psychoanalytic Treatment in a Sanatorium,' *International Journal of Psychoanalysis*, vol. 10, pp. 70–89 [1929]). Simnel put the stress on the *individual*. After a period of satisfying the needs of people whose deprivation had been very real, the milieu attempted to introduce frustration (and reality). This principle was adopted by William Menninger ('Psychoanalytic Principles Applied to the Treatment of Hospitalized Patients,' *Bull. of Menninger Clinic*, vol. 1, pp. 35–43 [1937]) and also by Bullard at Chestnut Lodge. Sivadon had already taken a somewhat different road by eventually aiming at the creation of groups by the patients (who could jointly express their antagonism toward the staff and so find cohesion as a group).

Stanton rightly points to Sullivan, who was among the first to introduce on his ward the principles of 'patient participation,' group therapy and a 'patient government.' Then comes Maxwell Jones, of course (*Social Psychiatry* [London, 1952]), with his explicit emphasis on the formation of a genuine community, with staff and patients on the same footing, in interaction and struggling toward decisions taken by all together. In America this was put into practice with psychotic people by Harry Wilmer (H. A. Wilmer: *Social Psychiatry in Action* [Springfield, Ill., 1958]); and Rapaport has elaborated this system (R. N. Rapaport: *Community as Doctor* [London, 1960]).

For the rest, this article provides a survey of some of the literature.

L. M. Lapenna: 'Delineating the Therapeutic Community,' *Mental Hospitals* (July, 1963).

A lucid survey of the division of roles – 'healthy' versus 'sick,' non-emotional, impersonal interactions between personnel and patients.

The author comes to the conclusion that among the group of doctors, nurses and male attendants major differences exist, not only in status but also in attitude, expectations and values. Thus a fragmented social field emerges. And that is the last thing that people with profound conflicts and 'disruptions' need.

Lapenna is quite forthright in urging the creation of an organization in which both *personnel* and *patients* can grow. The horizontal hierarchical structure (in which patients themselves ultimately participate as co-therapists), the daily community meeting and a new mode of formulating the role behavior of the personnel (including the 'doctor') are described in some detail.

D. F. Hooper: 'Changing the Milieu in a Psychiatric Ward,' *Human Relations*, vol. 15, pp. 111–123 (1962).

An attempt to induce some change and life in a ward with fifty women, most of whom were vegetating in passivity and were totally inactive. The nurses have no real emotional communication; and their behavior is characterized as 'involved superiority.' The rigid, status-bound, hierarchical setting yields the same type of relation between superior and subordinate. In fact, after the literal opening up of the ward, very little real change occurs.

H. A. Wilmer: *Social Psychiatry in Action* (Springfield, Ill., 1956).

Wilmer introduces Maxwell Jones's principles concerning psychotic clients. He argues:

> In the therapeutic community the hospital is conceptualized literally as a form of community, both of patients and of staff, and its pattern of life is designed to create an environment – a milieu – that reproduces as nearly as possible the types of interpersonal communication and action that exist in the outside world from which the patient has come and to which it is hoped he will be able to return as a useful member. Staff-patient and patient-staff relation take their form, like the relations of persons in the outside world, from common membership in the social group and the mutual responsibility that attends this membership.

Wilmer, too, sees clearly that the role of 'being sick' may be, among other things, a response to the expectation pattern of the staff (Wilmer alludes to what we call 'chronic-schizophrenic modes of being'). The point at issue is to change this whole pattern of expectation among the staff ('He's certain to be dangerous, he has no self-control, he can't be held responsible,' etc.). To achieve this:

> The treatment of the staff, therefore, is all-important. All this adds

up to the fact that a therapeutic community is, first of all, therapeutic for the staff.

The rigid roles enforced by the traditional hierarchy do not require the personnel to feel and think very much. There are ready-made solutions, patients' conduct can be disposed of immediately as 'clinical behavior.' The system is clear, the patient must adapt, and is treated as a quasi-thing 'rather than a living creature of the same order as themselves [the staff].' In this situation any real human contact is valued, of course, but it is not prescribed as an indispensable goal of the professional.

Wilmer stresses the daily community meeting as the place where the personnel can give vent to their own feelings and so arrive at an alteration of role. The milieu created 'permitted recovery, rather than driving patients deeper into insanity as, unfortunately, conventional hospital practices frequently do!'

Wilmer also takes up the concept of 'democracy,' which is often referred to in the literature on the 'therapeutic community.' There can be no question of democracy, obviously, for the patients cannot vote to get rid of the staff. The staff have to have authority – the way they use it is the crucial point.

E. F. Galioni: 'Evaluation of a Treatment Program for Chronically Ill Schizophrenic Patients – a Six Year Program,' in *Chronic Schizophrenia: Explorations in Theory and Treatment*, L. Appleby, J. M. Scher and J. Cumming, eds. (Glencoe, Ill., 1960).

A general account of a mixture of a 'total push program' as described by Myerson (A. Myerson: 'Theory and Principle of the "Total Push" Method in Treatment of Chronic Schizophrenia,' *Am. J. of Psychiatry*, vol. 95, pp. 1197–1204 [1939]) and the introduction of the principles of Maxwell Jones. A lot of group therapy, heavy pressure, with the aim in view of mobilizing the totally 'passively-turned-in-on-oneself' patients, and emphasis on the growing self-reliance of the ward: 'Administrative policy shifted away from direct central administrative control toward increasing ward autonomy.'

J. Kohler and L. Shapiro: 'Avoidance Patterns in Staff-Patient Interaction on a Chronic Schizophrenic Treatment Ward,' *Psychiatry*, vol. 27, pp. 377–389 (1964).

A confirmation of the rather obvious idea that staff seek contact with one another rather than incur the repeated frustration of being rejected by 'withdrawn chronic schizophrenics'! It is curious that these authors should continue to look for the answer in the appointment of *better qualified personnel*.

D. H. Clark, D. F. Hooper and E. G. Oram: 'Creating a Therapeutic Community in a Psychiatric Ward,' *Human Relations*, vol. 15, pp. 123–149 (1962).

Much in this article is wholly consonant with my experiences in Rose Cottage. The new approach led first to a phase of resistance: 'The whole ward appeared to be hanging on grimly to the old order which was so severely threatened.' There is a good description of the fear and bewilderment experienced by the psychiatric nursing personnel in the course of the change toward a more 'democratic' structure. What impressed me in this article were a number of conclusions that give food for thought:

1. If just one ward of a psychiatric hospital really does evolve toward a different structure, such a ward will become isolated, *will form into a group and display a sort of paranoid posture in the face of the remainder of the institution.*
2. What has been little analyzed is . . . the role of the 'reformer.' If he succeeds, a new community springs up. The trouble is that as soon as he departs, the ward gradually sinks back into the old (traditional) form of organization.

J. Kahne: 'Rehabilitation of Chronic Mental Patients,' *Psychiatric Quarterly*, vol. 37, p. 704 (1963).

Kahne also points out the importance of a more authentic relation between personnel and clients.

K. Kayser: 'A Therapeutic Community with Chronic Schizophrenics,' *6th Int. Cong. of Psychotherapy, London 1964*, pp. 52–59 (Basle/New York, 1965).

A brief report in which are described experiences similar to those which occurred in Rose Cottage.

A. Etzioni: 'Interpersonal and Structural Factors in the Study of Mental Hospitals,' *Psychiatry*, vol. 23 (Feb. 1960).

A study devoted to the formal, structural aspects of the organization of the mental hospital. With this main theme as a starting point, Etzioni sets out to analyze afresh the disruptions of communication between personnel and the attitude of 'nursing personnel' towards patients.

Etzioni objects rather strongly to the term 'hospital as a small society,' because so many factors are at work outside the hospital that make a functional autonomy of the institution ('functional autonomy means that all the basic functional needs of a social system are internally regulated') illusory. This also applies to the 'roles' played by various professionals. We should not forget, Etzioni says, that powerful factors are operative *outside* the institution ('the governors,' the 'board of management,' the 'health department') which very largely determine the role conduct of the personnel of a mental hospital (medical and nursing staff), their image and their prestige.

12. JOANE

I return to a concrete situation with a concrete person, a situation that went on for quite a time, for I am condensing in this chapter an experience that lasted for four and a half years. The person's name is Joane. She was one of the people signed to me for psychotherapy.

Why I have chosen her to write about will become clear to you as the story proceeds. My aim is once again to stress a central theme: weakness. The technical term in psychoanalytic jargon is 'ego weakness' (the opposite of 'ego strength'), and a lot has been published on the subject. It seems to me right, before I present you with some theory, to describe the experience in question.

I meet Joane for the first time on the day of her admission to Cedar Haven; and I greet her on the ward, where she is sitting somewhat forlorn, surrounded by her luggage. She is thirty-two, and looks rather attractive, though much younger than her years. The first session is, as always, an important one. When I ask her the reason for her coming, she replies: 'I'm weak. I feel pushed around by everybody. I must be able to decide things for myself. And I can't. My father and mother and my husband have decided everything for me. I can't make quick decisions and solve the problems the children put to me.

239

Then I feel paralyzed, numbed, and I have no idea what I ought to do. I've always tried to do what my parents said.'

Her troubles started soon after her marriage. She met her husband at a university where he 'discovered' her. She was very bashful and retiring and felt very inferior among her classmates. She quickly gave way to his insistence on having sexual intercourse and after a few months discovered she was pregnant. They were married and a son was born; two years later a second son arrived.

Joane felt that her marriage had misfired from the very start. Marriage, as she envisioned it, meant being completely managed and protected by a strong but tender husband. Her husband often left her alone, going off with his friends on weekends to play bridge. He also drank too much and found it hard to get up in the morning. He had a moderately well-paying job in a factory. Joane felt totally dominated by her husband, and gradually came to realize that she was unable to solve any practical problems without his continual help and support. She felt more and more isolated in the marriage and developed a strong resistance to sexual intercourse, which her husband sometimes urged upon her because he supposed that 'everything would then turn out all right.' Bit by bit she became tremendously angry with her husband, without ever giving vent to the anger.

From the outset her children made demands on her to which she was not equal. She describes them as 'nervy' and in phrases like 'They didn't behave properly.' When she was young, she herself had always been 'sweet' and tried to please her parents by being very quiet and obedient. Her children were nothing like that. They were noisy, ran around the house, and Joane never knew how to manage them. 'They were so much like boys.'

Both children asked immediately for a great deal of physical contact and that filled her with anxiety because she did not know how far she could go with them. With both children breast-feeding was a total calamity.

In order to cope with her difficulties she would sometimes fasten the children in bed with a strap. Later she started hitting them with a leather belt to force them to be quiet and do as they were told. Her husband was either unaware of this situation or he ignored the seriousness of it.

Several years after her marriage Joane found some support in a church she had joined. She became very active there as the chairman of a group of women. She sang in the choir. The warm colour of the stain-glass windows of the church gave her a feeling of home.

When for the first time she made some contact with people in the bible class, she felt that she was part of a group. She found the minister most helpful. When he met her he told her he would be able to help her with her marital problems. She sat next to him in the bible class, where he would often hand her the hymnbook. Although they were never alone together, Joane noticed at once that he was attracted to her. Sometimes she would see his hand trembling, and she gradually got the feeling that he was basing his preaching on the problems she confided to him from time to time.

The minister not only baptized the two children, but was always there to give her advice, and once a week she would ring him up. Over two years she had lengthy conversations with this man on the telephone, in the course of which he would give her advice and guidance.

Bit by bit her feeling grew that he was making countless allusions to her in his sermons. Sometimes she felt he was complimenting her for doing a good job, and sometimes she felt she was being criticized for tackling her problems at home in the wrong way.

One Sunday his sermon made it quite clear to her 'that the minister would soon leave his wife and then I would be his wife.' She had the idea that everybody in the church heard this, and that it was being said in the congregation that Joane would be rescued by a new marriage with the minister, and that this came from God.

Joane considered herself a complete washout as a mother and wife, and it was during this period that she began asking God to help her not to be so tensed up, so ridden with anxiety and uncertainty. While at prayer, she had a feeling on several occasions that God would help her and that he would even accept her if she was not strong and assertive. She told me:

During that prayer I felt completely accepted by God, a deep, authentic love that makes you feel completely accepted. If I could get that feeling back again, I should be sure of myself. And then I would stop having these outbursts of temper. I would feel secure in the love that I possessed, and I could transfer that love to my children, and so I could accept the children as I myself would feel accepted.

Eventually Joane told the minister what she had come to believe. The man became alarmed and put her in touch with a psychologist, who after several conversations decided that the case was 'much too serious for him' and referred her to a psychiatrist. Her husband, informed by the minister of his wife's condition, felt humiliated, especially because Joane had told several church members about her 'delusions.'

Over the next two years she had regular conversations, two or three times a week, with her psychiatrist, but concluded that therapy was not getting her very far. She gradually lost the 'delusions,' but according to her this was not a result of the psychotherapy but rather because absolutely nothing had happened. The minister was transferred to another church. The delusions gradually acquired a sort of dreamlike quality and the real nature of her marital situation once again became apparent:

I came to myself again, was amazed at my capacity for imagining things and was grateful for the memory.

She felt that her psychiatrist had given her little help, because during the sessions he usually remained seated behind his desk in silence, every now and again tossing in her direction a few phrases on the reasons for the intense distaste she experienced during sexual intercourse. This did not help her; all it did was strengthen the feeling that she was a complete failure as a wife and mother.

Once she threw her younger boy down the stairs. On various occasions before that she had lost control of herself in a bout of rage, but her husband had continued to ignore the seriousness of the situation. This time, however, it became clear that she had to be admitted to a hospital, and she landed in a psychiatric clinic, where she stayed for seven weeks.

She remembered very little of this period. She put on 30 pounds; and all she wanted to do was sleep. She was not really sure why she had been sent there; she just got used to the idea. When she got back home, things went from bad to worse. Her husband was despondent and felt rejected because of her 'delusions about marriage'; the new church that he obliged her to attend was too chilly and too big for her. Her home had gone. She gradually became more and more concerned about her bursts of temper: 'I sensed that these attacks were getting more and more frequent.' A tremendous amount of tension developed between her and her husband, and Joane was often utterly apathetic. She lived in a sort of fog, got a pretty big dosage of tranquilizers from her psychiatrist and slept most of the day. In the end there were heated scenes, and she is reported to have once threatened her husband with a knife. Her psychiatrist concluded that her condition was getting worse, and in consultation with her husband and parents arrangements were made to admit her to Cedar Haven.

Joane felt completely isolated and in despair. Her mind was gradually filled with thoughts of suicide. She also became convinced that her children would be better dead than growing up to become 'delinquents' because of their experiences with a 'psychiatrically sick mother.'

One Sunday morning a few years later she tried to sever her younger son's radial arteries with a razor. Her intention was to kill both children and then commit suicide:

But he woke up and started crying. Then I put the razor aside and bandaged his wrist. That was the end of the destruction. There was not even a feeling that I had done something wrong. My son was the one who irritated me most. I thought: Now I'm going to do something that no one would expect. I'm going to do something wrong. I was sick of myself because I'd never had the guts to do anything on my own, the guts to be an individual and have an opinion of my own.

When I asked her to tell me more about this, she went on:

I never rebelled when I was a teenager. I was always supposed to be nice and good, to my parents. I was quiet and
went to bed. When I picked up the razor, it was like saying
to myself: Do it *now*, do something *now* that nobody will
like. It was as if I was determined to be some sort of
individual.

For this story I have drawn on a great number of sessions. I
knew nothing of it when I met Joane for the first time, along
with her father, mother and husband. What follows now is a
part of their story.

The father strikes me as the most sensible of the three. He is
an elderly man, somewhat stooping and thick-set. He is not
given to many words, yet when he does speak, it is difficult to
interrupt him. In the contacts I have with him in subsequent
years Joane's father gives me no more than a few details about
his own youth. He apparently lost his mother when he was
very young and for some years lived with an uncle and aunt
on a farm near a large city. There is little that Joane's father
can tell me about his early years beyond the fact that his
father was a bohemian character who plunged from one
business venture into another. Throughout those years he had
been a very isolated person; and after that he made it his chief
purpose to show his disorganized and dissolute father that 'it
didn't have to be like that.' He went to college and at twenty-
five started his own business. He married and had three
children, two sons and a daughter, born in rapid succession.
When the marriage was about seven years old, his wife ran
away with another man. He said about this: 'I wasn't very free
and she was very passionate, she obviously needed more
affection.'

After his first wife had left him, the three children were
looked after by their maternal grandparents. The father slowly
built his business into a thriving firm employing about several
hundred people. He married his secretary, Joane's mother.
Her parents and grandparents had been country people. After
having worked for some years as a secretary, she married her
boss and agreed to take over the care of his three children.

After being married for several years she pressed to have a
child of her own. With some reluctance her husband con-

244

sented. The reason for her birth is movingly explained to me by Joane later on, when she starts one of the first sessions by saying: 'My father gave my mother the child she wanted to have.'

About Joane's very early years neither parent has very much to say. It was primarily her half-brother who had a lot to do with her. Her sister troubled herself less about her and was a reserved girl who went her own way. The parents describe Joane as having been very highly strung in junior high school; she was always quite terrified of examinations. She did not talk to her parents very much. The impression is of a quiet, rather gentle child, growing up in an old home with elderly parents.

At this point I shall interrupt the account given by the parents on their first visit in order to give you more particulars about the impressions both of them make on me. The mother is a few years younger than her husband and speaks with a high-pitched, plaintive voice. Behind the thick lenses of her glasses she appears at times to be crying. The impression she makes is of a helpless child – and very depressed. The father makes a more powerful impression, but there is something guilty about him. I notice how poorly clad both parents are. Joane's father is, after all, a man of some substance. The mother keeps telling me that she is just a simple country girl, points during the conversation – with some scorn – to her husband and says: 'You must ask my husband that.' When I insist on having more particulars about Joane as a small girl, the mother says: 'Oh dear, doctor, I don't know what I should tell you about it. We were both fairly old when Joane arrived, and we did not know how to bring up children. We still don't, even now.'

With Joane it is fairly easy to make contact. I see her four times a week, and she spends the first few months telling me in broad outline about the course her life has taken. Her account of her early years is the story of an only child. The distance between her and her half-brother and half-sister was considerable. She draws for me the house in which she spent her entire girlhood. She talks in a thin voice and sits huddled up in her chair. The drawing she makes of the house is vague, with thin lines; her handwriting is extremely childish. She talks much

245

more about her father than about her mother. She can only remember him as a man who worked hard, rose early and made his own breakfast. When he got home he was tired and remained preoccupied with his work. He usually retreated behind his newspaper, and Joane recalls her mother repeatedly admonishing her 'not to bother Dad' and above all to 'respect' him.

Joane describes her father as 'a big man.' She had the feeling that her father got much more tensed up when people came too close to him. His expression would change. His gestures seemed more relaxed if you kept your distance from him:

> That's how you can tell he doesn't want to be disturbed. Sometimes because he has a vacant expression on his face. He doesn't talk much. His whole appearance seems to be one of stress and strain.

Father's sole interest outside his work was weekend sailing. He went regularly for regattas, but Joane cannot recall that he ever took the family on a trip just for pleasure. The first time he took her with him on these races was when she was thirteen years old. She was then allowed to go because she 'had the right weight.' She remembers being allowed to lie on the fo'c'sle and that she was afraid because her father would curse and swear during the race. She cannot remember ever being caressed by her father or ever having sat on his lap:

> Father was God and I was full of respect for him. Father didn't wish to be disturbed.

Later on, when I speak with the father alone and try to get him talking a bit about his attitude at home, he confirms much of what Joane has told me. He tells how in his youth he went for an employee in a fit of fury, and it was only because colleagues forcibly restrained him that 'a murder was prevented. I would certainly have killed the man, and from then on became very much afraid of my own anger. I made up my mind to suppress my feelings and keep them under control in all circumstances.'

During my meetings with the father I can sense the truth of

much that Joane has told me. He is a sensitive man, very reticent, but also gives the impression of being explosive.

Joane tells me that for as long as she can remember her father and mother led entirely separate lives. She cannot recall any expression of tenderness between them. They never embraced each other. The mother was forever impressing upon her that giving physical expression to feelings of tenderness and friendship was just 'show'; when they sometimes saw people on the street walking arm in arm or with their arms around each other, her mother would always be irritated and say: 'It's all just for show. They do it to make an impression.' No friends came to visit her mother and father at their house, and Joane describes her parents as asocial. (This is confirmed later on by the father and mother.) She recalls the long evenings when her parents played solitaire, and it was typical of the family that not much was said. While she was in high school she went to bed every evening at about eight o'clock: 'I had nothing to do.' After supper – and the ritual of looking through the newspapers – she would go up to her room and play records, but they depressed her too much: 'I couldn't listen to Tchaikovsky.' She explains that by evening she was always very tired and sleepy. She gives me a glimpse into what this 'symptom' signifies when I ask her on one occasion to have a session later in the evening. When I inquire whether she won't be too sleepy for it, she replies: 'Oh no. At least I've got something to look forward to now.'

Even in the first few months of our contact Joane discloses to me that my listening with such understanding and sorting things out arouses intense feelings in her. Her whole body, she says, tingles as never before, and during the sessions she can feel an enormous desire welling up in her to touch me. She puts into words her yearning to be close to me, to touch my hair, face and chest, and the feeling is so strong that she often literally clings to her chair in order not to be overwhelmed by it. She begins to inform me about her idea that she comes across me here, there and everywhere on the grounds of the clinic. The experience of meeting someone who will talk to her and try to understand her and the feelings this evokes in her appear to be so strange and new that she is alarmed. Sometimes she exclaims: 'I can't understand all this, it's all so new. You're a doctor, after all, and I'm a patient. How is it, then, that everything becomes so personal?'

She is afraid the situation will get out of hand, that she will infect me with her emotions and longings and that a sort of explosion of feeling will occur between us, a fusing together, in which the formal relationship of doctor and patient will be completely destroyed. This alarms and confuses her a great deal. She simply cannot understand that I can go on quietly sitting there. She voices her great fear that I will not give her my approval, that I will reject her if she tells me about her physical yearnings. She will often ask me whether I am not too tired, too preoccupied, too tensed up to listen to her:

> I sometimes look at your face, yesterday your eyebrows were raised and your eyes were wide open. That meant I had to be careful with my feelings. You're very hard-pressed with consultations with other doctors. You won't want to be troubled with the foolish things I have to say. You have more important things to do.

Sometimes she describes me as an immovable stone, at other times as if I have the greatest difficulty in keeping very explosive feelings under control. Although any direct suggestion of a link with the experiences she had with her father seems to make little impression on Joane, she does give me more information about how she felt about her father:

> Yes, father had a way of walking that always gave me a feeling I must be on my guard. The look on his face was strained. Sometimes it was as though he didn't want to let people get too close. His muscles were tense. He said little and his whole appearance seemed tensed up. Particularly if something went wrong at work, he would be very tense at home. But he never talked to me or mother about what was going on at the firm. Mother never knew anything about that. Now I feel like a little girl who wants to run away to father and cry on his shoulder.

It is becoming clear to me as we go along that Joane is trying to give a form to this multiplicity of overwhelming experiences, to provide a formula that will make sense out of everything. It will not surprise you that she uses the same formula she had earlier used to try to define her relationship to the minister. Joane starts telling me of her growing feeling that I will marry her. Everything points to it. She believes that other patients on the ward are whispering about the prospective marriage. People are looking at her. All sorts of minor happenings point in the same direction. When I ask what 'marrying' means to her, she describes it as 'a deliverance sent by God.' Obviously she feels like a child and perceives me as a mixture of kind mother and strong father. Joane describes the feelings which a single movement, an understanding gesture or the sound of my voice are enough to arouse in her. A tidal wave of 'new feeling' flows through her and makes her completely helpless:

I'm afraid of this feeling, as though I were a puppet and you, by a single gesture or the sound of your voice, were pulling the strings. My heart thumps and I imagine to myself what it would be like to be married to you.

On the ward Joane is very isolated. There is no one with whom she can spontaneously communicate. When I am on evening duty, she will often ring me up in order to hear my voice. She will say:

I would have liked to go to your room. And if you should be asleep, then I would be able to touch you, your back, and run my hands through your hair.

Joane keeps expressing a wish to come running to me and to embrace me and be embraced by me. A burning desire for a physical blending together, a longing to be touched and kissed. Again she tells me that she cannot remember ever having sat on her father's lap.

During our sessions Joane will sometimes break off in the middle of whatever she is describing and begin to sigh and moan; and I find something in my notes to the effect that 'she looks at me like someone walking through a desert who suddenly sees some water.'

This desire to touch me gradually becomes so powerful and

dominates the psychotherapeutic sessions so completely that Joane arrives at a number of vague formulations designed to explain it all. She believes that I make certain gestures, seductive moves, in order to arouse desire in her. If I smoke a pipe during the sessions, she will whisper: 'Why are you making that noise?' Not without some difficulty we discover that the scarcely audible smacking sound evokes in her a longing to suck and kiss me. Sometimes, when I am bending foward, she expresses a desire to suck my breast. She also believes that the purpose of my various seductive gestures and noises could well be that I intend to satisfy my own physical desire for her.

Another theme that comes out quite clearly in our sessions is Joane's fear that I will take advantage of her. She says she is afraid that I am not really interested in her, but am only using her as a guinea pig, an object of research. Sometimes she will say: 'Do you want to marry me for my money?' By way of counterpart she makes known her wish that I should be completely independent, strong and protective and devoid of any need, so that she can be protected, managed and supported by me in total dependency.

Joane is slowly evolving the notion that God is commanding her to marry me. Thus she sends me a note:

> I still believe that God is calling me and that I must marry you. Please don't say 'goodbye' at the end of the session. And again, I feel you are protecting me.
>
> Joane

In the course of our sessions she tells me more about the feeling that comes over her. Not only is she going to marry me, but afterwards she herself will die. She describes it as a sort of love sacrifice, a surrender to me; and through her death she will be an example for others. As we talk about these feelings, it occurs to me that she is protecting and cherishing this developed 'world of delusion' and is begging me, sometimes in so many words, not to take it away from her:

> When you're away and I can't get to you, I feel lost. I feel utterly hopeless, I feel I am a part of you.

A few days later she makes everything somewhat clearer to me:

I feel God is giving me peace and strength. He has brought me here; and now I feel this waiting for you to ask me to marry you must be a period of testing, to find out whether I'm good enough for it. If I didn't have these ideas, I couldn't cope with things. In my marriage I got a tremendous sense of weariness, of being no good at all. I couldn't even keep the children's beds clean, I took no pleasure in living and I couldn't understand why it was so hard. To be able to laugh, not to be so exhausted, to enjoy the children, to lose your temper and see the anger go away, to feel kindly toward the person you're mad at. All this was beyond me. I felt there was something terribly wrong with me.

Joane feels sometimes that the 'church' and I have a sort of working agreement to save her. She has been to church and heard the minister there talking about the nobility and sufferings of man. He also said something about a 'stalwart figure.' Joane felt that he was really talking about her and about what was going on between her and me. She gradually begins to experience me as God and feels like a child. She asks on one occasion, in a whisper: 'Are you God?'

I notice how little connection she makes between these experiences and her relationship with her mother and father. Still, a number of patterns are slowly becoming clearer. She had indeed experienced her father as God; and she recalls how she would often sit on the sofa in the living room, staring at him. He would sit a long way from her, behind his newspaper.

I sat for hours watching him, but he never signaled me to come closer. I would have liked to sit on his lap and touch him, but I had an idea that he didn't want that. I can't remember ever touching Father.

When she comes running toward me and I try in one way or another to put some limit on her search for physical contact with me without making her feel rejected, she often says how surprised she is that I don't 'explode': 'I don't

251

understand how you can keep such a tight rein on yourself.' This she again associates with her father, who made her feel that he was always sitting on top of his emotions, as though he might explode at any moment. Sitting on her father's lap, then, entailed the risk that he might not be able to control himself and an incestuous sexual relationship might develop. At any rate that is the idea I have evolved about it.

In the months that follow it becomes increasingly evident in what world Joane is involving me, what function she assigns to me in that world of 'make-believe marriage.' It is a world in which everything points to a savior who will lift Joane out of her desperate isolation. The savior is a God, an ideal father- and mother-figure who protects and encourages, keeps watch, is present everywhere and at all times, directing and guiding. This world of hers finds expression in a number of examples and experiences she describes to me.

On the ward Joane acquires a roommate who can sometimes be aggressive. She copes with her fear of this companion in the following way: She tells me in the course of a session that there 'is now a television set, connected up to the head nurse and from there to your room. So you are keeping a lookout and I feel safe.'

One evening Joane tries to find the place where I live. She gets lost in the woods and is eventually found there by a male aide. She tells me: 'It was the dead of night, but I was not frightened. You knew that I was bound to come. You were all around me.'

Walking all by herself in Washington, she sees a white Volkswagen (there are thousands of them) and immediately she feels less afraid, because she is sure it is mine. I am keeping watch, she is not alone. She often experiences my consulting room as a warm, enveloping place of shelter where she can find security during the many sessions in which she lies speechless on the couch. It comes out later how terrified Joane is of living on the ward, the outbursts of aggression on the part of certain other patients, the group sessions conducted by the ward psychiatrist.

Her fellow patients are all so articulate – and Joane, who sometimes utters only one remark at these meetings, usually sits watching, silent and petrified, feeling everything around her as a threat.

Everything that Joane feels to be threatening in her surroundings, she appears to relate to me, in the sense that in the midst of the threat there dawns upon her the serene conviction of an approaching 'marriage.'

She sees me taking a walk with another schizophrenic patient; and during the session she comments:

D. is a patient to whom you're obliged to give some of your time, because you have to work as a psychiatrist. But still you walked past me to let me know that you preferred me.

So in this phase she is warding off feelings of great desolation and fierce jealousy.

This world of make-believe marriage and its variations Joane describes clearly on one occasion *in its functional significance*:

They're my crutches. I can't do without this fantasy, which is my reality – not yet. If none of this were true, I'd feel forsaken. If you were just an ordinary psychiatrist, seeing me every day as one of his patients, I'd feel lost and hopeless.

Joane often intimates that marriage is a defense against the overwhelming fear of being 'abandoned' and being reduced 'to nothing.' She is always bringing out the sense of 'nothingness,' which she feels deep down in her and which would sweep her away, if the fantasy were all untrue.

My activities in this phase of growing delusion in which I occupy such a central place are restricted mainly to keeping communication going; and this gives me the feeling that the world of delusion is her only bridge to reality. It seems to me in retrospect that I took the greatest care to preserve that fragile thread.

I invite her always to speak out freely and I interpret the 'marriage world' as an attempt to rationalize on the part of somebody who feels lonely and weak. From time to time I try to get her to say more about her experiences as a youngster, but here I come up against considerable resistance. It is as if

253

she is unwilling to admit the reality of those experiences. She will not take a critical look, stand back and consider things in a new perspective. It makes little sense to her, it would seem, to contemplate reality – the reality of the situation now, in relation to her husband and children, the reality of the relation to me and her fellow patients on the ward. Nor is she prepared to talk about her early years, about her home atmosphere (which seems to me enormously unreal, but which she refuses to describe in any detail). When I urge her to do so, she soon becomes terrified, shoots off into generalizations and comes out with some evasion: 'It wasn't different with us at home, really, than with so many other people.'

Having to speak about the role played by her mother Joane finds particularly threatening. As the years pass, it becomes clear to me why. I shall condense what she has to say about her relationship with her mother.

To Joane, Mother was the 'truth.' Her mother received Joane as a kind of gift from her husband. The birth was a difficult one; and the pregnancy was complicated by appendicitis, which soon after the birth necessitated an operation. Her mother frequently impressed on Joane the sacrifices she had made for her – how mortally dangerous childbearing had been. Joane felt that her mother was exhorting her to profound gratitude and loyalty.

Besides the theme: 'You should be grateful to me for the sacrifices I made for you during my pregnancy,' there was another: 'You must believe in me and obey me unconditionally.' What Mother said counted as 'the truth.' Mother defined the world for Joane. As Mother perceived the world, so the world *was*.

What I begin to realize from Joane's diffident, at times casual, comments on this relationship to her mother are the unlikely dimensions of what Helm Stierlin once called 'the adaptation to the stronger person's reality.' [1] Her mother defined Joane as 'weak.'

There is a great deal condensed in a single recollection. Joane once heard her mother say: 'I don't send my child out on an errand. I prefer to do it myself. That's much more efficient and it's quicker.' Joane puts a lot of store by this recollection, as it symbolizes an essential aspect of what she went through. She is regarded as an immature, ignorant, weak child, who needs to have explained to her what the world is about. There is really very little that Joane's mother lets the child experience for *herself*; but she is forever telling her daughter how her own experiences have led to a particular perception of the world.

I have been trying to initiate you via general observations; now I shall describe in somewhat more specific terms the world that the mother passed on to her daughter.

Everything at home has its proper place. The furniture is not to be shifted around. Joane recalls that her mother got very upset if anything was shifted.

> I once danced up and down on a bed that had been made. Mother then got very upset. She was afraid it would get broken.

Another recollection:

> Mother had made a pudding one day. I wanted to taste a bit and stuck a spoon into it. Then she was real mad at me.

Joane describes the house not only as a place of uncompromising orderliness but of almost deathly silence as well. Every expression of vitality is stifled, it seems. Joane's parents seldom speak to each other; and her description of the evenings, when the parents indulged in silent games of solitaire and Joane went to bed early and played records in her room, reflects a deep, depressive loneliness. The parents went out very little, seldom entertained friends and a party is something Joane cannot ever remember.

This must have been in sharp contrast to the rest of the community. Such social isolation certainly is counter to the life-style of most American business people, for whom the cocktail party and the dinner party are habitual. The father sought social contact with his business acquaintances on weekends, when he would sail his yacht. He would go racing and stay at his country club ... a life apart. Apparently he once took his wife to this club with him. She got a bit drunk and said things that endangered her husband's business interests.

After this incident her husband thought it better not to take her along. 'The world in which I had to keep my head above water was too competitive,' the father explained later. 'My wife couldn't take a drink. She gave too much away.' After that Joane's mother seems to have retreated more and more into the role of martyr for the cause. Outwardly, she played before her daughter the role of 'courageous resignation,' the woman who in quiet acceptance looks up to a husband whom she presents to her daughter as 'great.' 'You must always look up to him,' she would often say. 'We are happily married.'

What strikes me most, relying as I must on Joane's descriptions and what the mother has told me herself, is the persistent and flagrant denial of the mother's real feelings. In the conversations I had with her, more of the reality sometimes emerges. She is then an embittered, deeply depressed woman who knows very well how neglected she has felt:

> There's no point in talking about it anymore. It's all so hopeless, anyway. He has his business. I used to be of some help in the old days – when I was his secretary – but now I'm pushed aside. That's the way it is, and I like it that way.

Then she starts to brood on it, and as the sadness wells up behind her thick lenses, she begins to laugh, a queer, high-pitched laugh:

> Of course I've always made out to Joane that I was very happy, that things were all right between us. I asked her always to respect him. No, she never noticed anything . . . anything of the distance between us.

After one and a half years the delusional world of the 'prospective marriage' has clearly been stabilized, and its meaning has become more clear. With the help of the delusion Joane manages to keep going. She tries to deal with an overpowering terror which is mobilized by a direct confrontation with reality.

I want to give one more example of the way in which I handled the 'marriage delusion.' I would do it a lot differently today, but there is no point in slipping into a long technical discourse. Strategically, of course, the 'delusion' put me in a dilemma; and it occurs to me in retrospect that I was not nearly forceful enough in reminding Joane how things really stood, who and what I was and what she could and could not expect of me. I did not ignore this aspect, but was careful – perhaps too careful. I was feeling the anguish which Joane's previous history and abysmal feelings of inferiority evoked in me. I was very much affected by how much she needed her world of delusion and the extent to which it seemed to be the only bridge connecting her with me and with reality. To her I was now an ideal father, now an ideal mother; and it is certain that the whole experience gave her the opportunity to disclose in bits and pieces fragments of her life history. At the same time enough reality found its way into our relationship to give it the beginnings of a more realistic foundation. So in my strategy the delusion was a communicating bridge which at this stage I did not want to destroy, and the cloak beneath which there was a slow buildup of a more real psycho-therapeutic and personal relationship.

This point is important enough, I think, for me to discuss it more extensively. When I discussed with some of my colleagues how this 'transference psychosis' (that is the technical term) and delusion were developing, it was often suggested that I should interpret the defensive character of this delusion more directly and sharply. It was pointed out to me that my accepting attitude merely stimulated the flight into the dream. Thus I was promoting the radical turning away from reality that was so characteristic of Joane. Indeed it turned out later that dreaming and fantasizing were lifelong habits of hers. With her nose pressed to the window she would see the children across the road playing with one another, getting into mischief, shouting at their mother, but it was as if she could never fully grasp the reality of all this. She would see lovers walking hand in hand down the street and kissing each other, but again and again in her descriptive accounts it comes out that her mother forced her to deny the perception of these aspects of reality, especially aggressiveness and physical intimacy. All the time, it seems, her mother presented her with: 'Out there is the dream, in here is the reality, that's as it really should be.' The aggressive child, screaming and shouting its 'no,' the child who resists and asserts and defends its own individuality, *according to mother has no business to exist*. It is something unreal. It is something exceptional. And embracing is mad-and-bad behavior, a pose, a false notion of things.

What I am trying to describe here is a flowing together of dream and reality, a posture of *turning away from* what there is to see and experience in an active *turning toward* people. It is a posture of fantasizing, of being in the world and 'imagining things,' which Joane has been *taught*. Joane, as I have tried to understand her, has not withdrawn prematurely into a fantasy life owing to a 'constitutional sensitivity' to stimuli that she experiences as frustrating; *she has been systematically educated in this posture*. Mother is saying (with or without words): 'Believe in me, in my view of the world, unconditionally. Obeying, following, accepting and corroborating me in that way, you will be a good child and I a good mother.'

The mother admits to me later that she did not know how to bring up a child, what a good mother really was. So the mother survives as a person of some account, in the rigid application of what she considers to be 'good motherhood.'

Thus Joane was dreamy like this from way back. There was no essential difference in her outlook before and during the psychosis. I did not follow the advice to force her once and for all to face up to reality, to not allow her to go on turning away from it. The future will reveal whether I did right in this respect or not. There was really only one conscious reason why in this first phase I let her find her own way, in which she so often drifted off into fantasies and delusional convictions: I did not dare confront her with reality.

There may, however, have been an unconscious reason also for my treating Joane as cautiously as I did. Entering into the delusion and allowing it to unfold implied a satisfaction of symbiotic needs on my part. Living through the total dependency that Joane displayed, her striving toward a state of fusion between us, experiencing her immoderate yearning for the kind maternal breast and the protective embrace of the kind father – all this must have had an important psychological significance for me as well. She was my first patient at a time when I was adapting to a new country and a new environment; and my own loneliness may have given substantial impetus to satisfying my own dependency needs in a motherly concern for Joane.

Joane regresses only during her psychotherapeutic sessions with me; during the rest of the day one can see little about her that is out of the ordinary. On the ward and at occupational therapy she is regarded as not very disturbed.

The daily observation reports contain no relevant information. Sometimes, during a lull in the group session on the ward, she will suddenly come out with a telling remark that shows she can bring a lot of insight to a group situation. She works her way up to being a sort of group leader, in the sense that people expect her to come out with the right words at the right moment. But this is the extent of her participation.

For the rest, many find her 'mysterious,' some 'creepy'; one male aide is clearly afraid of her blazing fury, which sometimes forces its way out in brief, blind explosions. But I notice that a lot of the nursing staff and even her ward psychiatrist assume she is much 'better' than she really is. They evidently mean that Joane gives them little trouble – which cannot be said of the other female patients on the ward, who insist dramatically on attention. Physically, Joane is eye-catching enough. A good-looking woman with a childlike expression, a long neck, always walking on tiptoe as though hovering above the ground, and with a strange, unnatural laugh, with which she begins and ends every contact. Later on – when I see the family several times all together – the laugh becomes more comprehensible. It is a feature of the family. As soon as there is anxiety or some feeling has been stirred up, both the father and the mother break into a queer, whinnying, unnatural fit of laughter.

As the therapy enters its second year, Joane begins to describe her marital delusion more and more frequently in *functional terms* and gradually starts to confront reality. After minor frustrations she is beginning to give vent to her anger, and when I set limits to the exercise of her yearning to be cherished and protected, there are recurrent and violent struggles in my room, less blind and despairing now, like those of someone racked with thirst and battling toward a spring, but imbued with a cold hatred. Joane tries deliberately to create difficulties for me by jumping up suddenly and rushing at me. For the first time she can come out with sadistic fantasies. Carving up my chest with a knife, hurling me about the room by the penis, cutting my penis off. The delusion is breaking up, and that makes her more and more depressive. And what is coming out now, what has always remained hidden behind the delusion, turns out to be the opposite of everything that in the 'marriage world' manifested itself as hopeful and positive. Instead of being the elect, the chosen one, Joane is now the one forsaken and repulsed by me. My other patients really do interest me. Joane is nothing more to me than 'a case' for whom I have little sympathy and whom I am treating simply because I am paid to. More and more she is losing her belief in the delusion, the whole thing is 'untrue.' She comes crawling to her sessions now in a sort of dim despair and lies silent on the couch or sits turned away from me, slumped in a chair, staring out the window. For me, too, this is the most difficult phase of the therapy. Despair hangs heavily in the room – she does practically no talking. Altogether this process goes on for a very long time, more than a year. I, too, gradually develop a resistance to the sessions, 'forget' several; and all my attempts to get communication going come up against a wall of dogged negativism.

The sessions are mostly held at ten in the morning. I often see her lost in thought, making faces, whispering, at times making violently jerky movements. After a lot of trouble I manage in the end to get her talking. It then turns out that at nine o'clock she had attended a group session on the ward. No one paid much attention to her there. The atmosphere was fiercely competitive, and the conversation was dominated by a number of noisy female patients. It then appears that during her sessions with me Joane is going through the previous hour again, trying this time, in fantasy, to say what she would like to say, to show some fight, to assert herself: 'I can't express myself. I just sit there in silence, I must learn how to talk. Betty is always out in front.'

'Learning to talk,' introduces a theme which from now on is to dominate our sessions. Once the delusion has broken up, Joane reveals the extent of her feeling that she is 'nothing,' 'nobody.' Her feeling of personal identity, formerly 'the daughter of Mr. X.,' in the delusion 'the elect and future bride of Dr. Foudraine,' is extremely weak. There is absolutely no situation in which she really feels at ease. Everything is shot through with the terror of turning into nothing, an appendage, an addition, a puppet in the hands of the strong 'other.' She now begins to tell me more about her relationship with her mother; but as soon as she realizes the extent of her compliance, passivity and symbiotic captivity, there comes over her an attack of giddiness – a kind of sinking into nothingness – and then she tries, by clutching my hand and nestling up against me, to master this fear. I sometimes get the impression that only in the affirmation of her own physical nature is she able to recover the sense of being present, of existing. The world which Joane is now gradually disclosing to me is one in which she is continuously overpowered and dominated.

She feels like a fly in the web of other people, paralyzed by their energy and competence. She admits to herself that she can never attain to a thought, opinion, taste, choice of her own. She keeps describing herself as 'weak' and 'cowardly' and reveals to me a world of 'influencing,' of being-under-the-influence-of, in which it is only possible to follow lamely and be managed and manipulated, or else to react in blind protest. She teaches me something I have also experienced with other schizophrenic patients: that the world of delusional influencing is best interpreted in terms of the problem known as ego weakness. Thus Joane has been given little freedom *actively to explore the world and to make changes in it*. There are remarkably few areas in which she has ever felt *master of the situation*. Her experience in youth was of a continuous process of subjection, of *being subjected to things*; the plan of life is always being proffered to her, but *she did not herself have to travel, with all its ups and downs, the terrain of cause and effect*. This would have given her the ability to look ahead, to take stock of the total sum of consequences learned and caused by her own action.

This lack of strength inherent in herself makes even self-initiated activity in therapy a very difficult task.

Now that her longing to be born and nurtured anew is not being satisfied by me, and the dream of marriage has gone up in smoke, her negative feelings are coming powerfully to the fore.

The picture that Joane has built up of her father is derived partly, it is true, from her own observations and experience with him, but certainly it is much colored by the view of her father thrust upon her by her embittered mother. Joane finds these pictures difficult to distinguish. I will give you a few examples of how this is manifested in her relationship to me. She sees me as an authoritarian god who shows a great contempt for women. My work with her is motivated only by a wish to satisfy my own needs. Her state of dependency is my food and drink. To her I am a conceited cock. I fence myself off against her, she is really my support and so I trample over her and humiliate her.

We get to the stage of violent outbursts of rage. Sometimes, when I enter the cafeteria, Joane feels the desire welling up in her to fling a plate at my head. At other times she contemplates resorting to suicide, so as to tarnish my reputation. Once she wants to throw herself in front of my car, in order to dramatize how she feels in our relationship – ridden over, not respected in any way. To her I am the summit of egotism. It would seem on the face of it that this experience of the man corresponds well with what she went through at home in earlier days with her father. Indeed her father gave little consideration to his wife and to Joane. Her mother always referred to him as a god who had to be respected and not bothered when he came home in the evening.

My own contact with this man certainly does not give me anything like the same view of him. He is controlled, holds his feelings of aggression and tenderness studiously at bay, is pent up; but he has a certain air of integrity and he really is able to talk about his feelings. One notices with how much affection he can speak about his daughter. Joane assails 'the man' in a variety of ways, continues to describe her problems at home as a struggle between two down-trodden women –

a depressive mother who feels inferior and her devoted daughter – and a doctor who gave no time or thought to either of them.

These dynamics seem to be easy for her to comprehend and much less alarming than the process of getting an insight into her relationship with her mother.

Even so, the evidence is building up that Joane felt herself to be a complete plaything of her mother. Just as everything in the house appeared to have its permanent place, Joane is considered to be a total possession of her mother; and her opinions, judgments, observations have to be as Mother tells her they should be. The extent to which the mother crushes Joane's growing identity is impressive.

The situation that has emerged after three years of therapy is as follows: The marriage delusion has gone, and Joane is revealing herself as a woman who on any close contact with someone else develops a feeling of being overwhelmed by the other party. As it develops, the fear manifests itself in chaotic outbursts of rage. She sometimes throws herself to the ground during these attacks, and several times she has to be protected against herself. These tantrums are occasionally complicated by strong suicidal impulses. On her ward she displays much more emotion; she is now no longer the mysterious, extremely passive and taciturn woman who had previously eluded everybody's grasp. She used to communicate only with me, but now she is slowly developing somewhat more intimate relations with her fellow patients and the male and female aides on the ward. In doing so she drops her mask, and there is a growing awareness on the ward of her confusion and uncertainty. People are still obviously afraid of her. When she starts to speak at the morning meeting, the members of the group sit quietly and patiently listening to her; but evidently they are still startled to observe the degree of her confusion and isolation. At times she will speak only in barely understandable symbolic language, and many are struck by the impression this woman makes of never really having lived in the world of reality. She is now somewhat better able to express her yearning for physical intimacy, and she will sometimes ask one of the nurses 'for a little hug.' Her fury is reserved mainly for the male aides, who generally speaking are very much afraid of her. From time to time, because of some incident that is difficult to track down, she is capable of suddenly developing a blind hatred – an emotion that overpowers her and sweeps her helplessly away. Her lack of assurance in the face of the most simple tasks calls for persistent care and direction. Her yearning for dependence and security engenders great anxiety in her, for she then becomes, she says, 'immediately just like the other person I am dependent on.'

If, on the other hand, opportunities for autonomy, for independent action and decision-making arise, she again manifests considerable anxiety, because she is afraid of the loneliness in that autonomy; and a feeling grows in her immediately that she will cease to be accepted by the other person. For her, it would seem, autonomy signifies a total loss of affection and being made an 'outcast.' At the same time she experiences a childlike sense of security as a loss of her own identity. In all this tragic confusion the staff had an exceptional amount of trouble with her.

In this latest phase I get much more support from the personnel and the psychiatrist on the ward, now that they understand better with whom we are actually dealing.

In the course of our work Joane gradually put the bits and pieces together. She found an apartment. Her relationships with her children and with her husband were discussed at great length. The husband I saw only twice; he refused to get involved beyond that, and the marriage was eventually dissolved. Joane did indeed face up to reality, and after four years she had reached the point where we could part company and a psychoanalyst colleague could continue the psychotherapy. The latest information I have about her is positive.

I have told something of Joane's story (again, how do you summarize four years of therapeutic work?) by way of introduction to the next chapter. In it we shall concentrate our attention on a single theme: 'weakness.'

REFERENCES

[1] H. Stierlin: 'The Adaptation to the "Stronger" Person's Reality,' *Psychiatry*, vol. 29, pp. 143–152 (1959).

13. 'CHRONIC SCHIZO-PHRENIA' AND 'EGO WEAKNESS'

In this chapter I want to look more closely at the phenomenon of 'being chronically schizophrenic.' Once again I will make a selection from the extensive literature on this subject.

My initial premise is that the words 'chronic schizophrenic' amount to twenty letters of the alphabet and do not refer to anything concrete. They are 'nonreferential' words on a certain level of abstraction that give psychiatrists a chance to communicate with one another – to some extent meaningfully. Apart from this function – maintaining communication between fellow experts – the words do not mean much to me. The women I met in Rose Cottage, tied passively as they were to the nursing personnel and the institution as a whole, according to the definition surely could be described as 'chronic schizophrenics.' I would like now to focus attention on people in a given situation, living in a 'field' from which they cannot be detached – the culture of a psychoanalytically-oriented sanatorium. In this chapter we will examine not the question of how people *become* psychotic, but the question of why they *remain* so.

266

Ronald Laing (along with many others) sees being schizophrenic as a strategy for carrying on with life in a totally *unlivable* situation. He cites with approval the anthropologist, Gregory Bateson:

It would appear that once precipitated into psychosis the patient has a course to run. He is, as it were, embarked upon a voyage of discovery which is only completed by his return to the normal world, to which he comes back with insights different from those of the inhabitants who never embarked on such a voyage. Once begun, a schizophrenic episode would appear to have as definite a course as an initiation ceremony – a death and rebirth – into which the novice may have been precipitated by his family life or by adventitious circumstances, but which in its course is largely steered by endogenous process. In terms of this picture, spontaneous remission is no problem. This is only the final and natural outcome of the total process. What needs to be explained is the failure of many who embark upon this voyage to return from it. Do these encounter circumstances either in family life or in institutional care so grossly maladaptive that even the richest and best organized hallucinatory experience cannot save them?[1]

In another article Laing describes the psychotic mode of being as a process of regression. He calls it 'metanoia,' a journey inward and then a return (neogenesis) with an enriched and deepened mode of being oneself. A process of death and rebirth with reintegration on a higher level as the result. The point is that one is *not able to make this journey* (the 'metanoia sequence') within the original family, *nor in a psychiatric institution*. Laing's thesis is that one is not able to make the journey, one stops halfway, *because the culture of the institution prevents it*. This is a very provocative idea. I quote Laing:

These people are often removed from the miserable, mystifying context of their families to the equally miserable and no less mystifying context of the mental hospital without any existential change occurring.

267

So our 'treatment' impedes the journey, the possibility of attaining to deeper integration.[2]

We return to Leslie, Cathy, Isabel and the others, bogged down in Rose Cottage in a situation of being 'chronic schizophrenics,' despite their many years of psychoanalytic therapy. Since we are concerned with the question of why they got bogged down there is no need to investigate more deeply the original problems that led up to hospitalization. The issue is:

1. To what extent has the 'field' contributed to the conditions of the patients?
2. How has this come about? Where is the most obvious link that can best enable us to understand this process of stagnation?

As a frame of reference I prefer to select the literature that deals with the concept of 'self-esteem.' One can translate this term in many ways: the power of the self, self-appreciation, self-confidence, 'ego strength.' In the recent literature I have found particularly striking the work of Robert W. White.[3]

I will summarize his views on the subject. White is not only a good psychoanalyst, he is also a clear thinker and is able to express his ideas lucidly. He calls for a serious reconsideration of the merits of Freud's original *Instinkt model*. This model gave us an ordered, intelligible review of the child's development in terms of the phases of psychosexual growth. The theory described the child at the breast (oral phase), the child during training in continence (anal phase), the child pre-occupied with genital impulses vis-à-vis the members of his family (phallic phase) and the physically mature adult in the heterosexual relationship (genital phase). His description had great advantages because it classified and ordered a multiplicity of behavioral forms. But, despite its clarity, modern research has shown weak spots in Freud's original libido model.

A number of neo-Freudians – among them, Karen Horney, Harry Stack Sullivan, Clara Thompson and Erich Fromm – tried to explain the child's development in the light of a series of crises in the child-parent relationship. The theories they formulated replaced the libido model with an interpersonal one. (It was Sullivan in particular who made the most logical attempt to do this.) White argues that in fact the revisionists retained the oral, anal, phallic and genital prototypes while describing them differently and giving them different names. According to the neo-Freudians, each phase has its own typical problems – the problem of short supply in the oral phase, of obeying, conforming and rebelling in the anal phase, of rivalry, competition and genitality in the phallic phase.

Under the influence of thinkers like John Dewey, George Herbert Mead, Harry Stack Sullivan and the neo-Freudians White first states his chief propositions:

1. The child's emotional development cannot be adequately conceptualized by an exclusive libido-model, no matter how liberally we interpret this concept.
2. When the prototypes derived from libido-theory are translated into interpersonal terms, they still do not constitute adequate models for development.

So where the libido theory is concerned, White obviously sides with the neo-Freudians; but even their ideas and conceptual framework are too weak, he thinks, to cover essential aspects of the child's development. White proposes to use a new and supplementary model which he calls the 'competence model.' He believes that at this stage of our understanding of human development a *psychosexual*, an *interpersonal* and a *competence model* are needed in order to illuminate a number of facts.

The concept of 'competence' is certainly not new (White stresses this point repeatedly). It has grown and been distilled from the work of many authors in the fields of animal psychology, child development and personality theory. What, then, does White mean by the concept of 'competence'? He describes it more precisely as 'fitness' (or 'ability'). Thus he states:

The competence of an organism means its fitness or ability to carry on those transactions with the environment, which results in its maintaining itself, growing and flourishing.

People are capable of learning an inconceivable number of adaptational techniques. Many a learning theory was based on concept of 'drive,' and this turned out to be inadequate. Connected with the concept of 'drive' are such notions as 'deficiency,' 'internal stimulus-deprivation' and 'satisfaction.' Diminution of 'drive' became the primary motivational force for learning and unlearning certain behavior patterns. We learn what will help us to lessen a condition of need ('drive'). Research has shown that this way of looking at the problems of learning has its weak spots. Animals appear to have persisting tendencies to master their environment by actively exploring it and manipulating and controlling it. It seems these activities also occur when primary 'drives' *have been completely satisfied*. According to White, there has been a tendency to meet this theoretical weakness by postulating new 'drives,' such as an 'exploratory drive' or a 'manipulative drive.' But there are disadvantages to extending our arsenal of drives in this way. The main one is that in so doing we throw overboard the original definition of 'drive,' including Freud's original conceptualization of the 'instincts.' In its original meaning, the concept had considerable value and still has.

White proposes to interpret the restless, exploring, manipulative activity of the child as the expression of an energy which he calls 'effectance,' because the most characteristic aspect of this activity is to produce an effect on the environment. The accompanying experience he calls the 'feeling of efficacy.' Thus he defines competence as:

> the cumulative product of one's history of efficacies and inefficacies. It comes to operate in new behavior as a kind of set: We judge whether or not we can jump over the brook or carry out a proposed task. It also comes to be much cherished, so that we feel truly elated at new proofs of our ability, or deeply humiliated when we cannot do something we supposed was within our power.

White points out that we also find this concept of ability, or power, in Sullivan. (And in Adler too, of course!) But Sullivan never worked it out properly. He talks about a 'power motive,' which means:

> the expansive biological striving of the states characterized

by the feeling of ability applying, in a very wide sense, to all kinds of human activity.

A 'power drive' (Adler's 'struggle for power') comes about through the underlying sense of a *lack of power*. In other words, a 'power drive,' Sullivan would argue, is learned as a consequence of frustration of the need to be something or someone, to be capable, to have ability, to have power. Thus Sullivan describes the 'power drive,' the struggle to have power over others, as the result of a deep and oppressive feeling of incapacity, of impotence – an 'inner sense of powerlessness.' That feeling may be intensified by all kinds of setbacks in life.

A person who has a feeling of ability or power does not gain, and will not seek, dominance or power over someone. A person who manifests a 'power drive' does seek to dominate others.[4]

According to Robert White, man develops not only a sense of competence to deal with the nonhuman aspects of the world around him (technical competence) but also a sense of interpersonal strategy and its skills in relation with his fellow man. One has to learn what will and will not work with people in the society in which one lives.

In conjunction with these theoretical speculations White provides several descriptive accounts of the way he would wish to deploy this competence model in the various phases of the child's growth. Again in a very abbreviated form, I follow his conclusions closely.

THE ORAL PHASE

What it amounts to is that the situation: 'child fed by its mother,' is an excellent model for what happens during this phase. Everything has to do with feeding, the activity of sucking and the central position of the mother in her child's emotional development, are accepted factors.

But besides this oral model, White wants to present a competence model that will throw more light on the permanent exploratory, playful activities of the child. To describe the child's enormous urge to be active, especially in the latter half of the first year of life, White selects a description given by Gesell:

> The child wants to finger the clothespin, to get the feel of it. He puts it in his mouth, pulls it out, looks at it, rotates it with a twist of the wrist, puts it back into his mouth, pulls it out, gives it another twist, brings up his free hand, transfers the clothespin from hand to hand, bangs it on the high-chair-tray, drops it, recovers it, retransfers it from hand to hand, drops it out of reach, leans over to retrieve it, fails a moment, then bangs the tray with his empty hand. . . . He is never idle, because he is under such a compelling urge to use his hands for manipulation and exploration.[5]

This persistent motory, explorative activity can be explained, White argues, only with the help of his competence model.

THE ANAL PHASE

For White the anal model, comprising the liking for retention and evacuation of excreta and the struggle with the 'toilet-training' parental figure, is definitely inadequate. He quotes Erikson's account of ego development in this phase, giving a central place to the concepts of *autonomy* and *pride* versus *doubt* and *shame*.[6] Indeed, the struggle to become self-reliant would seem to be the most salient characteristic. Levy's accounts of early self-assertion and negativism are instances of this ability to say 'no' in the second year.[7]

Occupying a central place, therefore, are growth toward independence and the affirmation of one's own individuality. The tremendous playful activity made possible by the growth of the locomotory function, the achievement of mastering speech, give the growing child the opportunity to try out these capacities and keep knocking away at them. The restless activity leads, in the relationship to the parental figures, from one crisis to another.

The original prototype of the third phase of psychosexual development is said by Freud to come about through the increasing sensitivity to stimuli of the sex organs, which is expressed in autoerotic activities (erotic exploration of the subject's own genitalia) and a growing curiosity about matters of reproduction. The ideas Freud originally committed to writing on this subject have been deepened and broadened by many authors, including the neo-Freudians, on interpersonal lines. The three aspects of competence – the feasibility of physical locomotion, speech and the power of imagination – continue to expand. Now we come to what White has to say about this.

The child starts to realize its place in the family and its relationships with people in general and experiments with this growing capacity (White uses terms like 'social competence' and 'social power'), especially in relation to its peers. The child can play at being top dog, hit its friends, use threats and so on. It also develops a feeling for the roles it has to perform.

Once again White calls attention to a viewpoint that does not concentrate exclusively on the sex organs. A model *not* centered on sexuality, the competence model, again provides an important frame of reference for what happens in this phase. The original descriptions of the oedipal situation, in which 'sexual desires have to be relinquished,' certainly account for many of the feelings of shame and guilt, 'but they do not give as much reason to suppose that we could emerge with autonomy and initiative.' In this context White especially calls our attention to the concepts of *shame* and *guilt*. Much has been written about the subtle differences between these two types of feelings: I find White's view simple and clear. He argues that the sense of *shame*:

is always connected with incompetence. It occurs when we cannot do something, that either we or an audience thinks we should be able to do: when we cannot lift the weight, when we cannot hit the ball, when we offer to knock someone down and get knocked down ourselves.

273

It means belittlement and loss of respect. In contrast, guilt does not imply that one is unable to do something, it signifies that one has done, or is thinking of doing something within one's power that is forbidden.

White gives a good example of what he means. A youngster will play with his penis and mother may say: 'Don't do that, it's wrong (or dirty).' She may say it in so many words or indicate it nonverbally. That will produce a sense of guilt. But a parent-figure may also say: 'Come off it, don't kid yourself, that's only a tiny penis!' The result – shame.

THE LATENCY PERIOD

A great deal has been assigned to this phase by those who have employed a strongly interpersonal model. Sullivan, for instance, called it the 'juvenile era' – the period from six to twelve – a striking account, very much concentrated on the relationship between children themselves, in which the main problems are those of 'competition and compromise.'

White focuses on the variable crises which have to be struggled through and overcome on the way to acquiring a more powerful assertion of the self. Doing homework, accomplishing more adult tasks, in which one success can lead to another (and to approval), but in which frustration and a feeling of deep inferiority can also be engendered. Going in for competitive sports, participating in a group, can lead to being accepted easily and naturally, but also to taunting, ridicule and rejection. Seeking (and making) friends may open a way to the exchange of warm feelings of affection, but may also lead from one rejection to another and then to a retreat into isolation. Are these crises and experiences after the age of six very important to a person's development? White deploys all his originality and persuasion in answering that question.

He aligns himself with Sullivan and replies in the affirmative. This phase is of the greatest importance, he believes, because if something got warped in the early years at home (Sullivan's 'juvenile era') it is still open to correction, in the friendships formed during adolescence ('pre-adolescent friendship, which under fortunate circumstances might rescue young people who are otherwise destined for emotional trouble and mental breakdown'). Thus a few good friends and the first successful experiences in dating a member of the opposite sex (whatever may eventually go awry after this first successful strategy) enlarge the behavioral repertoire which in the end can open up a better alternative.

THE GENITAL PHASE

Here White points to the especially fine things that Erikson has written, combining as he does the libido model with the interpersonal one. But Erickson's views have certain short-comings. The account of sexual maturity is centered around the capacity for mutual orgasms, which actually entails a capacity for 'loss' of the ego: 'He who takes the ego to bed with him will never get a gold star for genital primacy.'

The major objection to this orgastic model White considers to be the meager stress on ego development during this period – which again he believes he can illustrate better with his competence model. For this phase White clearly lays the emphasis on *work*, on the ability *to perform a task*; and so he stresses for the genital phase what Erikson called the 'sense of industry.'

To sum up, then, we can say that for White the idea of 'competence' describes the whole field of learned or acquired behavior, behavior that will enable the child to handle its environment effectively. It includes the ability to manipulate, the growth of the locomotory function, the mastering of speech, a broad reconnoitering of the world and the learning of efficient patterns of action, including action in relation to one's fellows. He puts forward a source of motivation which he calls 'effectance motivation' and which finds its satisfaction in a sense of 'being efficient.'

As I stated before, White has always pointed out that his ideas are not original. What *is* original, in my opinion, is the way he ties together a variety of theories presented by earlier investigators.

New, too, is the central importance White gives to the explorative, playful forms of behavior that result in control of the surrounding world. That is of major importance for the growth and purposeful adaptation of the organism. Here White reveals his obvious kinship with the American philosopher John Dewey, who repeatedly stressed that it is through *action* and the *consequences of that action* that we learn to cope effectively with our environment.[8]

Now we must go on to take a look at the connection between the concept of 'self-esteem,' the concept of 'competence' and the ideas that many psychoanalysts have put forward regarding 'ego strength.'

THE CONCEPT OF SELF-ESTEEM

In White's view the psychoanalytic theory of 'self-esteem' has made too much use of infantile fantasies and instinctual energy and too little of a frame of reference with an action theory at its center.

For White it is very much a question whether the Freudian model of self-esteem, which depends on 'the volume of narcissistic supplies pumped in by the significant people in one's environment,' really provides an adequate explanation of the formation of self-esteem. He certainly does not underestimate the value of love and regard which the parents may show for the child, but believes that the concept of ego strength, self-confidence, Sullivan's (and Adler's) concept of 'power,' require an *action theory*. He emphasizes what the child and the man *do achieve* – what they can look back on as *successful action that they have undertaken*.

IDENTIFICATION AND COMPETENCE

In White's thinking there is a clear connection between the two concepts. A growing child constructs his behavior not just on a trial-and-error basis, but obviously imitates the behavioral patterns of adults and of his parents in particular. Identification, according to White, has to be seen as a form of imitation; but that does not mean the copying of someone else's behavior. He clarifies the characteristic difference between imitation and identification by comparing two phrases: 'wanting to do something that someone else has done' and 'wanting to be like someone else.' The latter phrase describes the concept of identification. The model here has a personal reference, and so identification is a particular form of imitation.

The copying of the model in this case is not the emergence of a number of specific patterns of action, *but has the character of wanting to be and trying to be like the model*. What White particularly emphasizes is that identification entails *a wanting or trying to be as competent as the model*. That is the point.

It is immaterial in this context what specific emotional bond, affectionate or aggressive, exists with the model. Various psychoanalytic writers have put the emphasis on the quality of the emotional link with the object, and this has given rise to some confusion. Anna Freud (identification with the aggressor) demonstrated a type of relationship in which fear and hatred of the model were clearly present.[9] In Freud's early thinking the concept of identification was bound up in the tender bond with the mother.

The confusion can be removed by using the concept of 'identification' to signify a process liable to occur in forms of relationship that can include many combinations of love, tenderness, fear and hatred. The only emotional quality playing a uniform role in the identification process would seem to be:

admiration of the model's competence. . . . We may dislike a side of him, yet admire and try to copy his poise and assurance in situations that would upset us. Or we may love him and admire and try to copy his lovable characteristics. The identification can go with several types of emotional relationships, provided they rest upon admiration.

White's views have brought us nearer to the concept of ego

strength, as elaborated by a psychoanalytic author. Obviously, the experience of one's own power and competence is based on a prior development of one's active engagement with the world, of experiencing consequences as they ensue from actions and of learning to control aspects of the world. So there emerges through the various phases of life a growing sense of being able to act efficiently, a feeling for and control of the strategy of interpersonal role relations and their complexity.

The time I have spent expounding White's views on the concept of competence appeared necessary because its significance for 'schizophrenic' people is so very central. What has particularly struck me about 'schizophrenics' is not just the degree of their emotional confusion, their conflicts as to sexual identity, their enormous, displaced aggression, but above all their sense of weakness in a complex world.

This meager sense of one's own capacity for action is in fact brought about by parents *who need their children in order to reach some sort of solution to their problems*. The symbiotic link with father or mother, a child's experience of being pushed to and fro on a battlefield occupied by contending parents, leaves no room at all for the development of a sense of socio-cultural competence. In my view a central importance must be ascribed to the overwhelming sense of ego weakness for the emergence of an ever-increasing passivity and surrender to fantasizing, which paves the way to delusional solutions when the problems of living call for real and purposeful action. It is not surprising that to Robert White fell the honor of giving the eighth Frieda Fromm-Reichmann Memorial Lecture.[10] She *had* stressed the same points: one's own action and its consequences, learning about reality, producing effect, the feeling of 'joy in being a cause,' [11] the sense of power that springs from being an effectively performing person. White arrives at the conclusion that *'weak action on the environment' is a very characteristic feature of being schizophrenic*. Weak self-assertion, poor mental concentration, an extremely feeble grasp of what is charactertistic about the other ('mastery of cognitive experience'), a very limited feeling of efficacy and competence, a paralysis of the feeling that one is able to take the initiative (with a tendency to avoid contacts), in short, *the inability to lead a life of one's own*, can easily be distilled from the enormous literature. This 'ineffectiveness in action,' then, stands at the center of the person's existence.[12] It results in a very narrow basis of self-confidence. White argued in his lecture:

> The world will be experienced as operating largely in ways that cannot be influenced. Having built up little power to control his surroundings, the person is bound to feel more or less under their control.

There are many possible ways of explaining this 'deficiency.' I shall not pursue the rest of White's argument in his lecture. What he has to say regarding the origins of the conditions, its consequences and manifestations (delusions of grandeur, total refusal of every form of action, etc.) I regard as fundamental.

In his paper White also focuses on what does and does not happen on the wards of mental hospitals. For him the secret of the success of the therapeutic environment experiments lies in the 'increase in the experience of efficacy.' Everything that stimulates action, doing something, participating in, producing effect, yields greater self-respect, and hence promotes the process of achieving relationships with others.

Needless to say, I am fully in agreement with White. This theme crops up in the literature over and over again, couched in terms such as 'role training,' the acquisition of 'social skills,' 'strengthening' and so on. So we may postulate as one of the central themes of the therapeutic environment *the strengthening of a weak ego. And at the same time postulate that the whole literature on psychiatric institutions describes forces that weaken the ego.*

With that conclusion my story takes a turn for which I want to prepare the reader. I want to remind you once more of the saying of the social psychologist Kurt Lewin: 'If you want to know how things really are – try to change them.'

The twist in my story centers on 'how things really are.' My conclusion is that things do not look promising *and that our 'reforms' in mental hospitals are not doing the job.*

The psychiatrist Hayward has pointed out that the psychiatric institution as a whole, and specifically via the actions of the psychiatric nursing personnel, constitutes a kind of 'auxiliary ego' which compensates, as it were, for the weak ego of the acutely psychotic person during the period he is in the mental hospital.[13] The various 'auxiliary egos' take over ego functions from the patient, who is also relieved of any burden of responsibility. Troublesome aggressive and erotic impulses are brought as much as possible under control. The institution as a whole and the nursing personnel in particular put their more or less strong 'egos' on loan. The aim of this procedure is to transfer this 'ego strength' to the patient. This 'lending procedure' must be discontinued at as early a stage as possible. Personal responsibility for the satisfaction of vital needs (this would be ideal), and the control of passion and instinct should be resumed by the patient, under constant encouragement, along with all those other activities that can restore to him his sense of his own 'efficacy,' his power of action. *But that is exactly what does not happen at the present time.*

Here are some observations from the literature that help to throw more light on the surreptitious undermining of ego strength characteristic of the mental hospital. Schwartz and Waldron remark that the danger of the mental hospital lies not in the community's excessive concern vis-à-vis the supposedly dangerous patient, but in the exaggerated concern for the patient vis-à-vis the presumably dangerous community. Overidentification with the patient and the underestimating of his reserve of ego strength lead to a sort of communication in which the patient is told, as it were:

> These people you have to deal with outside really are impossible, especially for someone as weak as you are. There really is not any use trying to cope with them. They ought to treat you the way we do, because that's really as much stress as you can handle.[14]

This communication the authors see as one of the most potent undermining factors.

The theme of the undermining of ego strength runs through the literature. The psychoanalyst Robert Knight, in a series of important articles on 'borderline states,' has said a number of things on this subject that are well worth adopting.[15] For instance, he states that in approaching a person living on the edge of disintegration it is essential to strike a balance between giving too little and too much support. The atmosphere in the hospital must on no account be such as to encourage a development resulting in 'a collection of sick individuals, each tending to regress in his own way and pulling others with him.' Like so many others, Knight has a list of recommendations. Because one finds essentially the same suggestions (they have been turning up in the literature for years) I cannot escape the impression that there is something rather hopeless about them, that somehow, sadly, the hard core of the problem has been missed. As far as they go, the recommendations are sensible enough. Knight is saying (I sum up a number of his publications): 'Don't be authoritarian and don't keep them in cotton-wool!' Along with his colleagues, Knight has interpreted and applied these insights at the psychoanalytic center of Austin Riggs.[16]

There is a growing understanding that 'a hospital should not be a succession of Sunday afternoons' and that, instead, an atmospheric pressure of expectancy must be created that will allow the patient to recover his ego and that will reinforce ego strength.

Before we once again return to Rose Cottage and my experiences there, I would like to round off this theoretical chapter with a summing up of my own. I consider the phenomenology of the being-in-the-grip-of-the-other, which is exhibited in delusions of persecution and being influenced, to be *an expression of this ego weakness*. Delusions and feelings of being persecuted and influenced may be explained *more extensively* by way of the projection principle – projection of aggressive and erotic impulses. I consider these forms of explanation as complementary, and I want to put ego weakness at the center of the problem.

We pursue the story of Rose Cottage. But first . . . an anecdote.

REFERENCE

[1] R. D. Laing: 'Is Schizophrenia a Disease?' *Social Psychiatry*, vol. 10, pp. 184–193 (1964).
G. Bateson, ed.: *Perceval's Narrative: A Patient's Account of his Psychosis* (Stanford, Cal., 1961).
[2] R. D. Laing: 'The Study of Family and Social Context in Relation to the Origin of Schozophrenia,' in J. Roamns, ed.: *The Origins of Schizophrenia; Proceedings of the First Rochester Conference on Schizophrenia, March 29–31, 1967* (Excerpta Medica Foundation, Amsterdam/New York, 1967).
[3] I make use of the following publications:
R. W. White: 'Competence and the Psychosexual States of Development' in *Nebraska Symposium on Motivation* (Univ. of Nebraska Press, 1960); 'Ego and Reality in Psychoanalytic Theory,' *Psychological Issues*, vol. 3, no. 3 (1963); 'Competence and the Growth of Personality,' *The Ego*, J. Masserman, ed. (New York, 1967).
[4] H. Stack Sullivan: *Conceptions of Modern Psychiatry* (New York, 1953).
[5] A. Gesell and F. L. Ilg: *The Child from Five to Ten* (New York, 1946); *Infant and Child in the Culture of Today* (New York, 1943).
[6] E. H. Erikson: *Childhood and Society* (New York, 1950); 'Identity and the Life Cycle,' Selected Papers, *Psychological Issues* (1959).
[7] D. M. Levy: 'Oppositional Syndromes and Oppositional Behavior,' in *Psychopathology of Childhood*,' P. H. Hoch and J. Zubin, eds. (New York, 1955).
[8] A summary of Dewey's work may be found in: *Intelligence in the Modern World: John Dewey's Philosophy*, J. Rattner, ed. (New York, 1939).
[9] A. Freud: *The Ego and the Mechanisms of Defence* (New York, 1946).
[10] R. White: 'The Experience of Efficacy in Schizophrenia,' *Psychiatry*, vol. 28, pp. 199–212 (1965).
[11] K. Groos: *The Play of Man* (New York, 1901).
[12] For an elaboration of these ideas, see also E. Becker: *The Revolution in Psychiatry* (New York, 1964).
[13] S. T. Hayward: 'On Being Ill in a Mental Hospital,' *Brit. J. of Medical Psychology*, vol. 36, p. 57 (1963).
[14] D. A. Schwartz and R. Waldron: 'Overprotection in a Mental Hospital,' *Psychiatry Quarterly*, vol. 37 (1963).
[15] R. P. Knight: 'Management and Psychotherapy of the Borderline Schizophrenic Patient,' *Bulletin of the Menninger Clinic*, vol. 17, p. 139 (1953).
The concept 'borderline' is somewhat vague technical jargon. It refers to people with a tendency to sidestep the problems their lives present in a psychotic way.

[16] R. B. White, E. Talbot and S. C. Miller: 'A Psychoanalytic Community' in *Current Psychiatric Therapies*, vol. 4, J. H. Masserman, ed. (New York, 1964).

NOTES

A selection from literature that is primarily concerned with the strengthening (or weakening) of the ego in the psychiatric institution:

E. Talbot and S. C. Miller: 'Some Antitherapeutic Side Effects of Hospitalization and Psychotherapy,' *Psychiatry*, vol. 27, pp. 170–176 (1964).

In this publication the 'patient community' that exercises a kind of suction is described: a suction which in fact reinforces the tendency to deviance. A summary of the contents:

Within the hospital, deviance is normal while normal behavior is regarded by the patient community as deviant. That is to say, the 'patient' is more or less forced to accept his 'illness' as the norm. Magical expectations regarding omnipotent doctors and nurses – the 'magic mountain effect' which follows from isolation, an absence of the normal expectations and the demands which society posits – bring the 'patient' to a condition of greater and greater preoccupation with himself. Thus the psychotherapy can lead to a 'cult of the psyche,' a concentration on personal feelings, and a much diminished concern for productive activities and interest in the 'outside world.' In the same way there arises a worship of spontaneity, the 'just let yourself go' sort of attitude, a blurring of the time perspective and of any preparation for the future. If nothing is done to counter this, the patient 'in care' may sink into an abyss of passivity.

E. Talbot and S. C. Miller: 'The Struggle to Create a Sane Society in the Psychiatric Hospital,' *Psychiatry*, vol. 29, pp. 65–172 (1968).

The problem is already reflected in the title. A struggle it assuredly is!

During four years at the Austin Riggs center the authors worked hard to get something done. A form of management by staff and patients together was organized, with committees, the right to elect representatives, work for everyone (no 'made work'). In addition, there were courses of instruction in various crafts and arts, aimed at involving the participants more as students than as patients.

In conclusion the authors express the hope (and expectation) that the mental hospital will not be a monastery, nor a 'cotton-padded milieu' that emphasizes only fragility, incompetence, helplessness, 'being different from the rest.'

J. Cumming: 'Communication: An Approach to Chronic Schizophrenia,' in *Chronic Schizophrenia*, pp. 106–120, L. Appleby, J. Scher, J. Cumming, eds. (Glencoe, Ill., 1968).

Here again Cumming focuses on *ego strengthening*, for which he holds the communication between the lower-echelon personnel and the patients to be of central importance. The staff's idea that one should not get involved results in an 'interpersonal distance.'

> This they do by reacting to each schizophrenic, not as an individual but as a member of a class, namely, patients, and by responding to overtures from the patient in terms of their own membership in a class of people, nurses or aides.

This form of 'efficient management' leads to chronicity. Authentic communication has an ego-rebuilding function.

J. Cumming and E. Cumming: *Ego and Milieu* (New York, 1962).

Authority needs to be placed in the hands of those who are closest to the patient. This is another account of the resistance put up by the 'old-line nurses' and the role confusion that results from new structures:

> In spite of preparation, ward staff can react sharply to the increased autonomy that self-government brings to patients. Attendants who no longer need to control the patients can feel useless and demoralized. This can be avoided by starting to give them the new therapeutic role of assistant in problem solution before they lose their traditional role of keeper.

Ego reinforcement calls for action and if the 'inferior personnel' (male attendants) are given no authority to make decisions, they will avoid *action* and *involvement*. The authors also warn against a sort of 'psychoanalytic' and overempathetic approach on the part of the personnel, which denies the patient the opportunity of becoming involved in new interactions. As soon as somebody starts 'psychoanalyzing,' the patient is no longer addressed simply as a spouse or a father, a temporarily unemployed truck driver or whatever.

What above all supplies the building materials for ego reinforcement is successful task fulfillment. Thus on the subject of role training these authors declare:

> In general, we may say that all personal problems are problems with the content of some role and that some patients will need to learn role elements they have never known, others to differentiate clearly between role elements that have always been unclear to them, and still others to master the correct role behavior when it is required.

And:

> To act successfully in an appropriate role is one of the elements

of ego identity. The resulting sense of 'fit' produces a pleasant ego feeling and thus tends to make such successful performance its own reward. If the hospital or day center is planned so that role learning takes place in a lucid social system, all patients can be expected to improve at least a little.

The authors also point out that we often do not sufficiently realize that people simply do not know how certain things have to be done. As an example they cite the case of a woman who kept stealing articles from shops. It was discovered that this woman simply did not know how to make a purchase!

R. Freeman and A. Schwartz: 'A Motivation Center,' *Amer. J. of Psychiatry*, vol. 110, pp. 139–153 (1953).

Strong emphasis on *activity*: 'Getting the patient involved in some relationship or activity rather than doing anything to or for him.'

W. N. Deane: 'Democracy and Rehabilitation of the Mentally Ill,' *Archives of General Psychiatry*, vol. 1, p. 1 (1963).

This article concentrates on the 'high-expectation atmosphere' that obliges (helps) the patient to emerge from his 'sick role.'

L. Appleby: 'Evaluation of Treatment Methods for Chronic Schizophrenia,' *Archives of General Psychiatry*, vol. 8, p. 8 (1963).

Here, too, the main accent is on the restoration of ego functions, responsibility, 'the reawakening of the ego.'

R. D. Scott: 'A Conceptual Model of the Hospital as an Aide to Everyday Handling of Psychotic Patients,' *Psychiatry*, vol. 25, pp. 208–219 (1962).

The most important passage seems to me:

> The functions of the patient's 'ego' get transferred into the hands of the staff. The staff become the keepers of this 'ego,' those who control its emotional expressions and whose duty it is to satisfy its needs.

Apart from the already existing nexus of problems, a patient discloses in this article how he 'feels himself devoured by the institution'—'communicating his utterly helpless feeling of being incorporated into the hospital as a whole.'

L. Appleby, K. L. E. Artiss, J. Cumming, Drye, Gyarfas, Stanton, E. Cumming, and others: 'Milieu-Therapy – a Dialogue,' *Mental Hospitals*, p. 337 (June, 1963).

An informative discussion among pioneers in the field of environmental therapy. They all agree that any attempt to reform the traditional bureaucratic hospital runs into a great deal of opposition. John and Elaine Cumming stress the 'ego regrowth' that results from more real expectations regarding 'social and interpersonal performance.' Ego regrowth is brought about: (1) through an enhanced possibility of controlling primitive impulses; (2) through the strengthening (acquired with 'success') of the 'executive competence side of the ego.' In the second aspect – 'competence training' (social-interpersonal – 'or whatever the patient is not good at') – lies the essence of the effect of a therapeutic environment, the Cummings believe.

Artiss and Appleby again point out the importance of a fundamental retraining of the psychiatric aide, which is not feasible, however, unless the whole social system of the hospital is changed. Stanton brings the word 'school' into this discussion: 'The climate of a helpful psychiatric institution should be more like the atmosphere of a boarding school than of a hospital.'

F. F. Main: 'The Hospital as a Therapeutic Institution,' *Bulletin of the Menninger Clinic*, vol. 10, p. 66 (1946).

To summarize his observations: Tradition has made of the psychiatric hospital a place where sick people are given shelter from the storms of life. They get the attention and care of the medical and nursing personnel. But in this conception of the hospital as a place of refuge all too often the patient loses his status as a responsible human being. Far too often he comes (in the institution) to be dubbed 'good' or 'bad' on the strength of his degree of passivity in face of the institution's demand on him to be 'obedient, dependent and grateful.'

The classic mental hospital (with its individual treatment for the individual patient by a doctor) creates an unrealistic milieu that leads to a 'state of retirement from society.' Isolated and dominated, the patient gets caught up in the wheels of the hospital machinery. Like Maxwell Jones, Main stresses how hard it is, in particular for the 'doctor' (accustomed as he is 'to playing a grandiose role among the sick'), to give up a little of his power and allow patients real independence. We must create a real situation with real responsibilities and real role expectations if the patient in care (who is thus already stigmatized) is to stand any chance at all of being able to manage in the world to which he will return.

R. N. Rapoport: 'Principles for Developing a Therapeutic Community,' *Current Psych. Therapies*, vol. 3, p. 244 (1963).

A lucid survey of a number of basic principles, with explicit consideration of the change in role behavior on the part of nursing personnel.

S. Boorstein: 'Ego Autonomy in Psychiatric Practice,' *Bulletin of the Menninger Clinic*, vol. 23, pp. 148–157 (1959).

An important article stressing the theme of ego reinforcement. The emphasis on everything that contributes to 'ego autonomy.' The stress on self-responsibility has much in common with what Scher described as a 'total push program.'

(J. M. Scher: *Archives of Neurology and Psychiatry*, vol. 78 pp. 531–539 [1957]).

L. Appleby, J. M. Scher and J. Cumming, eds.: *Chronic Schizophrenia* (Glencoe, Ill., 1960).

A lot of information is contained in this book.

K. L. E. Artiss and S. B. Schiff: 'Education for Practice in the Therapeutic Community' in *Current Psychiatric Therapies*, J. Masserman, ed., vol. 8, pp. 233–248 (1968).

This is a fairly recent survey in which, again, the principles of what can be called a 'therapeutic community' are defined. In a guarded way Artiss makes the point that psychiatrists who administer departments are conspicuous for sheer naïveté when it comes to questions of management and role relations in highly complex socio-psychological systems. A training program for psychiatrists who have to do this work is described.

R. White, E. Talbot and S. C. Miller: 'A Psychoanalytic Community,' in *Current Psychiatric Therapies*, vol. 4, p. 199 (New York, 1964).

Another account of how, by creating an atmosphere of demand and expectation, the patient can be prevented from lapsing into regressive inactivity. From this article comes the nice remark that 'A hospital must not be a succession of Sunday afternoons.' Besides the business of joining battle with regression (which even psychotherapy itself can induce), the emphasis is on creating a greater variety of social roles and stimulating 'conflicting areas of competence, skills, talents and abilities.'

M. J. Kahne: 'Bureaucratic Structure and Impersonal Experience in Mental Hospitals,' *Psychiatry*, vol. 22 (November, 1959).

This article concentrates on the formal institutional structure and ties up with Jules Henry's article, 'Types of Institutional Structure' (*Psychiatry*, vol. 20, pp. 47–60 [1957]), in which the mental hospital's formal structure is also investigated.
For Kahne the biggest challenge for the future evidently does *not* lie in the resocialization of the patient within the context of the hospital, but in the development of techniques 'which provide a reliable bridge to the outside world.' In fact Kahne sees everything that we have learned about 'chronicity' as a consequence of the social pressures in the hospital (knowledge that gives very little reason for optimism) more as a pointer to *future* developments.

G. F. Steinfeld: 'Parallels Between the Pathological Family and the Mental Hospital: A Search for a Progress,' *Psychiatry*, vol. 33, pp. 36–56 (1970).

It is hardly surprising that in this recent article the situation in the mental hospital should be compared with the original family situation, where psychotic behavior was the sole form of adaptation in a field of extremely confusing patterns of communication. The mental hospital is actually described as a substitute, *but equally pathological*, environment.

The author first stresses the work of Jay Haley (*Strategies of Psychotherapy* [New York, 1963]), which is based on a communication theory regarding human behavior. Many so-called symptoms can *also* be seen as ways in which one person holds another in a particular grip, manipulates the other in a certain way. This constantly happens in the mental hospital, with its dehumanization, confusing feedback or, in short, an atmosphere which Haley defines as:

> a kind of formless, bizarre despair overlaid with a veneer of glossy hope and good intentions concealing a power-struggle-to-the-death coated with a quality of continual confusion.

An example whereby the author demonstrates how the confusion in the mental hospital resembles original family situations:

The 'mother' (head nurse of the ward) sometimes undermines the authority of the 'father' (ward psychiatrist), and confusion prevails as to who really has the authority. This confused authority structure is magnified by manipulations on the part of the patient 'increasing the split between his parents, or parent surrogates, by acting helpless and despairing.'

A good deal of emphasis is placed on the element of 'consistency,' a uniform and consistent reaction by the staff to the various ways in which the 'patient' tries by way of his symptoms to impose some control over his environment. It is just this 'consistency' that is often so hard to arrive at. Frequently completely polarized reactions of 'punishment' and 'reward' increase the confusion.

When it comes to recommendations for a future alternative organization, Steinfeld is vague. Even this author, who is in fact saying that the inmates of a mental hospital suffer more as a result of their environment than as a result of their initial problems, can propose no clear alternative. I have added his article to the list of literature because this recent publication in one of the most authoritative psychiatric journals (*Psychiatry*) makes clear how devastating the criticism of the psychiatric institution is . . . and how vague the ideas regarding new types of remedial institutions still are.

ANECDOTE

A vacation took me back to The Nether-
lands. For sentimental reasons I stopped in at the hospital
where I had started my training (it seemed ages ago).

A senior male aide gave me an enthusiastic welcome. 'Oh,
yes – you went to America, didn't you? I heard something or
other . . . a clinic where they make a thing of talking to the
people.'

Yes, that was more or less it. 'Psychoanalysis they call it
there, psychoanalysis.' (I've got to say something.) 'I've got a
month's vacation. A few weeks and I go back.'

We paused and stood facing each other. 'Have you a
minute?' said the aide. 'I'd like to show you something.'

I followed him through the ward. There sat . . . Bart! I did
not recognize him at first. A well-dressed man who got up
with a laugh and shook hands. 'Dr. Foudraine . . . It's me . . .
Bart . . . Don't you remember? You went to America, didn't
you, to some sort of clinic where they work with people like
me?'

Suddenly I remembered. A man, usually naked, in an isolation room, the sickly smell of dried urine, a mattress in the
corner. He would often stand with a sort of imaginary sten-
gun, shooting all around him. 'Jesus! Bart,' I said, 'what's
happened to you? Why, you're looking fine!'

289

'Thanks to my friend,' said Bart, and he clapped the aide on the shoulder.

Later on I walked back with the aide. He saw my astonishment. 'How did that come about? What happened?'

'Well, indeed, doctor, it didn't bear thinking about, all those years. He was getting new medicines all the time, you know, dosage up, dosage down – well, you know what it's like. I thought, well now, I'll just go and have a chat with him. We used to walk every day, half an hour to start with, up and down the corridor. Bart just talking. You know . . . I started to get the hang of it. He'd had a hard time of it in the Indies and before that a very bad time with his father. Mind you, I'm only a layman, no psychiatrist, and yet . . . I thought: Hell, it's like he's shooting his old man. Later on I asked him over to my place. Just simply to have a meal with us. My wife was against it at first. But it was all right, and he just went on talking. He ran some errands for us too. Sometimes I would say: "Tell me, Bart, those voices of yours . . . do you still hear them?" And he would say: "Sure, but they're much softer now and I like to hear your voice much better." Anyway, I began to understand more and more about him, his life and so on. I felt a bit guilty, of course, it wasn't directly my business. One day he said to me: "You must come and lie in bed with me." I just said: "No, Bart, that won't do, that's homosexual."

'And now I'd like to ask you something. Only very recently a new psychiatrist came on the ward. Nice man, mind you, no complaint there. But . . . he has given new tranquilizers, and they're saying now that this whole improvement comes from the tranquilizers. What do you think? Do you believe that?'

I stood gazing at the aide's inquiring face. Then I could manage to do little else than say to him: 'Just let them talk, and carry on.'

Part 3

School for Living

14. ROSE COTTAGE, SCHOOL FOR LIVING

In Rose Cottage the work of building up the therapeutic environment had been in progress for about three years. Let us pick up the threads of the story, the 'natural history' of an attempt to achieve a new environment in which nursing personnel and chronic schizophrenic women (the latter all involved in individual psychotherapeutic relationships) might get a chance to grow, as personalities, toward greater self-reliance.

We take up our story again at a juncture when I was about to carry out a new experiment on the ward. The idea for this was born of certain observations which I would like to describe first.

One morning we were all sitting as usual in the small living room for our daily community meeting. There was a very lively atmosphere at our group session that morning. The issue was whether the patients were 'ill' or 'not ill.' Some of them disclosed that they had a 'mental illness.' Sylvia was groaning and moaning as usual, albeit with far less insistence (I have described her as the 'autistic one'), and said that she had 'a disease of the nerves,' following this up immediately

with the remark that she was in need of 'medical treatment.'
I said earlier that in many respects Sylvia made the impression
of someone giving a caricatured representation of 'a person
suffering from a disease.' As soon as she felt anxious and
unwilling to perform a particular task (or thought she
could not manage it), she started at once to complain that she
had a 'slight attack of the gallbladder' or a 'head cold' and
sometimes even 'an attack of appendicitis.' In her explosive
fits of rage she would often shout: 'I'm mentally insane, I have
got the schizophrenia!' Very often she would express a wish
to return to the mental hospital where she had been admitted
shortly after her psychotic disintegration at the age of sixteen:
'It was much nicer there, there were nice flowers and they gave
you electroshock treatments.' When I tried to persuade her
that those courses of electroshock treatment could not have
been of much benefit to her, she would reply with great conviction (her vocabulary had grown considerably): 'I don't
believe it. It's good for my nervous illness. My mother said so,
and the doctor said so.'

Betty also would complain about stomach ache and refer for
the umpteenth time to a 'streak of blindness' which was supposed to have developed at the start of what she called her
'nervous breakdown.' I had noticed for some time that her
language was a mixture of words that reflected personal problems, allusions to various relatives, and a great many references to the body, the body's functioning, a variety of possible
defects and innumerable medical treatments. The 'body'
words and the 'medical' words such as 'doctor, hospital, real
hospital, D.C. General, George Washington Hospital,
surgeons, stitches, hurting, stomach pains, injuries, blindness,
brain disease, mentally retarded, tumor, pregnancy, sick,
getting well,' etc., were poured out in a verbal barrage,
drowning out most of our efforts to involve her in a more
personal and educational type of dialogue. Betty seemed
completely oblivious to the fact that Rose Cottage, as part of a
psychoanalytic sanatorium, was a psychotherapeutic community in which she could get a better understanding of her
problems and her relationships to other people. She insisted
on addressing me as a 'medical doctor' (a fact I could do little

to alter) and that I was there to treat her *body*. Sometimes she would put me in the same category as obstetricians or surgeons. Betty made a mockery of my real function, that of a psychotherapist and administrator, and frequently startled me with remarks like: 'Doctor, do you think my body's a bit better now? Will I get better soon? My stomach feels quite all right today. Why are you still keeping me here?' Considering she had already been involved for four years in intensive psychotherapy, her failure to appreciate our psychotherapeutic-educative care constantly astounded me.

As usual Isabel spoke again that morning about her intestines, nose, pelvic bones, bowel movements and tired feelings in her legs. During this group session I had again been making several attempts to expound more clearly the difference between a bodily illness and emotional difficulties that lead to a disruption of the relationship with one's fellows. In order to make everything as clear as possible I had once more talked about real cerebral diseases and about the phenomenon of severe mental retardation. I tried again to explain to the group that these medical diseases were different, fell into a different category from *behavioral problems*, which were a product of psychological conflicts, of being lonely and anxiety-ridden, feeling unable to find and fulfill a satisfactory role in society. I had been talking about interpersonal problems and 'schizophrenia' and what I thought it was all about. But again that morning it was becoming obvious to me that my words were making very little impression. What struck me was how completely the 'medical patient' role had taken control of the identity of those around me, and to what extent they were prepared to play out that role and embrace it as a source of security. I had to remind myself that almost all the psychotic people at this group session had in fact, after their first psychotic disintegration, undergone some kind of *medical treatment*. Before being referred to Cedar Haven, most of them had indeed been given electroshock treatments and insulin cures. There could be no doubt that those treatments had previously been administered by doctors who, for the most part, were convinced that their patients were suffering from a mysterious 'disease' that had manifested itself as the result of various tensions, and (to enter still further into the thinking of these disciples of Kraepelin) some of them would have been certain that the 'disease,' assisted by the environment, 'popped up' more or less directly from a source in the 'hereditary constitution.' These women had, therefore, at an earlier stage, been treated as 'medical patients' and they had accepted it.

I looked at Sylvia, who probably had been told by her mother when she was four years old that she had a 'nervous illness' because she never said much and because her movements were awkward and stiff; probably because she dreamed a lot and because she expressed herself in a highly private way, cherishing her own private language and defying the process of socialization. I knew that her mother had taken her as a child to different famous neurologists, and that she had undergone various physical examinations. I do not believe that anything definite had ever been stated to her about what was organically wrong, but later psychiatrists expressed the view that she probably was 'autistic.' She had been sent to many private schools and foster families and when she was 16 she was labeled psychotic, because she felt that poisonous gas was all around her. From that moment on, she had become a hospital patient and had received electroshocks and insulin treatments before coming to Cedar Haven.

Sandy, sitting in the corner, mute as usual, had essentially the same career. Growing more withdrawn during her childhood, subjected to her mother's anxieties and projections, she had probably fought to retain some sense of individuality by becoming increasingly negativistic and defiant against what she called 'my mother's verbal forcing.' In the beginning of her hebephrenic career she herself seemed to have referred to her 'brain tumor,' and to me she expressed many times the views that she did not talk because she had 'an illness of the vocal chords' and that she could not make friends because her 'cerebrum was withdrawn.' In the course of her hospital career prior to her admission to my ward she had received 90 electroshocks and 200 insulin treatments and she must have overheard many discussions between doctors and her parents about 'Sandy's incurable schizophrenia.' I was told by

296

the parents that she might even have overheard a discussion about the possible usefulness of a lobotomy.

And so it was with most of the people in this group. They seemed in many ways to play the medical patient role. Whenever they were unable to face their problems and conflicts, they described their experiences in medical or quasi-medical terms. Looking around me, I felt overwhelmed by the confusion. I wondered whether I could ever break through this confusion and remake my ward into a meaningful educational and re-educational universe.

The ward at the time of this observation was functioning relatively well. Interactions between staff and patients were much more personal, and there was little left of an institutional impersonal atmosphere. Symbiotic parasitic relationships between personnel and patients had practically disappeared. There had been structural changes which increased the frequency of personal interactions among staff and patients. It had indeed become a group of people working together, each having a job, however small, and the daily morning meetings had become more lively. There were no white uniforms. The place looked and had the atmosphere of a big family. But the patients were moving very slowly.

What is described above can be summarized as follows. A number of chronic schizophrenic patients (some of them undergoing psychoanalytic psychotherapy for as long as ten years!) try to prove in their verbal and nonverbal behavior the legitimacy of their claim to the medical patient role. One patient, Sylvia, made this quite clear. Whenever she was asked to do something she threw a number of temper tantrums. When this did not prove convincing enough, she rushed to the window and slammed it with her fist until it broke. Her next move was to rush to the nurse, show her the bleeding wound on her arm and state: 'Medical treatment, if at all possible.'

I asked myself the question why these women, after being in intensive psychotherapy for a period of five to ten years, still had not caught on to the main message we were trying to communicate to them: 'You are here to learn about your behavior, your patterns of relationships with others, the faulty adaptive and communicational patterns you once learned in your nuclear family. You meet here psychotherapists who, though calling themselves doctors, are highly specialized educators who are willing to involve you in a learning experience, and those called "nurses" or "aides" are essentially assistant educators, equally eager to learn and unlearn.' The staff of this psychoanalytic sanatorium had almost constantly tried to communicate this basic message. Looking at my group, I was thoroughly discouraged because of the lack of results our work had produced. The message just had not sunk in. Most of the patients seemed totally oblivious to it. Their eyes and ears did not see or hear the ward as an educational world. They kept seeing and hearing it as a medical world. There remained a radical difference between my concept of why we were here and what we were doing, and the patients' conceptualization of the situation. Not only did they pour out words pertaining to the body, its defects and its treatments, but they seemed also to relish the words 'ill' and 'sick,' 'doctor' and 'patient.'

I decided to counteract this medical conceptualization. It would be interesting and worth trying, it seemed to me (having just read Szasz's *The Myth of Mental Illness*), to stamp out all the medical words like 'hospital,' 'patient,' 'doctor,' 'illness,' 'getting better,' 'normal,' 'well,' 'sick,' etc., and to replace them with educational words. My thought was that these medical words might, in themselves, be powerful enough to withstand our efforts to build up an educational environment meaningful to the patients.

We shall get to the theory by and by. For now I want to describe what happened.

I forbade the 'patients' to use this language anymore and proposed calling them 'students.' The term 'patient' was made taboo. Rose Cottage I described as a 'school for living'; and Julia was instructed to make a large board with the words THIS IS A SCHOOL FOR LIVING and to hang it on the wall of the room. The 'Nursing Office' sign we changed to 'Educational Office.' I asked the staff to go along with the experiment and named them 'assistant educators.' I told the new-born 'students' that the name 'hospital' had been an especially unhappy choice and made my apology for this. In short, I told them that we in Rose Cottage had come together in a 'school for living,' where they, the students, could learn what had gone wrong with their lives and how things could be made different. I called myself an 'educator' and declared even the words 'ill,' 'sick,' 'well,' etc., taboo. I told my baffled group of newly-baptized 'students' and the personnel that there was no such thing as 'mental illness,' that it did not exist, and that it would be better for them to regard themselves as *ignorant* about themselves and the forming of relationships with others.

It all happened spontaneously. Little did I know what the consequences of such an experiment would be. I could have predicted some of those consequences if I had realized that the right to *name* things, to define the language forms, is the right of the group and the culture and not the right of the individual. Artiss described this as 'the naming prerogative.' I had started to fool around with a key component of a given culture – its language. In his book *Milieu Therapy in Schizophrenia* [1] Artiss calls arrogating to oneself in this way the right to call certain things by a specific, *different* name a 'schizophrenic' kind of behavior.

I want to probe a bit further into Artiss's thinking on this issue of the 'naming prerogative.' He tries to make an aspect of schizophrenic behavior comprehensible by analyzing the *verbal transaction*. In 'normal' development the child accepts the parents' right to give it a name. This 'naming prerogative' indicates that there is a reciprocal role relationship between the 'namer' (the parents) and the 'named' (the child), a relationship that may also be described as obedience, respect, culturalizing. Operationally defined, it is the individual's 'tacit accepting of a role which is fundamentally *defined by others*, in return for their assuming a series of vital responsibilities concerning his welfare.' This is coupled, of course, with a 'battle'; but when someone develops into a 'schizophrenic,' something has gone wrong with that 'battle.' Here Artiss postulates that the *child* takes over the 'naming prerogative.'

He states:

The wise parent encourages the fantasy-life, at the same time

299

setting limits upon it. It should not interfere with the reality-demands. Junior may play 'Sir Galahad' out in the yard, but he may not plunge his wooden sword into the roast at the dinner table.

In the 'abnormal' (schizophrenogenic?) situation, according to Artiss, *it is the child who defines the situation and there is inadequate or insufficient counteraction from the parents.* Artiss argues that in the case of 'schizophrenogenic development' the battle for the naming prerogative is decided *in favor of the child.* The child dictates, so becoming a parent-figure vis-à-vis his father and mother. That leads later to a disastrous development of the child's growth.[2]

With his unyielding self-defined idea of what he is and what this, that and the other is (another way of describing omnipotence) 'the schizophrenic' naturally reaches a deadlock in the group, which because of his conduct rejects him as 'crazy.'

We can now pursue the account and the consequences of my action in taking over the 'naming prerogative.' The consequences will become clear when I describe the reaction of three groups: (1) my psychiatric colleagues; (2) the psychiatric nursing personnel; (3) the patients ('students').

I. THE REACTION OF THE DOCTORS

In the beginning the word innovations were treated as a joke. A crazy joke, but a joke nevertheless. It seemed something passing, a temporary loss of common sense. A visiting psychoanalyst, whom I naively informed about what I was doing, looked at me with concern and asked me whether I was in analysis. After assuring him that I was, he seemed obviously relieved.

The general reaction seemed to me to take the form of a compassionate ridiculing of the whole idea, through 'minimizing' or 'not taking it seriously.' Serious discussion about the background, the idea behind the innovation, remained absent and slowly the reaction took a more personal turn. The labels 'messianic,' 'grandiose,' 'superficial' and 'crazy' were applied to my efforts, together with demonstrations of friendship and the expressed hope that I would eventually return to the conceptual fold of medicine, or at least to its language. It was clear that somewhere the fun had to stop. The message that I received was somewhat as follows: To name a schizophrenic patient a 'student' is denying his despair and serious incapacity. In denying his despair I was not only denying the extent of what was called his 'psychopathology' but also my own despair about him. Calling schizophrenics 'students' then was a manifestation of some kind of bland denial on my part. I was acting as if I believed that those people would 'straighten themselves out by telling them to shape up.'

2. THE REACTION OF THE NURSING STAFF

The nursing staff caught on surprisingly quickly to the new terminology. They talked about it in a sort of tongue-in-cheek way, but with amazing tolerance. Soon they reported to me that they tried to avoid the awkward term 'student,' but as they also had to avoid the term 'patient,' they started to call people by their names. The frequency with which the term 'patient' was used certainly decreased. The head nurse told me: 'I think the introduction of this term "student," especially in the beginning, did a lot to boost morale and make the whole atmosphere more friendly and equal.' She told me she had many times overheard conversations in the dining room. Personnel of other wards were saying: 'This is the most ridiculous thing I have ever heard. How can someone in a mental hospital be a student?' The head nurse informed me that besides serving in the beginning as a sort of morale booster, the whole terminology also brought the personnel of my ward closer together. They became aware of their uniqueness, talked proudly of their ward and program and defended my views with great loyalty to personnel of other wards.

Sylvia, whom I previously described as being labeled 'autistic' and apparently deeply committed to the 'medical patient role,' reacted with great force, and was adamantly opposed to the idea of being called a 'student.' When she was called a 'student' she became very angry, threatened to throw a temper tantrum, and exclaimed: 'I do not want to be called a student . . . I do not like that word . . . I would rather be called a patient, if you please . . . this is supposed to be a mental hospital, is it not? . . . a hospital for the mentally sick. . . .' Constantly calling her a student and explaining my reasons for it gave rise to verbalizations such as: 'But I am supposed to be mentally ill. I have a disease of the nerves. I want a brain operation. I have a disease of the mind.' Challenging her further about this idea of a diseased mind made her more and more angry. 'But the mind is up there,' knocking on her head. After I began to call her 'student,' she sometimes burst out with sentences like: 'This is becoming a regular hell-hole around here. I do not like the tone of voice you are using.' Walking with her to my office (I became her therapist and called her hours with me 'educational hours') I engaged with her in the following manner. During our walk I said nonchalantly: 'Hello, student, how are you?' Whereupon she whispered 'patient.' To this I responded by whispering 'student' – whereupon she again whispered 'patient' . . . and we went on whispering stubbornly, each of us, the words of our choice.

Betty's language, which I described as both incoherent and extremely medical, did not change much, but she was clearly intrigued with the new words and at one time she used a silence in our group morning meeting to make the following statement: 'Doctor, are you serious about calling us "students"? Is this really a school where I am supposed to try to learn to live with others and with myself?' She sounded at this moment quite serious, reflective in an unaccustomed way as if beginning to realize and grasp something. The quality of her statement had something of the characteristics of an 'Aha-Erlebnis.' But before I could capitalize on this moment and show her my enthusiasm for her insight, she stopped me in my tracks by pouring out more medical words and body words than ever before. She told me later: 'To be called "student" makes me feel that I am on my own; that I am learning. The word gives you two feet to stand on. It makes you feel like a person, an individual. With that word you don't stand with one foot on the doctor. When I am called a "patient" I am a crutch on the doctor and the nurse. To be called "student" gives you an upstanding feeling.'

Isabel, who held everybody at arm's length by producing medical and body language in limitless quantities, once stated: 'How can I ever be a student? Then I cannot feel anymore like a hospital patient. For how can one say, "a state hospital student."' During an interview with Isabel conducted by one of the male aides on the ward, the following transaction was reported. The interviewer asked: 'Which would you prefer to be called, sick or ignorant?' Isabel: 'I don't like to be told that I am ignorant. I would almost prefer to be called sick. But there are some things that I am ignorant about.'

Cathy made the following remarks: 'To me to be called "student" means failure. It meant I was a failure getting along and getting friends. I would like to be called "patient." It is a more restful term[!]. Then I don't have to work and to exert myself. I just have to be here. Then I am here to be in bed and cured by a nurse and a doctor.' (At this moment she bursts into laughter.) 'You see, it brings out my difficulties in school. It makes me also think that you wish to be a teacher and I would like to think that you are curing me. To be called a "student" has made clear to me that I have to get out of here faster and that you are not willing to wait for us to get better.'

During an interview with a male aide the following dialogue took place:

Interviewer: What is the difference between being a patient and being a student?
Patient: Well . . . a patient, then you are waited on hand and foot, well . . . a student, you have to figure out your own ideas.
Interviewer: Do you think your life here is more like that of a student or patient?

Patient: If it were like a student I would leave.

Interviewer: If you had to be labeled, would you prefer to be called sick or ignorant?'

Patient: Sick.

Interviewer: Why?

Patient: Well, I would rather have somebody know I was ill than ignorant about a subject. I would be embarrassed if they called me ignorant.

Interviewer: I asked whether you would prefer to be called sick or ignorant. But 'sick' is a pretty mild word; would you prefer to be called crazy or ignorant?

Patient: Crazy.

Interviewer: Do you think this place should become more like a school?

Patient: No, I hope they don't start classes and all those things. They only annoy me.

Interviewer: Do you feel that this ward has changed?

Patient (laughing): Yes, it is much more like a school; it is going downhill rapidly.

With this I conclude my account of the experiment. All in all (up to my departure) it extended over two years. Once again I discovered how much one discovers when one tries to make a change! A background suddenly came to the forefront. Under the pressure of these semantic shifts and changes, what was already latently present in this social system became manifest.

What impressed me most was the extent to which most schizophrenic patients had committed themselves to a medical value and belief system. Their semantic 'map' being medical, they went by it, and the effort at linguistic change brought out clearly how much they adhered to it. They seemed to say: If I am addressed as 'patient' and am asked to name others as 'doctors' and 'nurses,' having received 'medical treatment' and finding myself in a 'hospital,' 'I am mentally ill' and tend to consider psychoanalysis as a rather confusing variation on the theme of 'treatment' and 'cure.'

We are now ready to summarize the problem. As long as the term 'mental illness' is taken for granted as the best shorthand label for deviant behavior, and as long as physicians who have become psychiatrists (psychoanalysts) together with nurses define their task as 'giving treatment' and aiming at 'health' and 'cure,' an essentially medical stage is set up and the various role players embedded in this medical culture will therefore perform their medical roles of 'doctors' and 'patients,' 'healthy' and 'ill.' The problem in Cedar Haven, which embraced the philosophy that the problems of psychotic persons were only quantitatively different from the problems of men in general, was more complicated because on the same stage another set of roles was being played; namely, the educational roles. These consisted of different role patterns and a different language. On this simultaneously operating *educational stage* the psychoanalyst and his assistants as educators were trying to involve persons in a learning process, and were aiming not at 'normality' or 'health,' but at personal maturation and a gradual unfolding of potentialities for living. This educational context and culture asked for role performances of educators and students and it is obvious that the role of the 'medical patient' with its expected passivity and helplessness was in sharp contrast to the expected role performance of the 'student' with its expectancies of initiative, responsibility and active cooperation. My experience and what I read of the literature helped me to see that much of the confusion in our clients is caused by ourselves. Our medical culture might produce so much medical background 'noise' that our main educational message does not get through. Stamping out medical words, then, was a small effort to reduce this background 'noise.' An example of this could be expressed in the following analogy. If I enter a hardware store and the salesman comes up to me and says: 'What kind of candy can I sell you?' I would undoubtedly be confused and I would resist the salesman's efforts to sell me candy in such an environment. I might not even trust the candy he shows me, lying there among the lawn mowers.

I am preoccupied with the idea that we are selling psychoanalytic-psychotherapeutic and reeducational candy in a medical hardware store. I have been wondering whether there would be more profit for all concerned if we could sell the candy in a candy store. This would lead us to the conclusion that we cannot deal adequately with people whose difficulty in living has such serious proportions as to merit the label 'schizophrenic' unless psychiatrists make up their minds to change their 'culture' – that is, their medical habits of action and language.

Such cultural reform is no mean task since we cherish our myths and traditions, however constraining they may be for all concerned. But, as Susan Langer pointed out: 'If we would have new knowledge, we must get us a whole world of new questions.' [3]

One of these questions was formulated clearly by Artiss [4] and serves well to conclude this chapter. He states:

What parts of our expectations concerning schizophrenia come to us from the world located within a traditionally medical model? How do our expectations control our treatment of the so-labelled person? How would our changed behavior effect such a person, if we were to label him in some other fashion, e.g., a person who has missed out on some vital socializing experiences and will remain culturally bizarre and rejected as 'crazy' until such time as he may have and integrate the before mentioned vital socializing experiences, whatever they may turn out to be?

In June 1965 I left for The Netherlands. The parting was painful.

REFERENCES

[1] K. Artiss: *Milieu Therapy in Schizophrenia* (New York, 1962).
[2] Artiss on the 'naming prerogative':

. . . the 'battle' between parent and child for the naming or defining prerogative may be crucial to the schizophrenic issue. . . . If it is a battle between parent and child, then presumably it must be won by the parent. If it does not have this outcome, then the child who takes the parents' prerogative *is* the parent. Therefore, he *is* anyone or anything he dictates and by that token 'outside the social law.'

Another logical extension would be to set up an hypothesis:

Non-schizophrenic child = history of battle for prerogatives won by parent.

Schizophrenic child = history of battles for prerogatives won by child – or no contest.

[3] S. K. Langer: *Philosophy in a New Key* (Boston, 1948).
[4] K. L. Artiss: 'Environmental Therapy,' in *Current Psychiatric Therapies*, J. H. Masserman, ed., vol. 4, p. 30 (New York, 1964).

307

15. THE SCHOOL-FOR-LIVING THEORY

As the years went by I had ample time to think about the experiment described in the preceding chapter.[1] I was astonished to discover how little there was in the literature dealing with the medical context which determines the background to our psychiatric activity and the character of our psychiatric institutions.

Let us start with the question as to what *type* of reform was described in the previous chapter.

The program of reform at Rose Cottage, taken as a whole, was nothing new. (The number of books that trace the process of change in any detail, though, is relatively small.[2]) The foregoing chapter does present a new aspect, however. While nothing in it is original in theory, attempting over a period of two years *to disencumber a ward of its medical mythology* is relatively new. So far I have not come across any account in the literature of a consistent attempt to carry through something of this kind in a mental hospital.

Did this experiment achieve anything? For me it certainly did. I learned a great deal from it. I have the impression, too, that it gave a powerful impetus to the resocialization of some of the Rose Cottage clients, besides having a very positive effect on the morale of the staff.

Now for the question of what *type* of reform. In order to submit it to closer analysis I propose making use of the ideas that Karl Popper has presented about this in his book *The Poverty of Historicism*.[3]

Popper describes two types of social action that bring about change in specific social institutions (large- or small-scale industry, church, insurance association, school, army, etc.). The first type he calls 'utopian' and/or 'holistic social engineering.' The second type he calls 'piecemeal social engineering.'

He is an outspoken champion of the latter type. Just as an engineer designs a machine, arrives at a new model or repairs the machine, so the social engineer is someone who controls certain existing social organizations, redesigns them or . . . reforms them. A social organization hinges on people, of course, but the blueprint of the organization is at least equally important. The 'piecemeal social engineer' is somebody who operates with bits and pieces, who makes reforms and introduces changes 'bit by bit.' He knows how little he knows, introduces his reforms step by step, learns from his mistakes and is 'always on the look-out for the unavoidable unwanted consequences of any reform.' He rejects the 'sweeping reform,' any *wholesale* change of traditional social institutions. For him such an approach is too complex; he would no longer perceive clearly what was cause and what effect. In short, he would no longer know what he is doing.

'Piecemeal tinkering' is in fairly sharp contrast to the work of the political activist, with his cry of 'everything's got to change!' This holistic or utopian social engineering tries to bring about changes in society as a whole. Of course, the piecemeal social engineer may be very ambitious, too. Reform of a constitution, a series of piecemeal reforms inspired by one general tendency (for instance, toward a greater equalization of incomes) – all this can still be called a 'piecemeal' method of reform.

Yet for Popper there is a difference in starting point and mentality. The giant steps taken by the holistic reformer often induce many unintended and frequently unexpected repercussions, which result in a sort of piecemeal *improvisation*, a kind of 'unplanned planning.' In contrast the piecemeal operator sets to work with greater caution, more critically, and is better prepared. Popper takes his indictment of the holistic, utopian reformers to considerable lengths: 'Of the two methods I hold that one is possible while the other simply does not exist, it is impossible.'

And again:

> One of the differences between the Utopian or holistic approach and the piecemeal approach may therefore be stated in this way: while the piecemeal engineer can attack his problem with an open mind as to the scope of the reform, the holist cannot do this; for he had decided beforehand that a complete reconstruction is possible and necessary.

Popper holds the holistic, utopian method of reforming society to be unscientific, or at any rate, 'conflicting with a truly scientific attitude.'

The demythologizing of medical mythology, the way in which the Rose Cottage staff put this into practice, the quite fierce reactions among medical colleagues and the staff on other wards – were these the consequences of a 'piecemeal' approach (albeit of the ambitious sort) or of a utopian, holistic approach? I am inclined to believe the latter.

I can now move on to a more theoretical discussion of the background of the experiment. The Rose Cottage experiment as a 'school for living' and the business of getting rid of medical jargon sprang from the idea that 'words' might be powerful enough in themselves to withstand our attempts to create a learning (and unlearning) environment. So we must first take a look at the question: Why replace words with other words? What's in a name?

The answer is supplied by a whole body of semantic literature, starting with Korzybski.[4] The power of words (more generally: certain linguistic systems) to light up part of our universe and to create specific meaning, specific possibilities of meaning, allowing certain possibilities of action, behavior and thinking, is impressive. Equally impressive is the power of words (linguistic systems) to obscure part of our universe, to obliterate and destroy certain possibilities of meaning and to paralyze certain types of action, behavior and thinking. Words can imprison and blindfold us as well as they can liberate us and make us to see and grasp. This has been stated before by three authors: George Herbert Mead, Edward Sapir and Benjamin Lee Whorf. To quote Sapir:

> Human beings do not live in the objective world alone, nor alone in the world of social activity as ordinarily understood, but are very much at the mercy of the particular language which has become the medium of expression for their society. It is quite an illusion to imagine that one adjusts to reality essentially, without the use of language and that language is merely an incidental mean of solving certain specific problems of communication or reflection. Matter of fact the 'real world' is to a large extent unconsciously built upon the language habits of the group. We see and hear and otherwise experience very largely as we do, because the language habits of our community predispose certain choices of interpretation.[5]

Kenneth Artiss directed my attention to the collaboration between Sapir and another linguist, Benjamin Whorf, which resulted in the intriguing (though unproven) Sapir-Whorf hypothesis which is known as the 'principle of linguistic relativity.' Chase formulated it as follows:

1. All higher levels of thinking are dependent upon language.

2. The structure of the language one habitually uses influences the manner in which one understands one's environment. The picture of the universe shifts from tongue to tongue.[6]

Whorf put is this way: 'Speakers of different languages see the cosmos differently, evaluate it differently, sometimes not so much, sometimes widely.' And: 'A change of language sometimes can transform appreciation of the cosmos.'[7]

This last statement in particular surprised me, for it was precisely what I had in view in initiating the experiment. I wanted the patients to appreciate, to grasp, to use the educational psychoanalytic cosmos as we tried to present it on our ward and as we are trying to present it in the psychoanalytic hospital in general. I wanted this educational universe to be within their grasp, within their ability to understand its meaningfulness, so that it would initiate and sustain the kind of action which seemed essential for successful psycho-therapeutic work.

Let us leave the experts in semantics and examine what can be found in the literature on this subject. There is remarkably little. People do, of course, create a 'therapeutic environment,' a 'therapeutic community,' but they overlook the fact that their workshop is still some sort of medical enterprise. 'Hospital,' 'patient,' 'nurse,' 'doctor,' 'treatment,' 'illness,' 'recovery,' 'cure' – all these words and requisites, white coats included, are taken for granted. To paraphrase Whorf: We do not notice it anymore, because this whole medical culture and language have become so much the background to our work that it is like air, whose absence we only notice when we are choking.

But the problem has not been neglected altogether. Thomas Szasz, in *The Myth of Mental Illness*, sets out to attack all kinds of 'myths' and to show how logically untenable they are.[8] In a brilliantly written book he upsets all the traditional ideas, the first among them being that 'psychiatry' is a special branch of medicine concerned with 'mental illnesses.' That idea holds true for organic diseases (epilepsy, tumor, dementia, neuro-logical or other diseases), but in the case of psychiatry a different process of development is called for.

According to Szasz, the confusion started with the cele-brated Parisian neurologist Charcot, who knew a good deal about diseases of the nervous system but understood little about people with 'problems in living.' He failed to distinguish the logical difference between a physical disease (neurological illness) and bodily-illness-imitating behavior (the 'hysterical' form of communication). This behavior has to be decoded and interpreted as an expression of psychological conflicts and a disruption in the building up of interpersonal relationships. When Charcot threw both categories together and defined (named) the second category (bodily-illness-imitating be-havior) on his own authority as 'mental illnesses' (*Nervöse Krankheiten*), the confusion started. Charcot believed that the people he used for demonstration purposes before crowded lecture room audiences (a circus act which alas! has been copied by many a professor in psychiatry and is still with us today) were *also* suffering from a physical disease, of which only the 'cause' still had to be discovered. Psychiatry became a special branch of medicine, and the role of 'medical patient' was offered to all those who (as Szasz drily puts it) 'played the game of life according to the wrong rules.'

The role has been accepted, but this expression of Christian neighborly love has had a destructive outcome. A vast medical game – 'doctor,' 'patient,' 'illness' – became an ingredient of our culture. Szasz suggests that this obscured the real issues, blocked the progress of psychiatry as a social science and had socially destructive results for all those who nominated themselves for this 'mental illness' role. Mental illness, according to Szasz, is a 'myth' and so is the fact that psychiatry (and psychoanalysis) is a medical speciality. Psychiatry is part of the social sciences. Its subject matter is the communicative behavior of man as a role-playing and rule-following symbolic animal. Psychiatrists deal with defects in the socialization process, engage their clients in a learning process, so that the origin of old rules can be investigated (and discarded) and new rules acquired, leading in turn to more efficient living and more gratifying interpersonal communication. Szasz criticizes psychiatry for waiting too long at the fork in the road, unable to make up its mind which way to go. The professional identity of the future psychiatrist is clearly defined by Szasz as a specialist in intra- and interpersonal communicative processes.

Ths psychodynamically oriented psychotherapist, group and family therapist, psychoanalyst, psychodramatist, social psychologist, cultural anthropologist – they are among those to whom the future of psychiatry belongs, and what they have accomplished until now has been in spite of the medical scaffolding of psychiatry and not because of it. If psychiatrists want to be 'humanitarian,' they must acquire the competence that will enable them to assist their clients in a process that helps them achieve a more efficient way of living and a more satisfactory type of interpersonal communication. As we shall see later on, these are not new ideas, but Szasz has been particularly clear and emphatic in advancing them.

For the moment I am sticking to the question of the medical organization, the medical culture of the mental hospital. The sociologist Goffman has also taken a clear stand on this subject. Goffman analyzes the logic and the consequences of the 'medical service model,' as deployed in the psychiatric institution. He first offers a fascinating analysis of the professional 'service model' in general – the giving of competent aid by a specialist.

The expert gives assistance to a client who presents a particular object for repair. Whereas this 'tinkering trade' used to be done primarily in the home, one of the changes that had appeared is the emergence of a 'workshop complex,' whereby the client goes to the person dispensing aid and leaves the object to be repaired wit him, later returning to pick it up.

When we consider the medical service model, the workshop is the hospital and the object the body – only we cannot leave it behind for repair and pick it up later. The problem is that this workshop-qua-organization is not a neutral environment at all, but can affect the person 'admitted' adversely. Goffman suggests that although hospitals claim to give service to people, this is highly questionable. It is not simply a matter of their financial interests. It is a fact that even a brief stay in a hospital can be a very traumatizing experience. Young children react, for instance, with 'separation anxiety.' According to Goffman, 'the workshop in such cases is not a benign, neutral environment but a hurtful one.'

Goffman then focuses on the mental hospital and the way in which the 'medical service model' is applied there. The medical service system is logically tenable in the case of, for instance, cerebral defects. The difficulty lies in the field of what in technical jargon are known as the 'functioning psychoses.' In the mental hospital social misconduct and genuine physical illness are brought together, which suggests that this combination is indeed possible within the same system. This would seem to be very illogical, though, and Goffman puts forward a number of arguments against it. All the facts connected with the processes that go on in a ward, the

314

dynamics, the disciplinary and administrative aspects, are expressed in the language of the medical service system. Goffman suggests that everything within this frame of reference must be distorted and that this gives a false picture of what is actually happening on a ward. Thus he states:

> Everything that goes on in hospital must be legitimated, assimilating it or translating it to fit into a medical service frame of reference. To effect this translation, reality must be considerably twisted, somewhat as it is by judges, instructors or officers and others in our coercive institutions.

What the patient does and what displeases the institution – not obeying the rules and requirements of the nursing personnel – may immediately be taken as evidence that one is 'not ready for liberty,' is in need of further 'treatment,' and has not so far been 'cured.'

This creates an extremely confusing situation. Patients and staff collaborate in a kind of performance ('an elaborate dramatized tribute') intended to confirm that a medical (psychiatric) service system is being applied and that the psychiatric personnel are rendering this service. So here again we have the 'medical game,' in which the patients are assigned a role confirming and supporting the medical identity of the staff:

> To get out of the mental hospital or to ease their lives within it, the patients must show acceptance of the place accorded them and support the occupational role of those who appear to force this bargain. The self-alienating moral servitude, some of which perhaps helps to account for some inmates becoming mentally confused, is achieved by invoking the great tradition of the expert servicing relationship, especially its medical validity.

His conclusion: 'Mental patients can find themselves crushed by the weight of a service ideal that eases life for the rest of us.'[9]

Goffman says the medical service system is all right for organic disturbances, but that when it comes to the functional psychoses the situation is untenable. Even the assertion that service is being offered is not correct. There is no evidence, he argues, to prove that admitting people to a mental hospital is justified in terms of its 'successes.' On the contrary, 'hospitalizing' probably does much damage to the prospects and potential for living of the person so 'admitted.' Apart from the *medical* service system, the *service system*, too, is inappropriate and inadequate. There is little real 'service,' the 'service' does not do what it *claims* to do. Thus: 'To be made a patient is to be remade into a serviceable object, the irony being that so little service is available once this is done.'

Kai Erikson, too, has made a substantial contribution to our understanding of the problem of the medical culture of the mental hospital. In his paper 'Patient Role and Social Uncertainty, a Dilemma of the Mentally Ill' Erikson first examines the role of the 'medically sick person,' a role which we have provided for people with deviant behavior even when no demonstrable disease underlies that behavior. If we nevertheless insist on assigning this role of 'medical patient,' and if psychiatrists (and psychiatry) persist in maintaining that their 'therapy' is a medical affair, then the role will continue to be played. When the 'patient' has some (indeed justifiable) doubt as to the legitimacy of this medical role definition and also has a sense of 'the public's' skepticism, he will resort to providing more *evidence*. Erikson uses the term 'validation' for this, alluding to the attempts made by a person to justify the medical patient role with illness-imitating behavior. In order to qualify properly for the 'medical-sick role,' a person will go into a spiral of 'validation': 'Convincing others of his "illness" is, therefore, the logical outcome of settling himself comfortably within the niche society has reserved for him.' Producing this spiral of 'evidence,' attempts to justify the role of 'medical patient,' can well lead to a permanent role definition of 'being sick,' 'making the model of medical patienthood an image for the future rather than the provisional shelter for which it originally may have been set up.'

All right, this sociologist is saying, if you think it's so logical to call a psychiatric establishment a 'hospital':

then the patient is likely to have an interested social logic that given the setting, it is only appropriate that he attains

316

the role expectations of the medical patient. As long as psychiatrists prefer to talk the medical language and so visualize human behavior as falling on a spectrum in which degrees of 'illness' are recognized as gradations between the polar states of 'ideal health' and 'total collapse,' and as long as the fundamental differences between psychiatric practice and medical practice are blurred, this situation is apt to continue.

This leads Erikson to conclude that it is about time psychiatry examined the whole situation on its merits and considered altering its approach, in order to create a more realistic position in our society for people *who simply find living a difficult and troublesome business.*

Erikson refers in his article to centers in Europe where according to him the atmosphere is far less medical: 'There is more emphasis there on re-education, on development and training (the therapeutic community), with its roots in outside society rather than in the hospital with its specialized medical culture.' Then comes the surprising statement that in Europe 'the patient is more of a student than a medical patient.'

We must take this idealization of Europe as wishful thinking, for in my opinion it simply is not true. Thinking in organic terms about the problems of the psychotic person remains predominant and the idea of psychiatry as a medical specialization seems to be an unassailable conviction. Anyone who is prepared to cast doubt on this takes the risk of being regarded as an oddity.

Let me quote another odd-man-out who has been mentioned before. It is the psychoanalyst John Rosen who has the same ideas on the subject. From his *Direct Psychoanalytic Psychiatry* (New York, 1962):

> The reader may notice the absence of the term 'doctor' and 'patient,' 'symptom,' 'diagnosis,' 'disease,' 'etiology' and other medical language from this book. These are deliberate omissions, to help emphasize my conviction that psychosis should not be viewed as a medical problem, nor its treatment as a medical matter. I say this in spite of the heavily medical orientation of psychiatry at the present

317

time, and in spite of my personal training and interest in medicine.

For Rosen, a 'psychosis' is a sort of dream and not a 'medical illness.' For the psychiatrist he has invented the name 'psychotrophist,' that is, a feeder of the mind. He does use the terms 'neurosis' and 'psychosis' as *substantives*, objects with thinglike properties. His clients are admitted to a *home*, surrounded by the assistant psychotherapists who are engaged twenty-four hours a day in a process that includes, besides providing insight into 'unconscious processes,' a great amount of effort at re-education and relearning or acquiring social skills.

Going back for a moment to the term 'mental illness,' we can say that as a name given to 'maladjustments' (another unhappy word) it does very little to help the individual thus labeled. Indeed it probably contributed to confirming his mode of being. As Kubany says in a recent article entitled 'Anxiety – Yes. Mental Illness – No': 'Whatever advantages may exist in having a unified concept called "mental illness," the disadvantages would seem to far outweight them.' [10]

It is not just a question of the social and legal discrimination that this term implies, it also gives rise to a demoralizing self-denigration:

> The label has a pervasive connotation implying that all facets of a person's mental functioning are impaired; some individuals are inclined to accept the condition as a crutch for evading moral responsibility; the label itself creates a fear which causes individuals who might normally seek help to avoid doing so; it connotes a medical model implying that, if the right pills are taken or prescribed treatment is followed, a cure will take place.

Thus Kubany finds the term 'mental illness' far from innocent. It should be possible to define the word 'accurately,' but the trouble is that laymen, and even professionals, *cling to the connotative meanings of the term*: 'To change these associations is semantically comparable to a leopard's changing its spots.'

Searching for a new way of defining, Kubany postulates

that we must give people wrestling with problems-in-living the feeling that they are part of a very much bigger group with the same problems. We have to look for a 'labeling system' that will make us realize we all have problems of adjustment. Some more so than others. It is certainly of first importance to get rid of the negative stigmatizing quality of terms like 'mental illness,' 'psychic illness,' etc., by altering our labels. A variety of adaptational problems of varying degree (thus avoiding diagnostic categories) would seem to be the best solution. The notion of 'adjustment' or 'adaptation' need not imply in advance *how* one should adapt, nor does it prescribe the form of such adaptation. The point is (and here I follow Kubany) that we must leave a person free to relate to his environment and adapt to it in the way he prefers. The idea of adaptation may well imply that an individual changes himself so as to fit better into his environment, but it equally allows for the possibility of a meaning which implies that the individual changes his environment so as to be able to function better in it.

Provisionally, that gives adequate support to the idea that formed the basis of the Rose Cottage experiment as a 'school for living.' The three authors cited (Szasz, Goffman and Kai Erikson) agree in their critique of the medical conceptual framework pervading the mental hospital and the confusion that results from it. They all describe how such a form of medical organization creates and perpetuates 'chronic-illness-imitating-behavior': a kind of role behavior that complements and supports the medical identity of the staff. Support has been found by quoting a number of authors (psychiatrists, sociologists, experts in semantics) for the rationale of the attempts described herein to eliminate the use of medical language. I have tried to show that medical classification of people who do not observe the cultural rules of the game is a historical anachronism and has had socially destructive results, and that this is most obviously expressed in conduct which in mental hospitals we call 'chronic schizophrenic.' I have also tried to show that my own findings have an *extra* degree of cogency in that they were arrived at in what was in many respects a unique psychoanalytic sanatorium lacking neither

319

in manpower and personal commitment nor in psychotherapeutic competence and care. It was definitely no obsolete
snakepit where I was working, not a state mental hospital,
where factors such as privacy, care and personal or group
psychotherapy are hardly present, if present at all.

I have indicated in what has been said already that I intend
to explore *this* aspect – 'medical' psychiatry and all that
implies. This chapter was the preamble.

REFERENCES

[1] It has been published in brief summary form under the title: 'Chronic Schizophrenia and the Medical Culture,' *Psychother. Psychosom.* vol. 17, pp. 133–152 (1969).

[2] See R. Rubenstein and H. D. Lasswell: *The Sharing of Power in a Psychiatric Hospital* (New Haven, Conn., 1966).

[3] K. Popper: *The Poverty of Historicism* (New York, 1964).

[4] A. Korzybski: *Science and Sanity*, 4th ed. (Clinton, 1958).

[5] E. Sapir: *Language* (New York, 1939).

[6] S. Chase: *The Tyranny of Words* (New York, 1938).

[7] B. L. Whorf: *Language, Thought and Reality* (Cambridge, Mass., 1956).

[8] T. S. Szasz: *The Myth of Mental Illness* (New York, 1961).

[9] T. R. Sarbin: 'The Scientific Status of the Mental Illness Metaphor,' in *Changing Perspectives in Mental Illness*, R. B. Edgerton and S. C. Plog, eds. (New York, 1969).

The quotations come from the essay: 'The Medical Model and Mental Hospitalization,' in *Asylums*, E. Goffman, ed. (New York, 1961).

[10] A. Kubany: 'Anxiety – Yes, Mental Illness – No,' *E.T.C.*, vol. 26, pp. 475–481 (1969).

NOTES

A selection from the literature, with special attention to the problem of 'chronicity' and the 'medical patient' role:

T. Parsons: 'Illness and the Role of the Physician: A Sociological Perspective,' *Am. J. of Orthopsychiatry*, vol. 11, pp. 452–461 (1951). A much-quoted publication because it contains a basic description of that form of deviant behavior which is called 'illness' and of the role expectations associated with 'being ill' in our culture.

Parsons describes four aspects of the 'sick role':

1. The first of these is the exemption of the sick person from the performance of certain of his normal social obligations.
2. Secondly, the sick person is, in a very specific sense, also exempted from a certain type of responsibility for his own state.
   This is what is ordinarily meant by saying that he is in a 'condition.'
   He will either have to get well spontaneously or 'be cured'

by having something done to him. He cannot reasonably be expected to 'pull himself together' by a mere act of will, and thus decide to be all right. He may have been responsible for getting himself into such a state, as by careless exposure to accident or infection, but even then he is not responsible for the process of getting well, except in a peripheral sense.

3. The third aspect of the sick role is the partial character of its legitimation, hence the deprivation of a claim to full legitimacy. To be sick, that is, is to be in a state which is socially defined as undesirable, to be gotten out of as expeditiously as possible. No one is given the privileges of being sick any longer than necessary but only so long as he 'can't help it.'

4. Finally, being sick is also defined, except for the mildest cases, as being 'in need of help.' Moreover, the type of help which is needed is presumptively defined; it is that of persons specially qualified to care for illness, above all of physicians.

K. T. Erikson: 'Patient Role and Social Uncertainty: A Dilemma of the Mentally Ill,' *Psychiatry*, vol. 20, pp. 263–275 (1957).

A good deal has been cited from this article in the text. I regard it as one of the most illuminating on the role of the 'mental patient.'

The term 'role validation' is introduced and defined as:
    the giving to a person certain expectations to live up to, providing him with distinct notions as to the conduct it considers appropriate or valid for him in his position.

The term 'role commitment' is defined as:

    the complementary process whereby a person adopts certain styles of behavior as his own, committing himself to the roles which seem to best represent the kind of person he assumes himself to be and best reflect the social position he considers himself to occupy.

Erikson uses the term 'role commitment' to indicate that a role is not only assigned, but that the person may actively and persuasively display certain forms of behavior so that the community 'is persuaded to accept these modes as the basis for a new set of expectations on its part.' This subtle bargaining process also occurs when somebody enters a mental hospital. In order to make the 'medical patient role' legitimate in the eyes of the community, sickness behavior has got to be produced. Erikson uses the word 'engineering':

    In their bargaining with society for a stable patient role and in the absence of clear-cut organic symptoms, a real illness which can't be helped is a most precious commodity.

Erikson describes (as others have) the way that the patient can suddenly shrug off this 'mental illness' role behavior (for instance, when taking part in the rehearsal or performance of a play). But after

> committing himself to positive constructive activity the patient tries afterwards like Penelope, who wove a cloak by day only to unravel it by night, to undo this constructive activity by a dramatic retreat into impulsivity and destruction.

An energetic attempt, that is, to produce helpless-dependent behavior so as to qualify once again for the 'sick role.'

D. L. Burnham: 'Identity Definition and Role Demand in the Hospital Careers of Schizophrenic Patients,' *Psychiatry*, vol. 24, pp. 96–123 (1961).

Burnham worked for a considerable time in Cedar Haven and in this article is clearly doing a balancing act. All around him he can see the more or less disastrous unfolding of 'patient roles' (which the hospital organization compels). He also gives a striking quotation from a poem by Robert Frost (*Collected Poems* [New York, 1945]),

> . . . nothing to look backward to with pride
> and nothing to look forward to with hope
> So now and never any different

and expresses thereby how precarious the situation of one's personal identity, the sense of one's self-reliance, is for the person hospitalized as 'psychotic.' With so much fragmentation, confusion and a feeling of ego weakness, the enforced role of 'patient' with its connotation of 'helpless' and 'not responsible' may be the final nudge into total regression. He sees this happening around him and gives some illuminating examples. I regard this article as one of the most convincing. Burnham also has a clear view of what happens if this whole institution-hospital-organization is suddenly removed.

From Sivadon comes the story of how during the German invasion of France the entire personnel fled and the patients had to fend for themselves. A follow-up after the war revealed that a lot of patients had not only survived but had organized various activities and fulfilled other social roles successfully and effectively.

From Hilde Bruch comes the example of a hospital with 'chronic mental patients' in Israel, which for economic reasons had to be converted into a work camp. Here, too, there were surprising and positive changes. 'Fresh role opportunities' were jumped at; and when a truck was presented to the 'workers' with a red cross on it: 'They objected vigorously that they no longer were patients and that the red cross should be erased.'

Despite his persuasive argument, when it comes to the *consequences* Burnham becomes hesitant. He asks the hospital to permit supplementary roles – supplementary, that is, to the only one there is to play, that of 'patient.' At this point Burnham begins to have doubts. Is that really possible? Which leads him to comment:

> For certain types of patients perhaps a hospital is not the proper treatment setting, and alternatives such as halfway houses, foster homes, work camps, clubs and day-hospital-schools might be more suitable.

But this idea is not worked out in any detail. Burnham still takes a positive line on the regression of a rigid personality structure – at any rate as a phase of disintegration. 'Patients have to get worse before they get better' may be going too far for him, but he admits there is such a thing as productive disintegration – a therapeutic (?) regressive phase.

Burnham sees the problem very clearly. My objection to his article is that he remains too cautious, does not present a real alternative and fails to draw the consequences. His proposal of 'supplementary roles' is therefore nebulous, and he describes a 'certain percentage of patients' whose fortunes are adversely affected by their hospital career.

G. R. George and R. W. Gibson: 'Patient-Staff Relationship Change with Environment,' *Mental Hospitals* (November 1959).

The account of a vacation taken with a number (20) of 'chronic schizophrenics' away from Cedar Haven, at a bungalow by the sea. In the psychoanalytic sanatorium the main emphasis was on *understanding*, on seeing and comprehending needs and attempts at restoring communication. The authors do not want to call it 'permissiveness'; but 'the primary emphasis was on understanding behavior rather than controlling it.'

Then came the discoveries made when patients and staff lived in a quite different environment. The authors describe a man (Albert) who for years had been wetting and defecating in his bed. On the ward that bed was efficiently cleaned and made up. The man's conduct during the vacation in the bungalow became a matter of intense personal concern, for patients and personnel were now living together for twenty-four hours of the day! It was becoming impossible for the group (and if it had gone on for long, for the bungalow's proprietor too!). It had now become not a 'psychiatric symptom' but behaviour that aroused strong feelings in the group. That manifestly made an impression, because the man stopped his objectionable behavior. And now it was discovered that this man could be very much more self-reliant and do much more for himself than had previously been believed. On the ward little had been expected of him – at least Albert had evidently taken the personnel's sympathy and attempts at understanding in such a way that he was unable to function at a more adult level.

In the new environment, during the vacation, the dividing line –

we (the staff) as opposed to them (the patients) – disappeared. The new surroundings compelled all to a genuine group experience, erasing this barrier, because everyone had his task and responsibility.

After the vacation Gibson tried to make changes on his ward: delegating responsibility to the patients, opening up the nursing office and so on. He came to the now familiar conclusion, which is interesting, because it was *not* arrived at in Cedar Lodge but during a vacation away from the 'culture' of the sanatorium. He even says so himself: 'In this case it was only that total change of milieu which gave us an opportunity to realize what was going on in the ward.'

Gibson then resolved to put into practice on his ward what he learned during the vacation:

> In any event, we believe that if we hope to maintain and improve our treatment program, a continuing search must be made to discover and correct the recurring antitherapeutic features of patient-staff relationships.

R. Sobel: 'Role Conflict and Resistance,' *Am. J. of Psychotherapy*, vol. 18, pp. 25–35 (1964).

In the psychotherapeutic relationship the client clothes the therapist with parental attributes ('parentification'); dependency and conflicts versus original parent-figures become visible in 'transference.'

But is this really all? Sobel stresses the significance of the 'role' of the 'patient' and of the 'medical patient' in particular. He tries to draw a distinction between the latter role and that of the 'psychiatric patient.' Where the 'medical patient's' role is concerned, Sobel refers us to the Talcott Parsons' analysis of it.

Sobel seeks to define the 'psychiatric patient' role in different terms (initiative, collaboration, learning) and suggests that *part* of the confusion in psychotherapy may be a result of the predominance of the medical model and the 'medical patient' role behavior expected of the client and produced by him. This behavior can be described as 'transference' or 'resistance,' while the possibility is ignored that the client could be persisting in his self-definition as a 'sick person' – a definition to which doctors who have become psychiatrist-psychotherapists have themselves powerfully contributed. So Sobel's advice is to explain to the client in the initial phase of the psychotherapy the difference between the 'medical patient' role and the 'psychiatric patient' role. In that way a form of working relationship can be structured more clearly from the very start.

J. H. Thrasher and H. I. Smith: 'Interactional Contacts of Psy-

chiatric Patients: Social Roles and Organizational Implications,'
Psychiatry, vol. 27, pp. 389–399 (1964).

This article contains a lot about roles. One sentence that struck me was:

> Some patients simply are convinced of the purely physical nature of their illness and restructure the patient role to be consonant with that of the medical patient.

A. M. Ludwig and F. Farrelly: 'The Code of Chronicity,' *Archives of General Psychiatry*, vol. 15, pp. 562–569 (1966).

The theme of being overwhelmed and imprisoned in the social role of the 'mentally ill person' with all the behavioral forms that this implies is elaborated and referred to as the 'code of chronicity.'

> This code, partially reinforced by staff and society, tends to perpetuate 'crazy' behavior, helps sustain a staff-patient barrier, leads to the acceptance and rationalization of continued hospitalization, and thus effectively eliminates any incentive for change, improvement, and eventual discharge.

The authors discuss the 'model patient' who is a cheap source of labor in the hospital and so becomes a sort of 'extra' to the staff. This behavior guarantees him a permanent niche in the institution. The person's self-definition as a 'victim of society' demanding total security as compensation is confirmed in the permissive atmosphere. I am in complete agreement with the authors when they say apropos of 'crazy behavior':

> . . . craziness does not remain fullblown constantly, but is a sometime thing. We have gained the distinct impression that patients may frequently turn their craziness off and on in both a predictable and nonpredictable manner. We believe that the aperiodic nature of many patients' 'craziness' effectively pays off for them in a variety of ways, not the least of which is continued hospitalization.

Hence 'craziness' can be used as a weapon against the staff (who have to remain 'human'). It is the weapon of 'if-you-upset-me, I'll-make-you-wish-you-hadn't.'

The authors also describe how the patients maintain this code among themselves and perpetuate each other's behavior. There is an account of the struggle to break through this wall of chronicity.

K. L. Artiss: 'Environmental Therapy' in *Current Psychiatric Therapies*, vol. 4, pp. 46–54 (New York, 1964).

In this article Artiss shows his interest in semantics (Sapir and Whorf). Besides the passage quoted in the text Artiss provides a clear indication that as the medical model and language disappear, the nurse of the future, for instance, 'may have dropped off part of her role, to be replaced by an appellation that suggests teaching or tutoring.' And he asks: 'What will happen to the white-coated Doctor making "rounds" with his white-clad and starched Nurse in their Hospital ward filled with sick Patients?'

It is intriguing to note that Artiss does not go beyond this hint.

16. 'MEDICAL'
PSYCHIATRY

In this chapter I want to probe further into the question of why psychiatry has become a medical specialty (including psychoanalysis) and why *organizations* such as mental hospitals, psychiatric-neurological departments of general hospitals and institutes of medical psychotherapy have been given a medical stamp.

I believe that psychiatry as we know it today is saddled with a problem, a skeleton in the closet, to prey on our will and constantly attack our peace of mind. It is an acute and troublesome problem which we have not shown much enthusiasm about tackling. For a long time now psychiatry has been a medical specialty. Modern psychiatrists still go through a medical training of from six to seven years. Some of them, after qualifying as psychiatrists, are then trained in psychoanalysis. The fact that they are medical doctors remains the core of their professional identity. Even psychoanalysis is defined – especially by the disciples of Freud – as a medical specialty, a part of medical practice.

The psychoanalyst who concerns himself with human behavior in a specific culture lives and works in a medical mode of conceptualizing problems. He is addressed as 'doctor,' talks to 'patients' and tries to find something to work with in the concepts of 'mental health' and 'mental illness.' He is compelled to describe the development of a psychoanalytic-psychotherapeutic relationship as 'treatment' and his patients present him with terms such as 'cure' or 'recovery' as their goal in therapy.

It is a fair question to ask if the psychiatrist who sees his work as embedded in a medical culture and meets human and existential problems with medical language is not losing sight of these problems. It is also fair to ask whether a medical culture and language do not thrust particular modes of conceptualizing upon him and so distort the real state of affairs which confronts him. A distortion that *makes him fail to ask the right questions and fail to define the problems in the right way.* Experts in semantics point out that language can muddy our vision of reality. They have shown that there is no essential connection between words and the facts or things to which these words refer. A particular type of wording is dictated by the culture in which we live; it is something agreed upon by a joint decision.

Korzybski and his disciples stress very much the difference between knowledge acquired by means of words or combinations of words (the 'intentional orientation') and knowledge obtained through direct experience of the actual world (the 'extensional orientation').[1]

Irvine Lee has summed up the principle thus:

> To be oriented *extensionally* is to realize the primary importance of life facts, to emphasize the roles of observation and investigation, to go to the facts first and to abide by them. To be oriented *intensionally* is to order behavior in terms of definitions, arguments, verbal proofs, and theorizings, essentially disregarding the existence of verifiable life facts. Fairy tales, fiction, myths, etc., may be considered intention-with-a-purpose. Verbalization which represents what goes on inside the skin must be analyzed as such and not in terms of its correspondence with fact-outside-the-skin.[2]

The basic response when someone gives you a verbal account of what things actually look like ought, according to Lee, to go like this: 'I don't know; let's see.' The simple but fundamental idea is *that a word cannot be equated with the thing it stands for*.

Everyone knows that we do not sit on a 'chair.' 'Chair' is a five-letter word. We sit on something which this word represents. There is no necessary connection between the symbol and what is being symbolized. Yet we often feel as though there were a necessary link. Foreign languages sometimes seem to us absurd, things are not being called by their 'proper' name. Sometimes people try to explain something to a tourist whose language they cannot speak by talking louder in their own language.

The trouble is that we frequently equate words with whatever it is they refer to and that the web of words we spin around the actual world (the 'world of words') leads us into short-circuit reactions that often result in misunderstanding and action that take no account of the real state of affairs.

To Korzybski belongs the famous comparison that the world of words stands in relation to the world of reality which we experience (the 'extensional world') as 'a map does to the territory it is supposed to represent.' Hayakawa later put it this way:

> If a child grows to adulthood with a verbal world in his head which corresponds fairly closely to the extensional world that he finds around him in his widening experience, he is in relatively small danger of being shocked or hurt by what he finds, because his verbal world has told him what, more or less, to expect. He is prepared for life. If, however, he grows up with a false map in his head – that is, with a head crammed with error and superstition – he will constantly be running into trouble, wasting his efforts, and acting like a fool. He will not be adjusted to the world as it is; he might, if the lack of adjustment is serious, end up in a mental hospital.[3]

Many writers – Ernst Cassirer [4] and Susan Langer,[5] for instance – have pointed out that as an 'animal symbolicum' man is an indefatigable map-maker.

Here first is a brief summary of Cassirer's argument:

Yet in the human world we find a new characteristic which appears to be the distinctive mark of human life. The functional circle of man is not only quantitatively enlarged; it has also undergone a qualitative change. Man has, as it were, discovered a new method of adapting himself to his environment. Between the receptor system and the effector system, which are to be found in all animal species, we find in man a third link which we may describe as the *symbolic system*. This new acquisition transforms the whole of human life. As compared with the other animals man lives not merely in a broader reality; he lives, so to speak, in a new *dimension* of reality. There is an unmistakable difference between organic reactions and human responses. In the first case a direct and immediate answer is given to an outward stimulus; in the second case the answer is delayed. It is interrupted and retarded by a slow and complicated process of thought. . . . Instead of dealing with the things themselves man is in a sense constantly conversing with himself. He has so enveloped himself in linguistic forms, in artistic images, in mythical symbols or religious rites that he cannot see or know anything except by the interposition of this artificial medium. His situation is the same in the theoretical as in the practical sphere. Even here man does not live in a world of hard facts, or according to his immediate needs and desires. He lives rather in the midst of imaginary emotions, in hopes and fears, in illusions and disillusions, in his fantasies and dreams.

Cassirer cites the philosopher Epictetus, who said: 'What concerns, disturbs, alarms man are not the things but his own opinions and fantasies about the things.' Cassirer ends up, therefore, defining man not as 'animal rationale' but as 'animal symbolicum.'

Susan Langer, too, has stressed very much this essential characteristic of man, his persistent need to symbolize. She writes:

The symbol-making function is one of man's primary activities, like eating, looking or moving about. It is a fundamental process of the mind and goes on all the time.

331

As 'symbolic animals' we are always making word-maps of the world, and we take over these maps from one another. Not every map is a good one – something we notice when we use them on a journey. A good map takes us to the right destination. To stay on course we need only to glance occasionally at the landscape. Thus Anatol Rapoport says that 'language is a representation of the world we live in,' and according to him there is but one human activity that compels us to keep on improving the map so that it will correspond better with the world landscape. That is scientific activity.[6]

In spite of the screen of words (symbols) standing between us and the world, there still are people, fortunately, who from time to time try to look behind the screen. A naive person (or scientific investigator) takes a fresh look at things, without preconceived ideas, without prejudgments. He does not deny the value of the screen of words. Worlds of experience are condensed in this screen, which makes it possible to transmit knowledge from one generation to another. But every so often (especially when certain problems in the world are not resolved, when 'things go wrong') someone pierces through the 'language-and-word screen' (the 'semantic map') and risks the anxiety that attends every new discovery.

Now back to medicine and psychiatry. It is certainly a fair question whether the language of medicine is sufficiently suited to the field of human action and behavior. We may well inquire whether this word-map does not make us keep losing our way through asking the wrong questions and doing the wrong things (that is, employing 'therapeutic treatments') which instead of resolving the problems, on the contrary exacerbate them. That is what the psychoanalyst Szasz and the sociologist Goffman would argue. Becker, too, has declared war on medical psychiatry. He even speaks in this context of a revolution in psychiatry – a revolution which he defines as the invasion of psychiatry by the social sciences. Again, Becker considers the medical model much too narrow; it is incapable of supporting a really preventive program and at most can render 'symptoms' less painful. The attack is also aimed at 'psychiatric syndromes,' which have to be reexamined and redefined.[7] Obviously, I am in agreement with Becker in believing that the revolution is in fact necessary but that opposition to it is going to be very considerable indeed.

Thomas Szasz, in a book published in 1961, *The Myth of Mental Illness*, has led the field in raising the whole problem of medical conceptualizing in psychiatry. He expressly says that while the notion of 'mental illness' had a historical justification during the nineteenth century, in the twentieth it must be regarded as having no scientific value. Szasz defines psychiatry as a pseudo-medical specialty and logically demolishes the medical edifice. In its place he puts a 'theory of personal conduct,' based on the productive hypotheses deriving from the social sciences (psychoanalysis, sociology, social psychology, communication theory) which have given us knowledge about man. He says, citing Karl Popper, that a science starts with hypotheses, which later become myths. A hypothesis is a provisional way of representing things. We must be bold enough to criticize these myths if instead of illuminating reality they obscure it and block new ways of formulating the issues.

Popper has repeatedly stated that science does not begin with facts which we collect and observe, which then lead to the discovery of 'laws.' [8] Science starts, rather, with an *idea* that focuses our vision on certain facts and so makes it possible to see them. We observe the facts through the glasses of our hypotheses. When those glasses keep making us see the same old facts and our conclusions lead us into activities which *do not resolve but rather exacerbate* the problems, then it is time to put on a different pair of glasses so we can begin to see facts in a different light and draw new conclusions that will compel us to new forms of social action. That it is indeed high time for this change in psychiatry should be apparent from the hotchpotch of activities which the present-day psychiatrist threatens to slip into. The psychiatrist P. W. Bridgeman has said: 'The real meaning of a word we can discover by watching what someone does with it, not from what he says about it.' [9]

The practices of the modern psychiatrist-neurologist are bewildering and diverse. Under the cloak of treating sick people as a 'medical expert,' he gives electroshocks and insulin cures, prescribes medicines, writes psychiatric reports and, last but not least, listens to people with difficulties and problems, either in groups or individually. As Szasz sees it, psychiatry is now confronted with the task of making up its mind. What psychiatrists do is communicate with people and at the same time subject the nature of this communication process (in a situation bound by certain rules) to a closer analysis.

In its 'operations,' therefore, psychiatry is in tune with all those sciences that concern themselves with interpersonal communication processes: sciences that describe man as a 'rule-following' and 'role-playing, symbolic animal.' The linguistic apparatus of medical-biological science, with its expressions like 'neurosis,' 'psychosis,' 'mental illness,' psycho-analytic 'treatment,' 'psychopathology,' etc., has not only led to thinking in substantives (whereas we should be thinking in terms of *processes*), but has also prevented psychiatry from growing into a component part of social science. According to Szasz, psychiatry is stuck with a scientifically out-of-date thought model. Psychiatrists may still look down their noses at the social sciences, but they cannot deny the crisis that exists in their own discipline.

According to Szasz, the confusion started with Charcot, who as a specialist in diseases of the central nervous system pronounced all those forms of behavior that simulated physical illnesses (for instance, neurological complaints) to be 'diseases' too.[10] Freud adopted this way of thinking without analyzing the logical error of it. Thus 'hysteria' became a 'nervous disease' with an obscure cause, and this way of defining hysteria became the forerunner of all the later 'mental illnesses.' From a social viewpoint the label 'sick' seemed humanitarian, a form of protection for people exhibiting certain kinds of behavior. Thus people who felt themselves unequal to certain tasks in life took refuge in the role of 'someone medically sick' and found security in that. Instead of dismissing such people for their 'histrionics' as malingerers or burning or persecuting them as 'devil-pos-sessed,' it seemed more humane to call these behavioral forms illnesses. But, says Szasz, the label 'sick' cut two ways. It not only led the victim into still greater confusion regarding the nature of his own problems, but also to a steadily intensifying definition of his 'being sick' that called for the complementary role of the 'doctor to the rescue.' So what people have done, according to Szasz, is to underscore the *similarity* in the behavior of the neurologically disturbed person and that of the person unequal to the problems of living and give more weight to outward similarities than to the *differences*.

Thus there emerged a medical-theoretical frame of reference that did much to hinder the correction of 'problems in living.' (It also led to the complete failure of the psychiatrist to take a stand in the face of a society that destroyed or made impossible human growth. The psychiatrist even concluded that his specialty had nothing to do with politics!)

What Charcot failed to do, then, was to draw a logical distinction between those forms of behavior that result from a bodily defect and those that are *learned* and determined socio-culturally. So the idea of 'mental illness' quickly took on a concrete meaning and was employed as such by Kraepelin, Bleuler and Freud in spite of the fact that the term, which was supposed to explain everything, clarified nothing at all. This led eventually to an obstinate attempt to classify syndromes (nosology), a conception of schizophrenia which still gives impetus to extensive biochemical research, mental hospitals where thousands are ensconced in the role of 'chronically medically ill' (a role security from which it is practically impossible to detach them), and doctors and neurologists who have been unable to launch a collective attack on these 'problems of living' and who are in no position to create a social organization that can set in motion new learning processes. (Despite the newer socio-psychological ways of thinking, a good many psychiatrists in mental hospitals are insufficiently equipped through lack of training to get a clear view, for instance, of the organizational problems connected with the building up of a therapeutic community, or to realize that there may be something wrong with their whole plant.)

The medical frame of thinking that defined psychiatry as a special branch of medicine centered on the study, diagnosis and treatment of 'mental illnesses' helped to produce nurses in white uniforms who, as a consequence of their training and the medical tradition, act in ways that increase the confusion and reinforce the illness role of their patients. Another damaging consequence has been the psychiatric university-clinic, where the Charcot-imitating white-jacketed professor makes his rounds past the beds and indoctrinates awestruck and equally white-jacketed residents with 'diagnoses' and 'clinical cases' that prevent any view the young residents might develop on the 'problems of living,' let alone any ideas they might have on how to approach them collectively and constructively.

At this point we will leave Szasz for a moment and take a look at how Freud tried to counter the confusion that had already arisen in his time. Unfortunately, Szasz does not deal with this in his book.

REFERENCES

[1] A. Korzybski: 'Outline of General Semantics' in *General Semantics*, collected by Baugh, Hansell (New York, 1938); *Science and Sanity*, 4th ed. (Lakeville, 1958).

[2] I. J. Lee: *Language Habits in Human Affairs* (New York, 1941).

[3] S. J. Hayakawa: *Language, Thought and Action* (New York, 1963).

[4] E. Cassirer: *An Essay on Man* (New Haven, Conn./London, 1944).

[5] S. K. Langer: *Philosophy in a New Key* (Boston, 1948).

[6] A. Rapoport: 'Integrating Knowledge and Action,' *E.T.C.*, vol. 27, pp. 7–27 (1970).

[7] E. Becker: *The Revolution in Psychiatry* (London, 1964).

[8] K. R. Popper: *Conjectures and Refutations* (New York, 1962).

[9] P. W. Bridgeman: *The Way Things Are* (New York, 1959).

[10] On this point Szasz has rightly been criticized. The medical model in psychiatry had started much earlier. Critical treatments of Szasz's work are, e.g.:

F. C. Thorne: 'An Analysis of Szasz' *Myth of Mental Illness*,' *Am. J. of Psychiatry*, vol. 23, pp. 652–657 (1966);
G. R. Moss: 'Szasz: Review and Criticism,' *Psychiatry*, vol. 31, pp. 184–195 (1968).

17. FREUD, 'MEDICAL' PSYCHIATRY AND 'MEDICAL' PSYCHO-ANALYSIS

While he was studying in Paris at Le Salpêtrière Hospital (from the autumn of 1885 to the end of February, 1886) Freud was greatly impressed by the work of the neurologist Charcot. When he returned to Vienna, he had every reason to accept Charcot's way of conceptualizing and naming the problems involved. Both were neurologists and their professional identity as medical men provided them quite naturally with a medical ideology and language: the language of 'cases,' diseases to be diagnosed and treated. The logic of this terminology prescribed inexorably that there should be patients (chiefly women, at first) who focused attention on themselves because they produced a sort of behavior that imitated physical illness. Logic also prescribed that these 'nervous diseases' awaited the discovery of a cause, a mysterious defect in the functioning of the body as a machine.

Freud's mentor, Brucke, impressed upon him the truth that the diseases he was likely to encounter in people must in the end be explained by the inexorable laws of physical-chemical processes. Freud had worked initially in the neuro-anatomical laboratory and so was schooled in the ideology of physical-physiological methods. He had already published quite a number of articles, especially in the field of the diseases of the nervous system. It makes little difference in this connection that Freud repeatedly described himself as a 'doctor against all inclination.' He did important work on the study of the central nervous system and once referred to himself as a good diagnostician – especially postmortem!

After the time spent with Charcot, Freud renewed his acquaintance with the work done by his colleague Breuer – work with women suffering from 'nervous diseases.' He discovered how they experienced release from their anxieties and hallucinations on purely psychological, humanly empathetic lines. Bodily symptoms (paralyses, etc.) seemed to be symbolic forms of expression and communication.

Freud became more deeply engaged in relationships with the women described to us in the *Studies on Hysteria*. He was confronted with relived experiences of hidden and unconscious conflicts. Freud the doctor became the brilliant psychologist.

The psychoanalyst Clara Thompson – rightly, in my view – has called the work of Freud as outlined in the *Studies on Hysteria* the most creative part of his life work in psychoanalysis.[1] His sensitivity for the functioning and meaning of symbols in human experience, his capacity for psychological reconstruction of suppressed memories, are impressive indeed. There is no need to cite examples. What concerns us here is the transition from the medical-professional identity and the safety provided by a familiar medical world of thought to the entirely new professional identity of the psychologist. This necessitated abandoning the old ways of thinking and creating a completely new language. This transition, with which Freud wrestled throughout his life, strikes us as a continuing crisis in his professional identity. What was he, or what was he becoming – doctor or psychologist?

Freud never fully succeeded in relinquishing his medical-professional identity and its world of thought and language, even though he called the extent to which he did succeed the main triumph of his life. Erik Erikson compares Freud with

339

Darwin, describes both men as 'lonely discoverers,' and in an essay, 'The First Psychoanalyst,' points out how in the early period of his studies on hysteria Freud examined recollections and more deeply hidden memories as though he were engaged in cutting the brain tissues of animals into thin slices.[2] But most striking of all is the fact that later on, when he had given up the medical and authoritarian hypnosis relationship, Freud made a deliberate effort to get the person (his patient) to open up and talk, only venturing to encourage him as he followed the person through the unfolding of his associations of ideas. So began the psychoanalytic technique of free association within a relationship of free collaboration between two adult persons in an attitude of respect.

Freud transposed his accounts of human pain and suffering into personal-psychological language, always accompanying this process with a certain *note of apology*, as though this mode of language might be thought literary and unscientific, and his medical colleagues might refuse to take this novel-writing Freud seriously. Yet this concern for professional security and prestige would also seem to be a kind of apology to the 'doctor within.'

The struggle was reflected in Freud's relationship with a rather fatherly friend, Wilhelm Fliess, who was an ear, nose and throat specialist. Freud met Fliess in 1887. The latter had developed certain theories about the connection between the nasal mucous membrane and the female sex organs. The correspondence between these two medical specialists, both occupied with raising a family and dreaming of great discoveries, dates from 1893. During the time the *Studies on Hysteria* were taking shape (they appeared at the end of 1895) Freud had frequent clashes with Breuer, a man who had meant a great deal to him as mentor and friend. When Freud was spurned by many medical colleagues in Vienna, Fliess was able to fill the gap and meet his loneliness. Freud began to idealize this friend in Berlin. They exchanged manuscripts, though their personal meetings were not so common.

The thing that is of interest is brought out in the introduction to this correspondence, written by Ernst Kris.[3] A lot more was involved in the idealizing of Fliess than the discovery of a father-figure and a potential ally. Freud also turned to Fliess whenever he felt himself becoming too much of a psychologist. It was as if he kept asking Fliess, the doctor, to keep him on the right medical (physiological) track.

Freud referred in one of his letters (May 25, 1895) to a dominating passion of his, 'a tyrant, to quote Schiller' (*'einen Tyrannen, mit Schiller zu reden'*). It was psychology, which became so dominant in Freud's encounters with the so-called neuroses. (*'Es ist die Psychologie von jeher mein fern winkendes Ziel, jetzt seitdem Ich auf die Neurosen gestossen bin, um soviel näher gerückt.'*) He voiced his conflict:

> I am troubled with two aims and aspirations: to discover how the theory of the psychic and its function takes shape if one introduces a quantitative consideration, a kind of economy of nervous resources (that is the physiologist-cum-medical man), and *also* secondly [my italics] whether we can get from psychopathology the returns for creating a normal psychology [*den Gewinn für die normale Psychologie*].

In this last remark we see Freud the psychologist coming through. When he was working out his repression theory and sharing with his patients their experiences of fear and anxiety, an anxiety which was caused by intense repression of early experiences, he asked Fliess for advice that would let him off the hook. Something chemical, menstruation: can't you offer me something physiological by way of explanation? From a letter of June 30, 1896:

> I have run into some doubts about my repression theory which a suggestion from you, like the one about male and female menstruation in the same individual, may resolve. Anxiety, chemical factors, etc. – perhaps you may supply me with solid ground on which I shall be able to give up explaining things psychologically and start finding a firm base in physiology!

Freud resisted explaining things on a psychological basis. He was greatly perplexed. It was with something like an exclamation of triumph that Freud, searching for those physical-chemical forces, the organic basis of psychological conflicts and other mechanisms, eventually came up with a sort of neurological model (the 'project') and sent it to Fliess. It was a kind of complicated radio set, full of nerve tracts, cells, transitions, forms of latent and free energy. Everything was accounted for, the conscious and the unconscious, the 'psychosexual group':

> Everything fell into place, the cogs meshed, the thing really seemed to be a machine which in a moment would run of itself. The three systems of neurones, the 'free' and 'bound' states of quantity, the primary and secondary processes, the main trend and the compromise trend of the nervous system, and the two biological rules of attention and defence, the indications of quality, reality, and thought, the state of the psycho-sexual group, the sexual determination of repression, and finally the factors determining consciousness as a perceptual function – the whole thing held together, and still does. I can naturally hardly contain myself with delight.

But a month later he expressed deep disappointment and could not understand why he should have sent the whole machinery to Fliess. Ernest Jones, in his biography of Freud, refers to the years 1888–1898 as a period in which Freud waged a hard battle before deciding to give up the whole idea of a correlation between physical and psychical activity:

> It is plain that there was for Freud a security in the knowledge of the anatomy and physiology of the nervous system.[4]

And yet – that security inherent in the medical identity and its conceptual frame of reference was something Freud never surrendered. He clung to it persistently. It was prominent in the recurrent predictions that one day it would be possible to find the physical cause of 'neurosis' and 'psychosis,' the belief in the possibility that 'hysteria' might some day be cured by administering a chemical substance! It also appeared in his frequent references to constitutional and hereditary factors that might determine, for instance, ego organization, intensity of drive and the sensitivity of the erogenous zones. It showed up most clearly, perhaps, in his clinging to such terms as 'disease,' 'sick person,' 'patient,' 'treatment,' 'cure,' and especially the words 'neurosis' and 'psychosis.' Freud's language, and therefore the language of psychoanalysis, was predicated on the assumption that the connection between psychological and biochemical processes might be found in the end.

Despite this, even in this early phase of his correspondence with Fliess, Freud admitted his real vocation in a letter of January 1, 1896. He told Fliess:

> I see that you are using the circuitous route of medicine to attain your first ideal, the physiological understanding of men, while I secretly nurse the hope of arriving by the same route at my own original objective philosophy.

A philosopher then – this is what Freud wanted to be.
Again, in a letter of April 2, 1896:

> As a young man I had no desire except for philosophical knowledge and at present I am intent on fulfilling that wish, now that I am gradually moving over from medicine to psychology.

The sentiments Freud expressed here prefaced the break with Fliess, who was determined to keep Freud on the right path of 'physico-chemical thinking' and offered him many suggestions that Freud had to reject.

The chief milestone on Freud's road to becoming a psychologist stands . . . at the end of his life. Yet even then he was uncertain. There is a final essay that seems to me of enormous importance in relation to the problems we have been discussing – an essay much neglected, however, in the literature. I mean *The Question of Lay Analysis*. It deals with the question: Can a layman (*Laie*), that is to say, a *nonmedical man*, be a psychoanalyst? The essay was written in defense of Freud's friend, the psychologist Theodor Reik, who had been accused of practicing psychoanalysis without the proper qualifications – a practice the Viennese authorities evidently regarded as the prerogative of medical men. So Reik was taken to court for practicing the art of 'medicine' without being authorized to do so, and Freud felt obliged to come to the aid of this fellow psychoanalyst and friend and to state more clearly what psychoanalysis really was (in the year 1926), who could justifiably engage in psychoanalysis and what his training should be. *He was also forced to take a clear stand on the question regarding which direction psychoanalysis would take in the future.* One may wonder whether this extremely important essay would ever have been written had circumstances not compelled Freud to produce it.

A few remarks are in order before we take a closer look at this essay. It is clear that nowhere in his work did Freud succeed in giving a satisfactory name to the job of being a psychoanalyst (nor, for that matter, to the person who enters into a personal and working relationship with the psychoanalyst, the person being analyzed). Educator-instructor was one term he used, but not for very long, as if he could never quite manage to part company with medical terminology. 'A secular pastoral worker' is what he called the psychoanalyst in the paper on lay analysis. (The psychologist Carl Rogers was later to use the terms 'counsellor' and 'client.')

Adler, fortunately, did not describe a medical-educational bureau – in my view a very confusing name – but a *Bertaungsstelle* (i.e., a consultative bureau). It is interesting in this connection to note how much more easily Adler solved the problem of transition from a medical ideology to the ideology of the social sciences. Obviously far less concerned than Freud about losing his professional prestige, he withdrew more rapidly from medical circles in Vienna and turned to educators and pastoral counsellors. Adler became the most used (and least quoted) psychologist. His contribution to ego psychology, his view of the individual and his repertoire of behavior conditioned by environmental influences, a life-style which in the relationship with the other avoids the experience of anxiety-ridden impotence (a sense of inferiority), was readily adopted later by Karen Horney ('neurotic trends') and by Sullivan ('self-system' and 'security operations'). Both of these writers had a definite inclination to take their stand from the start as social scientists. They have been called, justifiably, 'neo-Adlerians.'

The American, Harry Stack Sullivan, managed to make a

very original connection between Freud's ideas and the strong sociological and social-psychological tradition in America. However, he also had difficulty with the problem we are discussing now. He found the social psychologists a great deal less naive than the psychiatrists who connected everything with physical diseases, and he was inclined to favor a fusion of psychiatry with the social sciences – but still he recoiled from it, on grounds which were to be later defended in detail by others. Because there are genuine diseases (that mask themselves as problems in living – 'neurotic disorders'), and there is a sort of overlapping of the 'organic' and the 'functional' (problems of living), Sullivan saw no solution other than to equip the doctor with a sufficient working knowledge of psychiatry. He did not solve the problem. Helen Swick Perry is right when she says in an introduction to a work by Sullivan that he touched upon a dilemma but did not resolve it: 'This dilemma as Sullivan stated it in 1939 is still a central issue today.' [5]

Now for Freud's essay, *The Question of Lay Analysis*. Freud composed it in the form of a dialogue with an 'impartial person,' later defined in his Epilogue as 'a man of good intention and extraordinary integrity.'

Why he chose this particular form is clear enough. Freud addressed the interested parties *indirectly*. He must have realized that the question of who was to take over from him the heritage of psychoanalysis, who was to practice it, was a risky one. He must have known that the prevailing opinion among the doctors was that medical men should be the heirs of psychoanalysis. To raise the whole question at this late hour called for diplomacy, so as not to increase resistance. One might wish that Freud had been direct and forthright, had used more of his full authority to proclaim a viewpoint and a conviction that would have left no room for different interpretations. The reason why his friend Theodor Reik was being prosecuted was because the Austrian legal authorities took the medical terms literally. Since people spoke of 'neuroses' as 'nervous diseases' and of psychoanalysis as a way of 'treating' sick people leading to a 'cure,' it automatically followed that the layman was incompetent to carry out such a course of medical treatment. The semantic trap was wide open, the medical language led inevitably to a particular logic, the psychologist Reik became both victim and *cause célèbre*. Freud felt obliged to tackle the problem and began by arguing:

> It may perhaps turn out that in this instance the patients are not like other patients, that the laymen are really not laymen, and that the doctors have not exactly the qualities which one has a right to expect of doctors and on which their claims should be based.

He once more explained to his unbiased partner in dialogue what psychoanalysis really was all about: listening and talking, ostensibly not much more than an exchange of words. He then proceeded to expound to him something of psychoanalytic theory and technique.

In a brilliant introduction he maintained that the person who has gone through an analysis of his own has a knowledge of the psychology of the 'unconscious,' understands the art of interpretation (*die Deutungskunst*), commands the whole technique of building up a relationship, gradually overcoming resistances and handling relived emotional experiences (the 'transference') . . . and *is no layman in the field of psychoanalysis*. At this point Freud moved to the offensive and described medical training as just about the *opposite* of what the future psychoanalyst would need by way of preparation. Training in psychiatry does not come off much better. Those who practice this discipline, according to Freud, usually do little else but search for physical causes of mental disturbances and on that basis establish a kind of theory of diseases. For an adequate psychotherapeutic encounter with a neurotic person 'being schooled in medicine does nothing, but absolutely nothing at all.'

It was at this point, however, that Freud once again took a step backward, as though he himself dared not accept altogether the logical outcome of his own insight. He mentioned again the possibility that one day psychic disturbances might be influenced by 'an effect exerted on the biology of organs

346

and in a context of chemistry.' An old idea which apparently he could not bring himself to relinquish even when opposing the grave consequences of this kind of thinking.

After some very critical remarks about the 'medical charlatans,' doctors who assume the right to psychoanalyze after inadequate psychoanalytic training, and then think themselves bound to deny this right to psychologists whose preparation has been quite excellent, Freud declared that the real layman is the person who *is incompetent as a psychoanalyst*, that is, who is not adequately trained. Then Freud made his impartial interlocutor insist again on greater clarity: 'Yes, but the doctors, the doctors!'

At this juncture in the essay one senses that Freud knew how terribly isolated he still was. Here I want to employ my own interpretation. As I see it, Freud's sympathies by no means lay with his doctor colleagues, despite the fact that most of his pupils were doctors and had given him considerable support during his years of painful isolation. Again, he tried to be both candid and diplomatic. After some vague comments about 'consciousness of status and prestige' on the part of medical men, there was not much else he could do but approach the problem from the inside. His strategy is clear: he wanted to mention all the arguments which doctors were presenting to justify their position so that he could then, with penetrating logic, deliver the *coup de grâce* to all of them. With this strategy he did not succeed.

The doctor can indeed diagnose a real physical disease, concealing itself behind behavior symptomatic of a neurosis. But this was no real argument, for the doctor-psychoanalyst cannot stand in a medical and diagnostic relationship to the patient, anyway, and so must refer a possible organic illness for diagnosis to a specialist in internal medicine. The psychologist-psychoanalyst is bound to do the same. The other argument was the extent to which psychic disturbances are a direct consequence of a state of organic defectiveness.

Here Freud once again became confused and proceeded to talk about 'hereditary factors,' 'propensities' ('*Anlagen*') in the body that might determine the weakness of the 'ego,' the 'intensity of drive.' What he actually said was:

347

Without some such constitutional, congenital prompting a neurosis would hardly come into being. ('*Ohne irgendeine solche konstitutionelle, kongenitale Begünstigung kommt wohl kaum eine Neurose zustande.*')

Later on his doctor friends pinned him down on this statement.

His pupil, Ferenczi, later pointed out the danger entailed in such vague conceptions as 'constitution' and 'heredity.' These are concepts that can all too easily lead to premature and ostensibly simple explanations of phenomena (as, for instance, ego weakness) which call for a detailed examination of all the underlying psychological, interpersonal processes. In my view it has been clearly demonstrated just how complex the process of shaping and distorting personality growth within a given culture is and how little productive these organic hypotheses have finally been for the development of the psychoanalytic theory of personality.

The central point of Freud's argument emerged at the end of his essay when he returned to his great desire to see established a 'university of psychoanalysis,' an academic center where in addition to instruction in the achievements of psychoanalysis the main part of the education offered would be the study of 'cultural history, mythology, the psychology of religion and literary knowledge.' This center would also decide who is a layman (=incompetent) and who could become a psychoanalyst. (In his postscript, which he wrote later, he mentioned sociology as well!)

The effect of Freud's essay on many of his medical colleagues was bewildering. His fellow medical psychoanalysts felt completely let down. At a meeting in New York a resolution was drawn up in which psychoanalysis was declared to be a form of medical treatment. When one reads what was asserted in the course of this discussion by psychoanalysts like Ernest Jones, Wilhelm Reich, Oberndorff, Glover and many others, and as one analyzes this discussion in detail, one is struck by the appallingly slipshod character of the debate, the absence of any logic and the way the interests, status and prestige of the medical men override everything else. Freud's extremely important publication was treated in fact as a temporary mental aberration on the part of an aged man who would really do better to stop concerning himself with the future of psychoanalysis. The discussion sparked off is revealing and of great importance for the future of both psychoanalysis and psychiatry. It is all the more remarkable how little attention has been paid to it.[6]

I will follow the course of the discussion fairly closely. The list of speakers was headed by Ernest Jones, who reiterated how difficult it was for psychoanalysis to make a start and how hard it was to choose *who* was to become a psychoanalyst: 'Beggars can't be choosers.' His respect for the pioneer psychoanalysts, including the nonmedical ones, was considerable, and he had a clear-cut argument as to why there must be a proper training. But then he let the cat out of the bag when he started talking about the 'external organization of psychoanalysis,' by which he meant the relationship of psychoanalysis to the 'sciences.'

Which science merited priority here? The answer, according to Jones, was self-evident. Medical science. Jones enumerated the reasons: Freud was a clinical neurologist; psychoanalysis had, as it were, sprung up and flourished in the soil of neurology; one is faced with 'suffering patients' who are in need of help.

This line of argument had not much logical force behind it but Jones had something to top it up with: the 'psychoses' would always continue to be a medical affair. Then Jones resorted to a style of argument typical of the whole discussion. *Freud was pinned down to his own (old) organic-neurological ideas.* After all, the erogenous zones were 'physical,' the chemical basis of the libido, the functioning of the glands. (One wonders which glands Jones had in mind.)

Then the line of argument became historical once more: 'Great' doctors have done so much important psychological work (William James, Janet and – 'sun among stars' – Freud himself!). Jones had to make his position clearer and he opted for a middle way. But before doing so he felt compelled to make the point that it is often only by medical men that 'diagnoses' can be made. A venereal disease like syphilis can frequently present itself as a 'neurasthenia' – and then:

dementia praecox and paranoia wear a mask of hysterical phobia, catatonia one of conversion hysteria, manic-depressive insanity one of obsessional manifestations.

Thus for Jones there was no doubt a all as to whether these are 'diseases,' and as such he believed they called not only for a knowledge of clinical psychiatry but of neurology as well.

He then moved to his conclusion. Freud's position was clear: It was irrelevant whether a psychoanalyst studied medicine and took a medical diploma. He could manage without (and his lack of medical training even had certain advantages). Jones repudiated this position as too crazy for words, for once one conceded this ('the divorce between psychoanalysis and clinical medicine'), the barriers would be broken. After all, that would make it possible to regard 'psychical affections' as a nonmedical affair (a conclusion actually reached by Szasz in 1961!).

For Jones this was out of the question. If psychoanalysis were left to the nonmedical practitioner (psychologist), then problems of, for instance, biochemistry, heredity, 'somatic erotogenesis' (a completely obscure concept to me) would be beyond his knowledge.

From this point on Jones became more confused. The public had more confidence in the ethical standards of doctors, so medical training was good for the 'image' of psychoanalysis. According to Jones, doctors were 'responsible people,' especially in America, and there were too many nonmedical charlatans there to whom it would be better not to entrust psychoanalysis.

Then Jones came to the argument which, he said, Freud had dismissed much too easily, that is, that people in analysis may come up with complaints of a physical character. Jones cites a patient with cancer of the large intestine that was recognized in time, operated upon and removed. Of course, Jones admitted, the nonmedic could immediately refer such a patient to a doctor, but he might well feel a greater degree of hesitation, intent as he would be on the psychological significance of what his client was presenting him with. Therefore it was safer to be in analysis with a 'real doctor,' who would be more alert to notice something physically wrong. Thus Jones arrived at his conclusion that psychoanalysis must remain a medical discipline.

However, Jones did want to make room for the nonmedics. He proposed that the nonmedical psychoanalyst be allowed to work . . . but only if he were in continuous touch with a doctor. If there was the slightest chance, he should go on to study medicine.

The next speaker in this discussion was Oberndorff, who did the same thing as Jones, that is, he pinned Freud down to his organic-medical terminology and earlier ways of conceptualizing. In doing this he executed a maneuver aimed at depriving Freud's *idea of the future* of its visionary quality. Oberndorff suggested, in fact, that Freud was so angry at the poor reception given to psychoanalysis by doctors (certainly in Vienna) that *for that reason* he was now averse to medical science and would rather merge his psychoanalysis completely with psychology. But, Oberndorff argued, that was no longer necessary, since medical men had become much more tolerant (1930) and badly needed psychoanalysis as a component specialty (like bacteriology, radiology, etc.). He then began to beat the medical drum, talking about the relation of 'instinctive needs' to 'disturbances in the physiological function of the body,' and the 'obvious' connection of the 'psychoses' 'with medical problems – infection, exhaustion, intoxication.'

The compulsive force of medical semantics was quite conspicuous in the following passage:

> I think, too, that psychoneurotics are 'sick people' and not merely psychological oddities, in the handling of whom a knowledge of the general reaction of people in sickness is invaluable.

Oberndorff completely ignored the important vision of the future which Freud had unfolded in proposing his 'analytical college' for the training of the future psychiatrist-psychoanalyst. In Oberndorff's opinion the instruction would have to be medical, including, besides the principles of biology, 'a scientific knowledge of the sexual life and an acquaintance with the disease pictures of psychiatry.' Then Oberndorff made a final remark that reveals just how 'organic' his thinking really was. He implied that biologists and chemists would certainly be able to help us understand the 'libido,' talked literally about the 'chemistry of the psyche,' and in a literal interpretation of Freud's *metaphor* of the 'ego' and the 'unconscious,' said eventually they might be localized in the brain!

Then the psychoanalyst Harnik went so far as to declare: 'I don't believe that you can be a psychoanalyst without a knowledge of tape-worms!'

A classic example of how medical language compels one to adopt a particular mode of thinking is also provided by Schilder of Vienna.

> It seems to me unquestionable that the treatment of the sick is a matter for the physician. Everyone who suffers or (in the case of the mentally diseased) whose former personality would feel his condition as suffering, is ill. Anyone who seeks healing belongs to the physician.

This discussion among a group of resentful doctor-psycho-analysts indicates how little many of them grasped of Freud's vision of the future. Of course, those taking part in the discussion introduced their comments with all due respect and deference to 'the master' – but talk of 'disease' was still the order of the day.

Franz Alexander (at the time still in Berlin) emerged in this discussion as a distinctly and surprisingly original contributor. His whole argument made clear that he had read Freud's essay to good purpose and fully understood the consequences. He seized at once the essential point which Szasz elaborated later on:

> The problem of 'lay analysis' arises and can only arise because the position of psychoanalysis with regard to medicine is still undefined.

Following Freud, he not only defended psychoanalysis as *psychology* but also asserted that, if anything, it was medical science that could learn a lot from psychoanalysis and *not* the other way around. Alexander maintained that it would be much more justifiable to say that doctors should receive a psychoanalytic training than that psychoanalysts should have a complete medical training.

In the same vein as Freud, he considered what requirements should be laid down as essential to the training of the psychoanalyst. In his view such a training institute (Freud's 'analytical college') was by no means a utopian idea. He saw the task of psychoanalysis as consisting not in any demand for prior medical training but rather in the organizing of a really efficient training in psychoanalysis. (A very important pronouncement in 1930 – but one that had been fundamentally disregarded, and still is even now.)

It was obvious to Alexander that literature, mythology, etc. (unfortunately, he did not elaborate on the 'etc.'), were far more important for the 'study of the human mind' than a medical training. These statements are of so much interest precisely because in his later work Alexander did strongly emphasize human existential problems and their effect on the body's functioning. He came to be one of the pioneers in 'psychosomatics,' defective physical states (gastric ulcers, asthma, high blood pressure, headaches) closely connected with psychic difficulties.

I want to round off this exposition of an important discussion with the views expressed by two contributors who really did, I think, grasp Freud's vision of the future: Müller-Braunschweig, and the man who was the cause of it all, the psychologist Theodor Reik.

The striking thing about Müller-Braunschweig's line of argument is that he made use of terms like 'values,' 'norms' and 'ethics.' He even underlined the value of symbolism, the theory of giving 'sign-ificance.' Müller-Braunschweig was the only contributor to this discussion to touch on an essential point: namely, that man is a 'symbolizing animal,' that his 'unconscious' is full of symbols, images with significance, and that between those symbols and the things (or processes) they stand for there is not a causal relationship, but a relationship of correspondence, of sense and meaning.

Let me translate this idea into some concrete examples. A person may react to an employer with authoritarian traits as though he were his father, who previously acted toward him in a very tyrannical way. A husband may feel his rather peevish, demanding wife to be a potential danger because his mother had at one time buried him beneath her depressions. A mother can treat one of her children in an amazingly irrational way unless she comes to realize that this child bears some resemblance to her own brother, with whom she has been continually at odds.

Psychoanalysis is a process of *resymbolizing*, a tracking down of old symbols that continue to exercise an enormous influence. Müller-Braunschweig was the only one (and that is the surprising thing about this discussion) who touched on this problem. For him what was central to psychoanalysis was linguistics (he uses the terms 'science of language' and 'linguistic science'), and not the thinking in terms of the natural sciences that characterizes medicine.

Theodor Reik fought a losing battle . . . but with conviction. He said: Psychoanalysis is psychology. If we do not realize this to the fullest extent, we endanger the future of psychoanalysis. And our most useful forerunners and allies are the philosophers and great writers on the drama of human life. The forefathers of psychoanalysts are Plato, Spinoza and Nietzsche. We discover more psychological insight in the writings of Shakespeare, Sophocles and Dostoievski than in the whole of medical literature from Galen to Kraepelin.

But the pleas of Reik, Alexander, Müller-Braunschweig and some others were of no use. The discussion led to the following resolution (under majority rules) by the New York Psychoanalytical Society:

The practice of psychoanalysis for therapeutic purposes shall be restricted to physicians (doctors of medicine), who are graduates of recognized medical schools, have had special training in psychiatry and psychoanalysis and who conform to the requirements of the medical practice acts to which they are subject. Such practice of psychoanalysis embraces the treatment of individuals suffering from nervous or mental disease presenting symptoms which interfere with the efficient performance of their normal daily routine.

Nonmedical people were to be allowed to have training and apply psychoanalytic knowledge in specialist areas like criminology, anthropology, theology, pedagogy, but only 'for the more adequate interpretation and the better understanding of problems confronting them in these fields.' 'Giving treatment' is not allowed. In practice little came of this resolution, but the influence it has had on the development of psychiatry since 1930 has been very considerable. That is why I have given so much attention to this discussion.

Afterwards Freud wrote his 'Postscript on *The Question of Lay Analysis*'.[7] He retracted nothing – quite the contrary. He made his position sharper, better defined and more convincing. The following passage seems to me to be very important because here Freud pointed once again toward an ideal future:

My main thesis was that the important question is not whether an analyst possesses a medical diploma but whether he has had the special training necessary for the practice of analysis. This served as the starting-point for a discussion, which was eagerly embarked upon, as to what is the training most suitable for an analyst. My own view was and still remains that it is not the training prescribed by the University for future doctors. What is known as medical education appears to me to be an arduous and circuitous way of approaching the profession of analysis. No doubt it offers an analyst much that is indispensable to him. But it burdens him with too much else of which he can never make use, and there is a danger of its diverting his interest and his whole mode of thought from the understanding of psychical phenomena. A scheme of training for analysis has still to be created. It must include elements from the mental sciences, from psychology, the history of civilization and sociology, as well as from anatomy, biology and the study of evolution. There is so much to be taught in all this that it is justifiable to omit from the curriculum anything which has no direct bearing on the practice of analysis and only serves indirectly (like any other study) as a training for the intellect and for the powers of observation. It is easy to meet this suggestion by objecting that analytic colleges of this kind do not exist and that I am merely setting up an ideal. An ideal, no doubt. But an ideal which can and must be realized. And in our training institutes, in spite of all their youthful insufficiencies, that realization has already begun.

He declared himself against the resolution adopted in New York: 'The resolution passed by our American colleagues against lay analysts, based as it essentially is upon practical reasons, appears to me nevertheless to be impractical; for it cannot affect any of the factors which govern the situation.'

Well, that may be so, but the situation in 1973 has been substantially affected by that resolution. True, a number of psychologists and social psychologists have become psychoanalysts – a practice sanctioned eventually by the official training institutes of the International Association for Psychoanalysis. But far more important, the notion that psychiatry is a medical specialty has certainly *not* been weakened but on the contrary was confirmed and strengthened by this resolution. The visionary aspect of Freud's essay has been left in abeyance. His 'analytical college,' which was to have been an institution for turning out psychotherapists trained in psychoanalysis, social psychology and sociology, never came into being. If I have understood Freud rightly, he really wanted much more in the way of training: a familiarity with human symbolism, mythology, philosophy, the insights into the existential problems of people revealed in fictional writing. But – the wind of change is blowing. It is not accidental that Szasz has made such a stir. That commotion and the beginnings of a breakthrough are what the next chapter is about.

REFERENCES

[1] C. M. Thompson: *Interpersonal Psychoanalysis: Selected Papers* (New York, 1964).

[2] E. Erikson: 'The First Psychoanalyst,' *Yale Review* (September, 1956).

[3] S. Freud: *The Origins of Psycho-Analysis, Letters to Wilhelm Fliess, Drafts and Notes; 1887–1902*, M. Bonaparte, A. Freud and E. Kris, eds. (New York, 1954).

[4] E. Jones: *The Life and Works of Sigmund Freud*, vol. 2, pp. 152–167 (London, 1953–1957).

[5] H. S. Sullivan: *The Fusion of Psychiatry and the Social Sciences* (New York, 1964).

[6] The discussion is reproduced in full in the *Journal of Psychoan.*, vol. 8, pp. 74–284 (1930).

[7] S. Freud: *The Question of Lay Analysis* (London, 1947); 'Postscript to a Discussion on Lay Analysis,' in *Collected Papers*, vol. 5, J. Strachey, ed. (London, 1948).

NOTES

A book dealing with the problems discussed in this chapter has been written by Kurt Eissler: *Medical Orthodoxy and the Future of Psychoanalysis* (New York, 1965). A work by a deeply read man – but not, in my view, easy reading. It is difficult to ascertain his conclusions. At all events, he argues in favor of the nonmedical psychoanalyst and the latter's contribution to the development and extension of the psychology of which Freud and his disciples have laid the foundations.

T. S. Szasz: 'The Myth of Mental Illness,' *Amer. Psychologist*, vol. 15, pp. 113–119 (1960).

This is the preliminary article to Szasz's subsequent book: *The Myth of Mental Illness*. After explaining the position of psychiatrists, doctors and others who do believe that *ultimately* 'problems in living' can be attributed to physiochemical processes (more or less subtle neurological defects), he argues that *even for them* the term 'mental illness' is unnecessary and misleading: 'What these psychiatrists mean is that people with this label are suffering from a disease of the brain. If that is what they mean (and believe), things will be clearer when they say that and not something else.' The term 'mental illness' is then closely scrutinized as a sort of shorthand label for 'problems in living.' There are norms that determine what is 'deviant' in a culture; and these norms are defined by the person himself (the 'patient') or by the 'other' (relatives, psychiatrist, whether or not the latter is hired by an authority to correct the deviant individual). The term 'mental illness' is an invitation to normalize deviant behavior ('psychosocial, ethical and/or legal deviations') by way of *medical* action:

> Since medical action is designed to correct only medical deviations (deviation from the norm of the human *body's* structural and functional integrity), it seems logically absurd to expect that it will help solve problems whose very existence has been defined and established on nonmedical grounds.

Although medical practice bristles with values and ethics, this applies a fortiori to psychiatrists.

There is not a shadow of proof, according to Szasz, that people with 'problems in living' (who in their communicative activities 'are expressing unacceptable ideas, often framed, moreover, in an unusual idiom') 'have' something, have 'caught' something like a 'disease' and are 'carrying it about with them.' The problems presented by values, ethics, morality have a central place in psychotherapy. Szasz then probes into the why and wherefore of the term 'mental illness,' the function that this convenient term has had and still has. For human beings, living in relationship with others is difficult, full of struggle and strife. *It is not inherently 'harmonious.'* In earlier times people blamed devils and witchcraft for this difficulty, and the impersonal concept of 'mental illness' is a *successor* to the earlier explanations. As such:

> The concept functions as a disguise; for instead of calling attention to conflicting human needs, aspirations, and values, the notion of mental illness provides an amoral and impersonal 'thing' (an 'illness') as an explanation for 'problems in living.'

In the Middle Ages deviant behavior was 'explained' by witchcraft and 'treated' theologically; nowadays it is 'explained' as a disease and 'treated' medically.

Szasz is very much aware of the enormity of the problem of *how* the individual person should live in this complex society. Our growth in consciousness has given us an even greater 'burden of understanding' (Susan Langer). The point is that we cannot dodge this with false labels but must face up to it and take responsibility for it. In the old days this responsibility was ducked through the conviction that life was a matter of 'fate' or 'fortune,' decided by 'the gods.'

Even in this early publication Szasz presents himself to us as a very sensitive man who believes that now, in this phase of the development of mankind, we must not obscure the real problems and responsibilities behind the smoke screen of 'mental illness.' To Szasz the term is a 'social tranquilizer' supporting the fantasy that all would be well and satisfactory in human life, if *only* this tiresome 'psychopathology' and 'mental illness' could be eradicated. One final quotation:

> Our adversaries are not demons, witches, fate or mental illness. We have no enemy whom we can fight, exercise or dispel by 'cure.' What we do have are *problems in living* – whether these be biologic, economic, political, or sociopsychological.

T. S. Szasz: 'The Uses of Naming and the Origin of the Myth of Mental Illness,' *Amer. Psychologist*, vol. 16, pp. 59–66 (1961).

In this article preliminary to his book *The Myth of Mental Illness*, Szasz clarifies his standpoint and shows that he has something of a lead over his opponents (e.g., David Ausubel: 'Personality *Is* Disease,' *Amer. Psychologist*, vol. 16, pp. 69–75 [1961]). Szasz is very familiar with linguistics and logic. He names (in reference to Reichenbach) three functions of language: 'to transmit information, to induce mood, and to promote action.' The 'promotive use of language' in particular plays a major role vis-à-vis the 'mental illness' concept. The vagueness and ambiguous character of a given word make it eminently suitable for use in influencing people:

> Thus, psychiatric or sociologic descriptions and explanations may themselves present a barrier to recognizing and comprehending the very phenomena which they allegedly seek to elucidate, because in their formulations they frequently offer promotive statements in the guise of cognitive assertions. Or, to put it more simply, psychiatrists often *prescribe* conduct, while claiming merely to *describe* it.

T. S. Szasz: *The Manufacture of Madness* (New York, 1970).

Although this latest book by Szasz could be mentioned elsewhere, it seemed to me best to mention it here. Again a brilliantly written work, in which Szasz brackets the concept of 'being bewitched' (resulting in the witch-hunt as a form of social control) with that of being 'mentally ill' (insane, psychically sick, etc.), which has led to a *medical* witch-hunt of 'deviant people.'

There are, says Szasz, actions and types of behavior, and there are explanations; and the mode of explanation determines our procedures – our form of 'subjecting to the norm-control.' According to Szasz our medical explanation is wrong, and as a result institutional psychiatry is becoming a new version of the Inquisition! The conclusion, then, is clear: No 'improvements' are possible within the prevailing psychiatric-institutional system (for instance, mental hospitals) because the whole system is wrong.

H. O. Mowrer: 'Sin, the Lesser of Two Evils,' *Amer. Psychologist*, vol. 15, pp. 301–305 (1960).

Mowrer also criticizes the use of the word 'disease' as applied to

behavior that we commonly describe as 'neurotic' and 'psychotic.'
The omnipotence of medical science irritates him, because in his
view doctors certainly have no lien on 'treating' people in difficulties. He carries his annoyance to some lengths, for he describes
psychodynamic and psychoanalytic psychiatry as being in a state of
'virtual collapse and imminent demise.'
In my view these are quite unjustifiable statements, but his criticism
of medical conceptualizing is as fierce and as effective as Szasz's. He
reminds us yet again how Freud became hopelessly bogged down
in his medical thought model. He quotes from Freud's autobiography:

> My medical conscience felt pleased at my having arrived at this
> conclusion (that neurosis has a sexual basis). I hoped that I had
> filled up a gap in medical science which, in dealing with a func-
> tion of such great biological importance, had failed to take into
> account any injuries beyond those caused by infection or by
> gross anatomical lesions. The medical aspect of the matter was,
> moreover, supported by the fact that sexuality was not some-
> thing purely mental. It had a somatic side as well. . . . S. Freud:
> *Autobiography* (Norton, New York [1935]), p. 450.

But, says Mowrer, by the time of Freud's last publication, 'his Big
Idea had been let loose in the world and was no longer entirely
under his control.' To emphasize his point Mowrer introduces
some interesting quotations from a document of the American
Psychiatric Association (Committee on Relations between Psychiatry and Psychology: *Resolution on Relations of Medicine and
Psychology* [October 1954]). This document, reissued in 1957 with
the consent of the American Medical Association and the American
Psychoanalytic Association, reflects the state of affairs accurately
enough. The doctors affirm:

> For centuries the western world has placed on the medical pro-
> fession responsibility for the diagnosis and treatment of illness.
> Medical practice acts have been designed to protect the public
> from unqualified practitioners and to define the special responsi-
> bilities assumed by those who practice the healing art. . . .
> Psychiatry is the medical specialty concerned with illness that
> has chiefly mental symptoms.

And again:

> Psychotherapy is a form of medical treatment and does not form
> the basis for a separate profession. . . . When members of these
> [other] professions contribute to the diagnosis and treatment of
> illness, their professional contributions must be coordinated
> under medical responsibility.

Mowrer then reintroduces the notion of 'sin,' which seems to him
more meaningful than 'sickness,' and armed with this term, he

advances the argument in a very provocative way – but, in my opinion, far less constructively and fruitfully than Szasz.

K. Menninger: 'Advocacy of a Unitary Concept,' in *Chronic Schizophrenia*, pp. 59–69, L. Appleby, J. M. Scher and J. Cumming, eds. (Glencoe, Ill., 1960).

Menninger gives us a further survey of the way in which the classification theory of psychiatric syndromes originated. The deviant behavior (delusions of grandeur) that characterizes the last stage of syphilis aroused an appetite, as it were, for more 'disease entities.' So there appeared such terms as hebephrenia (1864), catatony (1874), and later on dementia praecox (1896) and manic-depressive psychosis (1899).

As early as 1820 one of the psychiatrist Esquirol's pupils (Georget) was explaining mental illness as a 'disorder of the brain.' So, too, Wilhelm Griesinger (1861) with his celebrated remark: 'Mental diseases are brain diseases.' Menninger points to a long-forgotten man Heinrich Neuman (1859), who propagated a notion of unity. Menninger translated him thus:

> Diagnosis is not simply the designation of a group of symptoms but the key to the comprehension of the case. . . . We consider any classification of mental illness to be artificial, and therefore unsatisfactory, and we do not believe that one can make progress in psychiatry until one has resolved to throw overboard all classifications and to declare with us: there is only one kind of mental illness.

Then Menninger comes to his own conclusions:

> The fact remains, however, that in the minds of many young doctors and in the minds of vast numbers of laymen, mental illness and particularly schizophrenia is a definite, specific, evil thing which invades the unsuspecting like a fungus or a tapeworm.

This statement seems to me perfectly true. This attitude is still with us. Menninger wants to get rid of the idea that people have some sort of 'disease' (going by this name or that), a disease which therefore must be combatted and 'expelled.' He thinks people live in varying degrees of isolation and unsatisfactory and disruptive relationships with others. Therefore the differences between the 'mentally ill' and the rest of us are not qualitative but quantitative. This conclusion is further elaborated in his book, *The Vital Balance* (New York, 1963).

18. BACK TO THE
DRAWING BOARD

The first draft of this chapter was written in 1966. In the process of giving it its final shape, I went through the most recent volumes of psychiatric periodicals and publications and found out that things are moving very fast indeed.

Thomas Kuhn has written about the conditions necessary for a scientific revolution.[1] He shows that there are periods when basic reliefs or ideas about a certain phenomenon shared by everybody begin to totter. People become skeptical. At the same time, in a tentative way, new ideas and new ways of thinking appear (usually they are not really new). Then the situation is ripe for a revolution, a sudden breakthrough, a change by leaps and bounds in scientific thinking, a 'discontinuous transformation' which leads to a fundamentally different way of conceptualizing certain phenomena and sets in motion a current of new (and fruitful) research.

The most recent reactions to the publications of Thomas Szasz (the great demolition expert of the medical model in psychiatry) indicate that he does not stand alone. Many are taking the same line and some are already starting to clear away the debris, preparatory to a new future.

Szasz's publications have caused a great deal of commotion,

362

though there is a tendency in the literature to belittle or brush aside the consequences of his penetrating analyses. His books *Law, Liberty and Psychiatry* (New York, 1963) and *Psychiatric Justice* (New York, 1963), earned him little popularity among 'forensic psychiatrists,' because he attacked the thesis of 'unaccountability,' the position of court psychiatrists, and the deprivation of liberty through the humanely intended insanity defense that resulted in incarceration in a mental hospital (a kind of life imprisonment). He considers the logical assumptions underlying these procedures as absolutely untenable.

His more recent book, *The Manufacture of Madness* (1970), has made him even more of an *enfant terrible*. In it the so-called clinical psychologists in particular are criticized as 'paramedical technicians' who 'test the patient's mind instead of his blood.' These are the people who long ago lost out to the hegemony of the 'doctor-psychiatrist' in dealing with people in distress who had no bodily illness. They are the 'laymen' for whose future as psychoanalysts Freud did battle.

One such psychologist, J. W. Albee, has made a number of statements that reflect the general feeling very well. He rightly points to the enormous shortage of (properly trained) manpower for helping people in existential trouble – the shortage of psychotherapists, group therapists, family psychotherapists, professionals who can lead and organize new types of institutes, known at present as 'community mental health center.' I think Albee is absolutely correct when he says that we cannot solve this problem of manpower *until we get a breakthrough in our understanding of 'mental disorder.'* He is quite concerned that the whole professional field that concerns itself with the care of the mentally disordered person and so with the problem of manpower planning in the area of mental health is dominated by the conception of *mental illness*. He stresses the fact that most disturbances (disorders) are primarily learned, deviant forms of behaviour to which the frame of reference provided by the illness model simply does not apply.

When the sickness model ultimately is laid to rest, society can set about training new kinds of professionals, closer perhaps to schoolteachers than to psychiatrists, to work with these disordered people in new kinds of institutions, closer perhaps to schools than to hospitals.[2]

Albee is angry about the position psychologists have occupied in medical centers (mental hospitals and the like). Despite the support they were given, they remain in the subservient position allotted to them by medical authorities. According to Albee clinical psychologists have been 'honored' guests, obedient slaves who adopted the values and language of their (medical) masters. They, too, talked about 'patients' with 'diseases' that require 'treatment.' Like Szasz, he calls the medical model 'a stone around our necks.' [3] Albee argues that of the old idea – that 'there can be no twisted behavior without a twisted molecule' – very little has survived.[4]

The medical model also comes under fire in a paper by Sarason and Ganzer.[5] The Middle Ages produced the religious model in which deviant behavior was seen as the expression of 'devils' and 'witches' by whom the individual was 'possessed.' As early as 1653, according to these authors, a sickness model (Johannes Weyer) appeared, and a hundred years later William Cullen invented the term 'neurosis.' He believed, like another British neurologist (Hughling Jackson), that maladaptive behavior was caused by a defect in the central nervous system, in the nerve cells (neurons).

To return to Albee, his various utterances reflect a basic theme – the training of a new type of professional, a new type of helper. Clinical psychology cannot be both an independent discipline and a 'health profession.' [6]

The extent of the controversy became apparent at the 124th annual congress of the American Psychiatric Association. An eminent psychiatrist, Roy Grinker, tried to pour oil on the troubled waters, but his arguments were far from convincing.[7] Albee again presented his viewpoint, which left nothing to be desired on the score of clarity.[8] He resumed his attack on the thesis that the cause of disturbed behavior is ultimately to be found in one form or another of physical disease. *He rightly defined the problem of 'being schizophrenic' as the central issue in the crisis of psychiatry today.* In this 'extreme' form of 'deviant' behavior the alleged biological cause *should* have been found by now. But, Albee concluded, research in this area has yielded nothing of substance. Recent summaries of the literature on this research (which devours millions of dollars) boil down to what he calls 'polysyllabic nonsense.' The researchers keep saying: 'We haven't found anything yet, but we're still digging.'[9]

I believe that the biochemical research still being financed in the field of 'schizophrenia' may well be the symbol of our obstinate attempts to *deny that human distress and confusion can take this form*. In a recent book, *Schizophrenie und Familie*, the German psychiatrist Kulenkampf says in his introduction:

> The elephant of biochemical, anatomical, genetic and other research, now being implemented all over the world, into the cause of schizophrenia has so far not even given birth to a mouse.[10]

The American Psychological Association, in a report concerned with the idea of the 'community mental health center' as an alternative to the mental hospital, is also critical of the illness model and gives an outline for the future. In the summary it is stressed that mental disorders are essentially different from physical diseases. They are an element in social systems (groups, family, etc.) of which the person in manifest distress is a member. The conclusion must be: Change these social systems so that the individual sending out the distress signals may again be able to live effectively as a person.[11]

The psychiatrist R. M. Kaufman takes a stand against these views.[12] He falls back on all the old positions: 'heredity,' researches in the field of brain metabolism, the presence of physical diseases, hormones, the function of the kidneys, biochemical research among those classified as 'schizophrenic.' To corroborate his opinion he mentions several 'great' men of the past – Kraepelin, Bleuler and . . . Freud! Kaufman's reasons for including Freud's essay *The Question of Lay Analysis* as supporting the medical model are the same arguments we discussed earlier. Kaufman simply cites all those passages in which Freud refers to the possible organic cause of being 'neurotic' or 'psychotic.'

In conclusion I refer you to a book, the very title of which – *Changing Perspectives in Mental Illness* – indicates what its editors (Plog and Edgerton) are after.[13] It comprises an extensive collection of articles, partly for and partly against the medical model in psychiatry. In their introduction the editors of this book declare that the tranquil and self-satisfied days of medical psychiatry are numbered: '. . . the walls of the psychiatric citadel are being shouted down by an astonishing multitude of voices.'

The core of the problem becomes more visible if we conceptualize deviant behavior as a consequence of the stress induced by living in a very complex society and regard such behavior as a cry of protest against restrictive norms and social conventions. This would *forcefully suggest the need to reform our society*.

The most provocative essay in this book is called 'The Scientific Status of the Mental Metaphor' by Sarbin.[14] This author, too, concentrates on the 'mental illness' label and the conceptual mode of reference and forms of action that are associated with it (isolation, degradation, surgery, chemical or psychological treatment, etc.).

Certain ways of thinking, Sarbin argues, are practically unalterable despite overwhelming rational arguments against them. They have become 'myths.' The 'myth of mental illness' has given doctors the power and the obligation to assess and to pass judgment on people with problems in living. Sarbin analyzes the history of this 'figure of speech' and the social consequences it has had. To him a semantic analysis is very meaningful. 'He has problems in living' has a dramatically different effect from 'He is a psychiatric patient with a mental illness.' Sarbin's historical analysis is cogent because he extensively examines the background of the illness model. In the sixteenth century Teresa of Avila introduced the notion 'as if sick' in order to save her fellow nuns (who as a result of their monastic existence were behaving in a rather 'crazy' way) from the fate of being burned by the Inquisition. The result was that the medical men of the time gradually assumed responsibility for treating people whose behavior was deviant and the priests retreated. Then the qualified 'as if' disappeared and the doctors pounced upon the notion of 'sickness' or 'disease.' The theory of the physician Galen (who thought that various body fluids were the cause of physical diseases) was now extended to cover human behavior that deviated from certain norms. Both conditions were caused by something *in* the body. Behavior came to be viewed as a 'symptom of disease' – inappropriate laughing or crying, spitting, taciturnity, lying, fantasizing and nonconformity were now assumed to be caused by 'internal pathology.'

This Galenic model was taken over by modern clinical psychiatry. Galen's 'body fluids' later became microbes, tumors, poisonous substances, endocrinological (hormonal) metabolic defects, etc. The question now became 'what' the 'cause' was located 'in'! The answer: in the 'mind' ('psyche'). In the nineteenth century, with the advent of neurology, the words 'mind' and 'brain' became closely associated and the term 'mental illness' was born.

Although 'ill,' generally speaking, did not have a negative, condemnatory connotation (one is not responsible for it), the expression 'mentally ill' soon acquired an unmistakable negative meaning. Those who 'had' this thing became a special sort of people for whom one was bound to feel fear or contempt or with whom one should sympathize. Sarbin maintains that we can now explode this metaphor, but to do so we will have to put forward an alternative: 'The time has come for replacing the old myth with a new metaphor.' A new name can help us to determine our strategy: namely, 'to reach out in the community and help those people who lead lives of quiet desperation, some of whom occasionally break out of their social entrapment with bizarre conduct or violence.'

This last quotation takes us to the heart of what confronts us: the challenge and the task of a future psychiatry.

REFERENCES

[1] T. Kuhn: *The Structure of Scientific Revolutions* (Chicago, 1962).

[2] J. W. Albee: 'The Relation of Conceptual Models to Manpower Needs,' in E. Cowen, ed., *Emerging Concepts of Mental Health* (New York, 1967).

[3] J. W. Albee: 'Manpower Needs for Mental Health and the Role of Psychology,' *Canadian Psychologist*, vol. 62, pp. 82–93 (1965).

[4] J. W. Albee: 'The Dark at the Top of the Agenda,' *Clinical Psychologist*, vol. 1 (1966).

[5] J. G. Sarason and V. J. Ganzer: 'Concerning the Medical Model,' *American Psychologist*, vol. 23, pp. 507–511 (1960).

[6] J. W. Albee: 'Give Us a Place to Stand and We will Move the Earth,' in *Mental Health Manpower Needs in Psychology*, Conference, University of Kentucky (Lexington, 1966).

[7] R. Grinker: 'Emerging Concepts of Mental Illness and Models of Treatment: The Medical Point of View,' *Amer. Journ. of Psychiatry*, vol. 125, pp. 865–870 (1969).

[8] J. W. Albee: 'Emerging Concepts of Mental Illness and Models of Treatment' in 'The Psychological Point of View,' *Amer. J. of Psychiatry*, vol. 125. pp. 870–877 (1969).

[9] R. Coles: 'The Limits of Psychiatry,' *The Progressive*, vol. 31, pp. 32–34 (1967).

[10] H. Blumenberg, ed.: *Schizophrenie und Familie* (Frankfurt/Main, 1969).

[11] M. B. Smith and N. Hobbs: *The Community and the Community Health Services*, Department of Psychology, Western Reserve University, November 22, 1966.

[12] R. M. Kaufman: 'Psychiatry: Why "Medical" or "Social" Model?' *Archives of General Psychiatry*, vol. 17, pp. 347–361 (1967).

[13] S. C. Plog and R. B. Edgerton, eds.: *Changing Perspectives in Mental Illness* (New York, 1969).

[14] For an extensive list of other articles by this author I refer the reader to the book: *Changing Perspectives in Mental Illness*.

NOTES

Most of the literature has been worked into the text. A few further examples of the attempts delineated in the literature to achieve a breakthrough to a new conception:

M. G. Field: 'Learning (and Relearning) Is the Name of the Game,' *International J. of Psychiatry*, vol. 8, pp. 659–661 (1969).

In a contribution to a discussion the author voices his mixed feelings regarding the right of 'the medical establishment' to concern itself with people with problems and in situations of conflict.

In this article, too, a theme crops up which is becoming more and more relevant: What sort of training does this kind of psychiatrist-psychotherapist really need? In the following passage (1969) it is almost like hearing Freud (1927!) speak again:

> . . . a special training curriculum, separate from the traditional medical one, might increase the availability of psychotherapists. Indeed, *the insistence on full medical training, most of which is irrelevant to the psychotherapist,* served to deflect from this critically needed profession many who by personality, temperament and inclination would be able to help patients.

R. Rubenstein and H. D. Lasswell: *The Sharing of Power in a Psychiatric Hospital* (New Haven, Conn., 1966).

Although this very informative book deals with attempts to reform a mental hospital (without marked success, however), there are passages indicating that the authors are not too happy about the medical model of the institution. There are typically hesitant statements such as the following:

> We must weigh the possibility that the traditional medical model is, in fact, inappropriate to deal with the problems of those who have gone down to defeat in the struggle for power. Our analysis suggests that when a hospital is transformed in the direction of a democratic community, many traditional medical elements are discarded or modified to such an extent that they are no longer recognizable; indeed, what persists as 'medical' appears to be less clearly justifiable. Perhaps a new specialized environment, elaborated from a new perception of the problem, might do a better job than the hospital.

There are one or two more quotations from the same authors in similar vein, implying that perhaps we are on the wrong track after all.

A somewhat more robust statement:

> The use of the medical-therapeutic model for coping with the predicaments of the defeated is, in part, fostered by the medical orientation of psychoanalysis and psychotherapy in the United States. The application of psychoanalysis to work with the psychoses has been carried out largely within the framework of a specialized branch of medicine, and in medically supervised hospitals and clinics, the only institutions in which psychotherapy of the psychoses has been systematically undertaken. It is conceivable that procedures of self-exploration, undertaken in specialized environments which do not conform to the medical

369

model, would undergo further developments impossible within medical and hospital contexts. The possibility of stimulating such experimentation is a potentially worthwhile and important consequence of developing specialized environments which depart from current approaches in psychiatric institutions.'

19. CLASSIFICATION, ALIENATION AND 'SECONDARY DEVIANCE'

Let's start at the beginning. If you happen to be narrow-chested, feel inhibited in action and self-assertion and the boys in the swimming pool, who have fine athletic bodies, tease you a lot as a scornfully 'superior' young man looking on, then a process of alienation sets in. We repudiate our own bodies, aspects of our own bodily nature are covered in shame, the 'appraisals of others' become 'reflected appraisal.' We end up alienated from our own body. We live in alienation. Mother frowns when the little girl touches her genitals. Father says: 'Hands on top of the blanket.' In short the 'other' through his verbal – but especially through his non-verbal – communication of censure and disapproval causes us to reject part of our own authentic selves. Ideal self-images are constructed that will obtain approval, parts of our own body (and this goes with our beliefs, ideas, opinions, convictions) turn into 'bad me' (Sullivan); and if things are very deeply repressed, Sullivan even speaks of a 'not me.' But parents and friends are only 'vehicles' of the culture, who hand on prevailing conceptions, opinions, norms and values.

371

The problem of alteration, confusion, self-alienation has engaged many philosophers. Freud was one of them. He was constantly concerned with the theme of self-alienation, of 'repression,' resulting from disapproval and prohibition.

Ortega y Gasset wrote of 'alteration' in these terms:

> To that degree, therefore, man, unlike the other creatures in the world, is never certain of his *'being-as-man,'* on the contrary, *'being-man' means precisely always being on the point of not being that, a living problem, being a total and hazardous adventure, or as I am given to saying: a quintessential drama!* For drama exists only when we do not know what is going to happen and each instant is pure risk and quivering danger. While the tiger cannot stop being a tiger, cannot de-tiger himself, man lives in constant peril of *de-humanizing himself.* Not only is it uncertain and possible for something to befall him as it does the other animals, but man is beset at times by the experience, no less, of *'not being man.'* And this is true not only in the abstract and for the species, but it applies also to our individuality. Each of us is always in danger of not being the *self*, unique and untransferable, *that he is.* Most people constantly betray that *self which they hope to be*; and to be completely truthful, our personal individuality is *a personality that is never wholly realized, a challenging utopia, an obscure legend*, which every person harbours in his heart of hearts. One can well understand that Pindar should epitomize his heroic ethics in the renowned imperative: *Genoio hoös eidi* – '*Become what you are.*' [1]

Becoming nonhuman, being turned into a thing, is also the theme that runs through the work of Karl Marx. His philosophy is a protest against alienation, against the process of dehumanization in Western industrial society. He stressed how institutions transform people and he concentrated especially on the system of production in a capitalist economy. His protest was against 'materializing,' the conditioning of needs for money and possessions. He called for the liberation of man, who is imprisoned in a production process that turns him into a thing and a slave of things. Eric Fromm sums it up like this:

Again it must be emphasized that Marx's aim is not limited to the emancipation of the working class, but the emancipation of the human being through the restitution of the unalienated and hence free activity of all man, and a society in which man, and not the production of things, is the aim, in which man ceases to be 'a crippled monstrosity,' and becomes a fully developed human being.[2]

I am not much disposed to getting submerged in the philosophers, and so will not go beyond mentioning the names of Sartre, Tillich, Gusdorf, Hegel, Kierkegaard, Buber, and of men of letters such as Pirandello and Rilke, all of whom have been deeply preoccupied with this theme – the reification of the unique individual, who is held captive in the straitjacket of what 'they' expect him to be.[3]

I find the following passage from Rilke's *The Notebooks of Malte Laurids Brigge* one of the most striking descriptions of alienation and being imprisoned in a role.[4] Rilke gives a description of a young man who discovers in the attic a chest with strange clothes in it, and dresses up as a kind of Turk. Then he admires himself in a mirror:

It was then that I first learned to know the influence that can emanate directly from a particular costume itself. Hardly had I donned one of these suits, when I had to admit that it got me in its power; that it prescribed my movements, my facial expression, yes, even my ideas. My hand, over which the lace cuff fell and fell again, was anything but my usual hand; it moved like a person acting; I might even say that it was watching itself, exaggerated though that sounds.

And again:

I seized in addition a large staff, which I made walk along beside me at arm's length, and in this fashion, not without difficulty, but, as it seemed to me, full of dignity, I trailed into the guest-room toward the mirror.

It was really grandiose, beyond all expectation. And the mirror gave it back instantly, it was too convincing. It would not have been at all necessary to move much; this apparition was perfect, even though it did nothing. But I wanted to discover what I actually was, so I turned a little and finally raised both arms: large, almost conjuring gestures were, I saw immediately, the only fitting ones. But just at this solemn moment I heard quite near me, muffled by my disguise, a very complicated noise; much frightened, I lost sight of the presence in the mirror and was badly upset to perceive that I had overturned a small round table with heaven knows what, probably very fragile objects. I bent down as well as I could and found my worst fears confirmed: it looked as though everything were in pieces. The two useless green-violet porcelain parrots were of course shattered, each in a different malign fashion. A box, from which rolled bonbons that looked like insects in silken cocoons, had cast its cover far away; only half of it was to be seen, the other had totally disappeared. But most annoying of all was a scent-bottle that had been shivered into a thousand tiny fragments, from which the remainder of some sort of old essence had spurted that now formed a spot of very repulsive profile on the clear parquet. I wiped it up quickly with something or other that was hanging down about me, but it only became blacker and more unpleasant. I was indeed desperate. I picked myself up and tried to find something with which to repair the damage. But nothing was to be found. Besides I was so hampered in my vision and in every movement, that wrath rose in me against my absurd situation, which I no longer understood. I pulled at all my garments, but they clung only the tighter. The cords of the mantle strangled me, and the stuff on my head pressed as though more and more were being added to it. Furthermore the atmosphere had become dim and as though misty with the oldish fumes of the spilled liquid.

Hot and angry, I rushed to the mirror and with difficulty watched through the mask the working of my hands. But for this the mirror had just been waiting. Its moment of retaliation had come. While I strove in boundlessly increasing anguish to squeeze somehow out of my disguise, it forced me, by what means I do not known, to lift my eyes and imposed on me an image, no, a reality, a strange,

374

unbelievable and monstrous reality, with which, against my will, I became permeated: for now the mirror was the stranger, and I was the mirror. I stared at this great, terrifying unknown before me, and it seemed to me appalling to be alone with him. But at the very moment I thought this, the worst befell: I lost all sense, I simply ceased to exist. For one second I had an indescribable, painful and futile longing for myself, then there was only he: there was nothing but he.

I ran away, but now it was he that ran. He knocked against everything, he did not know the house, he had no idea where to go; he managed to get down a stairway, and in his course stumbled over someone who shouted in struggling free. A door opened, several persons came out: Oh, oh, what a relief it was to know them! There were Sieversen, the good Sieversen, and the housemaid and the butler: now for a decision. But they did not spring forward to the rescue; their cruelty knew no bounds. They stood there and laughed; my God, they could stand there and laugh. I wept but the mask did not let the tears escape; they ran down inside over my cheeks and dried at once and ran again and dried. And at last I knelt before them, as no human being ever knelt; I knelt, and lifted up my hands, and implored them: 'Take me out, if you still can, and keep me,' but they did not hear; I had no longer any voice.

In this passage, steeped in profound symbolism, Rilke expressed the experience of self-alienation and imprisonment within a role.

And yet – it is one of the functions of a given culture to restrict an enormous variety of a person's potential forms of being to a number of social roles (husband, wife, father, mother, waiter, and so on). We encapsulate people in a job, in their vocational role and in prescribed and expected role behavior. Everybody has to be 'someone'; and the individual who as the 'eternal adolescent' refuses to be pinned down in one of the roles ('I'm this, but I'm something else as well'), refuses to conform to a stereotype, refuses to let himself be classified, lays himself open to suspicion and hostility.

We say, of course, that we admire a 'personality,' a 'character'; but he also makes us feel uneasy. We cannot predict what he will do and how he will behave.

So a person finds in the course of his existence a number of agreed-upon procedures and rules to which he is forced to conform by the community in which he lives. He finds himself in the various *roles* that he performs on the stage of life. It would appear that we are 'occupied' in succession by various roles, with which we more or less identify ourselves. We are always *en représentation*, we are never simply one with ourselves. The person who gives rein to some activity does so by virtue of this or that role, created for this or that occasion. Thus he can never be altogether responsible, in the degree to which he himself is partly absent.

There is an element of *exteriority* in our behavior (the actor is only a particularization of that exteriority), because we accept *names* as a principle of our activity and obey rules which do not proceed from the depths of our own being.

Thus a *role* is a *fonction de la personne*. An image designed for external use. The role (Jung's 'persona') exists as a social category independently of any given period or set of circumstances. One can resist it, it need not dictate our conduct in detail; but it exists, and its influence is the stronger *the less we are aware of its presence*. Along with his need for assurance, man also has a need to be able to depend on himself. Through various roles assurance is obtained. But this same fulcrum, partly an instrument of self-knowledge (the role as a '*forme d'intelligibilité de soi à soi*'), in part constitutes a hindrance to self-knowledge, to the extent, that is, '*où elle serait prise à la lettre, aceptée en bloc et comme un dernier mot*' – 'that it might be taken literally, accepted hook, line and sinker and as the final word' (Gusdorf). What is required is an equilibrium between what is called for by the environment and what we ourselves wish to be.

As I said before, there is an extensive literature on the problems confronting the person-in-a-role, from which he keeps on trying to free himself but in which he may also be imprisoned by the customs, rules, norms, values and expectations of 'the other,' '*die Leute*' – 'the people' (Ortega y Gasset).

Martin Buber (and his pupil, Hans Trüb), Ludwig Binswanger and others see liberation from the role, the persona, the '*moi-sociale*,' determined by '*les pensées des autres*' (Proust, Pascal), in the loving solidarity with the other. Buber's I-thou relationship: 'I become myself in you.' We find this also in what Binswanger has written about '*liebend-mit-einander-sein*' ('being-loving-with-one-another').

Listen to what the Dutch author Anna Blaman says in her novel *Op leven en dood*:

> She took from you all the decorum that the world outside thrusts upon one. She relieved you of the duty of being the adult representative of yourself, you were able to be the person you were, vulnerable or afraid, or just more aware of your self and more important than your place in the outside world permitted you to be.

The way human behavior is channeled from birth and directed along certain paths is a subject of the greatest importance in this respect. *How* the written and unwritten rules of the cultural game condition the individual from birth to develop *specific* forms of behavior, to see *certain* things (and not to see others) and to undertake *certain* forms of action. It is an extremely complex process. Jerome Bruner sees two lines of incidence.[5] The most striking is punishment and reward. Punishment can take many forms. The means of attack can be 'expulsion,' playing upon the 'fear of ostracism.' We threaten to expel someone from the group; a deep fear of being cut off and isolated forces the individual 'to conform.' Through a process of labeling (psychopath, delinquent, crazy man, dreamer, visionary) this process of expulsion as a sanction for, and a means of maintaining, certain rules in social systems (family, union, society) is put into effect. The other line of attack is the way people are conditioned (or 'programmed') *to see and conceptualize the world they live in*. This is the 'cognitive control' that constricts perception and with it the possibilities of action. Language and myth play major roles here. In recent years Ernst Cassirer and Benjamin Lee Whorf have done much to make us aware of this fact.

Bruner points out that language is first and foremost request-language. Naturally, it is expected of a child that he will learn to speak the language of his community. But there is a price to be paid for this. The child learns to think exclusively in the *forms* of that language, in the conceptions that are part of the language's grammatical structure. Here Bruner finds his way to Sapir and Whorf's hypothesis, although he favours a somewhat diluted version of it. He, too, believes that the language we speak predisposes us to think certain things, have certain perceptions and make certain associations. It imposes characteristic restrictions on all the members of the society speaking that same language.

The complexity of our whole world of experience, then, is coded, structured and made comprehensible in a particular way. Thus people within a given linguistic group are better able to communicate with one another, there being both linguistic and conceptual agreement. But it is a straitjacket, too. It reduces the variability of behavior and thinking and the formulation of new questions.

This raises the problem of social control: the subtle manner in which it is laid down in advance which forms of behavior are possible for people and which not, the way in which it is made clear to people 'what their place is.' To return to the psychiatrists, they play a very important role in this process of social control; and we should be aware of that. Szasz has written some penetrating essays about it.[6] I shall make use of them now.

If Szasz's assumption is right – that deviations from the biological norm may indeed be classified as 'illness,' but deviations from the norms and values of a society *cannot* be so regarded – then the psychiatric theory of classification comes very close to pronouncement of a verdict without setting out the substantiating facts. The psychiatrist as classifier is then passing judgment on the person classified. The psychiatrist becomes a mouthpiece of society's norms and his labels function as a social constraint, disguised in pseudo-medical jargon. In all his recent articles, in which the humanistic values of freedom, autonomy and individual responsibility have a central place, Szasz attacks medical-clinical psychiatry and its exponents and calls the latter accomplices of a society that is intent on preserving its socio-ethical values (and systems) and to do so makes use of *psychiatry and its 'catch-all phrase,' 'mental illness,'* in addition to every other means. In the unlikely event, therefore, that psychiatry persists in the future as a medical discipline, psychiatrists and psychiatry will continue, under cover of a 'health ethics' and the protection of the medical profession, to be an enormously powerful social factor in regulating people's conduct.

These warnings about the dangers of a society that manipulates human beings, conditions their behavior, directs it into certain prescribed channels and so lifts from people's shoulders the 'intolerable burden of freedom' are, of course, nothing new. In *The Organization Man*, written in the late 1950s, William H. Whyte said that although the team can be a splendid thing, and cooperative effort and belonging to the group can be a source of creativity, the social ethics of collectivism has led us to idolize 'the organization' until it has become more and more difficult to take one's stand as an individual *against* the organization. Yet the creative person (who wants to explore new paths) must be able to fight this 'organization.' The continuous pressure to yield to the organization, the security that is offered, the indoctrination of the team ideal, whereby it is intimated that *in ideal circumstances* there need be no conflict between the individual and the community – all that is very hard to resist; indeed, it is even hard to detect. And yet, Whyte maintained, there is a conflict between the individual and the community (and organization), and the ideology of collectivism cannot get around that conflict. The 'peace of mind' proffered by the benevolent organization is still 'surrender,' a giving up of one's own creative stance.[7]

What Szasz does in his work as a whole is to combat the organization of institutional psychiatry. He regards the whole 'mental hygiene movement,' deriving from Clifford Beers and defined by him in 1908 as 'work for the preservation of mental health,' as an attempt to suppress the autonomy of the individual. The aim of the social sciences (and psychiatry) became identified with predicting and keeping people's behavior under control; and this was to be done by a scientific elite who looked upon the 'mentally sick' as inferior.

Thus the 'mental health professional' is fundamentally authoritarian. His values are collectivism and 'social tranquility,' and the so-called social rehabilitation of the mentally ill means in fact turning a 'social misfit' into a 'socially useful citizen.'

It goes without saying that these ideas gained Szasz even more enemies than his whole analysis of 'medical psychiatry.'

I shall confine myself here to taking a closer look at his anlysis of the classification process in psychiatry. Man is the only animal who classifies, who sets down what he observes in categories. It is not just the research scientist who does this. Every human being gives names to things, and the motive underlying this is to obtain an element of control over the world he lives in. Every form of classification implies a hope of successful control. Being unable to classify goes hand in hand with a feeling of impotence:

> However difficult it may be to classify things, and especially to classify them accurately, it is even more difficult not to classify things: to suspend and postpone judgment and delay the act of classification.[8]

The business of classifying leads us to detect regularities, our symbolic identifications help us to avoid being constantly taken by surprise by the things that happen. We are able to predict them. Thus the aims proposed by the research scientist are 'prediction' and 'control'; and the naming and classifying procedures provide, along with hypothesis and theory formulation, the building material for that objective. This is the posture adopted by the rational person toward the world of things (rocks, stones, etc.), plants and animals.

But what are we doing with people, what are we doing *to* people, when we classify them as well? That human beings need to create order and regularity in a potentially chaotic universe and that the classification of things, plants and animals gives expression to that need is perfectly all right. Things, plants and animals care nothing, fortunately, about this classifying activity on our part. Among the mammals we can distinguish cows, but we affect the behavior of those cows only when we proceed to direct action: milking them or slaughtering them. Our symbolic action (our naming and classifying) has no effect on the cow: 'That which we call a rose by any other name would smell as sweet.'

With people it is different. To name, to classify, to label another person *affects that person immensely*. To call someone a homosexual, delinquent, schizophrenic, hysteric, neurotic, psychotic psychopath, neurasthenic and so on is most certainly action *upon* (or rather *against*) him.

Here again Szasz sees as the motive for making a 'thing' of people attempts by the psychiatric labelers to exercise control over the other person: 'To classify human behavior is to constrain it.' To attach a label to a person is to pigeon-hole him.

After this introduction we are in a position to turn to the work of the American sociologists, Scheff and Lemert, who both have a very original approach to the problem of 'mental illness' as a form of deviant behavior and likewise connect it with the theme of 'social control,' the norm-affirming reaction of society.

Thomas Scheff[9] starts his sociological analysis of what 'being mentally ill' really is by referring to the work of Howard Becker. Becker introduced the concept of 'deviance' in an original way:

> Social groups create deviance by making rules whose infraction constitutes deviance, and by applying those rules to particular people and labelling them as outsiders . . . deviance is not a quality of the act the person commits, but rather the consequence of the application by others of rules and sanctions to an 'offender.'
>
> The deviant is one to whom the label has successfully been applied; deviant behavior is behavior that people so label.[10]

The main question, then, is *what rules and norms* are infringed, that is, what *type* of conduct invites us to use, not the label 'criminal,' 'delinquent,' 'eccentric,' but the label 'mentally ill.'

To answer this question Scheff makes use of Ervin Goffman's work and describes the rules infringed as being in the nature of 'residual rules.' This is the network of often scarcely defined, often unwritten norms of behavior; behavior in situations that we might well take straight out of some handbook on etiquette. Goffman provides an extensive description and analysis of these infringed 'residual (social) rules.' [11]

At a cocktail party you may gaze out of a window for five or even ten minutes, but if you do it for fifteen, you begin to attract attention. The 'rules of the game' for parties do not permit it. But 'residual rule-breaking' need not of itself lead to labeling, classification and intervention by public bodies. A lot of people may 'act crazy' for a very long time without being officially stigmatized.[12] Scheff writes at some length about this. The deviant and disruptive conduct may be disclaimed and denied, for instance, or may be of a transient kind. A 'gloved hand' may be used ('informal control') to call the deviant person to order. The person can be normalized by means of informal sanctions (unfavorable comment, loss of prestige, disapproval, and so on), and in this method no 'public body' (or official) comes into it. The situation is consolidated or normalized at the level of primary deviance.

It is a very different thing when 'officials' (psychiatrists, etc.) enter the picture, especially if they form part of some institution or other. At this point there begins a social process that can turn this primary deviant behavior ('residual rule-breaking') *into a permanent form of role behavior*. First Scheff:

> Infringing the (often unwritten) residual rules may settle into a permanent role if – and this is the point – the conduct is defined as proof of 'mental illness.' The offender then assumes the status of a deviant person and begins to play the role of the mentally ill.

Scheff's book has a great deal to say about this process of 'living up to one's label,' and there is little point to giving a long extract from it here. Better to take a brief look at the work of the sociologist Edwin Lemert.

For Lemert, too, the starting point is the question of 'social control,' the way the citizen is compelled, informally or formally (by the competent authorities), to observe the rules of conduct applicable to a given community. Only Lemert inverts the proposition 'social deviance produces social control,' or rather, he posits *a new way for sociological research* by asserting that *social control also leads to deviant behavior* and – what is most important – gives a concrete form to such behavior, sustains *and renders it permanent*. He considers this reverse route a fruitful one for more intensive research and comes up immediately with a hit, in the shape of the notion of 'secondary deviance.'

Deviant conduct can have innumerable causes: disease, criminality, addiction, behavior arising from a family context or from a nexus of psychic problems – known at one time as the 'symptoms' of 'mental disorder' – and so on. This infraction of rules and norms (in the case of a physical disease, mainly biological norms) has been called *primary deviance* (Scheff's 'residual rule-breaking'). Against this 'transgressive' deviant behavior certain measures are taken: attempts at 'normalization' which, often conducted informally, fail. Whatever the causes of primary deviance may be, the 'official' reaction of the community can lead to a chain reaction with far-reaching consequences for the 'deviant.' By virtue of the labeling process, official censure, degrading, punitive isolation and before very long, a symbolic reorganizing of the deviant's attitude towards his own self begin to occur. 'But that's just how I am!' ('crazy,' 'schizophrenic,' 'psychopath,' 'delinquent,' manic-depressive,' etc.). The individual concerned is pinned down *to a particular social role*, becomes the bearer of a label, is placed 'at the disposal' of corrective authorities, legal or medical-and-psychiatric. This process of *adaptation to such regulative measures on society's part* then results in *'secondary deviance.'*

Lemert emphasizes the enormous consequences that this process of being frozen within a given role has for the (initially) 'primary deviant.' He stresses, too, how much behavior could be accounted for in terms of this secondary deviance.[13] The deviant person, once officially labeled and 'taken charge of,' *may* arrive at a type of role-conditioned behavior that will push the original problems pretty well into the background. The proposition becomes: 'deviance breeds deviance.' The so-called 'secondary deviant' begins to find more satisfaction in being deviant than in not being so. A delinquent *may* do some more housebreaking, for instance, because he thinks being caught will mean being looked after again and enjoying a kind of security. He *wants* to get back into prison. In my view the 'chronic schizophrenic,' as he is called, is a classic instance of 'secondary deviance.'

It is certainly possible in a particular context (say, the family or . . . the mental hospital) to assume the 'role' of the 'mad person' and become accustomed to it.[14] As a matter of fact, this was known a long time ago. In the literature of psychoanalysis people have talked about 'secondary disease gain.' The word 'secondary' may suggest that this is somehow less important. But for Scheff and Lemert it is very important indeed.

I believe that what I have already written about the residents of Rose Cottage is convincing enough to support the proposition that their behavior (within the context described) can be called an example of permanently role-conditioned conduct ('secondary deviance').

A recent provocative book by Braginsky and others argues that the behavior of people living as 'chronic schizophrenics' in a psychiatric institution is exceptionally intelligent, very rational and extremely purposive.[15] The purpose is . . . to stay there. They behave not 'crazy' enough to land in the closed ward – and just sufficiently enough (disturbed conduct) *not to be discharged*. One has only to enter certain mental hospitals (beautiful lawns, humane care and attention, workshops, beauty parlor and swimming pool on the grounds) to realize what tremendous security and safety they offer, which many people will not give up easily. The result is overcrowding, and the staff search desperately for opportunities to discharge these people to 'nursing homes' (the same situation, but not so luxurious) and 'halfway houses' (sometimes euphemistically referred to as 'resocialization centers,' a handsome expression, hardly ever justified by any real content).

Braginsky and his co-authors wonder, therefore, whether the 'patient' really is such a helpless victim of the enormous and fully sanctioned 'power' which the psychiatric hospital as 'total institution' has over them. It may well be that a lot of patients are more powerful than we think and exert a counterforce in the form of subtle sabotaging of their prospects for discharge by presenting conduct (secondary deviance) that Goffman has called 'impression management.' This manipulative type of behavior, geared mainly to maintaining oneself in the institution and living there as comfortably as possible, consists of 'making oneself invisible,' avoiding contact with a psychiatrist (not very hard to do, because the latter is usually not too enthused about patient contact himself) and simply 'acting crazy' at the right moment!

We shall illustrate just once more the problem of the 'crazy individual' who no longer desires to rejoin society, who performs the role of 'madman' more or less consciously, in order not to be confronted again with the problems that life (as we have arranged it) sets before him. Luigi Pirandello has handled the theme most penetratingly in his play *Henry IV*.

A man goes 'mad' and thinks he is Henry IV. His family hire a castle, bodyguards and servants for him and leave the madman to his delusion of being King Henry. But many years later the deluded man 'wakes up' and realizes that he must now make a decision. He is already gray-haired. The banquet of life has already been cleared away, his former fiancée is married. Pirandello has his main character say to a psychiatrist:

Now, doctor, the case must be absolutely new in the history of madness. I preferred to remain mad – since I found everything ready and at my disposal for this new exquisite fantasy. I would live it – this madness of mine – with the most lucid consciousness.

A little later in the play comes a passage full of symbolism:

This dress which is for me the evident, involuntary caricature of that other continuous, everlasting masquerade of which we are the involuntary puppets, when, without knowing it, we mask ourselves with that which we appear to be.

And later:

I am cured, gentlemen: because I can act the madman to

perfection, here; and I do it very quietly, I'm only sorry for you that have to live your madness so agitatedly, without knowing it or seeing it.

Now we must discuss the alternative. How might things be different?

REFERENCES

[1] Ortega y Gasset: *Zelfinkeer en verbijstering* (The Hague, 1949).

[2] E. Fromm: *Marx's Concept of Man* (New York, 1961).

[3] G. Gusdorf: *La Découverte de soi* (Paris, 1948).
E. Fromm: *The Fear of Freedom* (London, 1942).
L. Pirandello: *Naked Masks*, E. Bentley, ed. (New York, 1952); *Angst vor dem Glück* (Heidelberg, 1953); *Short Stories* (New York, 1959; *Humoresken und Satiren* (Heidelberg, 1956).
P. Tillich: *The Courage to Be* (London, 1952).
M. Buber: *Die Schriften über das dialogische Prinzip* (Heidelberg, 1954).
J.-P. Sartre: *Being and Nothingness*, Hazel Barnes, trans. (New York, 1956).

[4] R. M. Rilke: *The Notebooks of Malte Laurids Brigge*, M. D. Herter Norton, trans. (New York, 1949).

[5] J. Bruner: *On Knowing: Essays for the Left Hand* (Cambridge, Mass., 1962).

[6] T. S. Szasz: *Ideology and Insanity: Essay on the Psychiatric Dehumanization of Man* (New York, 1970).

[7] K. Kolle: *An Introduction to Psychiatry* (New York, 1963); W. H. Whyte: *The Organization Man* (Garden City, N.Y., 1957).

[8] T. S. Szasz: *Ideology and Insanity: Essays on the Psychiatric Dehumanization of Man* (New York, 1970).

[9] T. J. Scheff: *Being Mentally Ill* (Chicago, 1966).

[10] H. S. Becker: *Outsiders* (New York, 1963).

[11] E. Goffman: *Behavior in Public Places* (New York, 1963).

[12] For an extensive analysis of the stigmatizing process I would refer the reader to E. Goffman: *Stigma* (Englewood Cliffs, N.J., 1963).

[13] Lemert expounds his ideas at some length in *Social Pathology* (1958) and in a collection of essays published later. ('*Human Deviance, Social Problems and Social Control* [New York, 1967].) This latter book contains the relevant sociological literature which preceded Lemert in dealing with the problem of the deviant person and his behavior.

[14] A. P. Towbin: 'Understanding the Mentally Deranged,' *Journ. of Existentialism*, vol. 7, pp. 63–83 (1966).
See also J. Haley: 'Strategies of Psychotherapy,' 73, pp. 63–84, (New York, 1963).

[15] B. M. Braginsky, *et al.*: *Methods of Madness: the Mental Hospital as a Last Resort* (New York, 1969).

20. THE FUTURE

What, then, lies ahead? What are the alternatives for psychiatry and its institutions? I follow closely the suggestions given by Szasz.

The future will see a development away from medical science and toward psychology. A scientific study of man in his communal situation, with his past and his future and the struggle of his being human. Medical science can continue to be a branch of physical science, but psychiatry must get away from it. It must become a scientific discipline, concerned with values, norms, rules, ethical issues – a 'moral science.' What will emerge from the separating off of psychiatry from medicine is not an antimedical discipline but a nonmedical one, '. . . equally open to physicians and nonphysicians interested in the study of man and in psychotherapy.'[1] A complete breakaway from neurology must be part of this process of separation. Of course, the process will be a laborious one. With a bad marriage (psychiatry-neurology) the divorce proceedings are more often than not a tiresome affair. What is clearly taking shape is a discipline positioned between neurology and psychiatry. This discipline will concern itself with the diseases of the nervous system – in particular, of the brain – and the resulting adaptational dis-

388

turbances and defects in the capacity to symbolize. A component part of neurology, this discipline is already coming to be known as 'biological psychiatry' or 'neuropsychiatry.' This means that in practical, organizational terms there must be a separate kind of training for qualification as a psychiatrist and, concurrently with it, a training designed to produce competent psychotherapists.

I believe that if we throw the medical disease model overboard, we certainly will not lose anything of the psychoanalytic model. I agree with many others that the psychoanalytic model had too closed a character. (As though there were such a thing as a kind of defective personality system, of which 'being neurotic' was the inevitable outcome!)

Nor should we lose anything of what psychoanalysts and others have given us in order to understand people in distress, suffering in their present social situation and taunted by repressed memories. Freed now of the ballast of the disease model, we need a different approach that will give us new openings for more effective ways of prevention and intervention. An approach that will stimulate new organizations and new actions, enabling us to tackle adequately the enormous psychic problems (silently endured or voiced aloud) of so many.

We simply cannot hide any more behind the apologetic remarks that psychoanalytic psychology, social psychology, in short, the social sciences 'are still in an early stage.' We have an enormous amount of knowledge at our disposal. Only we have difficulty putting this know-how into practice. This is not the place to go into the knowledge we have acquired as a result of studying the social context (the family as a permanent social system and other societal structures) which evokes and perpetuates, even stimulates, deviant behavior. Studies of the context, for instance, within the setting of a psychotherapeutic intervention in a family, have already made more intelligible a lot of the ostensibly deviant and 'incomprehensible' behavior of one or more members of the group, behavior that we had once understood as *the only possible form of adaptive behavior within such a context.*

What we must concentrate on now is how to approach the

deviant to aid him more quickly and efficiently in the future. Of course, there are countless instances where we find ourselves in difficulties with people who infringe the social rules to an extent that forces us to intervene in one way or another. The nub of the problem is whether we can call a halt to the development of the disastrous role of the 'secondary deviant': that is to say, whether we can create institutions that will *not* proceed to clap the familiar labels on particular forms of behavior and will *not* be the kind of context that 'breeds' the process discussed in the previous chapter: namely, the development of the professional patient.

In tackling this problem I would opt for the simplest route, the route of establishing what our priorities are. I would first concentrate on the *training of a new type of therapist*. I believe that any discussion about the renovation of psychiatry (radical psychiatry, antipsychiatry or whatever one wants to call it) and futurological blueprints of 'institutions' still to be created remain meaningless, unless we first come to grips with the problem of training a new type of manpower.

Let us concentrate first, then, on the therapist (maybe he will still be called a psychiatrist) of the future. I see him as someone who having passed a preliminary qualifying examination (in psychology, medicine, sociology, pedagogics, social psychology, cultural anthropology) *undergoes a special course of study. First and foremost this would include the basic principles of sociology and social psychology.* The whole of psychoanalytic training would be a part of this. That means that the present psychoanalytic training institutes could simply disappear or at most put a finishing touch to the training to be outlined. At this point it is important to stress that without a socially (and politically) critical approach and training in ways of planning and implementing *change* (the strategy of change is still practically unknown territory) we shall *not* bring it off. We will go on scratching only the surface of the problem if we shut our eyes to societal structures and relations that give rise to serious disruptions within the family.

In the course of this study the student will enter a personal psychoanalysis and he will be supervised in his first psychotherapeutic experiences with individuals and systems and groups (married couples, families, organizations). The schooling in philosophy as an essential part of this training will be centered on developing a socially critical approach. It must be impressed on the future psychiatrist that there is a political aspect to his functioning and that he cannot do his job on a value-free basis. Quite the contrary. Ethical norms, such as respect for the individual, his freedom, his autonomy and his struggle for the greatest possible unfolding potentialities of being human, form the background to the future psychiatrist's training.[2]

Now the 'institutions.'

The mental hospital in its present form is, qua organizational form, rapidly becoming a historical anachronism. Goffman, who has recently hardened his stand against these bureaucratic colossi, deals with them quite critically. He states:

> In the last twenty years we have learned that the management of mental illness under medical auspices has been an uncertain blessing. The best treatment that money has been able to buy, prolonged individual psychotherapy, has not proved very efficacious. The treatment most patients have received – hospitalization – has proved to be questionable indeed. Patients recover more often than not, at least temporarily, but this seems in spite of the mental hospital, not because of it. Upon examination, many of these establishments have proved to be hopeless storage dumps trimmed in psychiatric paper. They have served to remove the patient from the scene of his symptomatic behavior, which in itself can be constructive, but this function has been performed by fences, not doctors. And the price that the patient has had to pay for this service has been considerable: dislocation from civil life, alienation from loved ones who arranged the commitment, mortification due to hospital regimentation and surveillance, permanent post-hospital stigmatization. This has been not merely a bad deal; it has been a grotesque one.[3]

But what, then, are we to do with all those leaf-enshrouded buildings in the country? It is my belief that after a long phase of transition we shall have to set aside these mental hospitals for *all physically sick (or handicapped) people whose behavior is in some way disturbed who need both medical care and support and guidance in their problems.* The person with a brain tumor with accompanying behavioral problems, the person suffering from epilepsy, (genuine) forms of imbecillitas mentis and idiocy. Likewise those with metabolic disorders with concomitant disturbances in symbolic functioning, delirious states as a result of alcohol intoxication or serious addictive conditions, and psychically disordered old people – a category with which we simply do not know how to cope for lack of adequate accommodations. And here I mean those elderly people whose behavioral disorder seems closely related to a definable process of cerebral decay. (But it is quite possible possible that including this last category would be a serious error. The kind of 'symptom' here is confusion during the night, bed-wetting, loss of decorum, severe loss of memory for recent events; in short, the confused states of senility. But is there a straight causal relation to changes in the brain? We may yet see some surprising discoveries in this respect. Creating the proper setting, keeping the elderly in our midst and giving them adequate psychological help may well lead to the disappearance of much disturbed behavior. Dumping them in mental hospitals, removing them from the com-community, could thus be a false solution.) There are also those with disorders caused by a cerebral hemorrhage or injury to the brain and the various forms of cerebral atrophy. One can stretch this category as far as one wishes. We've got enough accommodations; and the psychiatrist can find his place here as consultant in what one need now have no qualms about calling a 'hospital'.

At any rate, to maintain the situation in which the present-day mental hospital functions seems a most deplorable waste of money and devoted energy. The money poured into these hospitals ought to be used for primary preventive institutions. The mental hospital would then restrict itself to taking in and, in a human way, caring for people with organic disorders.

Now for something about the psychotherapeutic center. After my return from America I spent about three years running a center of this kind. It was small, had about thirty clients and a minimal staff: an ideal setting for the creation of a therapeutic community, with a daily community meeting, sports, painting, modeling, group psychotherapy, psychodrama sessions in the afternoon, individual psychotherapeutic care. I believe we gave the best possible care and a reasonably good after-care, and we certainly saw impressive results at times with previously totally deadlocked people. And yet – over the past few years I have learned that, besides the advantages, there are disadvantages to this sort of small community of people living together.

I do not doubt the great value such a setup can have for people: the clarification of here-and-now relational disturbances, the stress on shared responsibility for one another, on 'peer relationships,' the horizontal organizational structure, the openness of communication. In many respects it is an oasis of human solidarity, the more so as it approximates to the 'therapeutic community' in the strict sense (it is always a process of coming-to-be-a-community). But the drawback is that the nearer such a community gets to the ideal, the more protected and secure one feels in it. Despite efforts to counter this sheltered condition, the sense of security, of being well taken care of, creeps in. Society outside grows blurred, becomes more remote. What insights are gained would seem to be gradually annulled by an insidiously progressive weakening of the ego.

Another disadvantage is perhaps even more important. It relates particularly to people who are a part of this or that 'field' (marriage, family, long-term partner relationship) and break off as a 'pole' of this field, acquire the label 'sick' (neurotic, psychotic, etc.) and in isolation from that original field ('systematized' transactions) are getting 'treatment.' I see practically no advantages, only disadvantages in this way of tackling the problem. While admittedly a psychotherapeutic center, organized as a genuine therapeutic community, will be partly able to obviate the 'mental patient' role change (one of the advantages of these forms of nonmedical social organization), the problem of the *field* still remains. The so-called healthy husband will bring in his alcoholic wife, the tyrannical, sadistic and successful businessman who blocks any expression of feeling in himself will deliver his anxiety-ridden wife with an air of 'give her a cleaning treatment' and . . . go home. A stay in the psychotherapeutic center may then bring some improvement. But I have seen the improvement gained in a year of intensive psychotherapeutic work become undone after a week back home. The idea of geographically isolating one partner of a 'field' (the 'pole' which has let others and itself thrust upon it the 'deviant' label) and taking him or her into a community is illogical. Nor does it correspond to our present insights. The couple, the family, are permanent social systems, often imprisoned with rigid rules and forms of relationship. The compensation of one 'pole' is maintained thanks to suppressed, potential possibilities-of-being in the other. The decompensation of one of the poles supports compensation of the other pole or the system as a whole.

If this idea is right (and there is a considerable literature pointing in this direction), we must draw the right conclusion and create new forms of organization. I am conscious here of being engaged in an argument against the psychotherapeutic center. One should welcome the further development of these centers instead of launching into an argument that ends by concluding that some of their effects are undesirable and even crippling! And yet the conclusion seems inevitable. The sense of being 'in safe seclusion,' the stigmatization and isolation from a 'pathogenic' field (that, as a system, is not broken open so as to offer prospects for growth to every pole of this field), force us to consider new forms of organization, even for the psychotherapeutic center.

Now there appears on the agenda the new type of institution for a category of people for whom I have no label. People with 'problems in living.' The principle that runs through recent literature is community containment: keeping people within their natural community. This principle seems completely logical and I wonder whether after all that has been said it still needs to be clarified. At any rate, people who in their anguish send out s.o.s. signals – even when they say: 'Stop the world, I want to get off' – have something to tell us about the community in which they and we are living. They are indeed the 'loudspeakers of family trouble,' or better still, loudspeakers of the conflict-ridden subsystems of the community which block personal development and ultimately society's development. Instead of setting them apart (label attached) we might start to really listen to them. To me the most bewildering thing about my personal experiences with so-called schizophrenics has been to discover *how much* the most dispirited, isolated and confused person may have to tell us and teach us. I say 'bewildering' advisedly, because it is so appallingly seldom that anyone really listens to people so labeled.

The principle of 'keeping them within the community' and of quick and competent intervention is easier said than done. There is the manpower problem, first of all. But we shall not succeed unless we also face up to the question of how we can put into practice the principle of 'community containment.'

The last-quoted passage from Goffman on page 391 comes from a very recent publication, 'The Insanity of Place.' Goffman at once sets about answering the question we have just posed by first showing how tremendously difficult it will be. To jettison traditions alone is hard enough. To invent new solutions is harder. What shall we do about the person on the point of committing suicide? What shall we do about a maniacal condition? Goffman analyzes this latter situation.

The maniacal person leaves a trail of havoc in his family and his behavior in public and at work likewise tramples all the rules on 'how one should behave.' In this exuberant, energetic, unbridled activity (in which a great deal of aggression and sadness are given expression) there is no warrant for any transaction. A person in a state of maniacal excitation is hardly supportable within the family, since all the rules of conduct are infringed. At work the maniacal person (after an abortive attempt to calm him down) quickly becomes a 'center of distraction.' He is no longer taken seriously, and after every informal 'social control' has proved ineffective and attempts at correction have been abandoned, things reach a point where he is expelled from the group, and so there is created a 'real paranoid community for the paranoid.' [4]

Goffman takes this example and analyzes in detail what

all the consequences will be of not admitting the subject to a mental hospital. It is brilliantly done. In his article he then assumes a posture of sitting back and saying: 'Well now, psychiatrists, go ahead and resolve *that* problem with your "community-containment" philosophy!'

Indeed – how are we to solve this problem without resorting to some kind of 'social control' in the guise of this or that formal sanction? (Maniacal frenzy is just an example – all sorts of other examples might be given.) I see no reason why we should have to shy away from this problem. On the contrary, it is a challenge to us to get down to some thinking about the type of institution we *shall* have to organize. The literature on this is already extensive; and what emerges from it is the idea of a therapeutic institution called a 'community mental health center.' Other names such as 'crisis intervention center' or, recently, 'social intervention center' (Albee) also occur in the literature. There is currently some discussion about what is described as a 'day hospital' or 'day residence' (which the person 'in crisis' leaves in the evening). There is the term 'night clinic' – basically a place where help can be offered in the evenings and where it is possible to stay overnight for a short term. The principle at work here is still that of 'community containment.' The client remains in his job and his own living quarters and is not subjected to the process of prolonged separation from the source community in which he lives or works – however unviable that situation may be in itself. In The Netherlands there are social-psychiatric services where excellent work is being done by social workers and socio-psychiatric nurses in what are often very difficult circumstances. With these services, which often include a bureau for handling 'problems in living' and family difficulties, the tendency is again to establish a kind of 'center' – where everything has basically the same end in view. In his book *Beyond the Therapeutic Community*, Maxwell Jones has a sort of futurological chapter; and one cannot help noticing his perplexity.[5] Thus he says: 'Vast changes in the theory and practice of education are imminent [his allusion is also to the psychiatrist's training] and no one can conceptualize with any accuracy what will emerge in the next few decades.' He has a strong feeling that change is in the air. What in the future is to be the relationship between the psychiatrist and the educator? He offers no solution and uses terms like 'mental health' and 'mental illness'; but he does envisage a new type of psychiatrist: the 'community psychiatrist.' He wants to get rid of the old institutions, the mental hospitals (even the most modern). It is fascinating that he finds the term 'hospital' irritating and actually considers the old term 'asylum' (where one asks for 'asylum' and finds a place of refuge) much more candid. In fact he thinks in much the same terms as the authors cited in the previous chapter (Braginsky, etc.).

Life *is* difficult, sometimes unlivable, and for many people it becomes just too painful. A place of refuge *is* necessary at times; so why not set up some kind of village where people can find the courage to live again – or where they can remain? As for such terms as 'patient,' 'nurse' and 'psychiatrist' (in the old sense of the doctor-physician) and the role relations to which these give rise, it could well be that in future nothing will be heard of them anymore.

So Maxwell Jones concludes:

> We need to know far more about the whole process of learning, and it would then seem that in the future psychiatrists may well tend to integrate more closely with behavioral scientists, and also with the educationalists.

For Maxwell Jones this is an intriguing and exciting possibility for the future of psychiatry. In any case, he holds that whatever trouble we might take to 'democratize' the traditional mental hospital, we would still not come up with the right solution. It would be a drop in the ocean. We would just be bolstering and perpetuating old systems.

After this preliminary, a brief outline of the institution yet to be:

In the first place I have in mind something that will aim at *obviating the need to consign people to mental hospitals as they exist at the present time*: an institution that can offer to accommodate people in crisis, when presented by social psychiatric services and other bodies, by day or night – but on a short-term basis. From the moment of 'intake' and selection this institution must exude the atmosphere of a 'therapeutic community' geared to a speedy return of the client to society.

An institution free from a medical climate and language and pervaded by an ideology of 'social learning and unlearning' in the group processes created in the here and now. Not, that is, the guest house of a mental hospital, not a psychotherapeutic center, but a 'therapeutic community in the community.' This expression comes from Maxwell Jones. Precisely what he has in view is not clear to me. But that does not matter so very much. The feature of this new type of institution that seems to me most important is that it is located *in the community*. In this therapeutic center the principles of the therapeutic community are not abandoned but become part of a form of organization aimed at prevention and intervention. By prevention I mean in the first place a forestalling of the 'mental-patient-illness' role. By intervention I mean provision of aid to a person or group of persons in psychic need or distress as soon as possible. I certainly do not mean 'referral' after 'investigations,' not a traffic sign pointing to dead-end streets. The principle of direct aid (in the broadest sense) is now under full discussion, and there is no need for me to write at length here about its value.

The center will be imbued with an ideology which must not be a 'medical' one, but rather educational. There is something more to be said about this ideology. I share Laing's view that psychic trouble, certainly what we call 'insanity' (I leave demonstrably physical disease processes out of it), can actually be interpreted as a 'breakthrough,' a breakthrough to new ways of being human, which we are in the habit of describing as a 'breakdown.' [6]

As a matter of custom we have hung a negative label on what could also be evaluated as a positive phenomenon. 'Insanity,' 'senselessness,' may be a break *out of* a person's 'senses,' *out of* the 'games,' the hypocrisy, the caricatured rigidity and restrictedness that life has imposed on so many of us. The point is to guide and assist this breakthrough positively.

We came across this viewpoint in the works of Fromm-Reichmann; and there are many (surprisingly enough, those psychotherapists in particular who have worked intensively with 'schizophrenics') who think the same way. Recently, Carl Whitaker, a very experienced psychotherapist, has given prominence to this way of looking at things. He was asked in an interview why he felt so attracted to psychotherapeutic work with families in which enormous problems predominate: 'It really looks as though you are pleased at so much despair and confusion. It would even seem that you are congratulating the relatives on it!'

Whitaker replied as follows:

A: I honestly believe it. If a schizophrenic youngster comes in here and tells me what a horrible thing his mother and father did to him, I say, 'Look, you've got to give them credit. They made you crazy and you get something out of life. You're not out there dead like most of these characters carrying a briefcase.' I differentiate crazy from insane. The insane are what Christ called the 'whited sepulchers.' The ones who go to jobs every morning in gray flannel suits.

Q: A lot of people who work intensively with schizophrenics seem to get more of an appreciation of craziness and less of an appreciation of ordinary life.

A: It's true. I'm envious of people who have had an overt craziness. I've had my moments and shades and shadows, but never the full-blown creativity that some of these people have available to them.

They may never get around to using it, but they've got it right there. I think this is why the psychiatrist frequently gets into craziness with his mind. He's hoping to find it in himself.

And he goes further:

You can divide people into two groups: those who have been crazy and are trying to get over it and those who haven't been crazy and are trying to get there. And I'll say to a crazy person: 'You're stuck with two lives. I want you to stay crazy, but I also want you to live out there with those insane people, because that's the world you have to live in and you can get something out of that too.' [7]

Naturally, this viewpoint runs up against a lot of resistance, especially from those who believe they are in their 'right minds.' Besides the personal significance of a nexus of psychic problems as a breakthrough, there is also the other implication of this s.o.s. signal: namely, the call to take a look at ourselves and at the societal forms which we (and by 'we' I mean 'all of us') can no longer find acceptable. The authoritarian structures, the reduction of people to things, the creation of pseudo-needs (the fanatical advertising of goods in our consumer society), the aggressive-competitive and exploitative societal forms in our economic system (and destruction), the discrimination, environmental pollution, the totally antiquated divorce and abortion laws and above all our stubborn refusal to start birth control immediately. Those are just a few examples.

In round terms, the ideology I have been writing about is one that forces us into direct human (psychotherapeutic) and political engagement, and not into administering a whole battery of tranquilizers and a few more or less superficial, so-called restorative manipulations.

The institution I envisage also offers the possibility of bringing about a change in the system. A psychotherapy of the family as a whole is a constituent part of that. Knowledge of the family and marriage is increasing so quickly, and developments in this field are so fruitful, that we are in a position to say that family- and partner-therapy has moved out of the experimental stage. It is remarkable that we have been so tardy in getting down to a serious study of these natural groups (family and marriage) and in developing a psychotherapeutic technique for exerting a constructive influence on these 'fields' – an eye to change and new opportunities for growth for all members of the family. *It is to this development that we shall have to look for a central activity of the future, primarily preventive psychotherapeutic care and its structure-qua-organization.* Psychotherapeutic intervention in the transaction system called 'married couple' and 'family' should not be reserved for the happy few. To a substantial degree, social psychiatry is coming to be 'family psychiatry' (Howells).[8]

Thus the 'social intervention center' (the name I prefer for the moment) will as an institution be a tying together of the above-mentioned development of psychotherapeutic intervention in the family and marriage groups. The idea is a form of organization, an institution that is not allowed to 'institutionalize' clients. Of course, there is something illogical about that, for it will sometimes be necessary to admit people into this institution. The extent to which we are able to avoid the danger of 'institutionalizing,' of becoming a closed community, will depend on the way we set about things. It will depend on how we build up the staff and on the sort of staff that we want – and can train on the job.

I now propose to give a brief description of what we could aim for in practice. There are two categories of people in the running for the role of 'patient.'

I. THE ISOLATE

This is a category of people who are not involved, are not in permanent relationship with emotionally 'significant adults' (father, mother, marriage partner, homo- or heterophile partners, etc.). Of course these people have relationships that give an opening for conflict-charged 'transference' to develop (with, for instance, an employer or landlady); but we have not yet reached the stage of being able to influence these 'fields' on a sufficiently systematic basis. Still, some serious thinking is being done in the literature about this – witness the concept of a 'network therapy.' These people could offer a *group psychotherapy*.

The chief emphasis in what we are proposing is on restoring the capacity to engage in interpersonal relationships and on problems over work and the way in which conflicts between people can disrupt the work situation. Thus the emphasis is also on finding a job again quickly (and holding onto it).

Then there is the possibility, via psychodramatic techniques (role playing) within the framework of group psychotherapy, of some training in applying for a situation. It is precisely in applying for a job that the client so often goes in for rejection-courting maneuvers. People who have been admitted to mental hospitals are often confronted with an adverse reaction from the community. They are stigmatized. But the social role of 'patient' may also entail that one's response to each new move on the community's part is to behave in such a way that expulsion (or rejection) is *bound* to follow. A typical example is the conduct of the ex-patient who on his very first effort to apply for a job voluntarily and in some detail informs the employer 'that he has spent three years in a mental hospital,' so that he can then – not without a measure of satisfaction – put himself back into care, with loud protests about society's prejudices and his rejected job application. Such situations are foreseeable; and this type of behavior calls for very careful study and exploration.

To this category of 'isolated person' we can offer the facility of day- and night-admission. The danger is obvious. The whole notion of the social intervention center ceases to make sense if a large number of people in this category sit there all day, waiting for their group therapy session – let alone if we provide them with pottery work! Our task with these people will be to get them, as quickly as possible, to undertake a full day's work in the town, and to take steps to keep the question of accommodations and whatever else may be relevant under review. We shall then shift the group therapy as soon as we can to the evening or try to persuade employers to permit the person to attend group therapy sessions in the daytime. In any case the intention of getting the person to resume work and outside human contacts must be made clear at the time of selection.

2. THOSE WHO HABITUALLY PLAY THE ROLE OF 'PATIENT' IN THE MARRIAGE OR FAMILY SITUATION

This category of persons I shall call, for the sake of convenience, 'poles.' Here the 'deviant' makes it clear from his conduct that he is assuming the role of 'patient,' while at the same time it is being thrust upon him by the members of the group to which he belongs. We can offer these people *partner therapy* and *family therapy*. We shall want to take a psychotherapeutic approach to *marriage* and *family* as natural groups. The provision of a night-time facility for these *ostensibly highly disturbed people* (who are in fact 'poles' of fields) need not in itself be inconsistent with this point of view. It is very reasonable that a person who in his symptoms is sending out s.o.s. signals should sometimes get out of his immediate stress situation. But the selection and intake procedure must be fundamentally different in kind. From the outset we must communicate what we have in view – that this is a *field problem* – and must prepare the 'nonpatient partner(s)' for taking an active part in our psychotherapeutic activities. The 'nonpatient partner(s)' (or father and mother, etc.) must be confronted right away with a staff who really believe in this ideology and are seriously prepared to put it into practice.

It is easy to get quite discouraged about the current situation and adopt the standpoint once taken by Max Planck when he said:

> A new scientific truth does not triumph by convincing its opponents and making them see the light, but rather because its opponents eventually die. [9]

However, I believe that there is reason for more optimism that that. Everywhere in the psychiatric world change is going on – and especially among psychiatrists in training. In The Netherlands there is ferment on all sides. The latter category (the residents) are startled to discover how bad their training situation really is. (During a seminar I conducted in Holland it became clear to me that a lot of the residents had never even heard such names as those of Rosen, Sullivan, Séchehaye and Fromm-Reichmann. Some who had specialized in psychiatry for four years wanted further instruction at an institute for training in psychoanalysis, where they would have a chance to hear something about the work of these authors in the form of a short seminar. They knew little or nothing about social-psychological and sociological literature.)

Psychiatric nursing personnel are attempting to bring about changes in their status and training. Centers of medical education have begun to panic and to realize that there are grave faults in their structure and way of working.

Psychiatric social workers, trained at 'social academies,' are making a start with psychotherapeutic interventions on the family as a whole. Generally speaking, they are getting a training that looks a great deal better than that of the future psychiatrist.

The organizations responsible for looking after mental health are becoming increasingly uneasy and are organizing congresses where some search is being made for alternatives. The title of a recent congress in Holland was very revealing: 'Too Crazy for Words.' At last there is a healthy unrest in the psychiatric world. Articles are turning up in newspapers and periodicals. Directors of mental hospitals are in the process of 'getting with it.'

Not long ago I visited one such hospital and I came away with mixed feelings. I had respect and admiration for the humanity, spirit of sacrifice and courage with which many workers (from the director to the gardener) were setting about the job of making something really good out of it. They were saddled with enormous problems which society just threw in their lap. In the occupational therapy department the aide with great pride showed me the products that expressed what it is that preoccupies people in psychic distress. I saw the new gymnasium, where a retarded man was being stimulated in his sense of rythm and spontaneity. And yet none of it could change my conclusions; I retained the conviction that we are fundamentally on the wrong track.

The director gave away his 'philosophy' thus: 'Peter is here now for the fifth time,' he told me, 'and I said to him: "Man, you must think of it like this – a car, too, needs an overhaul every now and then. Change of oil and some new shock absorbers. Nothing to be ashamed of. A psychotic condition like this is bound to recur from time to time."' It sounded kindly and well meant. I felt paralyzed, because a polemical debate on the fact that this was not an authentic answer to the 'psychotic condition' seemed to me utterly senseless. The fact is that, at this stage, we cannot do without these psychiatric institutions, anyway. I am only afraid that we will make them bigger. For when one visits these 'villages' (which is what they most often are), one is immediately struck by how the director carries his visitor enthusiastically along with him and shows him the new 'plan for rebuilding and extension' displayed on the wall: 'Look, that's where I plan to have the new admissions unit. The mentally retarded will be going over to that new building there, this area will be entirely modernized. There will be our new theatre, the swimming pool and the gym.' The visitor in his bewilderment may then wonder whether the millions required for all these alterations might not be better expended in a totally different way. And who, for God's sake, is going to continue subsidizing all this, when the facts cry out that multiplying and enlarging these mental hospitals cannot possibly be the answer!

I realize that this final chapter has not got beyond being a very sketchy outline. I have ducked the whole problem of a new label for people in trouble. I have not talked, either, about the social and economic consequences that a fundamental reform of our provision of psychiatric care will entail. Enough sources of resistance to renewal have been specified as it is. And yet it is obvious that this will be a quite major source of opposition. The high annual income of medical specialists (with a number of 'nerve doctors' by no means lagging behind!), the fees which people in psychic trouble have to pay – in short, the whole financial side of the thing – is a political issue. Why political parties have remained so unaware of these (and indeed all the other) problems in psychiatry and have usually delegated them to a doctor member of the political assembly or medical secretary of state is for me just one of many mysteries. The answer is probably simple: lack of information or uncritical acceptance of the existing information. 'Doctor knows best!' Doctor did not, and does not, necessarily know best. He thought he knew and acted with conviction. Those who represent medical-clinical psychiatry (with the 'mental illness' myth in tow) wield enormous power in our society. Power over people without any physical disease, and yet in psychic and social distress. The big question is whether that power can be broken. And . . . whether we can succeed in resolving the stresses that result from the intensely conflicting values and norms in our society. We all maintain our private delusions. We distill them out of the collective delusions boomed in our direction by the media and firmly ensconced in rigid legislation. Of course, we can continue to duck the solution of these conflicts and tensions. Our favorite recipe for *not* resolving conflicts within a group is ... to look for a scapegoat. The scapegoat mechanism is an escape. Negro, Jew, homosexual and 'the mentally ill' are our lightning-conductors.

I recall from my high-school days a classmate who, when the math teacher had worked out a problem on the board, would stubbornly raise his hand and say: 'Sir, there's another way.' He was always allowed to go to the blackboard, and sure enough – there always was another way.

REFERENCES

[1] T. S. Szasz: *Ideology and Insanity; Essays on the Psychiatric Dehumanization of Man* (New York, 1970).

[2] The ethics of the psychoanalytical situation are expounded by Szasz in his book: *The Ethics of Psychoanalysis: the Theory and Method of Autonomous Psychotheraphy* (New York, 1965).

[3] E. Goffman: 'The Insanity of Place,' *Psychiatry*, vol. 32, pp. 257–389 (1969).

[4] See on this the essay 'Paranoia and the Dynamics of Exclusion,' in E. M. Lemert, ed.: *Human Deviance, Social Problems and Social Control* (New York, 1967).

[5] M. Jones: *Beyond the Therapeutic Community* (New Haven, Conn., 1969).

[6] I am grateful to W. F. van Leeuwen for having called my attention to an interview with Laing in the *Observer*, September 20, 1970.
An important account of a new type of institution is given by David Cooper in *Psychiatry and Anti-Psychiatry* (London, 1967).

[7] Conversation with Carl Whitaker in J. Haley and L. Hoffman: *Techniques of Family Therapy* (New York, 1967).

[8] M. Howells, ed.:*Theory and Practice of Family Psychiatry* (Edinburgh, 1968).
See also J. Boszormenyi-Nagi and J. L. Framo, eds.: *Intensive Family Therapy* (New York, 1965).

[9] M. Planck: *A Scientific Autobiography* (London, 1965).

EPILOGUE

As I read through the pages of the manuscript now lying in front of me, I realize that it has become a sort of odyssey. The story began on a personal note; and that is how I should end it.

In November, 1965, I returned to The Netherlands, full of enthusiasm, with my notes as a treasured possession, hoping to 'make my contribution.' The best thing, it seemed to me, was to make a start at the university. One needs to have a platform, a certain amount of financial security, time to write, to do some research. I soon discovered that the experience I had picked up in America shut more doors than it opened. I faced a lack of assurance among those who had secured for themselves a niche in the world of psychiatry and an element of indifference and envy that one has to be able to handle, or at any rate not provoke. One should bide one's time; not go knocking on doors and making propaganda as I did in my naiveté. The first conversations I had were so many blows to my unrealistic idealism. I faced a lot of disappointment and dismay during these few years. 'Good for growth' perhaps, but painful.

It soon became clear to me that no one was eagerly awaiting a Dutch-American messiah, and also that, with respect to the 'problem of schizophrenia,' understanding and interpretation had not changed fundamentally. It remained a sort of private hobby about which I obviously had 'different ideas.'

A number of psychoanalysts had managed to take over the chairs of psychiatry, which made for improvement compared with the previous situation. But, I had the impression, they scarcely knew how they were to organize the training of future psychiatrists. That is still my impression. The confusion has only just started to become apparent.

Why has all this been written, then, and for whom? Very likely for myself. All the same, I did want to share these ideas and reach a number of people with my story: people who would recognize themselves in these pages and people who would want to carry on. We must continue to move forward and find new ways. There is much reward for those who are prepared to choose what Freud once called 'that impossible profession.'

What concerns me most is why we do not see that those who are called 'psychotic' or 'schizophrenic' can teach us *most* about the human condition; why we have been so unprepared and unwilling to listen especially to them.

I hope we will do that in any case.

Index

Erikson, E. H. 215, 220 R.9, 272, 275, 282 R.6, 339 f., 357 R.2
Erikson, K. T. 316–19, 322N.
Esquirol 361N.
Etzioni, A. 238N.

Farber, L. 16, 24 R.7, 25 f.N.
Federn, P. 82, 95N.
Ferenczi, S. 212 f., 217, 220 R.7, 348
Field, M. G. 368 f.N.
Fliess, W. 340 f., 357 R.3
Foudraine, J. 117N.
Framo, J. L. 220 R.5, 407 R.8
Frank, A. R. 235N.
Freeman, R. 285N.
Freud, A. 282 R.9
Freud, S. 9, 14, 79–84, 86, 92 R.8, 95N., 268, 273, 277, 328, 334, 335, 338–56, 357 R.3, R.7, 360N., 363, 365, 369N., 372
Fromm, E. 268 f., 372 f., 387 R.2, R.3
Fromm-Reichmann, F. 10, 20, 60, 75 R.2, 82, 94N., 113, 121–25, 130 R.1, R.2, 130 f.N., 135, 150 R.3, 278; 398 f., 403
Frost, R. 2, 323N.

Galen 354, 367
Galioni, E. F. 237N.
Ganzer, V. J. 364, 368 R.5
George, G. R. 324N.
Georget 361N.
Gesell, A. 282 R.5
Gibson, R. W. 324N.
Glover, E. 348
Goffman, E. XVII, XX R.8, 152, 219, 232N., 314 f., 319, 321 R.9, 332, 381 f., 385, 387 R.11, R.12, 391, 395 f., 407 R.3
Goldberg, A. 174 R.2, 197 R.3
Greenblatt, M. XX R.7, 179, 197 R.2, 207, 220 R.4
Griesinger, W. 11, 361N.
Grinker, R. 364, 368 R.7
Groos, K. 282 R.11
Guntrip, H. 216, 220 R.10
Gusdorff, G. 373, 376, 387 R.3

Gyarfas 285N.

Haeine, R. W. 233N.
Häfner, H. 116N.
Haley, J. 288N., 387 R.14, 407 R.7
Harnik 352
Hayakawa 330, 337 R.3
Hayward, S. T. 279 f., 282 R.13
Hegel, G. W. F. 373
Heidegger, M. 92 f. R.12
Henry, J. 234N., 287N.
Hill, L. B. 95N., 99, 197 R.8
Hobbs, N. 368 R.11
Hoffman, L. 407 R.7
Hooper, D. F. 236N., 237N.
Horney, K. 14, 24 R.6, 268, 344
Howells, M. 400, 407 R.8
Humphry 220 R.1
Hunter, R. XX R.4, 233N.

Ilg, F. L. 282 R.5

Jackson, H. 364
James, W. 349
Janet 349
Jaspers, K. 85, 95N.
Johnson, A. M. 198 R.8
Jones, E. 342, 348 f., 357 R.4
Jones, M. XVI, XX R.6, 14, 144, 167, 185, 197 R.5, 208, 225, 233–36N., 286N., 396 f., 407 R.5
Jung, C. G. 13, 18, 80–83, 95N., 376

Kahne, M. J. 175 R.3, 222 f., 228 f., 232 R.2, 238, 287N.
Kaufman, R. M. 365, 368 R.12
Kayser, H. 238N.
Kemper, F. X
Kierkegaard, S. 26N., 373
Klapman 174 R.1
Knight, R. P. 280 f., 282 R.15
Kohler, J. 237N.
Korzybski, A. 310, 321 R.4, 329 f., 337 R.1
Kraepelin, E. 11, 21, 78–80, 83, 92 R.5, 335, 354, 365
Kraus, S. P. 235N.
Kris, E. 340